Financial Accounting
for Non-Specialists

CATHERINE GOWTHORPE

Financial Accounting for Non-Specialists

Second edition

THOMSON

Australia • Canada • Mexico • Singapore • Spain • United Kingdom • United States

THOMSON

Financial Accounting for Non-Specialists, 2nd Edition
Catherine Gowthorpe

Publishing Director
John Yates

Publisher
Patrick Bond

Development Manager
Anna Carter

Production Editor
Stuart Giblin

Manufacturing Manager
Helen Mason

Development Editor
Laura Priest

Typesetter
Photoprint, Torquay

Production Controller
Maeve Healy

Marketing Manager
Katie Thorn

Cover Design
David Brent

Text Design
Design Deluxe, Bath, UK

Printer
Canale, Italy

For more information, contact Thomson Learning
High Holborn House
50–51 Bedford Row
London WC1R 4LR
or visit us on the World Wide Web at:
http://www.thomsonlearning.co.uk

ISBN-13: 978-1-84480-205-0
ISBN-10: 1-84480-205-1

This edition published 2005 by Thomson Learning.

British Library Cataloguing-in-Publication Data
A catalogue record for this book is available from the British Library

Brief Contents

Contents

What is financial accounting?

There are two distinct strands to accounting in organisations: financial accounting and management accounting. Financial accounting is geared towards producing information that is useful to people outside the business. Management accounting, by contrast, produces the accounting information that managers in a business organisation use for internal decision making and control. This book is concerned principally with financial accounting.

Who is this book aimed at?

The aim of this book is to provide an introduction to financial accounting for students who are specialising in some other business discipline, or in a discipline for which some knowledge of financial accounting is useful. The book is suitable for students of:

- general business qualifications, for example: undergraduate and higher national diploma courses in business and finance;
- specific business disciplines such as marketing and human resource management where some fundamental knowledge of financial accounting is helpful;
- disciplines which lie outside the traditional business area. Students of, for example, engineering, fashion, fine and applied arts may all benefit from some knowledge of financial accounting;
- MBA and similar courses where study of financial accounting is required, although not at a specialist level;
- A and AS level business studies students may benefit from this book as background reading to their studies.

While the principal intended audience for the book comprises students taking a formal course of instruction at college or university, it is also intended that the book should lend itself to self-study by anyone who is interested in extending their knowledge of basic accounting. This could include people who are starting, or thinking of starting their own businesses. Also, the book could be useful for people who are already engaged in business but who are aware that they don't quite understand how financial accounting works.

The overarching aim of the book is to develop understanding of financial accounting. It is not, primarily, a book about how to do accounts. Some of the chapters do, indeed, require students to prepare fairly straightforward financial accounting statements. However, the principal purpose of this approach is to aid understanding; it is often easier to understand how accounting figures hang together if you have had some experience of working them out for yourself.

Special notes for the suspicious

Accounting and finance are often regarded as particularly difficult parts of the business curriculum. Lecturers in accounting are quite frequently presented with some quite seriously ingrained negative attitudes in their non-specialist students. Dealing with some of the most frequently encountered:

'Accounting is boring and it's not relevant to what I'm doing anyway'

Students who are primarily interested in the discipline they have chosen to study often have difficulty in appreciating why they should have to study accounting. A fashion student, for example, is likely to be much more interested in creative outcomes and in developing his or her own skills and deeper appreciation of the creative process. It is, however, the case that people who are successful in making careers in fashion (and other creative endeavours) have to be very much alive to the business environment in which they work. People who have forged successful careers in the creative arts are often surprisingly well-tuned in to all the business and accounting aspects of what they do.

'Accounting should be left to the accountants'

Students in other business disciplines who are looking forward to careers in, perhaps, retail management or marketing sometimes feel that accounting should be left to the accountants. It is one of the contentions of this book that accounting is, on the contrary, much too important to be left to the accountants. Business managers owe it to themselves to be able to interpret the reports that accountants present to them; they are vital aids to understanding what is going on in the business. Business managers should be in a position to question accountants from a position of strength about the information that is being presented to them. If they are not sufficiently knowledgeable to do this they risk being quite seriously restricted in their understanding of their business and their ability to make sound decisions.

It is important to appreciate that accounting is not an exact science. Accounting has emerged in its present day form, after many centuries of development, because there has been a need for it. It is, essentially, about communication between people and so it is vulnerable to all the impediments which hinder proper communication. For example, people sometimes tell lies and accounting can be used, very effectively, to tell lies. Accounting is often imprecise and its imprecision can be easily exploited by the unscrupulous. After studying this book, students should be more aware of the strengths and limitations of accounting as a means of communication.

'Accounting is all about maths, and I'm no good at maths'

Accounting undeniably involves dealing with numbers. However, the study of accounting rarely involves much beyond simple arithmetic. Specifically, the principal prior skills required of students of this book are the ability to add, subtract, multiply, divide and to calculate a percentage. Towards the end of the book students will be required to draw simple line graphs and to calculate compound interest. Most of these are skills that are covered at Key Stages 2 and 3 (for students who have come through the UK primary and secondary education system recently). There is nothing in this book (or indeed in many accounting textbooks) that requires knowledge of mathematical techniques beyond GCSE level.

What the study of accounting does involve, however, is the ability to understand what the numbers signify. This is a skill which some students find relatively difficult to acquire. The book, therefore, spends a lot of time from early on in developing that kind of understanding. It cannot be emphasised too frequently that this book is about developing understanding of accounting information.

'I won't be able to understand all the jargon'

Accounting is no different from many other spheres of fairly advanced human endeavour in that it has its own terminology. Jargon is often baffling to the uninitiated, but, inevitably, some of the jargon simply has to be learned. In this book, the author has tried to ensure that all unfamiliar terms are fully explained in the most straightforward terms possible. There is a glossary towards the end of the book which explains a lot of the more unfamiliar terminology so that students do not have to go hunting back through the book to find the original explanation.

Structure and features of this book

The book is divided into two parts. The five chapters in the first part provide an introduction to accounting and finance for business. Topics covered include sources of finance for business, business start-ups, some essential facts about companies and the role of accountants in business. Course tutors may choose to lecture on these topics, or, where time is limited, they may ask students to read these chapters as background material.

The second part of the book deals with financial accounting. From chapter 6 onwards, most chapters involve the study of some accounting techniques (and therefore the use of some manipulation of figures) but the overall objective is always to encourage understanding of accounting statements.

All chapters, apart from Chapters 1 and 5, contain at least one case study. These are often quite extensive, covering many aspects of the material covered by the chapter. Several of the cases incorporate more general business problems, so as to illustrate the close link between the conduct of a business and the information contained in accounting statements.

All chapters include an extensive range of exercises so that students can test their knowledge and understanding. Students are often worried and may become demotivated if the end of chapter exercises are too difficult. Therefore, the book aims to provide a good range of tests covering both the simple and more complex points presented in the chapter. If students wish to test their understanding with even more exercises, further examples are provided on the book's dedicated website (see below).

About half of the end of chapter exercises contain answers within the book. Answers to the remainder can be supplied by course lecturers who have obtained the Lecturer's guide (see below).

Supplementary material

In addition to the material presented in the book, the following supplementary material is available.

Dedicated website

The website can be found at www.thomsonlearning.co.uk/gowthorpefa2. The lecturer section is password protected and the password is available free to lecturers who confirm their adoption of the book. Lecturers should complete the registration form on the website to apply for their password. The following material is available:

For students and lecturers (open access)

- Multiple Choice Questions for each chapter
- Answers to Case Studies within the text
- Related Weblinks
- Additional Questions with Answers
- Additional Chapter – The Accounts of Manufacturing Businesses

For lecturers only (password protected)

- Answers to specific lecturer examples within the text
- Downloadable PowerPoint slides
- Additional Lecturer Questions with answers
- Comprehensive Teaching Notes
- Testbank of Multiple Choice Questions
- Additional Case Studies

Walk-through Tour

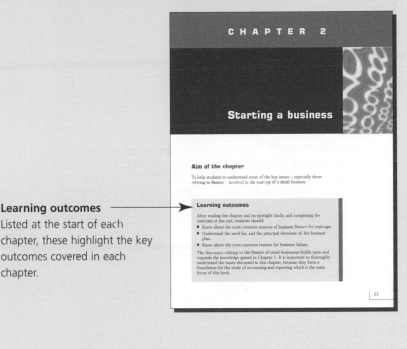

Learning outcomes

Listed at the start of each chapter, these highlight the key outcomes covered in each chapter.

Examples

Examples are dispersed throughout the text to illustrate the practical application of key concepts.

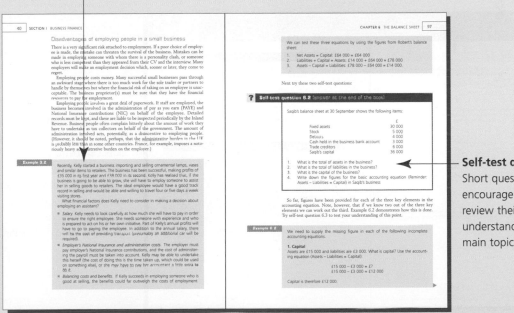

Self-test questions

Short questions which encourage students to review their understanding of the main topics and issues.

Spotlights

Mini cases which focus on decisions which have proved to be crucial for successful businesses.

Chapter summary

The end of each chapter has a summary of the main points and key concepts covered.

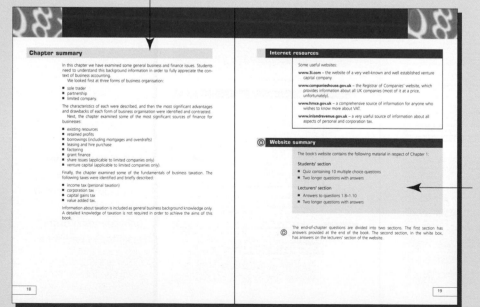

Website summary

Website summary sections direct students and lecturers to the companion website where additional resources are available to enhance understanding of specific topics.

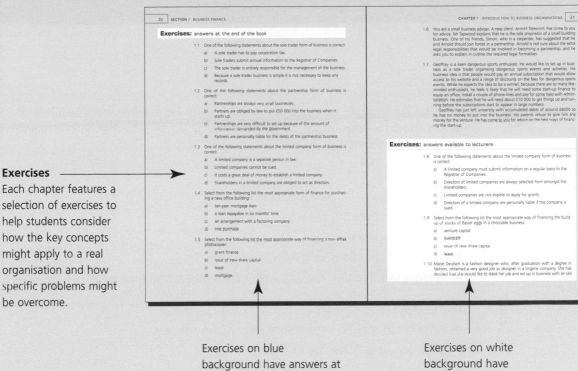

Exercises

Each chapter features a selection of exercises to help students consider how the key concepts might apply to a real organisation and how specific problems might be overcome.

Exercises on blue background have answers at the back of the book.

Exercises on white background have answers available to lecturers (on the website).

Case studies

Cases are provided in most chapters. They are based on realistic organisations and the accounting problems they might face. Each case is accompanied by questions to test the readers' understanding.

Accompanying Website

Visit the *Financial Accounting for Non-Specialists* 2/e accompanying website at **www.thomsonlearning.co.uk/gowthorpefa2** to find further teaching and learning material including:

For Students

- Multiple Choice Questions for each chapter
- Answers to Case Studies within the text
- Related Weblinks
- Additional Questions with Answers
- Additional Chapter – The Accounts of Manufacturing Businesses

For Lecturers

- Answers to specific lecturer examples within the text
- Downloadable PowerPoint slides
- Additional Lecturer Questions with answers
- Comprehensive Teaching Notes
- Testbank of Multiple Choice Questions
- Additional Case Studies

Business finance

Introduction

This section of the book examines issues in business finance relevant to different sizes of organisation. The first four chapters provide an introduction to issues in business financing. They should be especially useful for those students who are new to the study of business and accounting. Chapter 1 provides a general introduction to business organisations and their financing, examining characteristics of the different forms of business commonly found in the UK and elsewhere, and discussing sources of finance. Chapter 2 is concerned with business start-ups. Using a detailed case study, it examines some of the relevant financing and other problems that face the entrepreneur. Chapter 3 examines some of the problems and opportunities that face the growing business, and includes a description of some of the stages involved in business expansion. Chapter 4 examines the financing of limited companies, and extends the basic Chapter 1 coverage into a more detailed look at business financing via the stock market.

Chapter 5 aims to equip students with an understanding of the reasons why people need accounting information, the nature of accounting information and the role of the accountant. It provides an introduction to the rest of the book which is concerned with the acquisition of the skills that prospective business managers and proprietors need in order to be able to understand the information that accountants present to them.

CHAPTER 1

Introduction to business organisations and finance

Aim of the chapter

To introduce the most common forms of business organisation and to discuss the principal sources of finance for those organisations.

Learning outcomes

After reading the chapter and completing the exercises at the end, students should:

- Understand the differences between the sole trader, partnership and company forms of business organisation, including the advantages and drawbacks of each type.
- Know about some of the different sources of business finance available to commercial organisations.
- Know in outline about some important features of the business environment including the various ways in which tax is charged on businesses.

This chapter provides an introduction to the business environment and its financing. It is useful to know about the features discussed in this chapter as a background to the development of more detailed knowledge of accounting and finance in business which occupies most of the book.

The book focuses on the role of accounting and finance in commercial organisations. Accounting is also important for not-for-profit organisations and the public sector, but these are beyond the scope of this book.

Forms of business organisation

There are three common forms of business organisation: sole trader businesses, partnerships and limited companies. Other forms of organisation are encountered occasionally, but we will concentrate in this book on the three common ones. All three types of organisation are run with a view to making profits.

Sole trader businesses

A sole trader operates a business himself or herself, keeping any profits that are made (after deduction of tax). This is a useful form of business for certain types of trade or profession. For example, a plumber, carpenter, financial services adviser, tax adviser, writer or night-club singer could each operate as a sole trader business. Each of these offers a service to the public; each receives money in exchange for performance of the service. After deduction of the various expenses that are involved in running the business, any sum that is left over is the profit, all of which can be kept by the sole trader.

Example 1.1

Having finished his apprenticeship, Yasin sets up in business as a plumber. He pays for a listing in *Yellow Pages*, subscribes to a plumbers' trade association, installs a phone in his flat and waits to be contacted by members of the public and other businesses who require plumbing services. If there is a demand for his services (and there almost certainly will be; it is notoriously difficult to find a plumber) he will soon be called upon. Yasin charges fees for his services out of which he must meet business expenses.

What are Yasin's business expenses? They will typically involve: cost of tools, expenses of running a van, telephone bills, advertising (the *Yellow Pages* listing) and small amounts of administrative expense, such as paying for an accountant to sort out his tax affairs.

In order to keep his business affairs in good order, he will need to keep receipts as evidence of his expenses, copies of the bills he makes out to his customers, and bank statements. It is important not to mix up the business income and expenditure with his own personal items. Yasin or his accountant will summarise all the income he has received from customers and all the expenses of running the business on an annual basis. Income less expenses equals the profit of the business.

At an early stage, the tax authorities take an interest in Yasin's business activities. He will have to pay tax based upon the calculation of his profit. Later in the chapter we will examine the tax regime in a little more detail.

Characteristics of the sole trader form of business

The sole trader is the only person responsible for the management of the business. Although he or she may employ other people as the business gets bigger, all the decision making and risk taking involved in the business rests on the shoulders of one individual. If the business runs into financial difficulties or faces other problems, the sole trader is on his or her own in addressing them.

Sole trader businesses tend to remain fairly small. For people who are self-employed in the types of trade or profession mentioned earlier, this form of business can work very well. However, if the business is of a type that is likely to grow very much bigger, the sole trader form of organisation will need to be replaced by a partnership or limited company structure, which allows more than one person to act as manager.

If a sole trader overstretches himself or herself financially, perhaps by borrowing too much, or if losses rather than profits are made, he or she is liable for all the consequences as an individual. For example, a lender would be entitled to pursue repayment of a loan even to the point where the sole trader would have to sell personal property to repay it. In extreme cases, this can result in personal bankruptcy.

The sole trader business is relatively informal and easy to set up. The business does not require registration of a separate legal entity and so it is quite likely that no legal costs will arise. In the initial stages, at least, the principal administrative issues are likely to arise with the Inland Revenue authorities. A competent chartered accountant can mediate between the individual and the Inland Revenue to ensure that the correct amount is paid, and that tax does not become a problem.

Partnerships

A partnership is a business run by two or more people with a view to making a profit. Typically, partnerships are fairly small businesses, but there are certain types of business activity in which very large partnerships are operated. Professional partnerships, such as those between solicitors, may develop to be very large businesses indeed. There is a legal restriction limiting the number of partners in most types of partnership to 20; however, professional partnerships (solicitors, accountants, surveyors or architects for example) are exempt from the restriction. The very largest partnerships are such big businesses that people who have barely met each other are in partnership together.

Many different trades and professions may be run through the medium of a partnership; apart from the professions noted above, doctors, pharmacists, business consultants, shopkeepers, builders, hairdressers and almost any other type of trade or business activity could be run via a partnership.

Example 1.2

Winston and Winona are computer games enthusiasts. They both work as local government administrative officers and are bored with their jobs. They decide to start a business selling computer games; they will rent shop premises for retail sales, but will also run a mail order service from the room behind the shop. The business is established as a partnership with a business name of WW Wizard Games. The two partners decide that, as they will both be working full-time in the new business, they will share all the profits from the business equally.

As in the case of Yasin in Example 1.1, it will be necessary to keep some records of the business activities. It makes good sense to do so as it will contribute to good relations with the tax authorities. However, unlike the case of the sole trader, Yasin, there are some legal requirements governing the records that have to be kept by the business, and the way in which the business operates. Partnerships are covered by the Partnership Act 1890. This is a relatively straightforward piece of legislation that sets out a basic structure of legal relationships between partners, minimum record-keeping requirements and ways of resolving disputes between partners. For example, the Partnership Act states that profits will be shared equally between partners unless they make some other agreement between themselves. Winston and Winona have agreed in any case to share profits equally; this is a common arrangement where all partners are contributing equally to the success of the business. However, they could share profits in any way that seems appropriate.

Apart from the basic legal structure set out in the Partnership Act 1890, partners may decide to draw up a formal, legal agreement between themselves. Typically this would set out the details of the financial and legal arrangements that are to operate; it might, for example, state that Partner A will receive 60% of the profits of the business while Partners B and C each receive 20%. It may also deal with the actions to be taken in the event of a dispute between the partners. Not all partnerships bother to have a formal agreement of this type set up, but it can prove to be very useful if relationships turn sour.

Characteristics of the partnership form of business

The success of a partnership depends to some extent on the quality of the relationships between partners. Sometimes, people who are friends, or who are related to each other, set up a business partnership together. The pressures of running a business can sometimes place an intolerable strain on what has previously been a good relationship. On the other hand, where partnerships work well, they can be highly productive, especially if the partners have a range of skills that complement each other. Winona, in Example 1.2, is perhaps very good at selling over the counter, but lacks the attention to administrative detail that is required to run the mail order side of the business. If Winston is a good administrator, he will complement Winona's skills, and between them they will perhaps be able to run a successful business.

As well as sharing in the running of the business, the partners are likely to be able to command more resources to put into the business. At the start-up stage, each may have savings or other resources (such as equipment) which they can put into the business. If the partnership needs to borrow money, it may be in a better position to do so than the sole trader.

If the partnership loses money, or cannot repay loans, lenders are able to recover money owed by requiring the partners to sell items of property that they own personally. In this respect the partnership is no different from the sole trader, and the partners face the consequence of bankruptcy in the worst cases.

Each partner is liable under the law for the actions of his or her partners. If Winona makes a business decision that turns out badly and the partnership is left owing a large amount of money, both Winona and Winston are liable for the consequences of the decision. Winston could not claim that he knew nothing about the decision; he would still be equally liable with Winona. (It really is important for partners to know and trust each other thoroughly.)

A partnership business is not difficult to set up. However, partners should be prepared to go to the additional trouble and expense of having a clear partnership agreement drawn up with the help of a solicitor. It will make potential disputes in the future easier to resolve.

Limited companies

A limited company is a legal arrangement for regulating the ownership of business. A company is regarded as a separate person for the purposes of the law; so, for example, a company, unlike a partnership, can enter into a legal contract. This means that, if the other contracting person sues, he or she sues the company, not the owners of the company. The company itself becomes liable for its unpaid debts, overdrafts and so on.

This legal construction is an extremely important feature of the business world, in the UK and in many other countries. Because the company itself enters into contracts, takes out loans and so on, its owners are protected from any adverse consequences of the action. This is the concept of limited liability. It is an extremely useful and helpful device that protects shareholders from personal loss if the business runs into trouble.

Setting up a company (the process of incorporation) involves some legal formalities that must be followed strictly. It is therefore more difficult than setting up a sole trader business. However, the difficulties should not be overstated: there are specialist company registration firms, which, for a modest fee, take care of all the formalities. It need cost little more than £150 to set up a company.

After the company is incorporated, there are certain regular legal formalities that must be complied with. More details are given in the following sub-section.

Example 1.3

Winston and Winona decide to set up their business as a limited company, rather than as a partnership. The business is registered in the name of WW Wizard Games Limited. They divide ownership of the business between them; each owns exactly 50% of the shares in the business. Winona and Winston are both shareholders. Both are involved in the day-to-day management of the business and, as well as being **shareholders**, are also **directors**.

Characteristics of the limited company form of business

Shareholders are liable only for the amount that they have paid into the company in exchange for shares. This is the maximum amount which they can lose if the company is, for example, sued for not repaying its loans on time.

The legal formalities involved in setting up and running a limited company are more complex than for partnerships and sole traders. The directors of a limited company are responsible for making available to the public a certain amount of financial information about the activities of the company on a regular basis. They must do this via the Registrar of Companies, which is an agency responsible for the collection of data relating to companies. Any member of the public can obtain information about a limited company by visiting one of the offices of the Registrar of Companies or through its website (**www.companieshouse.gov.uk**). Regular filings include accounting information. Information that could remain private ina sole trader or partnership organisation must be made public by limited companies.

In small companies, shareholders (who are the owners of the company) and directors (who are responsible for managing it) are the same people. However, in larger companies it is frequently the case that most shareholders have nothing to do with the management of the company. Day-to-day management can be left in the hands of directors who are professional managers. Shareholders in very large companies often have virtually no contact with the company or its managers.

Sole traders, partnerships and limited companies contrasted

When setting up a business from scratch, the founder or founders must consider carefully which form of business organisation is most suitable for them. Usually, it is sensible to take professional advice on the matter as it can be advantageous for tax purposes to choose one form over another. Leaving tax to one side for the time being, the following are the principal advantages and drawbacks of the three different types of organisation.

Sole trader – advantages

- It is easy to start up as a sole trader.
- There are no legal formalities on start-up.
- The sole trader is self-reliant; he or she does not risk getting involved in the personality clashes that can occur where more than one person is managing a business.
- The sole trader does not have to share the profits from the business with anyone else.

Sole trader – drawbacks

- A sole trader bears all of the consequences of legal action against the business for unpaid debts and unfulfilled contracts. His or her personal property may have to be sold to meet business debts.
- A sole trader organisation remains small-scale.
- The sole trader bears the brunt of any losses or business difficulties.
- There is no co-manager with whom problems can be shared.
- If the sole trader is weak in some aspect of business expertise (such as ability to sell, to manage people or to keep track of business records) the business may suffer because there is no one available with complementary skills.

Partnership – advantages

- In a partnership, management is shared and the business can benefit from the complementary skills that the partners bring to it.
- Business decisions do not have to be taken alone.
- Business risks are shared, as are any losses that the business makes.

Partnership – drawbacks

- Partners are responsible in law for the consequences of each other's actions.
- Partners face unlimited liability; they must bear all of the consequences of legal action against the partnership. Their personal property may have to be sold to meet unpaid business debts.
- The profits of the business are shared between all the partners whereas a sole trader keeps all the profits for himself or herself (but note that a partnership business, which combines the skills of two or more people, should be able to generate higher profits than a sole trader).

Limited company – advantages

- The most significant advantage conferred by company status is the limitation of personal liability. Shareholders can invest in a business knowing that they will not be pursued for further contributions once their shares have been paid for.
- The limited company legal structure allows for shareholders to appoint professional managers as directors.
- A limited company's shares can be used to spread the ownership of the business among many people.
- Shares can be sold and bought so that transfer of ownership is relatively easy and straightforward.

Limited company – drawbacks

- Setting up a company requires adherence to a set of strict formal legal requirements, and will sometimes require professional advice.
- Regular filing of financial information with the Registrar of Companies is a legal requirement; this involves additional administration and means that members of the public have access to information that would remain strictly private in a partnership or sole trader organisation.

Finance for business

When starting a business the founder or founders must find a source of finance to pay for the setting-up costs, any equipment that is needed and, probably, for the expenses of the business for the period during which it is getting established. Most established businesses will also require finance from time to time to pay for such items as:

- Buying major items of equipment or land and buildings.
- Expanding the scope of the business (for example, opening new offices or conducting research into new product feasibility).
- Helping the business through difficult periods such as temporary recessions or decreases in sales.

In this section of the chapter we will examine the principal sources of finance that may be available to a business. Some are more appropriate than others for particular purposes.

Existing resources

When a business starts up, the founder(s) will almost certainly make an initial contribution of their own resources. This may be in the form of cash they have saved, or won, or been given. It could be in the form of motor cars or vans, premises or some other item of resource. Such initial contributions are known in accounting terms as capital introduced. We will examine financing business start-ups in much more detail in Chapter 2.

Where partners contribute to the setting up of a business, they may contribute unequal amounts depending on the resources they have at their disposal. In such cases, it may be decided between the partners that those who contribute more will receive an extra share of the profits to compensate.

Example 1.4

Jakes, Jones and Jessop form a partnership to conduct legal business. The total capital introduced by the partners is £190 000, constituted as follows:

Jakes – office building valued at £100 000

Jones – cash of £50 000

Jessop – cash of £30 000 plus office equipment valued at £10 000

The partners decide between them that they will allocate a 10% return on each of these contributions out of the profits made by the business, before dividing the profits equally between them. The business makes £49 000 in profits in its first year, which will be allocated between the partners as follows:

	Jakes £	Jones £	Jessop £
10% on Jakes' capital: £100 000 × 10%	10 000		
10% on Jones' capital: £50 000 × 10%		5 000	
10% on Jessop's capital: £40 000 × 10%			4 000

Remaining profit split equally between the partners:
£49 000 − (10 000 + 5 000 + 4 000) = £30 000.

	Jakes £	Jones £	Jessop £
Split equally	10 000	10 000	10 000
Total	20 000	15 000	14 000

The introduction of capital is possible at any point subsequent to the foundation of the business. Whenever the business needs more resources the founders may be able to make a further contribution.

Retained profits

As a business grows it makes profits. The owners of the business usually take out part of the profits as their reward for investing in it. However, they are not obliged to take out all the profits; they may leave some in the business to be invested to produce growth and further profits. The amount of profit left in the business is referred to as retained profits. This can be a very good source of funds for further investment as it is not dependent on any outside person or organisation.

Borrowed money

When thinking about potential sources of finance, borrowing may be one of the first possibilities that springs to mind. However, borrowing is not always the most appropriate source of finance for a business. In some circumstances it simply may not be obtainable. Many business start-ups would not be able to borrow money because no organisation would be willing to take the risk of lending it. Lenders need to know that: (a) the money they lend will be paid back eventually; and (b) the business will be able to pay a reasonable rate of interest on the borrowing. In order to do so the business needs to stand a good chance of being profitable.

The cost of borrowing

The cost of borrowing is the interest that must be paid on a regular basis to the lender of the money. Large institutional lenders may agree to lend money to the business but they will expect to receive interest payments on time and without fuss.

The risk/return relationship

Banks and other lenders do not always charge the same rate of interest. They make an assessment of how risky the lending is — i.e. how likely it is that the borrower will fail to repay. If the loan is perceived as more risky than average, the lender will either refuse to lend, or will charge a high interest rate on the lending. Sometimes, it may only be possible to borrow at extremely high interest rates.

Security

Sometimes banks and other lenders will not lend unless the loan is secured. A mortgage is a familiar example of a secured loan – familiar because at some point in their lives a lot of people take out a mortgage to buy a house or flat. Businesses often take out commercial mortgages to assist in the purchase of property in the form of real estate.

Overdrafts

Overdraft facilities may be obtainable through the business's bank account. An overdraft is most likely to be made available to a business if it can prove that the extra funds are needed only in the short term and that the business is fundamentally sound.

Example 1.5

Christmas Glitter Limited is an established business making Christmas lights and decorations. The period from July to the beginning of October each year is spent in frantic activity in the factory in order to build up the stocks of goods for sale in the company's three most important trading months — October, November and December. A lot of money is needed in July to October; materials have to be purchased and paid for, and staff costs are heavy because a lot of overtime is worked. At this time of year the business usually requires an overdraft. The company's bank manager is quite happy to provide overdraft facilities during this period because she knows from experience that by mid-November the company will have paid off the loan.

This is an example of a seasonal shortfall in cash, caused purely because of the nature of the business. A short-term facility like an overdraft tides the company over until it starts to generate cash.

It should be noted that an overdraft is a short-term solution. It is technically repayable on demand; this means that the bank can demand immediate repayment of the overdraft at any time. In practice, however, banks rarely demand immediate repayment.

Leasing and hire purchase

When a business makes a large purchase of an item that will be used over the medium to long term, it has to pay out a lot of cash at one time. Sometimes it makes sense to look at alternative ways of financing such a major item.

Under a leasing arrangement the business (the lessee) pays a regular amount to a lessor in exchange for the use of an item such as a piece of machinery. The lease often extends over a period of years. The lessor, usually a financial institution, pays for the machine, which is delivered to the lessee's premises and will, typically, remain there throughout its useful productive life. The lessor organisation is the legal owner of the machine but will probably never even see it. The lessee never owns the machine, but will use it, often for years, in the business.

Short-term leases are sometimes taken out on items such as photocopiers and cars. The items may be replaced regularly and each time this happens a new lease is negotiated. Again, the lessee never actually owns the item in question.

Hire purchase is a similar arrangement to the longer-term leasing described above, with the difference that, once the final agreed payment is made, under the terms of the agreement ownership passes to the purchaser business.

Factoring

Many businesses sell on credit – that is, they supply goods or services for which they are paid after a period of a month or two. The delay in receiving cash can be costly; if it is extended for too long the business may run into difficulties. Factoring is a way of speeding up the receipt of cash.

Example 1.6

Noone & Belfast Limited is a business that supplies major retail stores with home furnishings. The stores are slow to pay and sometimes the company has to wait up to three months to receive money that is owed to it.

The directors of Noone & Belfast decide to investigate a factoring arrangement. At the end of most months the company is owed about £200 000 by various stores that have bought goods but have not yet paid for them. The directors approach a factoring company which proposes the following arrangement:

- They will pay Noone & Belfast 80% of the amount owed to them at the next following month end (i.e. £160 000).
- The factoring company will do all of the administration work connected with collecting the debts.
- Each time Noone & Belfast are ready to bill a customer for goods supplied to them the factoring company will pay the company 80% of the amount billed.
- The remaining 20% less a handling charge will be paid over when the factor receives the amount due from the customer.

The advantages of this arrangement for Noone & Belfast are that they receive a one-off large amount of cash (£160 000), and thereafter, they will receive 80% of the invoice value as soon as they bill a customer. They will also be able to devolve most of the administrative work connected with collecting debts to the factor.

In exchange for the cash supplied up-front by the factoring company, and for the administrative work, there will be a handling charge. This could be 2–3% of the total amount billed; obviously the factoring company needs to be able to make a profit out of the arrangement.

Although the arrangement costs money, it may well be worth considering for Noone & Belfast Limited.

Grant finance

Businesses may be able to obtain grants from the government, local authorities or other agencies and funding bodies. Usually, grants would be awarded only in quite specific circumstances. For example, a local authority trying to encourage the growth of local business might allow companies moving into the area a rent-free period in local authority business units. Although this is not a grant of cash it is a saving on the expense of rental, and it may well entice businesses into the area.

Grant finance is very advantageous in that it usually does not have to be repaid. However, there may be strings attached. In the example above, a business taking advantage of the rent-free period might have to undertake to stay in the area for a further minimum period of time of, say, three years.

Financing companies: Share issues

A company (but not a partnership or sole trader business) can raise additional finance by issuing more shares for cash. If the company is doing well, it can offer existing and potential shareholders a sound investment opportunity.

In Chapter 4 we will examine share issues in much more detail.

Financing companies: Venture capital

Medium-sized companies may be able to seek finance from venture capitalists. A venture capital company invests for limited periods in growing companies in order to give them a short to medium-term financial boost. Usually, the venture capitalist buys into the shares in the company, and will often provide management expertise as well.

Example 1.7	

Hawthorn and Hayward Limited has been in business for five years, and has experienced very rapid growth during the whole of that period. The company's directors are now looking to expand into European markets and are seeking both additional finance of around £250 000 and specific expertise to help them. They approach a venture capital organisation, Bizexpand, for help.

Bizexpand's adviser explains that his organisation would buy shares in Hawthorn and Hayward in exchange for a cash sum of £250 000. Bizexpand would consequently become a significant shareholder in the company. In addition, one of Bizexpand's specialist staff would take up a directorship in Hawthorn and Hayward. The new director would be appointed because of his or her expertise in opening up European sales markets.

The arrangement is planned to last for between two and three years. At the end of a maximum period of three years, Bizexpand would sell its holding of shares (hopefully at a handsome profit) and the specialist director would move on.

Investment by a venture capitalist can be very helpful to a growing company, because it usually combines a sizeable input of cash together with advice and expertise in areas that will benefit the company.

Short-, medium- and long-term finance

It is important for businesses to match their needs for finance with the most appropriate form of finance. Using an overdraft to buy a new office building, for example, would be highly inappropriate. Taking out a ten-year commercial mortgage, on the other hand, would probably be the most sensible course.

Table 1.1 categorises the different sources of finance discussed earlier into short-term, medium-term and long-term sources.

Table 1.1

Terms of sources of finance			
	Short-term	*Medium-term*	*Long-term*
Existing resources	✓	✓	✓
Retained profits	✓	✓	✓
Borrowings	✓	✓	✓
Mortgage			✓
Overdraft	✓		
Short leases	✓		
Long leases and hire purchase		✓	✓
Factoring	✓		
Grant finance	✓	✓	✓
Share issues		✓	✓
Venture capital		✓	✓

Fundamentals of taxation

Taxation is a fact of life for most people and businesses. In this section we will take a brief look at the most common taxes levied on the different types of business which we examined earlier in the chapter.

Income taxes (personal taxation)

Sole traders and partners in business partnerships make profits (they hope) which are chargeable to tax. The tax that is levied is not a specific business tax; it is charged according to the individual's own circumstances at income tax rates.

Example 1.8

Cerise and Cherry are partners in a discounted clothing business. Under their partnership agreement Cerise takes 60% of the profits and Cherry takes 40%. In the tax year 20X5–20X6 the partnership profits are £30 000. Neither partner has any other source of income.

Cerise will be entitled to 60% of the profits: £30 000 × 60% = £18 000

Cherry will be entitled to 40% of the profits: £30 000 × 40% = £12 000

Each partner will include her share of the profits in her personal tax return. Each woman will be liable for income tax on her share less any attributable personal allowances. National Insurance contributions will also be payable.

Corporation tax

As the name implies, this is a tax levied on companies. Directors are paid a salary for working in the company, and they will pay income tax and National Insurance on the amounts they earn (just like any other employee). The company itself, however, is liable to corporation tax on its profits.

The company's profit is calculated (income less expenses = profit) and then corporation tax rates are applied. In recent years in the UK, corporation tax rates have tended to fall. Currently, in the 2004–2005 tax year, the basic corporation tax rate is 30% with a small companies' rate of 19%.

Capital gains tax

If an item such as an office building is sold at a profit, capital gains tax is likely to be charged. Capital gains tax applies to both individuals and companies, and so would be levied on sole traders, partnerships and limited companies.

Value added tax

Value added tax (VAT) is the UK's principal form of indirect tax; it is a tax on the purchase of goods. As private individuals we frequently pay VAT on goods and services that we purchase; we have no choice in the matter, and because prices are charged inclusive of VAT we do not usually even notice that we are paying the tax.

What about VAT from the point of view of a business? Businesses act as collectors of VAT, which they pay over on a regular basis to the government authority that collects it, the Customs and Excise. The operation of VAT is demonstrated in Example 1.9.

Example 1.9

Palfrey and Bennett Limited is a retail business that sells men's clothing from a series of high street outlets. The company adds a charge of 17.5% (the standard rate of VAT) to all the items that it sells. The company's customers pay the tax.

At the end of the three-month period ending 31 March 20X5, Palfrey and Bennett completes a VAT return. Total sales before VAT for the three-month period are £100 000. VAT at 17.5% is £17 500. The amount of £17 500 is known as output tax.

Palfrey and Bennett has itself, however, paid VAT on the purchases it makes. During the same three-month period it has bought goods totalling £70 000 before VAT. VAT at 17.5% is £12 250. The amount of £12 250 is known as input tax.

The quarterly liability to the Customs and Excise is calculated as follows:

Output tax for the quarter	17 500
Less: Input tax for the quarter	12 250
VAT payable	5 250

The company must complete a VAT return immediately following each quarter. In this case, by the end of April 20X5 it must send the VAT return to the Customs and Excise together with payment of £5250. The Customs and Excise authority is very strict indeed about deadlines.

Each of the businesses supplying Palfrey & Bennett will also be obliged to fill in VAT returns and make payments to the Customs and Excise. People in business often complain about the large administrative burden imposed by accounting for VAT. However, once a business has set up systems to cope with VAT, filling in the VAT return is usually straightforward.

Very small businesses are not obliged to register for VAT. However, if total sales for a year exceed £58 000 or are expected to exceed that amount, it is compulsory to register for VAT.

This section has provided only a very general introduction to the taxation of businesses. For the purposes of this book it is regarded as general background business knowledge. Detailed knowledge of tax is not required for any part of the material that will be covered in the rest of the book. In almost all cases, the exercises ignore the effects of taxation in order to avoid adding an unnecessary layer of complication. However, readers should bear in mind that the effects of taxation can be a significant factor in the real world.

Chapter summary

In this chapter we have examined some general business and finance issues. Students need to understand this background information in order to fully appreciate the context of business accounting.

We looked first at three forms of business organisation:

- sole trader
- partnership
- limited company.

The characteristics of each were described, and then the most significant advantages and drawbacks of each form of business organisation were identified and contrasted.

Next, the chapter examined some of the most significant sources of finance for businesses:

- existing resources
- retained profits
- borrowings (including mortgages and overdrafts)
- leasing and hire purchase
- factoring
- grant finance
- share issues (applicable to limited companies only)
- venture capital (applicable to limited companies only).

Finally, the chapter examined some of the fundamentals of business taxation. The following taxes were identified and briefly described:

- income tax (personal taxation)
- corporation tax
- capital gains tax
- value added tax.

Information about taxation is included as general business background knowledge only. A detailed knowledge of taxation is not required in order to achieve the aims of this book.

Internet resources

Some useful websites:

www.3i.com – the website of a very well-known and well established venture capital company.

www.companieshouse.gov.uk – the Registrar of Companies' website, which provides information about all UK companies (most of it at a price, unfortunately).

www.hmce.gov.uk – a comprehensive source of information for anyone who wishes to know more about VAT.

www.inlandrevenue.gov.uk – a very useful source of information about all aspects of personal and corporation tax.

 The end-of-chapter exercises are divided into two sections. The first section has answers provided at the end of the book. The second section, in the white box, has answers on the lecturers' section of the website.

Website summary

The book's website contains the following material in respect of Chapter 1:

Students' section

- Quiz containing ten multiple choice questions
- Two longer questions with answers.

Lecturers' section

- Answers to exercises 1.8–1.10
- Two longer questions with answers.

Exercises: answers at the end of the book

1.1 One of the following statements about the sole trader form of business is correct:

a)   A sole trader has to pay corporation tax.

b)   Sole traders submit annual information to the Registrar of Companies.

c)   The sole trader is entirely responsible for the management of the business.

d)   Because a sole trader business is simple it is not necessary to keep any records.

1.2 One of the following statements about the partnership form of business is correct:

a)   Partnerships are always very small businesses.

b)   Partners are obliged by law to put £50 000 into the business when it starts up.

c)   Partnerships are very difficult to set up because of the amount of information demanded by the government.

d)   Partners are personally liable for the debts of the partnership business.

1.3 One of the following statements about the limited company form of business is correct:

a)   A limited company is a separate person in law.

b)   Limited companies cannot be sued.

c)   It costs a great deal of money to establish a limited company.

d)   Shareholders in a limited company are obliged to act as directors.

1.4 Select from the following list the most appropriate form of finance for purchasing a new office building:

a)   ten-year mortgage loan

b)   a loan repayable in six months' time

c)   an arrangement with a factoring company

d)   hire purchase.

1.5 Select from the following list the most appropriate way of financing a new office photocopier:

a)   grant finance

b)   issue of new share capital

c)   lease

d)   mortgage.

1.6 You are a small business adviser. A new client, Arnold Tapwood, has come to you for advice. Mr Tapwood explains that he is the sole proprietor of a small building business. One of his friends, Simon, who is a carpenter, has suggested that he and Arnold should join forces in a partnership. Arnold is not sure about the extra legal responsibilities that would be involved in becoming a partnership, and he asks you to explain in outline the required legal formalities.

1.7 Geoffrey is a keen dangerous sports enthusiast. He would like to set up in business as a sole trader organising dangerous sports events and activities. His business idea is that people would pay an annual subscription that would allow access to his website and a range of discounts on the fees for dangerous sports events. While he expects the idea to be a winner, because there are so many like-minded enthusiasts, he feels it likely that he will need some start-up finance to equip an office, install a couple of phone lines and pay for some help with administration. He estimates that he will need about £10 000 to get things up and running before the subscriptions start to appear in large numbers.

Geoffrey has just left university with accumulated debts of around £8000 so he has no money to put into the business. His parents refuse to give him any money for the venture. He has come to you for advice on the best ways of financing the start-up.

Exercises: answers available to lecturers

1.8 One of the following statements about the limited company form of business is correct:

a) A limited company must submit information on a regular basis to the Registrar of Companies.

b) Directors of limited companies are always selected from amongst the shareholders.

c) Limited companies are not eligible to apply for grants.

d) Directors of a limited company are personally liable if the company is sued.

1.9 Select from the following list the most appropriate way of financing the build-up of stocks of Easter eggs in a chocolate business:

a) venture capital

b) overdraft

c) issue of new share capital

d) lease.

1.10 Marie Deutsch is a fashion designer who, after graduation with a degree in fashion, obtained a very good job as designer in a lingerie company. She has decided that she would like to leave her job and set up in business with an old friend from college who also trained as a designer. Marie has heard that it is more sensible to set up as a limited company because it would mean that she and her friend would not be personally liable for the debts of the business. However, she says she is sure that there must be some strings attached, and would like you to tell her about any disadvantages in limited company status.

CHAPTER 2

Starting a business

Aim of the chapter

To help students to understand some of the key issues – especially those relating to finance – involved in the start-up of a small business.

Learning outcomes

After reading the chapter and its spotlight study, and completing the exercises at the end, students should:

- Know about the most common sources of business finance for start-ups.
- Understand the need for, and the principal elements of, the business plan.
- Know about the most common reasons for business failure.

The discussion relating to the finance of small businesses builds upon and expands the knowledge gained in Chapter 1. It is important to thoroughly understand the issues discussed in this chapter, because they form a foundation for the study of accounting and reporting which is the main focus of this book.

Financing the small business

All businesses have to start somewhere. They mostly start small and are usually based upon a bright idea that occurs to one person, or sometimes, to a small group of people. The idea may be brilliant but impractical in business terms, or it may have occurred to lots of other people so there will be a high level of competition in the market, or it may be so good and original that it is going to make its owner a millionaire.

The basic business idea may arise out of a need for a product or service that cannot, apparently, be found, or cannot be found at the right price.

Example 2.1

Julie has a full-time job. She has two children, aged five and seven, at the village school which closes at 3.15pm each day, two hours before the end of her own working day. Julie cannot be there to collect the children, and no other member of the family is available at that time to help out. After trying various unsatisfactory arrangements for having the children collected, she concludes that the only way to solve the problem is to set up a business to run an After School Club on the school premises, so that the children of working parents can play in properly supervised conditions.

In this example, there is a perceived need for a service that does not currently exist. Provided that the need is shared by a sufficient number of people, and that the service can be provided economically, there is a business opportunity here.

Sources of finance for a new business start-up

In Chapter 1 we examined sources of business finance in outline. Below we look in more detail at some typical sources of finance that might be used to finance the start-up of a new business.

Any business start-up is likely to require an investment of money in order to make it work. Money is needed for some or all of the following:

- purchase of equipment
- supporting the owner and family while the business gets going
- paying for premises
- paying for staff
- expenses like business rates, insurance, running costs of cars, etc.

It can be very difficult to make realistic estimates of some of these costs. Later in the chapter we will begin to look at how to estimate costs. For the moment we will assume that some money and/or other kinds of resources are going to have to be contributed to the business in order to get it started. (Other kinds of resources could include, for example, use of a car or van that is already owned by the individual starting the business, or a contribution of free labour by members of the family.)

Where does the money come from?

Existing cash resources

Existing cash resources may be available in the form of savings and windfalls. In fact, the arrival of an unexpected windfall may even provide the impetus for the starting up of a business.

Example 2.2

Tim wins £120 000 on the National Lottery. He has always wanted to have a retail business, but has never had enough spare cash to be able to seriously consider setting one up. Now, because of this windfall, he has enough money in hand to be able to give up his job, and to invest in the lease of premises and the purchase of stock that he needs to get his business off the ground.

This scenario can probably be dismissed as completely unrealistic (although, after all, somebody has to win). More likely is the case where the prospective business person has some savings, or is made redundant and receives a sizeable sum of cash or is conveniently left some money in a will.

Also possible, depending upon the nature of the business, is self-financing through part-time work. In practice, many small businesses are financed in this way.

Example 2.3

Sasha completes her degree in fine art, producing several very good pieces of work at her degree show. Two of the pieces sell, and Sasha is offered an exhibition at a local art gallery. However, even though she may be comparatively successful in her working life as an artist, it is highly unlikely that she will ever earn enough from her work to be able to provide herself with a decent living. Very few artists earn much at all. Sasha takes a job for 15 hours per week in an art materials shop. This pays just enough to allow her to spend enough time producing her work for the exhibition, although she is very hard up indeed.

Family or friends

If the prospective business person has no resources it is possible that his or her family may be prepared to support the business in its early stages. Sometimes this can be through a handy injection of cash, or the loan or gift of an item of equipment. Very often, a supportive partner will agree to cover living costs from his or her salary during the early stages of the business.

It should be clear that the chances of obtaining this kind of financial support will depend upon the previous record and good standing of the individual.

Example 2.4

George wants to start a business supplying animal feed. He needs approximately £25 000 for renting premises, buying a second-hand goods vehicle and enough stock to get the business going. However, he is well known in the family as an unreliable spendthrift with an unfortunate tendency to lie and cheat. He has borrowed small sums of money from his parents and brother in the past and has failed to repay them. In the circumstances they are unlikely to be prepared to lend him anything at all.

Even if finance can be obtained in this way, there may be a downside. If the businessman borrows from his nearest and dearest, and then loses the lot in a reckless business start-up, family relationships can be scarred or even terminated. Business failure can, and often does, contribute to the breakdown of long-term relationships.

Grant finance

Grants can be an excellent source of start-up finance, as they usually do not need to be repaid. However, they are available only for quite specific purposes and will almost never serve to finance all of the expenses of a start-up. Also, once a grant is given, the granting authority will normally keep quite a close check on the progress of the business.

The chances are high that grant finance will not be available, but it is well worth checking just in case. Grants may be available for quite specific purposes. For example, in areas of high unemployment it may be possible to obtain a grant for employing local people.

In Example 2.1 involving Julie's childcare business (which is a real-life example), grant finance was obtained successfully. The business would have gone ahead without it, but at the time the government was making generous grants available to any business creating additional childcare places, and a grant was obtained to cover the cost of providing equipment and for the first year staffing costs. However, although the grant was 'free' in the sense that a cheque for several thousand pounds was obtained and did not have to be paid back, there were strings attached. The progress of the business was monitored frequently by a local business agency and this involved the keeping of quite detailed monthly accounts, and attending monitoring meetings.

Commercial borrowings

Generally speaking, anyone proposing to start up a small business will be reluctant to borrow money from external sources, such as banks, if it can possibly be avoided. There are several sound reasons for this reluctance. First, banks charge commercial rates of interest on loans. This can add substantially to the costs of a business start-up and can make the difference between potential success and failure.

Secondly, bankers will not lend to just anyone. In fact, they usually will not lend to anyone who does not have a record of success in business. This is not a problem if you are embarking on start-up number ten, with nine successful businesses to your credit, but, realistically, most people without a good track record in business are likely to face a polite refusal when they ask for a start-up loan.

Thirdly, bankers want to know that their loans will be repaid. They will maximise the likelihood of repayment by insisting upon security for the loan. This means that an arrangement is made so that, if the loan is not repaid on time, the bank can take an item, or items, of at least equal value from the business or the individual in settlement of the debt. The bank will usually insist upon a legally binding agreement, known as a charge, to ensure that the loan gets repaid.

Example 2.5

Des starts up in business with a bank loan of £50 000. He owns his own home, and, to cover its interests, the bank requires a legal charge over Des's house. The business goes bust after two-and-a-half years, still owing the bank the original £50 000 plus £3000 in unpaid interest. Because the bank has the legal charge, the house must be sold to meet the debt, and Des and his family will, effectively, be evicted and may be made homeless. Bankers are only human, and an individual bank manager may try very hard to find an alternative course of action. Nevertheless, the charge is a legal document, and the bank is quite within its rights to insist upon repayment via the sale of the house. After all, Des went into this with his eyes open; he knew the risks and should be prepared to take the consequences.

If security is not available in any other form, bankers may ask for a guarantee from someone who is sufficiently wealthy to repay the loan if the business fails.

Example 2.6

Suleman wants to borrow £25 000 from the bank for a business start-up. He owns virtually nothing himself, so there is no question of setting up a legal charge as in Des's case. However, his father is a successful businessman who considers it very likely that his son has inherited his business ability. He signs a guarantee for Suleman's loan. If the business fails, still owing the money to the bank, then the bank will require Suleman's father to settle the debt.

This type of arrangement is fine, provided that the guarantor (that's the person giving the guarantee) thoroughly understands the possible consequences if the business fails. In Example 2.6, Suleman's father is an experienced businessman who knows exactly what he is agreeing to when he signs the guarantee. However, there have been unfortunate cases where the guarantor has not understood that he or she stands to lose a very large sum of money if the business goes bad.

A secured loan is less risky, from a bank's point of view, than an unsecured loan. The nature of the loan and the value of the security tends to affect the interest rate. The greater the risk, the higher the rate of interest. Therefore a loan made by a bank on good security will carry a lower interest charge than an unsecured loan.

We are now going to examine an example of a business start-up in an extended case study that divides into two parts. The first part looks at a very low-key start-up requiring little finance.

! SPOTLIGHT 2.1 Business start-up (Part 1)

The idea

Pete has a full-time job as a clerk in a factory office, working from 9.00am to 5.30pm Monday to Friday. Having left school with very few qualifications he has little scope in his present employment for promotion, and his earnings are relatively low. Until recently Pete and his partner, Angie, enjoyed a reasonably good standard of living; she also had a clerical job and the two salaries together allowed them to live comfortably. However, their circumstances have changed recently with the birth of their twin daughters. Angie has her hands full and is unlikely to be able to return to work until the children start school; it is not really worth her while to go back to work in the meantime because childcare for two children would eat up a large proportion of the additional income she could bring in. Besides, she thinks children do better if they have a parent with them full-time.

Pete wants to find a way of earning more money. He and Angie have a mortgage of £65 000 on a flat currently valued at £80 000. They have savings of £3000 kept in a 'rainy day' account on 90-days deposit. The flat looks very small now that there are four in the family but there is no realistic chance of moving to anywhere larger without an increase in income. Given the lack of promotion opportunities in his present job Pete has been looking around at ideas for self-employment. A recent visit to the gardens of a stately home has given him an idea. On the day that he and his family visited, a vintage car rally was taking place and there were large crowds of people around. Pete joined a long queue to buy two cups of coffee from a mobile stand. The refreshments facilities clearly did not match the demand and Pete could see the opportunity to make money.

On the way home he thought it through. He could use the family savings to buy a small mobile coffee stand. If he could borrow his brother's van he could take the stand around at weekends to antiques fairs, car rallies and the like. At the stately home he had paid £1.50 each for the cups of coffee – surely it must be possible to make money?

Financing issues

Peter's business idea is low-key in that it involves very little initial capital outlay, and very little risk. His immediate action plan would look like this:

- Find out about: (a) cost of mobile coffee stand; (b) any charges for setting up a pitch; (c) cost of coffee, cups, sugar etc.
- Discuss plan with: (a) Angie; (b) brother.

One week later

Pete has been busy. The first thing he did was talk the plan over with Angie. She was worried about the possibility of losing their savings, but Pete thinks that there would be very little risk involved. He has also asked his brother, Dave, about borrowing the van. Dave is a plumber and uses the van mostly during the week. He doesn't want to put a lot of extra mileage on the van, and points out to Pete that there will be times – about one weekend in four – when he's on call and will need the van. Pete agrees to pay his brother a reasonable charge for the hire of the van. This will reflect the mileage covered, and also the fact that there will be an additional insurance charge because the van is being used for a business other than plumbing.

Pete has looked at the cost of coffee machines. He cannot afford one of the bigger models, but has discovered he can save some cash by buying a second-hand reconditioned model. This would cost about £2000. For £100 he can buy sufficient coffee, plastic cups and so on to get started, but he doesn't know quite how long they'll last. He does some homework on possible venues, and discovers that the charges for pitches vary quite a lot. However, there is a small garden show due to take place only about 20 miles away, and the organisers are asking only £35 for the pitch that Pete wants.

He talks it through with Angie again. She is still worried. It isn't just the possible loss of the savings; Pete has succeeded in convincing her that if he can't make a go of the business the machine can always be sold on again, and the potential loss is small. She spends all week alone with the twins while Pete is out at work, and she doesn't want to have to cope alone for much of the weekend as well. Pete doesn't really have an answer to this objection, but suggests that she might get her mother or sister to come and stay to take the pressure off. Pete and Angie have an argument over this, but it concludes with her saying that he might as well try it out for a couple of months to see what happens. The next day Pete goes out and buys the coffee machine and arranges to borrow the van from his brother for the day of the garden show.

What are Pete's chances of success?

Factors in Pete's favour include the following:

- He doesn't have to borrow money, and the start-up is very low cost.
- The business idea is simple and will fit in with his existing job.
- He has the support (although not wholehearted) of his immediate family.

Factors working against Pete include:

- He hasn't investigated the business idea thoroughly. What about the competition? Owners of competitor stands might object to a newcomer.
- He hasn't attempted to estimate how much profit the business might make, or thought very clearly about how much he will charge per cup of coffee.
- He should probably have done more research on possible venues.
- Angie may be going to find it very difficult to cope alone at weekends. In addition, Pete doesn't seem to have considered the fact that his plan means that he will see very little of his family, and also that he is committing himself to working six or seven days a week.

Summary

Not all of the above factors relate to finance. We would need to know a lot more (and so would Pete) to be able to assess realistically his chances of success. From a financial point of view, Pete is unlikely (unless he's particularly unlucky or incompetent) to lose a lot of money. However, he should really be thinking more carefully about the business start-up than appears to be the case. It is clear from the case study that Pete's attitude to risk is more relaxed than Angie's. This could be an advantage, up to a point, in that he won't waste time and energy in worrying too much about the progress of the business. However, past a certain point, his attitude could lead to recklessness.

The business plan

Spotlight 2.1 shows a business start-up that has not been properly thought out. Pete should have produced a business plan. If he were seeking financing in the form of a loan or a grant he would certainly have to produce a quite detailed plan. However, even though he is not looking for finance it would be well worth his while to produce a plan. It would help him to clarify his ideas about the business, and give him some idea of its chances of success.

The business plan normally includes most or all of the following elements:

- Description of the business concept.
- Detailed description of the product or service that the business will offer.
- The market for the product or service, including market research and analysis of the competition.
- Profile of entrepreneur. A personal profile detailing relevant experience (including possibly a CV) and an analysis of personal strengths and weaknesses.
- Initial investment required. Type and cost of equipment, premises and similar items.
- Details of other people involved. If the plan is to employ people straight away, details are required of how they will be recruited and how much it will cost to employ them.
- Insurance requirements. Any relevant legal issues.
- Professional advisers. Details of the type of professional advice that may be required and how much it is likely to cost.
- Detailed financial projections. A budget will be required for at least the first year, showing the projected profit and cash flow.

The 'budget' is a statement of anticipated future income and expenses. 'Profit' is the amount left over after all the expenses of a business have been taken away from income. 'Cash flow' is the movement of cash in and out of the business.

Comparing the information in Spotlight 2.1 with the requirements of the business plan, we can see that Pete has some of the information he needs, but should really do a lot more investigative work before starting the business. The second part of the case study follows Pete's first 18 months of trading.

SPOTLIGHT 2.1   Business start-up (Part 2)

Pete's business after 18 months

Despite the absence of a proper plan for his business, Pete has managed to muddle through the first 18 months and has succeeded in making some money. He met several unexpected problems and had some bad luck:

- The coffee business is dependent on the weather. At Pete's first venue, the garden show, the temperature was very high and the ice cream vans did excellent business. Pete, on the other hand, had a disappointing day and didn't even manage to cover the costs of the pitch.

- Because Pete hadn't investigated the market he didn't understand how important the position of his pitch would be. The best pitches at a lot of venues are taken by experienced vendors and people like Pete lose out. However, he started attending smaller events and found that he could make more money that way; sometimes his is the only coffee stand, and he has had some excellent days' takings.

- Pete was involved in an accident when driving Dave's van to a venue. The immediate result of this was that he lost a day's takings, but the longer-term problem was that Dave refused to lend him the van again once it was repaired. Pete has therefore had to hire a van and it has cost him a lot of extra money.

- Pete didn't keep proper control over the cash coming in from the business. At the end of each day he put all the banknotes in his wallet, mixed up with his own money, and would use them for spending money. From time to time he would bank any surplus in his and Angie's joint bank account. After several months in business Dave persuaded him to go to see his accountant, Norris. Norris told Pete that he must keep the money from the business separate from his own money, and must count up and record each day's takings. Norris has sorted things out now, but he's just presented Pete with a bill for £550. He tells Pete that £300 of this cost came about through having to sort out the mess that resulted from Pete not keeping proper records.

The new plan

Despite these problems Pete loves running his own business. He really enjoys chatting with the people he meets at the venues, and he and Angie both like having the extra income. He likes the feeling of not having a boss telling him what to do, and he even enjoys the risk and uncertainty of running his own business.

Pete decides that he wants to give up the clerical job and go into full-time self-employment. He decides that he wants to open a coffee shop in the town centre. Pete is more confident now and he's sure he can make a go of it.

There's a small shop to let on the edge of the main town centre shopping area; Pete rings the commercial estate agent who is dealing with the premises and finds that he could take out a five-year lease at a rental of £7500 per year. The shop would need refurbishment, but Pete's brother Dave (who has got over the trauma of having his van wrecked and is now on good terms again) knows a lot of people in the building trade who would do a good job at minimum cost.

Pete gets home from work and tells Angie about his idea. Angie is extremely unhappy about it; she becomes very agitated, loses her temper and starts shouting. She has got used to Pete working most weekends, and the extra money is really useful. If they were careful they could think about moving house sometime next year. She can now see that Pete really wasn't risking much in setting up his coffee business 18 months ago. But now, it seems crazy to her that Pete should even think about giving up his job to take on such a big risk as a proper coffee shop.

Financing issues

Pete has a great deal more to think about this time. He will need to find some external finance for this venture. Norris, the accountant, says that he can help him prepare a business plan to present to the bank manager, and that Pete should start thinking about the type of costs involved in setting up this venture.

Pete comes up with the following list of costs:

- rent
- refurbishment costs
- new equipment (coffee machinery, tables, chairs, crockery and so on)
- insurance
- business rates
- advertising
- wages (he will need to employ somebody else part-time for the busiest times of the week)
- coffee and other catering supplies
- electricity, water and phone bills.

He shows this list to Norris who says 'Well, so far so good, but there are some other things you haven't thought of. What about legal fees for setting up the lease? And I'll be putting in a bill for advice on your business plan, as well as the charges for doing your tax return. Also, if you get a bank loan for the start-up there will be a charge for interest.'

Other issues

Pete has a lot more work to do before he can decide whether or not this new business idea will work out. What about the competition? Are there other coffee shops in the area? Will there be a demand for food or snacks, as well as for coffee? Is the coffee shop really in the right location to attract customers? How much money does the business need to make to cover costs and to ensure that there is enough for the family to live on? Also, how is he going to persuade Angie that it's a good idea? If he can't get her support should he go ahead with the new business?

This second business idea of Pete's is very much more risky than the first. He's managed to make money out of the first business, although he's muddled through rather than following a proper plan. He's made quite a few mistakes, but he's learned something about running a business and has found that he enjoys being self-employed. However, if he takes on this business and it fails, what's going to happen to him and his family?

Why do businesses fail (and why do some of them succeed)?

It can be quite difficult to estimate the failure rate for businesses. Researchers have estimated that, of every ten businesses started up, only two will still be in existence after five years. The government produces insolvency statistics (**www.insolvency. gov.uk**). In 2003 there were over 36 000 individual insolvencies in England and Wales, and over 14 000 corporate insolvencies in England, Wales and Scotland.

Failure factors

The Association of Business Recovery Professionals (**www.r3.org.uk**) regularly surveys failed businesses to find out the reasons why they did not succeed. The main reasons are:

- poor management
- lack of working capital
- lack of long-term finance
- bad debts
- loss of market.

Poor management

As we saw earlier, Pete didn't really understand about managing the money in his business; he could have run into serious trouble with the tax authorities if his brother had not suggested consulting an accountant. His failure to manage properly could have taken many other forms: for example, failing to take out the right kind of insurance. Some people who go into business are brilliant at product ideas, or providing the service that is the basis of the business, but are no good at day-to-day management. They may be both untrained and inexperienced in management.

Lack of working capital

Essentially, lack of working capital means running out of money. The bank manager might allow the business to borrow some money on overdraft, but overdrafts always have a limit. Once the limit is reached, closing the business down may be the only option available.

Lack of long-term finance

There is no money to invest in the long-term future of the business. For example, a new machine is required but the business cannot afford to buy it outright and no one will lend the money. In the short term the business may be able to struggle on, but long-term survival is unlikely.

Bad debts

Bad debts are not a problem for a business like Pete's where cash changes hands at the point where the product is purchased. However, if a business supplies on credit (that is, ships the goods to the customer before payment is received) and a big customer will not or cannot pay up, that can result in failure.

Loss of market

This can happen when a competitor business sets up successfully and takes away some of the market share. For example, a florist's business two streets away from a hospital will probably do well. However, if a rival florist opens up in a shop right next door to the hospital this will almost certainly result in a major impact on the existing florist's business.

This list is all very depressing, especially for anyone who is seriously thinking about setting up a business. However, many businesses do succeed and prosper. The factors that tend to lead to success include adequate financing, a cautious approach to risk-taking, existing management experience and sheer good luck.

Chapter summary

This chapter has covered some of the important elements of starting a business. We have seen that financial considerations are just part (although an important part) of the decision to start a business.

We have established a foundation for the study of business finance and accounting. The rest of Section One of the book deals with the financing of larger businesses. After that we will turn to a more detailed study of accounting matters.

Internet resources

Some useful websites:

www.businesslink.gov.uk – answers some frequently asked questions about small businesses in the UK.

www.dti.gov.uk – the website of the Department of Trade and Industry containing vast amounts of useful information about all aspects of business in the UK.

www.r3.org.uk – the website of the Association of Business Recovery Professionals.

www.about.com/business – A US site providing useful advice about a range of business issues, including start-ups.

www.startbusiness.co.uk – includes a very useful guide to the contents of a business plan

www.insolvency.gov.uk – includes a lot of information about business failure in the UK.

 The end-of-chapter exercises are divided into two sections. The first section has answers provided at the end of the book. The second section, in the white box, has answers on the lecturers' section of the website.

Website summary

The book's website contains the following material in respect of Chapter 2:

Students' section

- Quiz containing ten multiple choice questions
- Two additional questions with answers.

Lecturers' section

- Answers to exercises 2.3 and 2.4
- Two additional questions with answers.

Exercises: answers at the end of the book

2.1 Erika is planning to become a self-employed graphic designer working from a small one-room office in a new development in the middle of town. You are a small business adviser and she has asked you for help in producing her business plan. You decide to prepare a list of questions to ask Erika at your first meeting, based on the major headings that you would expect to see covered in the business plan.

2.2 Ben has a degree in public relations and a huge list of useful contacts in the aerospace business, which he has established over a period of several years while working for Amis & Lovett, a large PR agency. He would like to set up his own PR agency. He plans to employ a new graduate and a secretary immediately in order to avoid being regarded as a 'one-man band'. He is confident that his savings (£45 000) will tide him over the first couple of months while he finds enough work to get started. List the main risks that you see in Ben's plan for the new business start-up.

Exercises: answers available to lecturers

2.3 Ashok has been left £100 000 by his grandma in her will. He plans to start a haulage business and will use part of the money to purchase an HGV. He already has an HGV licence. His wife will run the administration side of the business, initially from home, until they can afford to lease an office. Advise Ashok on the principal types of expense that you think he will face in running his haulage business.

2.4 Choose any two of the following businesses and, for each, write a list of the main expenses you think would be involved in running them as a profit-making business.

a) Childcare facility catering for children from three months to five years.

b) University cafe serving light snacks and lunches.

c) Internet-based travel agency.

d) Advertising agency.

e) Firm of estate agents.

CHAPTER 3

The growing business

Aim of the chapter

To assist in understanding some of the problems and opportunities that face the growing business, especially those related to finance.

Learning outcomes

After reading the chapter and its spotlight study, and completing the exercises at the end, students should:

- Know about some of the important stages in business expansion.
- Understand some of the problems and opportunities presented by business growth, including issues related to employment, developing the business organisation and moving into new markets.
- Know about the typical money management issues that face the proprietors of successful and growing businesses.
- Appreciate that business growth inevitably involves risk.

Introduction

In Chapter 2 we looked at some of the evidence about business survival. The evidence is not particularly encouraging in that the majority of new businesses will fail. In this chapter we will look at those businesses which survive and, to a greater or lesser extent, prosper. Prosperity and growth bring problems of their own. Sometimes established businesses are simply unlucky: perhaps key staff leave, a competitor offering a cheaper product or service becomes established, or some unforeseen event takes place such as accident or illness of the business proprietor. Sometimes, on the other hand, problems arise that the proprietor(s) of the growing business are simply unable to handle, such as growth that proceeds too rapidly or inability to cope with changing circumstances.

However, although problems may arise, there are also increased opportunities arising from growth. If a business does really well its original owners may be able to sell their stake and realise large amounts of cash. If the original objective in setting up the business was to become seriously rich, such owners achieve their ambition. For owners who decide to remain involved in the business, new opportunities may arise for business expansion. As a business grows and builds up a track record of success it becomes easier for it to borrow money in order to fuel further growth. Often, people who start and run successful businesses thrive on the new challenges and would not choose to give up their involvement even if they were able to retire early with large sums of cash.

In this chapter we will examine the phases of growth from a small to medium-sized business, charting some of the major milestones in business development. Financial management issues are often significant in the development of the growing business, and we will look at several relevant examples.

Stages in business growth and expansion

Employing people

In the previous chapter we examined a sole trader business. Many businesses do not grow past the point where they generate an income for one person and his or her dependants. A self-employed tradesperson, such as a plumber, small builder or garden designer may have no particular need or wish to expand the business to the point where employing another person becomes necessary. However, some business people will see the need for expansion, and employing another person is often the first step towards expansion.

Advantages of employing people in a small business

There is an opportunity to increase the skills base of the business. As we noted in the last chapter, one of the reasons why businesses fail is because of poor management. A sole trader is particularly vulnerable to this type of problem; he or she has to marshal a range of skills including selling abilities, financial management skills, organisational ability, self-discipline and so on. If any one of these is missing the business may fail. One way around the problem of missing skills is to either go into partnership with someone whose skills are complementary, or, in some cases, to employ a person who can contribute skills lacking in the proprietor.

Employing people is likely to increase the volume of trade in goods or services. Two pairs of hands can achieve more than one. If the right person is employed, he or she may be able to contribute to the profitability of the business.

Example 3.1

Kingsley is a self-employed furniture designer who undertakes commissions for the provision of original, well-designed furniture for businesses. He started up in business two years ago, and he has been very successful in generating work. He now has more than he can easily cope with. He is working seven days a week from early morning until late at night and his relationships with friends and family are suffering. Also, he has received some unpleasant letters recently from suppliers, including a threat from the electricity utility company to cut off his supplies unless he pays his bill within seven days.

It is pretty clear that Kingsley needs help. Administering a small business can take a disproportionately large amount of time. While Kingsley may not be ready to take on a full-time administrator, he should examine the possibility of employing a part-timer who can keep control of the paperwork. This would, presumably, free up part of Kingsley's time so that he could get on with more productive work.

The other area in which he probably needs help is in the design work. This is a much more difficult issue to resolve than the administration. People award Kingsley design commissions because they like his work. If he delegates some of the work to an assistant the design values may suffer. Unless Kingsley is prepared to carry on working all hours, he will have to make a decision on whether he keeps the business very small by turning down any commissions that he cannot manage himself, or, alternatively, whether he is prepared to share the design work with someone else. The first course of action involves a risk; if he turns down too much work the supply of commissions may dry up altogether. The second course of action also involves a risk; will the quality of work suffer? Also, does Kingsley have the necessary management skills to control the work of one or more designer employees?

Disadvantages of employing people in a small business

There is a very significant risk attached to employment. If a poor choice of employee is made, the mistake can threaten the survival of the business. Mistakes can be made in employing someone with whom there is a personality clash, or someone who is less competent than they appeared from their CV and the interview. Many employers will make an employment decision which, sooner or later, they come to regret.

Employing people costs money. Many successful small businesses pass through an awkward stage where there is too much work for the sole trader or partners to handle by themselves but where the financial risk of taking on an employee is unacceptable. The business proprietor(s) must be sure that they have the financial resources to pay for employment.

Employing people involves a great deal of paperwork. If staff are employed, the business becomes involved in the administration of pay as you earn (PAYE) and National Insurance contributions (NIC) on behalf of the employee. Detailed records must be kept, and these are liable to be inspected periodically by the Inland Revenue. Business people often complain bitterly about the amount of work they have to undertake as tax collectors on behalf of the government. The amount of administration involved acts, potentially, as a disincentive to employing people. (However, it should be noted, perhaps, that the administrative burden in the UK is probably less than in some other countries. France, for example, imposes a notoriously heavy administrative burden on the employer.)

Example 3.2

Recently, Kelly started a business importing and selling ornamental lamps, vases and similar items to retailers. The business has been successful, making profits of £35 000 in its first year and £38 000 in its second. Kelly has realised that, if the business is going to be able to grow, she will have to employ someone to assist her in selling goods to retailers. The ideal employee would have a good track record in selling and would be able and willing to travel four or five days a week visiting stores.

What financial factors does Kelly need to consider in making a decision about employing an assistant?

■ *Salary.* Kelly needs to look carefully at how much she will have to pay in order to ensure the right employee. She needs someone with experience and who is prepared to act on his or her own initiative. Part of Kelly's annual profits will have to go to paying the employee. In addition to the annual salary, there
will be the cost of providing transport (presumably an additional car will be required).

■ *Employer's National Insurance and administration costs.* The employer must pay employer's National Insurance contributions, and the cost of administering the payroll must be taken into account. Kelly may be able to undertake this herself (the cost of doing this is the time taken up, which could be used on something else), or she may have to pay her accountant a little extra to do it.

■ *Balancing costs and benefits.* If Kelly succeeds in employing someone who is good at selling, the benefits could far outweigh the costs of employment.

Suppose the total cost of employment is £30 000 per year; provided the employee can generate additional business that makes more than this amount in profit then it makes good business sense for Kelly to employ him or her. There may be other less obvious benefits: if Kelly gets flu and has to spend a week in bed the business, at the moment, grinds to a halt until she is better. If she could depend upon an employee, the business could be kept going more or less as normal.

Developing the business organisation

As a business grows and starts to employ more people, the way in which it is organised becomes more of an issue. There is a tendency in most business organisations to establish manageable units according to the functions they carry out. For example, in a typical manufacturing organisation it may be appropriate to establish separate departments for marketing, production, despatch, design, personnel, accounting and general administration. In the early days of the business only one or two people will be employed in each function, and the business proprietors are likely to retain firm control over all of the operations of the business. However, as the business grows, it becomes increasingly difficult for its owners to control every aspect of its functions. It is important for proprietors to be able to recognise when this stage has arrived, and to be prepared to delegate control to others.

Professional management

People who have started up successful businesses are often very reluctant to concede any part of their control to others. However, in most cases, it eventually becomes necessary to employ professional managers – people who have the experience and knowledge to manage functions such as marketing and personnel. Conflict sometimes ensues between the managers and the founders of the business as they disagree about the right way to manage change and growth.

Communication issues

As the business grows and departmental structures emerge, a range of communication problems can arise. Departments develop their own identities, and can, if not properly managed, become narrow in outlook, fighting territorial battles with other departments to protect their own status. Where this type of 'in-fighting' occurs, the overall objectives of the business tend to be forgotten.

Growth in bureaucracy

As we have already noted in this chapter, a certain amount of unavoidable record-keeping and administration is imposed on businesses by government regulation. As businesses grow and organisational functions separate, the business itself starts to require more complex records. An accounting department is usually required in order to keep the financial records straight. Some kind of authorisation and control procedures are inevitably required, but a great deal of management skill is needed to make sure that the generation of paperwork does not get out of hand. Organisations with excessive administration procedures may ultimately fail because they have become too inwardly focused. For example, staff become demotivated by the requirement to produce what they see as excessive paperwork. Perhaps the need for prompt and thorough organisational reporting starts to take priority over activities such as production quality control and establishing new sales contacts.

Moving into new markets or products

Expansion and growth of a successful business usually involves moving into new areas. Sometimes, this means expanding the range of products and/or services on offer, or new opportunities may arise to expand the market that the business serves. Clearly, there is always a risk involved in taking this kind of action. Some examples of typical business expansion decisions are examined in the following sub-sections.

Borrowing to finance expansion

Expanding a business involves additional costs, which can be substantial. The managers responsible for making the decision on whether or not to expand the business need to think carefully about all of the costs and potential benefits involved. Borrowing is often an attractive option, but the risks should be properly weighed up. The next example looks at a typical expansion decision.

| Example 3.3 |

Lucinda and Lister are sole (and equal) shareholders and directors of L & L Limos Limited, a company that runs a small fleet of limousines for hire for weddings and by celebrities visiting the local area. Each year the business has gradually expanded its total sales as its reputation for reliability has grown. There is no direct competitor for their service in their own town, and, increasingly often, the firm is asked to undertake business in neighbouring towns and cities. Quite often the directors have to turn business away because all of the available cars are booked. Expanding the fleet and taking on new drivers seems like an increasingly attractive option.

How could this expansion be financed? The following costs would be involved: (a) the purchase or leasing costs of new vehicles; and (b) the employment of drivers, plus related costs. Also, the expansion might incur additional administrative costs (because more bookings would be made, more invoices would be generated and so on), and perhaps additional premises costs. The limos have to be housed securely in garage premises, and it might be necessary to expand the space available.

The directors need to look at the costs involved and think about financing. Several options may be open to them:

■ *Investment in new vehicles.* Buying the limos outright involves a substantial capital outlay and it might be preferable to lease the vehicles. However, if the directors want to borrow to finance outright purchase of the new limos they may well be able, as an established business, to obtain a bank loan quite easily. If they do not wish to take the risk of borrowing, they may be able to lend their own savings to the company.

■ *Investment in other costs of expansion by using existing resources* If there is spare cash available in the business, financing the expansion could be a good use for the funds.

■ *Financing via a flexible overdraft facility*. The directors need to prepare a cash flow budget that will reveal any points in the year at which short-term finance may be needed to cover shortfalls.

The directors face the risk that they have misjudged the market. If they invest in expansion and the demand for services is less than they thought, they may severely damage the future prospects of the business. Another risk is that, if they borrow money, interest rates could rise and become more of a burden on the business.

Amalgamating businesses to create expansion

Amalgamation of two or more businesses can be an attractive route to growth. For example, the managers of a business may decide that they wish to expand their business to a different city or area of the country. Starting up a new branch from scratch may be difficult, perhaps because the competition is well established. In such circumstances it often makes sense to try to join forces with a similar business in the area. Similarly, where a business wishes to expand the range of services it offers, the least-cost option may be to amalgamate with an established business.

Example 3.4

Linus, Lonsdale & Co is a firm of accountants established about ten years ago by Peregrine Linus and Paula Lonsdale. The business has always made a profit, and in recent years profitability has tended to improve. At a recent society of accountants' local meeting they met a sole practitioner, Liz, who is looking for an opportunity to merge her practice with another. She finds it difficult to cover the range of services that people expect from an accountant these days, and would like to take her own business into a partnership arrangement with another small practice. She specialises in capital gains tax and inheritance tax advisory services.

Bringing the two firms together would create a larger firm with three partners. If their range of skills is complementary the larger practice could, potentially, provide a better service to clients than at present. Also, a larger firm is in a better position to take on larger businesses as clients.

An amalgamation of businesses like this would probably involve some costs (for example, it might be necessary to enlarge the premises) but these would probably be fairly modest. The combined business could be more effective and better placed to expand in the future.

What risks are involved? The principal risk for the two firms is that the amalgamation does not work because of differences in style between the partners. The three partners must be able to get along harmoniously and, ideally, should have skills that complement each other. In a small firm it is very difficult to ignore major personality clashes.

Takeovers

In the previous example the amalgamation under consideration would involve the owners of the two businesses entering into partnership together. All of them would retain an ownership interest in the expanded firm. Takeovers, by contrast, involve buying out the interests of most, or all, of the existing owners. Where a business decides to attempt a takeover of a limited company (the 'target company'), for example, the shareholders in the target company are approached to see if they are willing to sell their shares. Where there are few shareholders this process can be relatively straightforward. If both buyer and seller(s) are willing, and a suitable price can be agreed, the takeover can go ahead. The result will be an expanded business, but the original holders of the shares will no longer have any financial or other interest in it.

The next example looks at a typical proposed takeover. Some of the business risks involved in takeovers are explored.

Example 3.5

Lupine Leisure Limited is a very successful manufacturer of sportswear. The company has grown rapidly since it was established five years ago, and it has built up a substantial cash surplus. The company's managing director, Lex Lupine, is highly entrepreneurial and is full of ideas for expanding the company's range of interests. The company's goods sell in a competitive market where big discounters and retailers are able to put pressure on suppliers to cut prices. Lex is unhappy with the margins that the company makes. He would like to break through into the retail market so that the company would control not only manufacturing but also the retailing of the products.

The options available to the company are to:

- Finance the opening and management of a small chain of retail stores.
- Acquire a small chain of retail stores (Lex has his eye on a particular chain that he thinks is ripe for takeover).

In both cases the medium-term plan would be to build aggressively upon a small-ish local network of stores to expand rapidly into neighbouring areas and, within five years, have nationwide representation. (Lex likes to think big.) When Lex presents the options to the other directors, he points out the advantages of the takeover approach: 'The beauty of it is that we can do this very quickly. We don't have to look around for suitable retail stores, and then arrange leases and employ managers and staff and so on. If we buy the chain it's all set up and in place. We can then concentrate on improving the overall management – we'll keep the decent managers and get rid of the rest – and we'll be in prime position to take up all the profit that's going.'

There are several potential risks in this situation. First, Lex may have misjudged the situation. He is seeking to integrate the supply of goods with their retailing, but the expansion into another area of the supply chain may not work well. The directors of Lupine Leisure are clearly good at running a manufacturing company; they may not have the necessary skills and experience to run a retailer successfully.

Secondly, there is a risk that, because of lack of knowledge, the company could pay too much for the retailer. If the retailer is a takeover target it may be because of some inherent weakness in its operations.

Thirdly, Lex wants to 'keep the decent managers and get rid of the rest'. However, what often happens in such situations is that the managers in takeover targets become concerned about their future prospects in the new, larger organisation. The good managers, who have portable skills and can easily get new jobs, tend to leave. The managers who stay may be the people who cannot easily transfer, perhaps because they are near to retiring age, or because they simply do not have the requisite skills and experience to attract another employer.

Finally, because of the apparent attractions of the scheme to take over the retailer, the directors of Lupine Leisure may not be giving sufficient thought to alternative uses for the company's cash resources.

Making money

As we have seen, the evidence is that most business start-ups do not succeed. However, those that do succeed may flourish and make money for their proprietors. In this section we will look at some of the issues and problems related to money management that arise for the owners of successful businesses.

Extracting cash

How do business people actually take money out of their businesses? We saw in the previous chapter, in the case study concerning Pete, that business resources must be kept strictly separate from personal resources. A business must be able to declare its profits for taxation purposes, and in order to do that, must have an orderly system of record-keeping. The business entity concept of accounting describes the necessary separation of the business and its proprietor.

Sole traders and partners in partnerships take money (and sometimes goods) out of the business in the form of drawings. Sole traders and partners usually need to take drawings from their businesses to pay their normal living expenses.

Where the business is set up as a company, the situation is slightly different. Directors are employees of the business and usually receive a salary for their work, just like any other employee. Where the directors are also shareholders they receive cash in the form of a dividend, which may be paid once or twice annually. Many companies have just one or two shareholders and directors who are the same people. The proprietors of such companies usually receive cash, therefore, in two forms: salaries and dividends. There are tax advantages to be gained by getting the balance of salaries and dividends just right; usually the business's accountant advises on the correct combination.

Managing cash within the business

One way of helping the business to grow is to keep past profits to fund future growth. Most business proprietors, therefore, aim to keep a balance between the amount of cash they remove from the business and the amount that is left in to fund growth. Spare cash in the business should be put to good use to help create future wealth – if it lies more or less dormant in a low interest bearing bank account, it is not being well used. Business proprietors and managers need to manage the position carefully so as to ensure that the business does not run short of cash when it is needed, but also that it is properly used to optimise the overall profitability of the business.

Exit strategies

Although people starting new businesses rarely bother thinking about it, it is important at some stage to start thinking about the most effective way of exiting a business. Serial entrepreneurs, whose principal interest is in start-ups, may be the exceptions to this generalisation; they will often have a vision of the length of time they wish to devote to the business before bailing out and starting on a new venture. However, all proprietors of successful businesses will need at some stage to evolve an exit strategy by addressing some of the following questions:

- When do I want to retire/leave?
- Who should take on the business when I go?
- How am I going to prepare for the transition to new management?
- Should I just sell my stake in the business?
- Is it saleable?
- Who is likely to buy it?

The problem is one of turning business wealth into hard cash which can be taken away by the retiring proprietor. This is more feasible for some kinds of business than for others. Businesses that manufacture or trade in goods, which have machinery, premises and a good brand name may be quite easy to sell. For example, earlier, in Example 3.5, we looked at the possibility of buying a chain of retail shops in preference to setting up shop businesses from scratch. As well as the shops, the fittings, the stock and so on, the retail chain would have a recognised brand name and, probably, some degree of customer loyalty. Factors such as loyalty and brand name are brought together under the general heading of goodwill in business terminology. Goodwill refers to all those intangible factors that are hard to quantify, but which add value to a business. Brand names, in particular, are powerful and valuable signifiers of a set of attributes to which customers are attracted.

By contrast, businesses that rely upon the particular skills and expertise of their proprietor may have little value once the proprietor decides to leave the business. In service businesses, there may be little left apart from desks and chairs once the proprietor (along with any remaining cash) is removed. For this type of business there is a particular challenge in building it up to the point where it can be continued without the original founder. The founder of the business may not want to let go of an enterprise that he or she has nurtured from day one, but part of ensuring the business's longer-term survival is to ensure that effective successors are identified and that they are given the space and opportunity to develop the business.

Some of the issues explored in this chapter are examined in the following spotlight study.

❗ SPOTLIGHT 3.1 A successful business in danger

In this spotlight study we will examine some of the problems that can face even a successful business. The business context is that of a partnership, but some of the problems could also be found in a sole trader or company structure.

Chris and Anwar have been in partnership for over eight years running a computer consultancy business. Both men are in their mid-40s. They first met up almost 30 years ago at Sixth Form College where they studied computing at A level and founded a computer programmer's club. After that, they went to different universities and then gradually lost touch. However, almost ten years ago they met up again at a school reunion and started talking about their dissatisfaction with their respective jobs. At the time Anwar was employed in computer sales; although his job was well paid with high levels of commission, he really felt the time had come to run his own business. Chris had had various programming and consultancy jobs but he, too, was unhappy at the time because of an unsympathetic boss.

A year or so after their chance meeting, Chris and Anwar had taken the plunge into self-employment. Eight years on they remain the sole partners in the business, but now they employ nine consultants, three secretaries and a bookkeeper. The business has been successful and profitable almost from day one; the partners have complementary skills and have continued to work harmoniously together. Anwar is the public face of the firm; he has a 'larger-than-life' personality, is immensely sociable and extrovert, and has been able to build up a huge range of useful contacts in many industry sectors. The firm has never been short of work; in fact, the consultants all have to put in long hours to fulfil the existing contracts. Chris is the details man; he organises the provision of consultancy time to ensure that the contract requirements are met and is in charge of the management of all administrative matters. His technical knowledge is more advanced than Anwar's and he is involved hands-on in every contract the firm takes on. Despite having such different personalities, Chris and Anwar get along very well both personally and in business. They see each other socially, their families get along well and their sons go to the same school.

Now, however, the business has reached its first major crisis. About a year ago, Anwar suffered a fairly serious heart attack. He was advised to cut back on his hours of work, to give up smoking and to lead a much healthier life. It's been a huge struggle, but he's managed to kick the smoking habit; cutting back on work, however, has been much more difficult. Anwar loves his work; he cannot imagine life without it. Chris has encouraged him to leave earlier, to take on less and not to work so much at weekends. The trouble is, though, that the business is so absorbing and there's always so much to do that he hasn't really noticed that Anwar is putting in just as many hours as before.

One morning Anwar doesn't come into the office and Chris gets a phone call from the hospital. Anwar has suffered a much more serious heart attack; he will need major surgery and there is no question of him returning to work for many months. For the first time, Chris is really on his own.

A couple of days later, Marcia, one of the firm's best consultants, drops into Chris's office to tell him that she's leaving. She's got a good offer from one of the business's competitors. The initial salary is less than she's getting at the moment, but she's been promised a partnership position in a year's time. She says she's sorry to have to add to Chris's troubles by leaving at this point, but she has been in negotiations with the rival firm for a couple of months now. Chris tries to persuade her to stay, but Marcia's made her mind up. As she explains: 'The thing is, Chris, I've been here five years, and you and Anwar have never so much as mentioned me joining the partnership. I know I've done well here financially, but I'm still just an employee and I always will be as far as you're concerned.'

Chris is completely taken aback by this development. He really doesn't know what to do. Neither he nor Anwar has ever thought about inviting someone else to join the partnership. They've just assumed that the staff must be happy because they're earning so much money.

There's another problem, too. For the last three or four years, the business has been severely short of office space. The consultants spend most of their time out of the office visiting and working at clients. However, they all need some office space for the time they spend designing and planning solutions to clients' problems, liaising with equipment suppliers, and dealing with general administration. There has been a severe shortage of desk and storage space, and the business records are in a mess. Three months ago, Anwar and Chris started looking around for office premises to buy. Almost immediately they found the perfect solution – a three-storey office block not far from the existing offices. There would be enough space for all the staff on the first two floors, and the third floor could be let to provide some investment income. The purchase is going to be financed partly in cash, and partly by a mortgage secured on the value of the property. The partners are due to exchange legally binding contracts on the office building next week.

Later on Chris starts thinking seriously about the future for the first time. What's going to happen if Anwar doesn't get better, or if he can't return to work full-time? How will he, Chris, manage? He knows he doesn't have the skills or the sheer force of personality to take on Anwar's role as the public face of the firm. He shrinks at the thought of going out actively looking for business. He doesn't enjoy taking people out to lunch, like Anwar does, and he knows that he's no good at selling. He's always been a 'backroom' person.

What about the future of the firm? If Marcia leaves to become a partner elsewhere, perhaps the other consultants will follow her example and go too. What about the new office building? Should he go ahead and buy it on behalf of the firm?

Chris now thinks that perhaps he and Anwar should have thought about this sooner. And another thing: even assuming that Anwar's operation proves to be completely successful, and he's able to return to work full-time, what should they do about the future? One day they'll want to retire from the firm with a large enough amount of money to allow them a very comfortable retirement. What's the firm actually worth? Would he and Anwar be able to sell it?

The worst thing is that, for the first time since they set up the business together, Chris feels that he cannot discuss the business with Anwar. It wouldn't be fair to burden him with the problems when he's so ill.

Chris is very much in need of advice. What action should he take, both immediately and in the medium term?

Spotlight discussion

The partnership between Chris and Anwar has been very successful up till now; it appears to be based upon a sound working relationship that is enhanced by the partners' complementary skills. Anwar deals with the aspects of the business that require good people skills, while Chris is more of a technician and administrator.

Now, however, the partnership and therefore the business, is in danger. While the immediate problem relates to Anwar's state of health and the question mark over his future contribution to the business, there is an emerging problem with staff that has been building up, it appears, over a long period of time. High salary levels have not, evidently, been enough to keep Marcia committed to the business. She wants to be involved in running the business, and to be entitled to a profit share, and she is prepared to take the risk of leaving in order to put herself in the running for a partnership position. If Marcia feels like this it is quite possible that some of her colleagues feel the same way, and they may also be thinking about leaving.

One major problem that faces Chris is that he cannot take significant decisions without the involvement of his partner. Ideally, he needs to wait until Anwar returns, or at least, is sufficiently well to discuss the problems facing the business. The decision to buy the new premises, however, was taken jointly by them both, and Chris probably ought to go ahead with that. If the basic property investment is sound, it is unlikely that the partnership would lose money in the long run. Chris will probably have to organise the details of the move into the new premises himself, but then he would probably have handled that area of work in any case.

Decisions have to be made in the near future on the following:

- Employing someone to replace Marcia.
- Possibly employing someone to take over parts of Chris's work while he stands in for Anwar.
- Reallocating parts of Anwar's work to other consultants.

In the medium term decisions must be made on the following:

- Creating an employment and incentive structure in the firm that will allow it to retain staff.
- Agreeing on ways in which the ownership of the firm can be spread more widely, with a view to easing the retirement of the two existing partners and allowing them to withdraw the value of their equity from the firm.

If Anwar is unable to return to a full-time role within the business, the problems become even more pressing. Chris knows that he doesn't have the right mix of skills to take his partner's place. If the firm is to survive, he must ensure that Anwar's role in the firm is taken over by someone else. This may mean, ultimately, appointing from outside, merging with another similar firm, or allowing the firm to be taken over.

What is the business worth to Anwar and Chris? The spotlight study is a good illustration of how an apparently successful business could easily fade away as a result of an unforeseen event. This is a service business that depends for its survival on the partners and the quality of the staff they employ. Without the people, the business has very little substance or worth.

If the partners want to be able to take cash out of the business when they retire they need to plan their exit strategy carefully. The strategy will almost certainly involve admitting other people into the partnership. New partners admitted to an established business usually have to buy their way in, either by contributing a share of their salaries over a period of years, or by contributing a lump sum. These contributions compensate the existing partners for giving up part of the ownership and control of the business. If the strategy is managed well it provides several advantages:

- The partners who originally established the partnership are compensated for the share of the business which they transfer to new partners.
- Gradually, the skills base of the partnership can be broadened, making it more resilient to changing circumstances.
- The possibility of joining the partnership provides an incentive for staff.
- The business can survive even if the original partners leave it.

Risk

Risk has been mentioned at several points in this chapter. Each of the business decisions outlined in the examples involves taking a risk; this is an unavoidable factor in running a business. For example, a business may have to make a momentous decision about whether or not to invest several millions of pounds in a new factory. This type of decision clearly involves potentially major risks. Getting it wrong could bring about the downfall of the business.

All business people have to take risks. Sometimes their decisions prove to be wrong. More rarely, the decisions prove to be disastrously wrong. Successful businesses minimise their risks as far as possible, but risk cannot be eliminated. Financial analysis can help business managers to understand the range of possible consequences of their decisions.

Chapter summary

In this chapter we have discussed the problems and opportunities presented by business growth. Specifically, we examined the advantages and drawbacks, and the most significant risks involved in employing people, developing a more complex business organisation and expanding the business into new products and markets.

We examined three approaches to business expansion:

- borrowing to finance expansion
- amalgamating businesses to create expansion
- takeovers.

Next, we looked at the issues involved in making money in a successful business, and ways in which proprietors of businesses actually extract money for their own use, including drawings by sole traders and partners, and dividends and salaries receivable by company shareholders and directors. This section concluded by examining exit and succession management by the proprietors of smaller businesses.

The spotlight study developed several of the issues discussed in the chapter, in particular the problems involved in managing a successful service business constituted as a partnership. The study involves consideration of problems relating to the following areas:

- complementary skills in a partnership
- personnel management
- succession management
- broadening ownership
- exit strategies.

The chapter concluded by considering the element of risk that is inherent in all business decisions.

 The end-of-chapter exercises are divided into two sections. The first section has answers provided at the end of the book. The second section, in the white box, has answers on the lecturers' section of the website.

Website summary

The book's website contains the following material in respect of Chapter 3:

Students' section

- Quiz containing five multiple choice questions
- Two additional questions with answers.

Lecturers' section

- Answers to exercises 3.3 and 3.4
- Two additional questions with answers.

Exercises: answers at the end of the book

Note: the principal objective of the following exercises is to set students thinking about some of the financial and other issues involved in business growth and development. No specific knowledge of particular types of business is required to answer these questions. Use imagination and common sense to think through the problems.

3.1 Nancy is a self-employed hairdresser. She runs a salon with the assistance of one untrained employee who takes bookings, tidies and sweeps up, and makes tea and coffee for the clients. Nancy would like to expand the business; this would involve employing a fully trained stylist. There is sufficient space in Nancy's existing premises for another person to work.

Advise Nancy on the costs, risks and potential benefits involved in employing a stylist.

3.2 Oleander Enterprises Limited is a small holiday company run by its two principal directors and shareholders, Libby and Lisa. The company organises exclusive (and expensive) holiday tours of French chateaux. During the four years since it was set up the company has gone from strength to strength. It now employs six people and it makes substantial annual profits. The company has a cash surplus and the directors have been considering ways of using the surplus to expand the business, possibly by starting up operations in new countries. Recently, the directors have been approached by Loretta, the managing director of another holiday company, Oxus Orlando Limited, which organises holiday tours in Turkey. Loretta is the principal director and shareholder of Oxus Orlando. She would like to sell her company and retire on the proceeds. Advise Libby and Lisa on:

1. The advantages and drawbacks of expanding by buying into another company.

2. The type of information they will require in order to be able to make a decision on whether or not to buy Oxus Orlando.

Exercises: answers available to lecturers

3.3 Norman and Naylor Partners is a business that runs corporate events. Sam Norman and Sally Naylor founded the business about five years ago and it has been very successful. The partners share profits equally. It now employs five full-time staff and calls upon a pool of up to 40 additional staff who can be employed part-time for specific events. Sally is several years older than Sam, and would now like to pull out of the business. She plans to take out her share of the value of the business with a view to buying and running a vineyard in Italy.

Identify the business problems and risks that Sam must deal with as a result of Sally's decision. What are the financial implications (in broad terms) for the partners?

3.4   Lionel is an experienced chartered surveyor with many years of experience. He is employed by a large property company where he receives a good salary and a performance-related bonus. He has recently been approached by an old friend, Leo, who is one of three partners in a firm of surveyors. The other two partners are nearing retirement age and they have decided that they need to bring in some 'new blood'. The partnership has been in operation for nearly 20 years and has carved out a sizeable niche in commercial property management. Leo tells Lionel that the partnership has been valued by a business valuation specialist at £1 200 000, a figure that includes goodwill of £500 000. If Lionel accepts the invitation to join the partnership he will be required to pay £300 000 in cash for a quarter share of the business. In exchange he will be entitled to 25% of the profits made by the partnership in the future.

1.   Explain to Lionel what is meant by the term 'goodwill'.

2.   Advise him on the type of information he will need to examine in order to be able to make a decision on whether or not to buy into the partnership.

3.   Identify the main elements of risk involved in Lionel's decision.

CHAPTER 4

Large businesses

Aim of the chapter

To understand the context in which large businesses operate and in particular, the financing of quoted companies and the decision on whether or not to finance expansion of a company via a stock exchange flotation.

Learning outcomes

After reading the chapter and its spotlight study, and completing the exercises at the end, students should:

- Understand the operation of the UK stock market.
- Understand the reasons why companies choose to have their shares publicly quoted, and understand the fundamentals of what is involved in listing.
- Know about the advantages and drawbacks of operating as a listed company.
- Understand the need for information about listed companies, know about the principal sources of information concerning them, and be able to obtain relevant information.

Before we begin, a note about financial jargon. In this chapter we will examine several important aspects of the financing of companies, especially via the issue of shares. This will involve assimilating quite a lot of financial jargon and terminology. Remember to consult the glossary at the end of the book where necessary.

The jargon used in the financial news on television and radio, and in the financial press, can be very off-putting for the novice. However, once some basic items of terminology have been learnt, it soon becomes possible to read and understand the financial news. After a short time, it ceases to be such an effort, and may even, believe it or not, become interesting.

Sources of finance for companies

As explained in Chapter 1, there are many possible sources of finance that businesses may be able to obtain. Some of these, however, are available only where the business is structured as a company.

Issue of shares

Upon the initial formation of a company, ordinary share capital is issued to the first shareholders of the company. In the case of small businesses, the number of shareholders is usually low, often no more than one or two people. As companies grow, they may issue more shares to other people. Private companies (companies with 'limited' after their name) are not permitted to issue shares to the general public or to have their shares quoted on a stock market. Public limited companies (companies with 'plc') after their name, on the other hand, are permitted to issue shares to a wider public. Some plcs are quoted on a stock market and so are able to issue their shares widely to the general public. It is important to note that not all plcs are quoted companies, but that only plcs (and not private companies) may have their shares quoted on the stock market.

The ordinary shares of companies are often referred to as equity shares. They have a nominal value such as £1.50p or 25p; this is the basic denomination of the share. Shares that are quoted on a stock market have a share price representing a market value that is, usually, greater than nominal value. For example, a listed company has 5 000 000 shares with a nominal value of 50p each and a market value of £3.75. This gives the company a total nominal value of 5 000 000 × 50p = £2 500 000; this is the nominal value of its issued share capital. The total market value of the company (its market capitalisation) is 5 000 000 × £3.75 = £18 750 000.

Don't worry if this seems confusing at the moment. We will return to the same point later in the book when we examine accounting for limited companies in more detail.

Rights of shareholders

Ordinary (equity) share capital entitles its owners (shareholders) to a vote which they can exercise at the general meetings of the company. Usually, the only general meeting of a company is the annual general meeting (AGM) at which shareholders vote on such matters as appointment of directors, appointment of auditors, and on whether or not to accept the annual accounts that are presented at the meeting. In almost all cases, AGMs are extremely dull affairs, often poorly attended, but occasionally something interesting happens at the AGM of a major company, triggering a report about the AGM in the financial press.

The other principal right of shareholders is to receive dividends. Dividends are paid out to shareholders, often on a regular basis; they constitute the income received by shareholders on their investment. Very large companies usually have two regular payment dates each year for dividends (an interim dividend and a final dividend). The company's directors decide upon the level of dividend to be paid out; it is usually expressed as an amount in pence per share: for example, 'the directors have declared an interim dividend of 5p per ordinary share in issue'.

Benefits of limited company status

The liability of shareholders in companies is limited. That means that, even if the company fails, the shareholders cannot be called upon to contribute any further cash.

Because the capital of limited companies is split up into many shares, it is possible for a shareholder to sell a very small proportion of the total share capital of the company to another person. This can be useful where, for example, the original shareholders of a company have decided that they wish to spread the share ownership more widely, perhaps to other family members.

Usually, if a business becomes really large, a limited company is the only realistic business vehicle for it. It allows for multiple shareholders, each owning perhaps a very small proportion of the total business. Sole traders, for obvious reasons, usually own very small businesses. Similarly, partnerships, except in a few special cases, tend to be small or medium-sized businesses. The special cases tend to be professional firms (such as firms of accountants, lawyers, architects or other professionals) where very large partnerships do exist. In most cases, however, if a business grows to be very large, it will be in the form of a company.

Sometimes, the directors of a company may choose to raise finance by obtaining a listing on the stock exchange. This involves selling shares to a wider public than family, friends and business associates. In the next two sections we look at various aspects of the operation of the UK stock market.

The UK stock market

A stock market is a place where stocks are traded. So, what are the stocks referred to in the term 'stock market'? The UK stock market trades in, principally, the shares of quoted companies. Quoted companies comprise both UK based companies and overseas companies that have a quotation in the UK. The market also trades in British government bonds (these are known as 'gilts' or 'gilt-edged stock') and other types of shares and company bonds (also known as loan stock or debentures).

So, where is this 'place' where stocks are traded? In former times the principal stock market location in the UK was the trading floor of the London Stock

Exchange. This was located in the City of London where the agents of people and organisations wishing to trade in stocks and shares met in person to arrange transactions. This physical location is no longer necessary following the far-reaching reforms and reorganisation of trading implemented over the last fifteen to twenty years. Transactions in shares now take place electronically.

The London Stock Exchange (LSE) is a powerful organisation that regulates the trading in shares and organises their listing. The LSE operates in two principal capacities: as a 'primary market' and as a 'secondary market'.

Primary market

The primary market function allows companies to raise capital via the LSE. In order to exploit the capital raising potential of the LSE new entrants to the market apply for a listing and, if successful, float the company on the stock market. This means that they are entitled to offer shares – either newly issued or existing shares – to the public.

Companies which already have a stock market listing may decide that they need to raise more finance. Such companies can issue more shares and sell them for cash.

Secondary market

The secondary market function allows trading in shares to take place between willing buyers and sellers. This is an extremely useful function providing for liquidity in shares. Liquidity means, in this context, that shares can be bought and sold easily. High liquidity is extremely attractive to investors; it means that they are not tied into their investment over long periods, but can liquidate (turn into cash) their investment whenever it suits them to do so. One of the problems of investing in unquoted companies is that it can be difficult (or downright impossible) to sell the investment to anyone else.

Organisation and operation of the London Stock Exchange

The LSE's market is split into two: the main market and the Alternative Investment Market (AIM).

The main market

The main market is the most important element of the market provided by the LSE. Companies on the main market have a full listing and are subject to the full range of regulation applicable to listed companies. In order to obtain a listing on the main market, companies normally have to have been in business for at least three years and to have a full record of accounts for that period.

The Alternative Investment Market (AIM)

AIM is a market that deals in shares of smaller and/or newer companies than those eligible to obtain a full listing. Many relatively small companies choose to obtain a quotation on this market. Investing in these companies is potentially riskier than investing in companies with a full listing because: (a) the business venture may be inherently riskier; and (b) the shares of AIM companies are often relatively illiquid – that is, they may not be traded very often or in very large volumes. This could make a holding of shares in an AIM company relatively more difficult to sell. However, some AIM companies are highly successful; they may move on to a full listing once they have built up a trading record.

Share prices

There are over 2000 UK companies quoted on the LSE at any one time, plus several hundred overseas companies. Although many companies have been listed for years, the list is constantly changing as new companies come to the market (at a rate of some 200–300 per year), and existing companies leave (because they have failed and go into liquidation, or because they are taken over, or because their directors decide to de-list).

Shares in quoted companies have a market price that can fluctuate a great deal. Shares in the larger, better known companies are traded very frequently, and their price can change from minute to minute. It is possible to obtain share prices with a delay of approximately 15 minutes from many sources nowadays. One of the best and most reliable is the LSE's own website (**www.londonstockexchange.com**). Shares in smaller companies, especially those on AIM, may be traded infrequently – i.e. their trading volume is low. Prices for such shares may remain relatively static with long periods of inactivity.

Share prices will tend to rise when a company is doing well, or when some piece of good news is announced (for example, the company has obtained new business or it has sacked an incompetent director). Conversely, bad news often results in a fall in share price. However, sometimes movement in share prices has relatively little to do with individual companies' activities and is the result of general market sentiment. For example, in the early part of 2000 share prices were generally high, but they fell during the middle of the year as the dotcom bubble burst. This 'bursting of the bubble' affected dotcom companies most severely but there was a more general loss of faith in high technology companies and in the market in general. There was a huge general drop in share prices following 11 September 2001. This affected all companies, but those involved in aerospace, insurance or tourism were particularly badly affected.

Stock market regulation

All companies are subject to regulation. The Companies Acts contain many legal stipulations about, for example, the internal constitutional arrangements for companies, the appointment and remuneration (that is, payment) of directors, the filing of accounts with the Registrar of Companies and the form and content of accounts. In addition there are other sources of regulation, including accounting standards which contain detailed requirements about specific items in the financial statements. However, listed companies are subject to another level of regulation in the form of a detailed rule book that used to be controlled by the LSE but is now regulated by the Financial Services Authority (FSA). The rules include, for example:

- A requirement for listed companies to report, via interim financial statements, half-yearly as well as annually (and in some specific cases, three-monthly – also known as quarterly – reporting is required).
- A requirement to include, alongside the annual financial statements, a chairman's statement.
- Regulations about building up large holdings of shares.
- Regulations about notifying the market of major events or large transactions.

Stock market indices

The FTSE

Anyone who watches television news, or who listens to radio news, will have heard the (usually) brief reports about the financial markets which sound something like: 'Bad news on the financial markets. The Footsie 100 fell 13 points to close at 5345.5.' While the first sentence makes sense, the second sounds like gibberish to the financial novice. Let's pick the important pieces out of the statement. 'Footsie' is the usual verbal reference for 'FTSE' which stands for 'Financial Times Stock Exchange'. The FTSE organisation, which is owned by the London Stock Exchange and the *Financial Times* newspaper, runs a series of indices both for the UK stock market and worldwide.

The FTSE 100 is an index that rises and falls in line with the value of the top 100 listed UK companies. The index started originally with a value of 1000. Each of the 100 constituent companies figures in the index according to the relative size of its capital. The minute-by-minute changes in the value of the 100 companies' share prices are fed into the index calculations. For most interested observers, daily tracking of the index value tells them all they need to know, but it is possible for people and organisations who are deeply involved in investing to find the current value at any time during LSE trading hours.

So, if the index falls by 13 points, it reflects an overall, average fall for the day in the share prices of those companies that make up the index. Some of the companies' share prices may have gone up; some will have fallen; but, overall, the average movement for the day is slightly downwards.

The reported index total (5345.5) is only really helpful to a person who keeps a regular eye on the movements in share prices. The index figure on its own means very little.

Which companies are in the FTSE?

At regular intervals the FTSE committee reviews membership of the FTSE 100; the principal criterion for membership is size, which, of course, fluctuates. The committee also reviews membership of the other principal stock market company classifications, and there are indices for the following:

- FTSE 250 – these are the 250 companies that are next in order of size after the FTSE 100.
- FTSE 350 – these are the FTSE 100 and FTSE 250 together.
- FTSE All-Share – the FTSE 100 and FTSE 250 plus a group of smaller, but still significant companies classified as FTSE SmallCap.
- FTSE Fledgling – these are fully listed companies that do not qualify in size terms for the FTSE SmallCap.

- FTSE TechMark – these are companies listed on the TechMark part of the LSE, which is a separate market introduced in 1999 for shares of high tech companies.

Information about the current values of all of these indices, and the rules that operate for their calculation, can be found at the FTSE website: (**www.ftse.com**).

Flotation and other types of share issue

Floating a company

As noted earlier, between 200 and 300 companies become publicly quoted each year. The process is time-consuming (it can easily take up to a year to organise and carry out) and may deflect directors' attention from running the business. A great deal of professional advice is required in order to conduct a successful flotation. Corporate finance advisers, stockbrokers (usually referred to simply as 'brokers'), lawyers and professional accountants are involved in ensuring that the process is successful.

Flotation for most companies involves a placing of the shares. This means identifying prospective buyers (usually institutional investors such as pension schemes, life assurance companies, venture capitalists, investment trusts and asset managers), and arranging to sell a portion of the shares. In the case of a placing, there is no invitation to the general public to buy into the new shares. An offer for sale, by contrast, does involve a general invitation to the general public and the institutions to buy shares in the company. It involves preparation of a detailed prospectus containing a great deal of information about the history and prospects of the company.

In either case, once the shares are floated they can be bought and sold in the secondary market. However, in most cases of smaller companies coming to the market for the first time, the principal or only buyers of the new shares are likely to be half a dozen or so of the well-known institutional investors.

Other types of share issue

New issues

Once a company has been floated successfully it may issue further blocks of shares in order to raise new capital. If there is sufficient demand for the shares, the new issue is likely to be successful.

Rights issues

It is commonly the case that, where a listed company wishes to raise cash via a new issue of share capital, it will do so via a rights issue. A rights issue is an offer to existing shareholders to purchase additional shares. It is usually expressed in terms such as 'a one-for-three rights issue'. This would mean that for every three shares already held in the company, the shareholder could buy one additional share. Taking up the rights issue allows an individual shareholder to retain the same percentage shareholding as before, as the following example illustrates.

Example 4.1

Wendover Household Goods plc has a total issued share capital of £1 000 000 £1 shares, the current market price of which is £5.30 each. It requires a fresh injection of capital to finance the building of a new factory to produce the company's revolutionary range of cleaning products. Wendover's corporate finance advisers tell the directors that the best way of raising the money is via a rights issue. They suggest an issue of one-for-four at £4.40.

An issue of one share for every four held will result in the issue of an additional 250 000 £1 shares. Each of these will be sold for £4.40, resulting in a cash inflow for Wendover of £1 100 000 if all the rights are taken up.

Jeannie Lemmon is one of Wendover's principal shareholders. She holds 170 000 of the issued shares. How much will Jeannie have to pay if she takes up the rights issue? She will have the opportunity to buy 170 000 ÷ 4 = 42 500 shares. She will have to pay, therefore, 42 500 × £4.40 = £187 000 if she decides to take up the rights issue.

As in Example 4.1, it is usually the case that the rights issue price will be pitched below the current market value of the share in order to make it attractive to shareholders. If the rights issue fails (in that existing shareholders do not take up the issue) then it would be possible to try to raise additional capital by a placing or an offer for sale. However, existing shareholders could be assumed to have a particular interest in the company; if they are not interested in investing more money in the company, it is even less likely that outsiders will wish to do so.

Mergers and acquisitions

Where a full-scale effort is made by one company to purchase a majority of another company's shares, this is referred to as a takeover bid. What happens is that the bidding company offers to purchase shares from existing shareholders at a stated price. The existing shareholders do not have to accept the offer, so it has to be pitched at a price that will make it sufficiently attractive to induce a large number of the existing shareholders to sell. Takeovers are a common feature of the stock market environment. A hostile bid refers to a bid by one company that is rejected by the target company's directors. Not all takeovers, however, are hostile.

The consequences of a successful takeover bid are often far-reaching. The purpose of a takeover, in principle, is to allow a better quality management to take on the control of the operations of the target company. Ideally, takeovers should lead to improved efficiency and better returns for shareholders of the company that is taking over the other. In practice, it appears that takeovers do not always have the desired effect.

Mergers and acquisitions (M&A) is a general term referring to any bringing together of companies either by agreement or as a result of a hostile bid. Both 'mergers' and 'acquisitions' have specific meanings for accountants, but it is beyond the scope of this book to examine those meanings.

To list or not to list?

It may not be easy for the directors of a limited company to decide on whether or not to list. There are advantages and drawbacks.

Advantages of listing

- The principal advantage of listing, of course, is that the company can raise more finance for new projects and investments.
- Listing increases a company's general profile and credibility and may enhance its reputation.
- Listing may allow the founder members of a company to turn their hard work in the past into cash by selling part or all of their holding of shares.
- Listed companies shares can, in most cases, be liquidated easily. Listing is, therefore, likely to increase the pool of potential investors and may increase the value of the company.

A 2001 survey carried out jointly by the LSE and Eversheds (a firm of business lawyers) found that the most popular reason cited for seeking flotation was 'to raise funds' (mentioned by 64% of respondents), followed by 'to increase the company's profile and credibility' (mentioned by 23% of respondents).

Drawbacks of listing

- A listed company is in the public spotlight. Financial journalists are likely to become much more interested in a company's activities once it is listed. This may work to the company's advantage when everything is going well and the publicity is welcome. However, if the company is struggling, or if it is engaged in some controversial activity, publicity may be a major drawback.
- A listed company may become a 'takeover target'. A company can take over another company by buying up a majority of the shares in order to obtain control over it. The directors of the target company usually find themselves in a difficult position in these circumstances and they often lose their jobs.
- There is increased pressure on companies' management to produce consistent and ever-improving results. This pressure may result in short-termism, where investment in the long-term future of the company may suffer in order to produce the kind of short-term results that satisfy City commentators.
- Obtaining a listing is not cheap. A great deal of accounting and legal work must be paid for, plus underwriting costs. The total costs usually amount to at least 10%, and occasionally as much as 20%, of the amounts of cash raised by the flotation.
- The additional layers of regulation are onerous and compliance with them can be very expensive. It is usually necessary to employ additional staff.
- Movements in the company's share price can be worryingly difficult to explain or predict.

In the LSE/Eversheds' survey referred to earlier, the principal drawbacks to being a public company were identified as 'additional reporting requirements and associated costs' (mentioned by 57% of respondents) and 'volatility of share price, often with little correlation to business fundamentals' (mentioned by 18% of respondents).

The role of information in stock markets

Information is the lifeblood of stock markets. People, including those who represent the institutions that buy shares (for example, pension funds and insurance companies), need to have some assurance that they are buying shares that have some underlying value.

Sources of information about listed companies' shares

Published financial statements

All companies, whether listed or unlisted, are required to produce annual accounts for the benefit of shareholders. They are also required to file certain information (although not the full accounts in all cases – there are various exemptions for small and medium-sized companies) with the Registrar of Companies. However, the reporting requirements are more onerous for listed companies. All listed companies must produce an annual report, which has to be made available to interested parties. These are often very long and elaborate documents, running to many pages and involving high quality paper and design work. In addition to the full annual report, listed companies produce interim financial statements, which report results for the six-month period immediately following the year-end.

The reporting requirements mean that investors, potential investors and anyone else who is interested can obtain information about a company at approximately six-monthly intervals. It takes time, however, to compile this information. Most listed companies publish an annual report, at the earliest, some three to four months after the company's year-end.

How reliable is the information? There have been many cases of investors and others being misled by financial statements that were inaccurately or fraudulently prepared. All large companies are required by law to have an annual audit of their financial statements carried out by an independent firm of auditors. Although the audit process is not foolproof, and although it in no way guarantees accuracy, it does provide investors with some assurance that the financial statements are fairly stated.

The internet

The internet has emerged in the last few years as a very useful source of information about listed companies and their activities. Although not all listed companies have websites (and the law in the UK does not, currently, require them to have websites), most do.

There is no standardisation of content on websites, but, typically, a corporate website includes:

- Information about the activities of the business (this is often very extensive).
- The latest annual and interim financial statements.
- An archive of annual and interim financial statements.
- E-mail contact details.
- A constantly updated share price (sometimes via a link into the stock exchange's own website).
- Links into other useful websites.

A company's website can be a very useful source of information. However, the quality of website construction and content varies enormously. Some are out of date, dull, difficult to access and badly designed.

Many companies listed on stock exchanges outside the UK also have websites. Before the late 1990s it was often very difficult to obtain information about overseas companies; by contrast, nowadays, it can be very easy. Most US companies have extensive websites and it is becoming increasingly common to find good corporate websites among continental European companies.

As well as companies' own websites, there are many other sources of information available nowadays. The Hemscott Group website (**www.hemscott.net**) provides information about all UK based companies listed on the London Stock Exchange, including companies listed on the Alternative Investment Market. Some of the information is available by subscription only, but a large amount is freely available.

The financial press

The best and most extensive coverage of company activity and general financial news available in the UK is undoubtedly provided by the *Financial Times* (FT), which is published six times a week. Anyone who reads the FT thoroughly on a daily basis before long will be a fount of financial knowledge. Most business and accounting students will find that making a conscientious attempt to read the FT fairly thoroughly once a week will add considerably to their general financial knowledge.

Some Sunday papers and broadsheet daily papers (e.g. *The Times* and *The Guardian*) contain good coverage of financial and accounting issues.

The spotlight study for this chapter examines various aspects of the flotation decision.

SPOTLIGHT 4.1 Going public

The directors of Gropius & Garner Productions plc are about to hold one of the most important board meetings in the company's history. A few months ago the founding shareholders, Brendan Gropius and Amelia Garner, suggested to the board that it was time to think about 'going public', by obtaining a listing on the stock exchange.

Brendan Gropius is the company's managing director, and Amelia Garner, who is a chartered accountant, is the finance director. They founded the company, which produces television commercials and documentaries, nine years ago. Since its foundation, the company has produced strong results; it has grown very rapidly and now employs almost 150 staff. The shares are currently held as follows:

- Bernard Gropius, 40%
- Amelia Gardner, 30%
- Sigmund Gropius (Bernard's cousin), 15%
- Karl-Heinz Muller (Amelia's brother-in-law), 15%.

As well as Bernard and Amelia, Sigmund and Karl-Heinz also hold directorships. There is one further member of the board who does not hold any shares: Judy Segal, who has overall responsibility for the production of commercials and documentaries.

Bernard and Amelia propose that 300 000 of the 700 000 shares currently in issue should be sold. Each director would sell shares in proportion to his or her total shareholding as follows:

Director	Shares currently held	Shares to be sold (3/7)	Shares remaining
Bernard (40%)	280 000	120 000	160 000
Amelia (30%)	210 000	90 000	120 000
Sigmund (15%)	105 000	45 000	60 000
Karl-Heinz (15%)	105 000	45 000	60 000
Total	700 000	300 000	400 000

In addition to the 300 000 existing shares that would be sold, the company would issue a further 200 000. The directors have been advised by their corporate finance advisers that they could probably raise around £10.50 per share on flotation, after taking into account all the costs of issue.

There are two principal reasons for the proposal to obtain a listing:

1. Bernard and Amelia are both paid large salaries for their work as directors of the company. However, they are both interested in selling a substantial part of their shareholding now, while share values in the market generally are high. The sale would allow each of them to realise a substantial amount of cash, which they could then invest elsewhere. They would both like to plan for an early retirement in about 5–8 years time.

2. The company plans to move into children's entertainment programmes because there are very substantial profits to be made from this area of the market in programmes. This will require a substantial investment of resources. Borrowing money to fund the expansion would be a possibility, but both Bernard and Amelia feel that the time is right for a flotation.

Judy Segal, the sole director without a shareholding, is concerned about the proposal. She can see, of course, that her fellow directors all stand to gain substantial sums by selling their shares, but she is not sure that the flotation will be advantageous to the company in the longer term. She would like the company to remain as an independent operator, and she has been alarmed by a spate of recent takeover announcements in the business press. She fears that, once floated, the company could be swallowed up rapidly by one of the bigger companies.

Bernard assures her that there is no particular reason why Gropius & Garner should become a takeover target. The company is well managed and has a good record of producing profits even in difficult times. He can see nothing but advantages from the move.

Discuss the advantages and drawbacks of stock market flotation for the company, taking into consideration the following questions:

- Would the company be at risk of becoming a takeover target?
- Are Bernard and Amelia being unreasonable in wanting to cash in their shares?
- Is Bernard correct in seeing only advantages in the flotation?

Spotlight study solution and discussion

In order to assess the advantages and drawbacks of the proposed flotation, it would be sensible first to assess the financial impact of the deal.

Would the company be at risk of becoming a takeover target?

A company is usually only at risk of becoming a takeover target if more than 50% of the voting shares are available for purchase. This deal involves the issue of a further 200 000 shares. Added to the existing 700 000 shares, this gives a prospective total of shares in issue of 900 000. How many of the shares will be retained by the current directors?

Holdings now (before flotation)	700 000
To be sold on flotation	300 000
Retained after flotation	400 000

So, the directors will hold 400 000 of 900 000 shares (i.e. less than half of the issued share capital). If another person or company wished to take over Gropius & Garner it would be technically possible to do so. Judy's concerns are, therefore, realistic in the circumstances.

In total, 500 000 shares will be sold. If the corporate finance advisers' estimates are approximately correct, this would mean that 500 000 × £10.50 could be raised, i.e. £5 250 000. The sale of the shares belonging to the directors will raise 300 000 × £10.50 = £3 150 000 and new capital raised for investment in children's programming will be 200 000 × £10.50 = £2 100 000.

How much money will the directors make?

- Bernard holds 40% of the shares currently in issue, and so he will be entitled to 40% of the proceeds of the directors' shares: 40% × £3 150 000 = £1 260 000.
- Amelia holds 30% of the shares currently in issue, and so she will be entitled to 30% of the proceeds: 30% × £3 150 000 = £945 000.
- Sigmund and Karl-Heinz each hold 15% of the shares currently in issue, and so will each be entitled to: 15% × £3 150 000 = £472 500.

Clearly, all the directors (except Judy) stand to make substantial sums out of the flotation. All will retain large holdings of shares in the business, and so they could potentially make more money out of selling more shares in the future.

Is it unreasonable of Bernard and Amelia to want to sell their shares?

Flotation on the stock market is a common way for founders of a company to turn part or all of their investment into cash. As both Bernard and Amelia are thinking ahead to retirement, the proposal to float the company makes perfect sense from their point of view.

Is Bernard correct in only seeing advantages in the flotation?

Because Bernard stands to gain a substantial sum of cash from selling part of his shareholding he is, perhaps, not very likely to dwell on the potential drawbacks of the flotation. However, Judy has pointed out one significant drawback in the form of a potential takeover bid. If the company were taken over the existing management might not be able to hold on to their lucrative directorships. Even if they did, they would find that they no longer have complete control over the company's activities.

Other possible drawbacks include:

- Increased public attention which is not always welcome. Following flotation the company would find itself subject to much more media interest than before.
- The company would have to start producing interim financial statements as well as a full annual report, and there are various other forms of additional regulation that would come into play. A listed company incurs additional costs in complying with regulation.
- There might be pressure from the City to produce better and more consistent results.

Most of these drawbacks are unavoidable. The company could help to minimise the possibility of takeover by floating rather fewer shares than originally intended. If 400 000 of 900 000 shares were to be made available, this would leave a majority in the hands of the four shareholder/directors. The company could, of course, still be vulnerable if one or more of the four were persuaded to sell all or part of their holding.

Chapter summary

The chapter started by examining some aspects of the financing of companies by the issue of shares, including the rights of shareholders, and a brief reprise of some of the benefits conferred by limited company status.

The role of the UK stock market as both a primary and secondary market was then discussed. A brief description of the main market and the Alternative Investment Market was included, followed by an introduction to stock market regulation. The FTSE indices were then briefly described and discussed.

Flotation of companies, new issues in established listed companies and rights issues were described. There are advantages and drawbacks to listing on the stock market, and these were detailed and discussed.

Finally, the important role that information plays in stock markets was flagged, and some of the principal sources of information about companies were described, including published financial statements, various internet resources and the financial press.

The spotlight study examined a company contemplating a listing. This involved assessment of the financial consequences of listing, both in terms of rewarding the company's founders and in raising fresh capital for investment.

Internet resources

Some useful websites:

www.ftse.com – explains the operation of the FTSE indices and reports regularly updated values for the main indices.

www.fsa.gov.uk – the website of the Financial Services Authority.

www.hemscott.net – provides a large quantity of useful information about UK based companies listed on the London Stock Exchange.

www.londonstockexchange.com – provides information about all companies currently listed on the LSE (including current share prices) and about the activities of the exchange itself. For example, at the time of writing, the website contained the LSE/Eversheds' survey report referred to earlier in the chapter.

Links to individual company's websites are often provided through the Hemscott site and through the LSE site referred to above. If there is no obvious link it is worth contacting the company by phone (phone numbers are obtainable from the Hemscott data) to ask if they have a corporate website.

The end-of-chapter exercises are divided into two sections. The first section has answers printed at the end of the book. The second section, in the white box, has answers on the lecturers' section of the website.

Website summary

The book's website contains the following material in respect of Chapter 4:

Students' section

- Quiz containing ten multiple choice questions
- Three additional questions with answers.

Lecturers' section

- Answers to exercises 4.5 to 4.8
- Three additional questions with answers.

Exercises: answers at the end of the book

4.1 Ashton Longton plc, a listed company, has issued share capital of £8 000 000 comprising shares of £1 nominal value. The current quoted price per share is £3.85. What is the company's market capitalisation?

4.2 The Alternative Investment Market is a market for:

   a)   companies that do not currently wish to proceed to full listing

   b)   companies that promote alternative lifestyles

   c)   British government securities

   d)   overseas companies without a trading history.

4.3 Warminster Toys plc has a total issued share capital of £3 000 000 in 50p shares. The company decides to make a rights issue of one-for-five at a price of £5.42 per share. To take up the rights the holder of 50 000 shares will have to pay:

   a)   £27 100

   b)   £135 500

   c)   £54 200

   d)   £271 000.

4.4 Yolande Brighton is the managing director of Brighton Bestwines plc, a company that supplies the licensed trade. The company has been very successful but has now reached the point where it needs to expand its warehousing capacity if it is to continue growing. The directors have been contemplating applying for a quotation on the Alternative Investment Market (AIM). The company will issue a further 500 000 shares (it already has 1 000 000 shares in issue). It hopes to be able to sell the shares at around £2.50 each. The directors have invited you to their board meeting to discuss the flotation. They are keen to raise the finance, but one or two of them are wondering about potential drawbacks to being quoted on the AIM, and they would like you to give them an outline of any possible problems they face. Prepare a list of potential drawbacks for discussion at the meeting.

Exercises: answers available to lecturers

4.5 Amery Chorlton plc, a listed company, has issued share capital of £4 000 000 comprising shares of 25p nominal value. The current quoted price per share is 98p. What is the company's market capitalisation?

4.6 Interim financial statements are:

   a)   first drafts of the final financial statements of listed companies

b) provisional financial statements that are awaiting audit

c) half-yearly financial statements produced by listed companies

d) audited financial statements awaiting directors' approval.

4.7 Willoughby Wooster plc has a total issued share capital of £1 000 000 in 25p shares. The company decides to make a rights issue of one-for-two at a price of £2.70 per share. To take up the rights the holder of 30 000 shares will have to pay:

a) £40 500

b) £10 125

c) £20 250

d) £7 500.

4.8 Tatiana, a friend of yours, has recently been left approximately £50 000 of listed company investments in her grandmother's will. She has been trying to read the *Financial Times* in order to see what is happening to her investments. She has found some information about three of them:

1. Turtlehammer plc rose to 215p on speculation of a hostile bid from a competitor, but fell back to 210p by the end of the day's trading.

2. The share price of Teddington Tilmain plc has risen by 26p following the announcement that it has obtained an important new export contract.

3. Tolson Tortellini plc has announced today that it is making a rights issue of one-for-four at £2.30.

Tatiana frankly admits that she doesn't understand any of this. She asks you to explain each of the pieces of news in terms that she can understand. She would like to know if any of it is likely to be good news for her. Also, she would like you to tell her if the *Financial Times* is the only source of information about her investments.

CHAPTER 5

The role of accounting in business

Aim of the chapter

To understand the reasons why people need accounting information, the nature of accounting information and the role of the accountant.

Learning outcomes

After reading the chapter and completing the exercises at the end, students should:

- Understand why accounting information is produced.
- Be able to identify the principal groups in society who need and use accounting information.
- Know about the principal characteristics and features of accounting information.
- Understand the distinction between financial accounting and management accounting.
- Know about the functions that accountants perform in the production of accounting information.
- Appreciate the reasons why business managers should be able to understand accounting reports.

The need for accounting information

Quite simply, accounting information is produced because people need it. The reasons why they need it vary from one group of people to another. In this chapter we will examine the range of reasons for the production of accounting information and the nature of the information produced by commercial businesses.

First, we will re-examine the three types of business organisation introduced in Chapter 1, considering in each case the range of accounting information that might be required and the purposes for which it is needed.

Sole trader

A sole trader business, because it usually remains small, is not complex in its organisation. There is one manager, the sole trader, who may employ a few staff. The sole trader does not have to make information about the business's profitability generally available. In fact, the only consumers of financial information about the business are the taxation authorities (the Inland Revenue) and, possibly, the Customs and Excise (if the sole trader is registered for VAT).

Annual information

Tax returns to the Inland Revenue have to be made once a year, within the stipulated deadline. The sole trader needs to prepare simple accounting statements to accompany his or her tax return. There will be a statement showing the calculation of profit or loss for the year, and, possibly, a statement that shows the resources owned by the business. These statements are known as the **profit and loss account** and the **balance sheet**.

The profit and loss account shows the revenue for the business for the year, less the business expenses. The remainder is either a profit or loss. The balance sheet is a statement of the resources owned and controlled by the business at a single point in time. It also shows any amounts owed, for example, loans taken out from the bank and payments due to suppliers of goods.

Every business has a year-end date. The profit and loss account is prepared for the year ending on that date, and the balance sheet shows the statement of resources less amounts due on the same year-end date.

Quarterly information

If the sole trader is registered for VAT, a quarterly VAT return will have to be prepared. As explained in Chapter 1, this contains a summary of sale and purchase transactions that have taken place in the quarter, and a calculation of input and output tax, in order to arrive at the net amount payable to the Customs and Excise. Failing to meet Customs and Excise deadlines for submission of the return and the amounts due must be avoided at all costs, so the sole trader business has to be able to keep accounting records sufficiently well to be able to provide the required information quickly.

Accounting information within the business

As well as information provided for external authorities, there will almost certainly be a need for more frequent information to help the sole trader manage the business efficiently, and to assist him or her in making decisions. At the simplest possible level this means keeping an eye on the state of the bank balance.

Example 5.1

Deva runs a small nursery specialising in tender plants. Most of her business is via mail order. Every three months she pays rent for the premises, comprising two glasshouses, a yard and a small office. The quarterly rental is £1500.

Before writing the cheque to the landlord Deva must know whether or not there is enough money in the bank account to cover the £1500 payment. If there is not, the cheque may be returned because of lack of funds (i.e. it bounces). A business manager cannot afford to accumulate unopened bank statements; he or she needs to know how much is in the bank so as to be able to anticipate any difficulties in meeting payments, or to ensure that any surplus is transferred to a high interest account.

At a slightly more sophisticated level, it is usually helpful for most small business owners to understand how the business is doing on a regular basis. A sole trader should keep records of sales and receipts of cash, and of the payment of expenses. From these it should be possible to prepare a simple monthly statement of profitability. This will not be used for reporting outside the business; it is an internal document for the sole trader's own use.

Recording and summarising information

In most cases, sole trader businesses do not employ an accountant. It would be far too expensive, and, besides, because accounting information needs are relatively modest, there would be little point. If the sole trader is equipped with some basic knowledge of record-keeping, has the time to do it, and is sufficiently well organised to keep the records straight, the cheapest and most straightforward option is to do the job himself or herself.

Some sole traders pay a bookkeeper for a few hours a week to keep the records straight. Where staff are employed it is particularly important to keep good records and to make accurate calculations of pay, income tax and National Insurance contributions due. In almost all cases, the sole trader is well advised to use the services of a qualified accountant for assistance with preparing annual financial statements, preparing tax returns and ensuring that the correct amount of tax is paid. Unless some very complex advice is involved, this kind of service can usually be purchased for a few hundred pounds each year.

In summary, the sole trader produces financial information to be used outside the business by the Inland Revenue and, probably, the Customs and Excise. No other external party can require information from the sole trader. Financial information for internal use will be produced as frequently as necessary to provide the sole trader with the information needed to run the business.

Partnership

A partnership, as we have seen in Chapter 1, does not need to make financial information generally available to the public. However, it must, in the same way as the sole trader, prepare annual financial statements that form the basis for tax calculation by the Inland Revenue. Also, quarterly financial information will probably have to be made available to the Customs and Excise in the form of summaries of sales and expenses and input and output tax totals supplied on the VAT return every quarter.

In most respects the information requirements are, so far, very similar to those of a sole trader. However, there is one important difference: in a partnership the annual profit and loss account provides the profit figure that will be split between the partners in accordance with their profit-sharing arrangements. The annual accounts, therefore, take on an additional dimension of importance in a partnership. The partners themselves need to be satisfied that the accounts have been prepared properly and that they present a reasonably accurate profit figure.

Audit

In some cases, the partners may decide to have an audit conducted to ensure that the annual accounts are properly prepared and fairly stated. There is no legal stipulation for audit of partnership accounts, but partners may decide, in drawing up the partnership agreement, that an audit should be carried out annually.

So, what is an audit? It is an independent examination, by a properly qualified person, of the financial records and financial statements of an entity. One of the important qualities of a well-conducted audit is that the auditor should be independent of the management of the business he or she is auditing. A partnership requiring an audit would appoint a professionally qualified auditor to conduct the examination of the records and give an impartial opinion on whether or not the annual financial statements have been properly drawn up. The opinion takes the form of an audit report which is attached to the financial statements. In addition to providing reassurance to the partners themselves, the fact that an audit has been conducted may be reassuring to the Inland Revenue. However, it should be emphasised that there is no legal requirement for the audit of partnerships (or of sole traders).

Accounting information within the business

We saw earlier in the chapter that sole trader businesses will find it helpful in running their businesses to produce accounting information such as monthly statements of profit. Partnership businesses tend to be larger than sole trader businesses (because more people are involved) and the need for internal accounting information may be greater because of the increased size and complexity of the business. As a business increases in size, its managers will usually find that they need more detailed information to help in decision making.

Example 5.2

Poste, Ponsonby and Peppard is a partnership of solicitors. As well as the three partners, the practice employs three other qualified solicitors and several administrative staff, including a full-time bookkeeper. The partners have a monthly management meeting at which they make decisions on important issues. In order to help them, they have instituted a system of internal financial reports. The bookkeeper prepares the reports, which are confidential, to be seen only by the partners.

The principal reports are:

- profit and loss account for the month
- billings summary for each solicitor for the month
- summary of hours worked by each solicitor for the month
- list of client invoices unpaid.

These reports allow the partners to see whether any of the solicitors are falling behind target in their monthly billings. They also allow for an assessment of profitability so that if, for example, monthly profits are tending to fall, the partners can take stock of the situation and decide whether action is necessary.

The list of unpaid client invoices informs the partners of any clients who are taking an excessively long time to pay. They can then make the necessary phone calls and send out letters to prompt the client to pay up.

Limited company

Accounting information needs within the sole trader and partnership types of business organisation are, essentially, very similar. However, the picture changes when we examine accounting for limited companies.

Provision of financial information outside the business

As we noted in Chapter 1, limited companies are required to publish financial information via the Registrar of Companies. Because everyone has access to the information held at Companies House, the information is potentially available to a very large number of people. In fact, the financial information of most companies remains undisturbed because there are very few people who are interested in it, apart from the shareholders. The company's shareholders are informed, in any case, of the financial condition of the company because they are entitled to receive a full set of annual accounts.

However, it is possible that other groups of people, apart from the shareholders, could be interested in the information. People or organisations who have been asked to lend money to the company are likely to be interested in its financial status. People who are affected by a company's existence (for example, those living near the premises of a chemical company that regularly breaches environmental legislation) may also take an interest. Later in this chapter we will consider the different categories of people who might be interested in a company's financial information.

Companies are required to submit tax returns and VAT returns, and financial reports must be made available to the Inland Revenue and Customs and Excise in the same way as for sole trader and partnership organisations.

Separation of ownership and management

In smaller companies the shareholders and directors are often the same people. Because they are engaged in the day-to-day management of the business, directors who are also shareholders really do not need annual financial information to tell them what is going on. They have access to as much internal financial information as they need.

However, the position is different for shareholders who are not directors. In large companies, most of the shareholders are remote from the activities of the business; they receive dividends and an invitation to the annual general meeting (AGM) of the business, but have no other contact with it. If they are shareholders in a listed company, they will be able to follow movements in the share price by consulting the financial press, but they are not entitled to the regular detailed internal financial information that the directors use in managing the business.

The relationships between the company, the directors and the shareholders are depicted in Figure 5.1. The diagram demonstrates the separation between the ownership of the company and its management. Shareholders appoint directors

Figure 5.1   Separation of ownership and management in a limited company

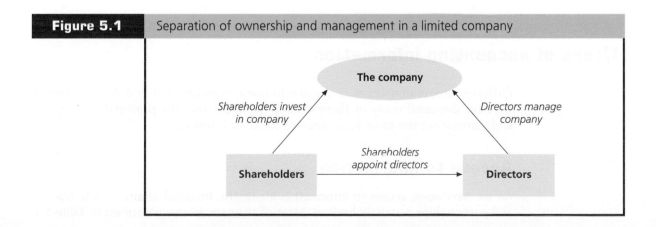

(who in larger companies are professional managers) to manage the company on their behalf: the directors act as agents of the shareholders, or (to use an old-fashioned term) as stewards on their behalf. The stewardship function requires directors to act in the best interests of the company at all times. In order to demonstrate good stewardship, they should report on a regular basis to shareholders – hence the requirement in company law that full annual financial statements are sent to shareholders.

Clearly, where shareholders are remote from the management of their company there is potential for the directors to take action that benefits themselves rather than benefiting the shareholders. This is one of the potential problems of the agency, or stewardship, relationship. For example, a current, and recurring issue, is that of directors' remuneration in very large companies. Criticisms are often voiced in the press of the very large increases in salary and substantial bonuses that directors award themselves. Shareholders are in a position to take action if they do not approve of directors' remuneration packages (via their votes at the AGM) but, in practice, they rarely challenge the directors.

If directors wish to manipulate financial information they are well placed to do so. How can shareholders be sure that the annual financial information they receive has not been distorted in some way? The mechanism that is used in company law is the requirement for audit by an independent auditor. Until recently, all companies, whatever their size, were required to have an audit of their annual financial statements. The requirements have, in recent years, gradually been relaxed by the government so that smaller companies are now exempt from regular audit. However, shareholders in exempt companies can still require an audit if they wish for the reassurance it provides.

Accounting information within the business

With the exception of the very large professional partnerships permitted by law, all larger businesses in the UK are constituted as limited companies. As a company grows in size, its management needs ever larger quantities of internally generated accounting information in order to keep control of the business and to make good quality decisions. Larger companies, especially those involved in the complexities of, say, manufacturing or banking, tend to produce highly complex and sophisticated information for use by management.

Users of accounting information

Different groups of users of financial information can be identified. In this chapter we have discussed many of them already. Table 5.1 lists the principal user groups and summarises the most likely reasons for their interest.

Access to information

As we have seen, access to information about the financial affairs of sole traders and partnerships is strictly limited. Most of the user groups identified in Table 5.1

Table 5.1

Principal groups of users of financial information	
User group	*Reason for interest in financial information*
Shareholders	To assess the performance of management in their role as stewards of the company
	To use the information to make decisions on whether or not to sell the investment in the shares of the company, or perhaps whether to buy more shares in the company
Potential shareholders	To make decisions on whether or not to invest in the shares of a company
Investment analysts	To assess the performance of the company in order to be able to advise their clients on investment strategy
Lenders and potential lenders	To assess the ability of the business to make repayments and to meet regular interest payments
Employees and trade unions	To assess the viability of the business and the extent to which it is likely to be able to (a) continue to offer employment; (b) increase pay and improve employees' conditions
Suppliers	Where suppliers offer credit terms, they need to be able to assess the likelihood of being paid promptly
Special interest groups	In the case of an environmental activist group, for example: to assess the extent to which the company has set aside funds for environmental clean-up operations
Government: tax collecting agencies	To assist in the assessment and collection of taxes
Government: other agencies	To assist, for example, in the collection of national statistical information
Financial journalists	To obtain information about a company's activities and profitability which will be of interest to the journalist's readers
Academics and students	To assist in the study of business activity
Customers	To assess the likelihood of the business continuing in existence, and continuing to supply the goods or services required by the customers
The general public	Anyone, not covered by any of the categories above, who has an interest in the activities of the company

would not be able to gain access; the exceptions are the government agencies concerned with the assessment and collection of tax, and lenders who are likely to be in a position to be able to demand financial information would not normally be available.

Because company financial statements are made publicly available, however, all these categories of users have access to them. In many cases the user groups are making important decisions on the basis of the information, answering questions such as:

- Should I sell my shares in this company?
- Should my bank be making an overdraft facility available to this company?
- Is the company doing well enough to make it safe for me to carry on working for it?
- How risky is it to supply goods on credit to this company?
- How well are the current management looking after my interests as a shareholder?

Company accounting information is called upon to be useful to a wide range of users in making decisions. In the next section of the chapter we look at the characteristics of useful financial information.

Characteristics of useful financial information

Ideally, financial information produced by businesses should have the following key characteristics:

- *Relevant*: to the decision being made. For example, the information should be prepared shortly after the events being reported so that it is not out of date by the time it is used.
- *Reliable*: the information should be properly prepared and free from error or bias in its preparation.
- *Comparable*: where financial statements from more than one period are concerned, the information should be prepared on the same basis, so that it is comparable.
- *Understandable*: the information in the financial statements should be capable of being understood.

In practice, it is not always possible to achieve information that fulfils all of these characteristics. In large and complex businesses collecting accounting data and processing it into a set of financial statements is a time-consuming process. By the time it is published (usually three to four months after the year-end date in a very large company) circumstances may have changed and the information may be of limited use for decision making. Also, the information that is reported is all historical – i.e. it relates to events that have already occurred. The extent to which past events are a reliable guide to the future is questionable in a fast-changing business environment.

Accounting information should be understandable, but, again, this is not always easily achievable. The financial statements of very complex organisations tend, inevitably, to reflect that complexity. People who are reasonably knowledgeable about business matters should be able to comprehend financial statements, but even their ability to understand is sometimes tested by the complex financial statements of major listed companies.

Financial accounting and management accounting

There are two distinct strands to accounting in organisations. **Financial accounting** refers to the processes and practices involved in providing users external to the business with the information that they need. Companies, because they provide a relatively large amount of information to outside users relative to partnership and sole trader entities, tend to devote substantial resources to financial accounting. This type of accounting is also referred to as **financial reporting**, and both terms are used in this book. **Management accounting** is the accounting that a business organisation carries out for its own internal uses. It assists management in controlling the business and in making decisions.

Both financial and management accounting use information generated by the accounting system of the business. Clearly, the accounting systems of businesses are likely to vary enormously depending upon the complexity and size of the business organisation. However, all accounting systems have certain characteristics in common. The flow of information in an accounting system and its relationship to financial accounting and management accounting is demonstrated diagrammatically in Figure 5.2.

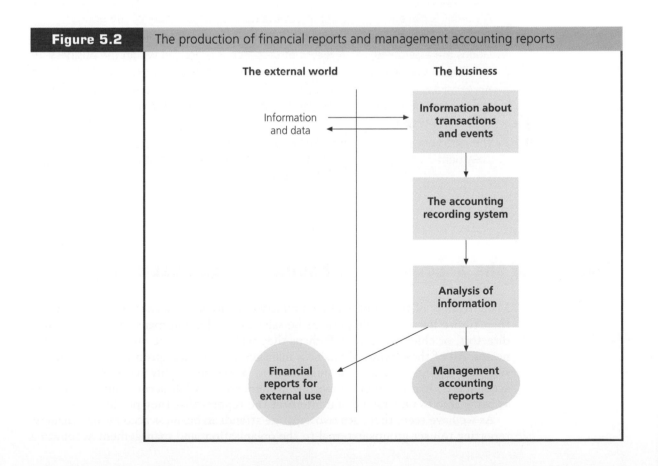

Figure 5.2   The production of financial reports and management accounting reports

Data and information about events and transactions flow in and out of the business. For example, when a business makes a sale of goods to a customer that it supplies on credit (i.e. the customer is not obliged to pay cash straight away) the events and information flows set out in Table 5.2 take place. At each stage details about the event are 'captured' by the accounting recording system. Periodically, data that shares common characteristics (e.g. all sales invoices) are analysed and the analysis is used to produce reports for both financial and management accounting purposes.

The principal purpose of this book is to assist business and other non-accounting students to understand the important elements of financial accounting reports. Therefore, we are not concerned with the details of data capture, recording and analysis for accounting purposes. These areas are the province of accountants. Unless students are so captivated by the accounting and financial understanding they glean from this book that they decide to change direction and become accountants, detailed knowledge of accounting systems really is not necessary. However, it is helpful to have some outline understanding of the way accounting information is gathered in order to produce the reports.

Table 5.2

Events and information flows relating to the sale of goods

Event	Information flow
An order is placed	Data about the nature and quantity of the goods required flows into the business and is recorded
Goods are assembled, packaged and sent out	A record of despatch is produced within the business and is sent out with the goods to the customer
An invoice is raised through the business recording system	The invoice is sent out from the business to the customer – information leaves the business
The customer sends payment	Information is received in the business and is recorded. The cheque is banked – information again flows out of the business

The role of the accountant in business organisations

Many readers of this book will be aiming for a career in business management. In their future lives they will perhaps be sales or production managers, or personnel directors, or chief executives. Perhaps they will at some stage own their own businesses. All of these types of business manager and business proprietor work alongside accountants and use the information, often on a daily basis, produced by accountants. It is therefore important to understand what accountants do, as well as being able to understand and interpret the reports that they produce.

As we have seen, there are two separate strands in business accounting: financial reporting to user groups external to the organisation, and management accounting for reporting to managers within the organisation. This variation in function is reflected in the organisation of the accounting profession and in the training of accountants.

The accounting profession

The accounting profession includes the following types of accountant: independent accounting practitioners and accountants in business.

Independent accounting practitioners work outside industry and business in professional practices. These are the accountants who provide taxation and accounting services to a wide range of businesses. If they are registered auditors, they are authorised to carry out the audits of companies and other organisations.

Accountants in business are the accountants with whom business managers work in organisations. Broadly, they are either financial accountants or management accountants, depending upon whether they specialise in the external or the internal provision of accounting information.

Professional accountants may have one or more accounting qualifications. These days almost all professional accountants have a university degree, although it is not necessarily in accounting or a related subject (the author of this book, for example, is a chartered accountant with a degree in Russian). After university they enter into a period of three or four years training with an employer during which they take some very tough examinations. Not everyone who embarks on accountancy training will manage to qualify because the examinations are so demanding.

The following are the principal professional accounting bodies in the UK which have their own qualification systems:

- ICAEW: the Institute of Chartered Accountants in England and Wales (members have the letters ACA or FCA after their names).
- ICAS: the Institute of Chartered Accountants of Scotland (members have the letters CA after their names).
- ACCA: The Association of Chartered Certified Accountants (members have the letters ACCA or FCCA after their names).

The members of these organisations are found in both professional independent accounting practice and in business. Students of ICAEW and ICAS usually train in professional accountancy firms. Students of ACCA are found in both professional and business environments. Usually those who go into business specialise in financial accounting and reporting rather than in management accounting.

Finally there is CIMA: the Chartered Institute of Management Accountants (members have the letters ACMA or FCMA after their names). As the name of this organisation implies, its members work principally in management accounting, and its students train exclusively in the business environment.

People who have trained as accountants are often found at the most senior levels in business organisations. It is not unusual in the UK to encounter chief executives and senior directors who started their careers as accountants before moving into more general business management.

Why do business managers have to understand accounting reports?

As we have seen earlier in the chapter, and in the four previous chapters in this section of the book, accounting information is necessary to business organisations. To summarise, accounting is used to provide:

- Financial reports about companies for a range of user needs.
- Management reports in all types and sizes of business organisation to assist management to: control business operations; plan for the future; make decisions; and find out how the business is performing.

In business organisations where there is more than one manager, decisions tend to be taken collectively by directors or partners. It is very often the case that accounting information feeds into business decision making. In order to be able to make informed decisions non-financial managers must be able to understand the financial information that accountants present to them.

Accountants occupy a service function in the business, but the service they provide is a very important one. Poor financial reporting and control can be the downfall of an otherwise successful business.

Chapter summary

This chapter has provided a framework of information about accounting, which underpins the remainder of the book. First, the need for accounting information was examined in the context of three different types of business organisation: sole trader; partnership; and limited company. Each organisational type needs to make some information available to people or organisations outside the business. In addition, accounting information is needed to assist management in running the business.

The provision of information to outsiders is a much more important issue for limited companies than it is for partnership or sole trader organisations. The general public has access to company financial information through the medium of the Registrar of Companies. As well as filing information at Companies House, companies are also obliged by law to make annual accounting information available to their shareholders. The chapter explained the important issue of the separation between the ownership and management of limited companies, which is especially noticeable in larger companies.

There is a long list of potential users of accounting information: shareholders, potential shareholders, investment analysts, lenders and potential lenders, employees and trade unions, suppliers, special interest groups, the government, financial journalists, academics and students, customers and the public at large.

The chapter went on to discuss the characteristics of useful financial information: it should be:

- relevant
- reliable
- comparable
- understandable.

The distinction between financial accounting and management accounting was described and discussed, and then the role of the accountant in business organisations was described. There are several different professional accountancy qualifications and the main ones were noted.

The chapter concluded with a brief discussion of why business managers need to be able to understand accounting reports.

The end-of-chapter exercises are divided into two sections. The first section has answers provided at the end of the book. The second section, in the white box, has answers on the lecturers' section of the website.

Website summary

The book's website contains the following material in respect of Chapter 5:

Students' section

- Quiz containing five multiple choice questions
- Two additional questions with answers.

Lecturers' section

- Answers to exercises 5.5–5.8
- Two additional questions with answers.

Exercises: answers at the end of the book

5.1 One of the following statements about the regulations governing a sole trader business is correct:

a) A sole trader does not need to supply any accounting information about his or her business to anyone.

b) A sole trader must employ an accountant.

c) Sole trader businesses are exempt from completing VAT returns.

d) A sole trader must submit a tax return annually.

5.2 One of the following statements about the regulations governing limited company businesses is correct:

a) All limited companies are obliged by company law to have an annual audit.

b) A limited company must send annual accounts to all of its shareholders.

c) All shareholders have unlimited access to their company's management accounting information.

d) The general public can access information about a company only by applying in writing to the directors.

5.3 Podgorny & Weaver Limited is involved in the wholesale supply of fashion goods to retailers. The company directors have a monthly meeting to discuss strategy and to make decisions. The directors are presented with the following reports prepared by the company accountant each month:

- List of amounts owed by the retail businesses that the company supplies.

- Summary of the value of fashion goods items currently held in stock.

- Summary of the orders received during the month.

- Profit and loss account for the last month.

Explain how the directors would be able to make use of each of the reports listed in order to improve the management of the company.

5.4 A group of environmental activists is interested in the activities of Burnip Chemicals plc, a company that has been regularly fined in the past for emitting toxic waste into the river running past the factory premises. What kind of information would the activist group be seeking about the activities of the company? To what extent are the annual financial statements likely to be helpful to them?

Exercises: answers available to lecturers

5.5   One of the following statements about the regulations governing partnership businesses is correct:

a)   Partnerships are obliged to have an annual audit of their financial statements.

b)   Partnerships must prepare annual financial statements as the basis for the calculation of tax.

c)   At least one of the partners is obliged to hold a bookkeeping qualification.

d)   Each partner must submit his or her own VAT return.

5.6   Which of the following statements is correct? The stewardship function requires directors of limited companies to:

a)   Act at all times in the best interests of the company.

b)   Allow shareholders to see detailed accounting records upon request.

c)   Hold regular monthly meetings to answer shareholders' questions.

d)   Consult the shareholders over particularly difficult management decisions.

5.7   Ponderosa & Smythe plc is a shoe manufacturing business, specialising in children's shoes. The finance director has just received the following letter from a shareholder who has recently bought some shares in the company:

'Dear Mr Pershore

I have just read a most interesting article in the *Financial Times* about the decline in the market for children's shoes. The article suggests that, because of demographic changes, the market will decline by 3–4% each year over the next ten years. In the circumstances I think our company should branch out into women's shoes. I would like the directors to discuss this at the next board meeting. Could you please send me a copy of the sales budget for the coming year, so that I can see whether or not you have taken the declining market properly into account.'

What are the principal points that the finance director should make in response to this letter?

5.8   Mohsin, a bank manager, is looking at an application for a loan from Boxer Burstall Limited, a local company. The company has included a copy of its most recent annual accounts, which are for the year ending 31 December 20X6. The accounts show that a modest profit has been made in the year. It is now March 20X8.

1.   What type of information will Mohsin be looking for from the annual accounts to help him in making a decision on whether or not to lend the money?

2. How relevant is the accounting information that the company has provided to Mohsin's decision?

3. Is Mohsin entitled to request any further information?

SECTION TWO

Financial accounting

91

Introduction

This section of the book is concerned with the provision of accounting information to interested parties external to the business. This type of accounting is usually referred to as financial accounting, and the process of communicating accounting information to external parties is known as financial reporting. Non-specialist students, who constitute the principal intended readership for this book, are quite likely to find that they will never be required to prepare accounting information during their working lives. However, it is highly probable that they will, sooner or later, have to read and understand accounting information. This section of the book aims to equip students with the skills to understand the principal features of financial accounting statements, so that they can interpret the message that the statements convey to an informed reader.

The first few chapters in the section demonstrate the way in which profit and loss accounts, balance sheets and cash flow statements are prepared in practice. The examples and exercises involve students in learning the basics of how to prepare such statements, and it may seem at first glance that this approach runs counter to the book's aim of fostering understanding. However, financial statements are difficult to understand without some basic knowledge of how they are prepared, and of how the statements fit together. Therefore, Chapters 6 to 10 cover the basics of financial statement preparation, but a recurrent underlying theme in these chapters is the significance of the information. Chapter 6 examines the balance sheet, while the focus of Chapter 7 is the profit and loss account. Chapters 8 and 9 examine some of the principal categories of adjustment that are made to the financial statements, and also some of the key principles that underlie financial accounting. Chapter 10 introduces another significant financial statement: the cash flow statement

The first four chapters in the section are oriented towards financal accounting in small unincorporated businesses. Chapter 11 introduces some of the real world complexities of financial accounting and reporting by limited companies. In this chapter we examine both financial and non-financial reporting, and we start to examine the principal features of the annual reports of listed companies. Various forms of accounting regulation are introduced, and the recent and growing phenomenon of corporate reporting on the internet is examined. Chapters 12 and 13 are entirely concerned with the significance of financial accounting information; they are two of the most important chapters in the book. Various means of analysing and interpreting accounting information are introduced in these chapters.

Each of the chapters in this section of the book includes a case study that can be attempted once a reasonably sound understanding of the chapter content has been reached.

@ Extra case studies

An extra case study is available on the lecturers' section of the website for use by those students who have gained a sound understanding of the content of Chapters 6 to 9 inclusive (The Hayseed Gallery).

In addition, two extra case studies, both available on the lecturers' section of the book's website, are referred to at the end of Chapter 13. Both relate to real examples of the financial statements of UK listed companies.

CHAPTER 6

The balance sheet

Aim of the chapter

To enable students to understand how a balance sheet is prepared.

Learning outcomes

After reading the chapter and completing the related exercises, students should:

- Understand the terminology used in a balance sheet.
- Be able to draw up a balance sheet for a sole trader from a list of account balances and explanatory notes.
- Be able to understand and comment on the basic information conveyed by a balance sheet.

Balance sheet basics

A balance sheet is a financial statement that shows the position of a business at a single point in time. It shows the assets, liabilities and capital of a business. We will now look at these three elements in more detail.

Assets

Assets are resources controlled by a business, which it will use in order to generate a profit in the future. Examples of such resources include:

- Cash in the form of notes and coins, and cash kept in bank accounts.
- Amounts of money that people or organisations owe to the business. Such amounts are described in accounting terminology as debtors.
- Items bought by the business to sell on to somebody else, or to process or transform in some way to make saleable goods. Such items are known as stock or inventory (note that 'inventory' is a term more commonly used in the USA and in international accounting).

Cash, debtors and stock are categorised as current assets. This description reflects the fact that they do not remain static for long. For example, debtors usually pay their bills within a short period of time, stock is sold and then replaced, and the business bank account balance changes very frequently.

Items bought (or sometimes leased) by the business, which will be used over a long period of time are known in accounting terminology as fixed assets. 'Fixed' implies that the assets stay in the business for a long time (not that they necessarily stay in one position). Examples are buildings (and the land they stand on), which are bought to house the activities of the business, vans and lorries that can be used for transporting goods and people, and computer hardware and software.

Liabilities

Liabilities are amounts that the business is obliged to pay to other people or organisations. Examples of liabilities include:

- Amounts owing to people or organisations that have provided goods or services on credit (i.e. they provide the goods or services without expecting immediate payment); these amounts are known as trade creditors.
- Amounts owing to the government in the form of taxation, for example, corporation tax or value added tax (VAT).
- Loans that will have to be repaid in due course to banks or other lenders.

All of these liabilities are known as creditors. The convention in drawing up a balance sheet is to subdivide liabilities into two major categories: (a) long-term liabilities (amounts that do not have to be paid for a year or more after the date of the balance sheet); and (b) current liabilities (amounts that are payable within one year of the balance sheet date).

Capital

Capital is the amount invested by the owner(s) of the business. There may be one or more owners: as we have seen in earlier chapters, in a sole trader business all of the capital is invested by a single owner or proprietor. In a partnership the ownership is split between several individuals.

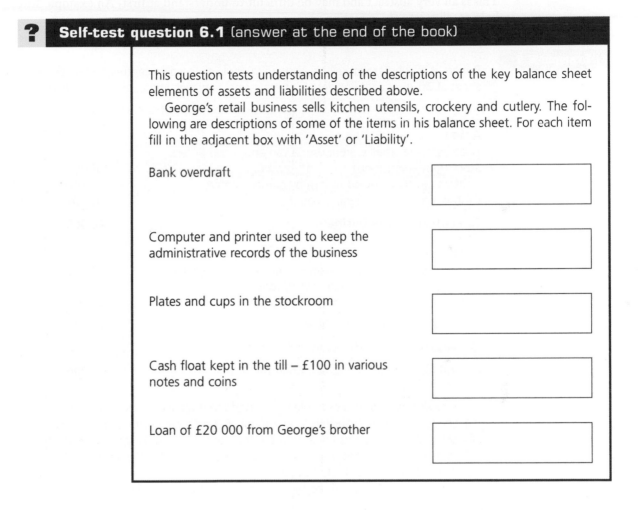

? Self-test question 6.1 (answer at the end of the book)

This question tests understanding of the descriptions of the key balance sheet elements of assets and liabilities described above.

George's retail business sells kitchen utensils, crockery and cutlery. The following are descriptions of some of the items in his balance sheet. For each item fill in the adjacent box with 'Asset' or 'Liability'.

Bank overdraft

Computer and printer used to keep the administrative records of the business

Plates and cups in the stockroom

Cash float kept in the till – £100 in various notes and coins

Loan of £20 000 from George's brother

The accounting equation

A key feature of balance sheets is that they balance. Obvious, perhaps, but what does 'balance' mean in this context? At any point in time a business should be able to provide a complete list of its assets and liabilities, each having a monetary amount. The resources available to the business are the total of assets less the total of liabilities. The total of the net resources is owned by the owner(s) of the business.

Therefore, it is possible to express the basic elements of a balance sheet in the following equation:

Assets less Liabilities equals Capital

Or, using arithmetical terms:

Assets − Liabilities = Capital

This is all very abstract and may be difficult to understand at first. An example will help to illustrate the equation.

Example 6.1	

Robert is a wholesaler selling gardening tools to garden centres. His balance sheet at 30 June contains details of his assets, liabilities and capital, as follows:

	£
Assets	
Fixed assets (a small warehouse, a van and a computer)	60 000
Stock (gardening tools)	8 000
Debtors (amounts owed to him by garden centres)	4 000
Cash in the business bank account	6 000
Total assets in the business	**78 000**
Liabilities	
Trade creditors (amounts owed to the firm that supplies Robert's business with gardening tools)	6 000
Other creditors (amounts owed to the bank)	8 000
Total liabilities in the business	**14 000**
Net assets (total assets less total liabilities)	64 000
Capital (Robert's resources tied up in the business)	**64 000**

We have a value in this example for each of the three elements of the accounting equation: assets, liabilities and capital. Robert's capital in the business is £64 000. Although assets come to more than that (£78 000) a total of £14 000 will have to be used up in paying liabilities. £78 000 less £14 000 equals £64 000 which is the amount of Robert's capital.

Summarised under the three basic elements, Robert's balance sheet looks like this:

	£
Assets	78 000
Liabilities	14 000
Net assets (assets less liabilities)	64 000
Capital	64 000

It is therefore logically true (Assets − Liabilities = Capital) that:

1. Net Assets = Capital, and that
2. Liabilities + Capital = Assets, and that
3. Assets − Capital = Liabilities.

We can test these three equations by using the figures from Robert's balance sheet:

1.   Net Assets = Capital: £64 000 = £64 000
2.   Liabilities + Capital = Assets: £14 000 + £64 000 = £78 000
3.   Assets – Capital = Liabilities: £78 000 – £64 000 = £14 000.

Next try these two self-test questions:

?   Self-test question 6.2 (answer at the end of the book)

Saqib's balance sheet at 30 September shows the following items:

	£
Fixed assets	30 000
Stock	5 000
Debtors	4 000
Cash held in the business bank account	3 000
Trade creditors	6 000
Saqib's capital	36 000

1.   What is the total of assets in the business?
2.   What is the total of liabilities in the business?
3.   What is the capital of the business?
4.   Write down the figures for the basic accounting equation (Reminder: Assets – Liabilities = Capital) in Saqib's business

---

So far, figures have been provided for each of the three key elements in the accounting equation. Note, however, that if we know two out of the three key elements we can work out the third. Example 6.2 demonstrates how this is done. Try self-test question 6.3 to test your understanding of this point.

Example 6.2

We need to supply the missing figure in each of the following incomplete accounting equations.

1. Capital
Assets are £15 000 and liabilities are £3 000. What is capital? Use the accounting equation (Assets – Liabilities = Capital):

$$£15\ 000 – £3\ 000 = £?$$
$$£15\ 000 – £3\ 000 = £12\ 000$$

Capital is therefore £12 000.

2. Assets

Capital is £6 000 and liabilities are £18 000. What is the total for assets? Use the accounting equation (Assets – Liabilities = Capital)

$$? - £18\,000 = £6\,000$$
$$£24\,000 - £18\,000 = £6\,000$$

Assets are therefore £24 000.

? Self-test question 6.3 (answer at the end of the book)

Amy's balance sheet at 31 August contains total assets of £58 000 and total liabilities of £30 000. Use the accounting equation to find Amy's capital.

Drawing up a balance sheet

In this part of the chapter we will look at a business start-up example to see how the balance sheet develops from basic transactions. We will use the accounting equation looked at in the previous section and we will be using the accounting terms described earlier in the chapter. Therefore it is important to have gained a basic understanding of what has been dealt with so far in this chapter. It may be helpful to run through it again, and to do some or all of Exercises 6.1 to 6.10 at the end of the chapter, before moving on to learn how to draw up a balance sheet.

Example 6.3

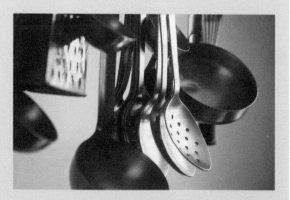

Salma has run a successful business in garment retailing for several years. Early in 20X3 she sells the business to a large retail chain, and makes a profit of £150 000 after tax. She is not ready to retire yet, and decides to start a new business. She spends several months researching possibilities, and decides to set up a retail business selling designer kitchenware. The business will be called 'Kitchen Kit'. Salma signs an agreement to rent premises from 1 February 20X4, planning to open her shop on

26 February. Rent is payable in arrears, so Salma will not have to pay anything until the end of March. In the rest of this example we will look at how Salma's balance sheet is prepared, and how it changes from day to day as she undertakes more transactions.

Day 1

On 1 February Salma opens a bank account, depositing £100 000. What are the accounting implications of this transaction?

Effectively, Salma's business is 'born' on 1 February 20X4. We can apply some of the terminology from earlier in the chapter to the first transaction:

An **asset** is established – the balance in the bank account of £100 000. Salma's **capital** in the business is the amount she has just put into it – i.e. £100 000.

At this point, we have two of the basic accounting equation elements, as follows:

$$\text{Asset (£100 000)} = \text{Capital (£100 000)}$$

Using this information, we can draw up a balance sheet at 1 February 20X4:

Kitchen Kit: Balance sheet at 1 February 20X4

	£
Asset (bank account)	100 000
Capital	100 000

This simple balance sheet follows certain conventions that are accepted as the norm in accounting in the UK and many other countries:

1. It has a heading showing the name of the business and the date of the balance sheet.
2. It is in vertical format – that is, the figures are arranged in a column.
3. It is headed by a £ sign, telling the reader which currency is being used.
4. Assets are stated first. Where there are liabilities these are stated below assets. Finally, at the bottom of the balance sheet, capital is reported.
5. The key totals are underlined.
6. The balance sheet is that of the business, rather than of Salma herself. From its beginning, the business has a financial existence separate from Salma's personal financial affairs. (This is known as the 'business entity' concept).

Later on in this chapter, and in subsequent chapters, we will encounter many balance sheet statements that are much more complex than this one. Nevertheless, all of the statements will obey these basic conventions.

Days 2–8

Salma needs to stock her shop in time for the opening on 26 February. First, she has arranged for a builder to come into the shop to install a counter and some shelving. She pays him £6500 on 8 February. What are the accounting implications of this transaction?

The counter and shelving are likely to be used in the business over a long period of time. Therefore, they are regarded as fixed assets, and will be classified as such in the balance sheet of the business. The business's cash resources are depleted by £6500, but fixed assets increase to £6500. The transaction involves an exchange of a current asset (cash) for a fixed asset.

A balance sheet drawn up at 8 February following the payment to the builder is as follows:

Kitchen Kit: Balance sheet at 8 February 20X4

	£
Fixed assets	
Counter and shelving	6 500
Current assets	
Asset (bank account)*	93 500
Total assets	100 000
Capital	100 000

*The balance on the bank account was £100 000 before Salma wrote the cheque for £6500. After she has issued the cheque the bank account balance drops to £93 500.

Note that the accounting equation remains valid: assets = capital.

Day 9

Salma needs to stock the shop. She has ordered various items of kitchenware that are delivered on 9 February. Because Salma has several years of experience in business and a good credit record she has been able to obtain credit terms from suppliers, and will not have to pay for the stock until 9 March. The cost of the stock is £72 000. What are the accounting implications of this transaction?

The business has acquired a new type of current asset in the form of stock. Note that it is classified as a current asset because it is not expected to remain in the business for a long period (unlike the counter and shelving). However, in this case there is no effect (yet) on the bank account because immediate payment for the goods is not required. So what has occurred?

A current asset of £72 000 arises, and current assets in the balance sheet will increase by this amount.

A current liability of £72 000 arises.

Taking this transaction into account the balance sheet of the business at 9 February 20X4 is as follows:

Kitchen Kit: Balance sheet at 9 February 20X4

	£	£
Fixed assets		
Counter and shelving		6 500

	£	£
Current assets		
Stock	72 000	
Asset (bank account)	93 500	
	165 500	
Current liabilities		
Amounts owed to supplier	(72 000)	
Net current assets		
(£165 500 – 72 000)		93 500
		100 000
Capital		100 000

What is going on here? Why are there so many more figures in this balance sheet compared to the previous one? Don't panic. Most of the changes from the previous balance sheets have been made in order to make the balance sheet statement clearer and more useful to the reader. Starting at the top of the balance sheet at 9 February:

- Fixed assets are the same as before at £6500.
- Under current assets we now have the new asset of stock. There are now two categories of current asset so it is helpful to summarise current assets by means of a total figure of £165 500.
- We have now introduced the new category of current liabilities which comprises the £72 000 which is due to be paid for the stock in one month's time.
- It is a convention, when drawing up balance sheets, to show a total for 'net current assets' – that is, current assets less current liabilities. In this balance sheet the total for net current assets is £93 500. Because the balance sheet is getting a little bit crowded with figures at this point, we pull the figures related to current assets and current liabilities to one side and show them in a separate column. Once the reader gets used to this convention it makes understanding what is going on in the balance sheet very much easier.
- Note that the current liability figure is shown in brackets. This is in order to emphasise the fact that they are being deducted from assets. It is not strictly necessary to do this, but it may help understanding by creating an obvious distinction between the figures relating to assets and those relating to liabilities.

Note that the accounting equation remains valid, but that it is now slightly more complicated because of the introduction of liabilities:

$$\text{Assets } (£165\ 500 + £6500 = 172\ 000) - \text{Liabilities } (£72\ 000)$$
$$= \text{Capital } (£100\ 000)$$

Day 10

Salma has invested in stock to sell in the shop. Once she pays for it in one month's time she will have a cash balance of £21 500 (£93 500 – 72 000). She realises that there will be many further demands on her cash in the short-term, for example: newspaper advertising, more stock purchases, purchase of a cash register, installation of a burglar alarm and so on. She realises that she is likely to need more cash, but she does not want to draw any further on her personal resources. She borrows £20 000 from her mother. This is a loan without a fixed repayment date, but her mother is happy for it to be a long-term arrangement. On 10 February Salma pays £20 000 into the bank in the form of a cheque from her mother. What are the accounting implications of this transaction?

The business has boosted its cash resources by £20 000. On the other hand, there is now a long-term liability. A balance sheet drawn up on 10 February will be as follows:

Kitchen Kit: Balance sheet at 10 February 20X4

	£	£
Fixed assets		
Counter and shelving		6 500
Current assets		
Stock	72 000	
Asset (bank account)*	113 500	
	185 500	
Current liabilities		
Amounts owed to supplier	(72 000)	
Net current assets		
(£165 500 – 72 000)		113 500
Long-term liability		(20 000)
		100 000
Capital		100 000

The bank account was £93 500; it now increases by £20 000 to £113 500.

Note that the accounting equation remains valid:

$$\text{Assets } (£6500 + £185\ 500 = £192\ 000)$$
$$- \text{ Liabilities } (£72\ 000 + £20\ 000 = £92\ 000)$$
$$= \text{ Capital } (£100\ 000).$$

Summary

Each transaction that we have examined makes the balance sheet a little more complicated – and by 10 February, when the example ends, the business has yet to make a sale. However, it is not necessary, or even useful, in practice, to spend time drawing up a balance sheet every time a transaction is made. Balance sheets are drawn up on a periodic basis – at least once a year, possibly as often as once a month, but practically never on a daily basis. We have examined Salma's balance sheet after each transaction simply in order to demonstrate how an individual transaction can alter asset and liability balances.

It is important to note that the basic balance sheet totals (£100 000 for net assets and £100 000 for capital) have remained the same throughout the period. All that has changed is the composition of the assets and liabilities of the business. Next, we will briefly examine the possible events that could alter the balance sheet totals.

Changing the balance sheet totals

What would it take to alter the balance sheet totals for Kitchen Kit? Let's look at the possibilities. First, the value of capital, and therefore of net assets, could increase. This would happen in either of two situations:

1. The owner (or owners) of the business might put some more of their own personal resources into it. In Salma's case she might, for example, sell her house or her car and put the money into the business bank account. This would increase both net assets and her capital by an equal amount.
2. The business increases its net assets by making a profit. Any organisation run on commercial terms will attempt to make profits. In Salma's case she will do this by selling kitchenware at prices greater than the price she paid for the goods. The difference between selling and cost price must be sufficiently large to cover all categories of expense, such as rent, rates, advertising and administration.

Alternatively, the value of capital, and therefore of net assets, could decrease. This would happen in either of two situations:

1. The owner (or owners) of the business take out some of the resources they have put into it. The owner(s) will want or need to remove some part of the assets (probably in the form of cash). Net assets decrease and so does capital. The removal of assets is traditionally known as drawings. (The issue of owners extracting cash from their businesses is discussed at greater length in Chapter 3.)
2. The business decreases its net assets by making a loss. If goods are sold for amounts that do not, overall, cover the costs of the business, a loss will be made and net assets, and capital, will be depleted.

In the example above, the business has not yet reached the point where it is open for trading. No sales have been made and, therefore, no profit exists. We will examine what happens when sales are made in a subsequent chapter.

More practice with balance sheets

Example 6.3 for this chapter examined a new business start-up to illustrate the basics of preparing a balance sheet. This section applies the knowledge gained from the earlier part of the chapter to established businesses that are preparing balance sheets at the end of an accounting period.

Each business – whether a company, a partnership or a sole trader (like Salma) – has a year-end date, at which point it prepares its annual accounts. Conventionally, year-ends tend to fall at the ends of months (31 December,

31 March, etc.) but there is no rule about this. It would be quite acceptable to have a year-end of 3 January, for example.

The next example deals with preparing a balance sheet for an established business.

Example 6.4

Dipak has been established for several years in a business selling computers for home use and for small businesses. As well as selling standard systems he also builds PC systems to customers' specifications and sells a limited range of software packages, printers and fax machines. He runs the business from shop premises that he owns on a freehold basis.

Dipak's business has the following balances at its annual year-end, 31 August.

	£
Freehold premises	53 000
Shop fittings and equipment	6 300
Cash	60
Loan from brother (no fixed repayment date)	8 000
Stock of PCs	48 000
Printers, modem cards, etc.	9 650
Bank overdraft	13 750
Debtors (amounts owed by businesses for computers)	5 250
Dipak's capital	99 130
Software	15 000
Creditors (due to suppliers)	16 380

First, we need to establish which categories each of the balances fall into – asset, liability or capital:

	£	Category
Freehold premises	53 000	Asset
Shop fittings and equipment	6 300	Asset
Cash	60	Asset
Loan from brother (no fixed repayment date)	8 000	Liability
Stock of PCs	48 000	Asset
Printers, printer supplies, modem cards, etc.	9 650	Asset
Bank overdraft	13 750	Liability
Debtors (amounts owed by customers)	5 250	Asset
Dipak's capital	99 130	Capital
Software	15 000	Asset
Creditors (due to suppliers)	16 380	Liability

Note: It may be helpful to refer back to the definitions and examples at the beginning of the chapter if any of these classifications are unclear.

Classifying assets

Seven of the items on the list are classified as assets. Which are fixed and which are current? Remember that stock, debtors and cash are categorised as current assets.

The first two items on the list are fixed assets – i.e. freehold premises and the shop fittings and equipment; these have been, and will continue to be, used in the business for a long time.

There are three categories of stock in the list. These will be added together to arrive at the total for stock:

	£
PCs	48 000
Printers etc.	9 650
Software	15 000
Total stock	72 650

As well as fixed assets and stocks, Dipak's business has debtors (amounts owed to the business by customers) of £5250 and cash of £60.

Drawing up the balance sheet

Having done the preliminary work on classification, we can now prepare the balance sheet at 31 August.

Dipak: Balance sheet at 31 August

	£	£
Fixed assets		
Freehold premises		53 000
Shop fittings and equipment		6 300
		59 300
Current assets		
Stock	72 650	
Debtors	5 250	
Cash	60	
	77 960	
Current liabilities		
Bank overdraft	(13 750)	
Creditors	(16 380)	
	(30 130)	
Net current assets (£77 960 – £30 130)		47 830
		107 130
Long-term liabilities		
Liability (loan from brother)		(8 000)
Net assets		99 130
Capital		99 130

Dipak's balance sheet – what does it say?

It should always be remembered that balance sheets are intended to be useful to people as ways of communicating important information about a business. When involved in the difficulties of fitting the figures together and getting the balance sheet to balance it can be difficult to remember that the point of the exercise is to communicate a message.

So what is this balance sheet telling us? We know that Dipak is in business, and we know that he sells computers; that is why the business has stocks of computers, software and so on. But does the business need to have quite so much stock? Let's say the average price that Dipak has paid for a PC is £600. That means that he has approximately 80 systems (£48 000 divided by £600) in stock. How long will it take to sell these items, and will they be out of date soon? Similar questions could be asked about the printers and the software.

Dipak owes his creditors more than £16 000. Presumably they will expect to be paid very soon. How is he going to pay them? The business has a large overdraft with the bank. Will the bank let him borrow more money on overdraft? Even if the debtors were to pay up straight away, there would still be a problem. Does Dipak have more resources of his own that he can put into the business?

Trying to understand this balance sheet leads to asking a lot of questions, which cannot currently be answered. In order to answer the questions we need more information. In the next few chapters we will be looking at other accounting statements that provide more information about businesses.

In the meantime, it is important to bear in mind that the purpose of balance sheets (and accounting in general) is not to provide number puzzles for business students, but is to provide information that actually means something in the context of the real world.

Chapter summary

This chapter has explained the basics of preparing a balance sheet. The main accounting terminology used in the balance sheet has been described, and the accounting equation (Assets – Liabilities = Capital) should by now be familiar.

Students who have worked through this chapter thoroughly should now be able to draw up a balance sheet from a list of balances provided.

The communications aspect of the balance sheet statement has been recognised and discussed, and it should now be possible for students to ask informed questions about the meaning of specific balance sheet statements.

The end-of-chapter exercises are divided into two sections. The first section has answers provided at the end of the book. The second section, in the white box, has answers on the lecturers' section of the website. It is important to work through as many as necessary in order to achieve complete understanding of the chapter content, before moving on to the next chapter.

Finally, the chapter contains a case study that examines a business start-up example. Answers to the case study requirements can be found on the students' section of the website.

Website summary

The book's website contains the following material in respect of Chapter 6:

Students' section

- Quiz containing ten multiple choice questions
- Six longer questions with answers
- Answer to case study 'Balance sheet basics'.

Lecturers' section

- Answers to exercises 6.14–6.21
- Four longer questions with answers.

Exercises: answers at the end of the book

6.1 Alexander's business manufactures and sells biscuits to supermarkets and grocery shops. Below are descriptions of some of the items in his balance sheet. For each item fill in the adjacent box with 'Asset' or 'Liability'.

Cash kept in a tin in the factory office

Oven

Bank loan, repayable over 5 years

Plastic packaging for biscuits

Flour and sugar

Amounts payable to supplier of dried fruit

6.2 Amir has a consultancy business that he runs from rented offices. The following are descriptions of some of the items in his balance sheet. For each item fill in the adjacent box with Fixed asset, Current asset, Long-term liability or Current liability.

Value added tax (VAT) payable to Customs and Excise

Office computer

Amount due from Lomax plc for consultancy work carried out by Amir

Bank overdraft

Bank loan to be repaid in three years' time

Amount payable to stationery supplier

6.3 Brian's balance sheet shows totals for assets of £83 000 and £36 500 for liabilities. Use the accounting equation to find the total for Brian's capital.

6.4 Basil's capital in his business is £43 650. The business assets total £188 365. Use the accounting equation to find the total for liabilities.

6.5 Brenda's business has fixed assets of £12 000, current assets of £8500 and total liabilities of £17 300. What is Brenda's capital?

6.6 Brigitte's business has fixed assets of £27 000, current assets of £16 000, current liabilities of £12 000 and long-term liabilities of £10 000. What is her capital in the business?

6.7 Bryony's balance sheet shows the following totals:

	£
Fixed assets	35 840
Current assets	16 500
Current liabilities	12 000
Long-term liabilities	6 000

Which of the following is Bryony's capital in the business?

a) £70 340

b) £1 340

c) £46 340

d) £34 340.

6.8 Benito's balance sheet shows the following totals:

	£
Fixed assets	39 497
Current assets	26 004
Current liabilities	16 777
Capital	33 058

Work out the missing figure for long-term liabilities. (Hint: first, work out total liabilities using the accounting equation.)

6.9 Blanche's balance sheet shows the following totals:

	£
Fixed assets	36 609
Current assets	38 444
Current liabilities	26 300
Capital	39 477

Which of the following is the missing figure for long-term liabilities?

a) £61 876

b) £9 276

c) £15 012

d) £67 612.

6.10 Callum's balance sheet at 31 July shows the following:

	£
Fixed assets	18 337
Stock	12 018
Debtors	365
Cash	63
Bank overdraft	3 686
Creditors	2 999

a)   What is the total of assets in the business?

b)   What is the total of current assets?

c)   What is the total for liabilities?

d)   What is Callum's capital?

6.11 Ciera's business has the following balances at 31 December:

	£
Stock	18 600
Creditors	23 700
Cash in bank account	13 000
Long-term loan	20 000
Fixed assets – premises	39 000
Amounts owed by customers	6 500
Amounts owed to Inland Revenue	3 800
Ciera's capital	29 600

Prepare Ciera's balance sheet at 31 December. Use the format shown in the chapter – i.e. start at the top with fixed assets, then work down the page presenting current assets, then current liabilities (remember to show a total for net current assets), then long-term liabilities. Capital is shown at the bottom.

Remember to line up columns of figures neatly, and to use a proper heading for the balance sheet.

6.12 Dan's balance sheet at 1 May is as follows:

	£	£
Fixed assets		30 000
Current assets		
Stock	15 000	
Debtors	5 000	
Bank account	18 000	
	38 000	
Current liabilities		
Creditors	(16 000)	
Net current assets (£38 000 – £16 000)		22 000
Net assets		52 000
Capital		52 000

(1) On 2 May Dan pays £1500 for an office computer to help him keep the business accounts. (2) On 3 May Dan pays a creditor £3000. Explain how his balance sheet will be affected by the two transactions and show the new balance sheet at 3 May after taking account of both transactions.

6.13 Ernest runs an art gallery. He organises exhibitions at which painters and sculptors show their work. If a piece of art work is sold, Ernest takes a commission of 50% of the selling price. He banks the cash and then pays out what is due to the artists. He held a successful exhibition in November, and is planning the next one for January. Each time he holds an exhibition he pays for advertising and sending out leaflets to people on his mailing list, and also for wine and soft drinks on the opening night of the exhibition. Putting on the exhibition in January will cost him around £4000. Ernest has the following assets and liabilities at 31 December:

	£
Gallery premises	68 000
Cash at bank	18 600
Amounts payable to artists	16 560
Office equipment	2 260
Amounts payable to printers for publicity material for recent exhibition	1 600
Capital	70 700

1. Prepare Ernest's balance sheet at 31 December.

2. Write a brief assessment of Ernest's business position as shown by the balance sheet.

Exercises: answers available to lecturers

6.14 Adrian owns and runs a restaurant. The following are descriptions of some of the items in his balance sheet. For each item fill in the adjacent box with Fixed asset, Current asset, Long-term liability or Current liability.

Restaurant tables

Wages owed to waiter

Bank account containing £3850

Tax bill due to Inland Revenue

Restaurant premises

Mortgage (i.e. loan) from bank to buy restaurant premises

Food supplies in kitchen fridges

Amounts due to baker for bread supplied over the last month

6.15 Bernie's business has liabilities of £63 000. His capital is £28 000. What is the total for assets?

6.16 Bjork's capital in her business is £97 000. The total for current liabilities is £31 000. There are no long-term liabilities. What is the total for assets?

6.17 Bashir's balance sheet shows the following totals:

	£
Capital	68 350
Fixed assets	79 403
Current assets	16 276

Which of the following is the total of liabilities in Bashir's business?

a) £131 477

b) £27 329

c) £5 223

d) £164 029

6.18 Benedict's balance sheet shows the following totals:

	£
Current assets	716 237
Current liabilities	426 663
Long-term liabilities	100 000
Capital	1 373 424

What is the total for fixed assets?

6.19 Carmela's business has the following balances at 18 October:

	£
Amounts due from customers	16 303
Fixed assets – machinery	12 722
Amounts payable to creditors for materials	6 868
Bank balance	6 993
Cash on the premises	120
Amounts payable to the Inland Revenue	396
Long-term loan from sister	1 800
Fixed assets – office computer	1 060
Stocks of goods	17 721

Prepare the balance sheet for Carmela at 18 October. (Note: no figure is given for Carmela's capital – it has to be calculated from the information given above.)

6.20   Diana's balance sheet at 28 August is as follows:

	£	£
Fixed assets		13 500
Current assets		
Stock	10 300	
Debtors	1 200	
Bank account	1 000	
Petty cash	600	
	13 100	
Current liabilities		
Creditors	(6 400)	
Net current assets (£13 100 – £6 400)		6 700
Net assets		20 200
Capital		20 200

1.   Diana has saved up some money for her holiday, but decides to put it into the business instead. She pays a cheque for £2000 into the business bank account on 29 August.

2.   On 30 August the business receives a cheque for £600 from one of its debtors.

Explain how her balance sheet will be affected and show the new balance sheet at 30 August after taking account of both transactions.

6.21   Erik has a retail business selling china and glass ornaments from a small shop in a town centre. He has the following balances at his year-end of 30 November:

	£
Freehold premises	16 800
Shop fittings, computer, till, etc.	8 300
Cash – float in till	600
Loan from mother (no fixed repayment date)	2 000
Stock	10 300
Bank overdraft	3 800
Creditors – due to suppliers	3 200
Creditors – due to Customs and Excise for VAT	800
Capital	26 200

Note that the amounts due to suppliers include £2200 owed to one company, Ornamental Glass Products Limited. The company has been waiting for payment for this amount since August and Erik has been rung up on several occasions by the company's chief accountant requesting immediate payment. Erik has an overdraft limit of £4000.

1. Prepare Erik's balance sheet at 30 November.

2. Erik has asked you to advise him on whether he should ask the bank manager for an increase in his overdraft limit. Assess Erik's position at 30 November as shown by the balance sheet.

CASE STUDY 6.1 Balance sheet basics

Part 1: Business start-up – the first balance sheet

Following completion of her degree course in textiles, Isobel Buchanan was unable to find a job that really used her skills and knowledge. For the last five years she has worked in a clothing firm where she deals with import and export paperwork. She has maintained her interest in textiles, and continues to produce creative work, but the experience of some of her university friends has convinced her that she does not want to face an uncertain future as an independent textile artist or designer.

Recently, however, events have occurred that have encouraged her to think about leaving her employment to set up a new business. Isobel attended a regional training course on changes in the law affecting businesses that import from outside the European Union. At the coffee break she was introduced by a colleague to Ivan, who runs his own importing business. Ivan has been investigating the possibility of importing hand-made rugs and carpets from the Middle East and India where he has several contacts. He does not want to go into the retail business himself and is examining the possibility of selling his goods wholesale to retailers. He has identified an outlet in London, but is also looking for possible selling opportunities in Scotland. Isobel expresses an interest in seeing the samples and she and Ivan arrange to meet the following week.

At the meeting, Isobel is very impressed by the samples; the quality of the work is very fine and the patterns and colour combinations are striking and unusual. She begins to wonder whether she could set up a retail outlet herself in Scotland. She doesn't know anything about business start-ups or finance, but her uncle, Andrew, is an accountant, and she decides to ask his advice.

Andrew has been of the opinion for a long time that Isobel is more likely to make a success of a career in commerce than in the creative arts. Before she went to university he had tried to persuade her to do an HND in finance or a degree in accountancy, but without success. So, when Isobel outlines her business idea to him he is very receptive and listens carefully. To her considerable surprise he offers to provide her with some financial backing in the form of a loan at a commercial rate of interest. Isobel, who had been wondering how she could possibly persuade a bank to give her a commercial loan, is very keen to take up the offer.

Several months pass. Andrew, although wanting to help his niece, is, after all, an accountant. He insists on Isobel producing a reasoned business plan before he will lend the money. She finds this difficult, but at last succeeds in writing a plan that Andrew finds acceptable. Isobel is prepared to risk her own savings of £10 000 (which she has built up over the last five years with a view to putting down a deposit on a flat) but the business plan shows that she will need a great deal more than that. Andrew and his wife pay the legal fees to have a proper loan agreement drawn up. The terms of the loan are that they will lend Isobel £40 000 immediately, with a further loan of up to £40 000 available if it is needed. The interest rate is variable, tied to commercial bank rates, and is currently at 6%. The £40 000 is to be paid off at the rate of £5000 at the end of each financial year over an eight-year period. However, no repayment will be expected in the first three years of the business while it is getting established.

Andrew and his wife Hannah are well off, and have no children of their own. They intend that their four nieces and nephews should be the main beneficiaries of their wills. Although they want, and expect, to have the loans to Isobel repaid, if Isobel loses all or part of the money they intend to deduct the loss from her share of the inheritance. Hannah thinks they should tell Isobel this so that she won't have to worry too much about paying the money back. Andrew, on the other hand, thinks that it will do Isobel good to have to treat the loan as a proper commercial liability; she is more likely to run the business sensibly if she's forced to worry about meeting the repayments.

On 1 March 20X1 Andrew and his wife give Isobel a cheque for £40 000 which she puts into a bank account that she has opened for the business. On the same day she makes a bank transfer of £10 000 from her own savings account into the business account. Isobel has handed in her notice at work and is ready to take the plunge into self-employment. She decides to name the business 'Buchanan International Designs'.

Part 1: Requirements

a) What are the principal risks that Isobel faces in her new business start-up?

(Note: it may be worth briefly reviewing Chapters 2 and 3 before answering this question)

b) Prepare a balance sheet at 1 March 20X1 that includes the effects of the transactions described in part 1 of the case study.

The answers and discussion relating to these requirements can be found on the student section of the book's website.

Part 2: Subsequent transactions

While some business start-ups can be run from home (for example, where people are using their skills in consultancy businesses), a retail business will almost always need shop premises. Isobel knows that the location of her premises will be a key factor in her success (or failure), and she spends a long time looking for a small shop in a suitable location which she can afford to rent. The main streets of towns and cities tend to be occupied by major retail chains (e.g. Boots, Next, Marks & Spencer) and it becomes clear to Isobel early on in her search that she cannot afford even a small shop in the city's main shopping streets. Two or three streets away, however, there is a cluster of smaller shops and galleries specialising in selling art and antiques. Isobel finds a basement shop in this area that has almost exactly four years left to run on its lease.

The cost of the lease comprises two elements. First of all, a sum of £10 000 is payable immediately for the purchase of the right to occupy the premises for four years. This is known as a **lease premium**. After that, there is an annual rental of £14 000, which is payable quarterly in arrears (i.e. at the end of each three-month period during which Isobel occupies the premises). At the end of four years, if she is still in business, Isobel will have to leave the premises, or negotiate a new lease with the landlord. On 2 March 20X1 Isobel pays a cheque out of the business bank account for £10 000 for the lease premium.

The shop is in reasonably good condition, but lacks any kind of display facilities. Isobel commissions a carpenter to produce two wall-mounted display racks and some hollow plywood boxes over which goods can be displayed. The racks are installed on 3 March 20X1 and Isobel writes a cheque to the carpenter for £4500.

Another major purchase is the first consignment of rugs and carpets which Isobel buys from Ivan, the importer. A retail business needs sufficient stock in order to start trading; in Isobel's business it is important to have a wide range of designs for customers to select from. Therefore, she has had to allow quite a large amount of money in her initial business plan for stock purchase. The merchandise comes in four main size categories: small rugs, larger rugs and two sizes of carpet. Isobel expects to be able to sell a larger number of the rugs and so her initial purchase is as follows:

	Cost (£)
30 small rugs at £100 each	3 000
10 larger rugs at £300 each	3 000
10 small carpets at £750 each	7 500
10 larger carpets at £1000 each	10 000
Total purchase of stock	23 500

Ivan delivers the rugs and carpets to Isobel on 4 March so that she can get the shop organised and the displays set up prior to the opening on 10 March. He gives Isobel an invoice for £23 500 which will require payment by 1 April.

Part 2: Requirements

a) Prepare a balance sheet for the business at 2 March 20X1 to reflect the effects of the lease transaction.

b) Prepare a balance sheet for the business at 3 March 20X1 to reflect the effects of the display racks transaction.

c) Prepare a balance sheet for the business at 4 March 20X1 to reflect the effects of the stock purchase transaction.

@ The answers and discussion relating to these requirements can be found on the student section of the book's website.

CHAPTER 7

The profit and loss account

Aim of the chapter

To enable students to understand how a profit and loss account is prepared and how it fits together with the balance sheet.

Learning outcomes

After reading the chapter and completing the related exercises, students should:

- Understand the terminology used in a profit and loss account.
- Be able to draw up a profit and loss account for a sole trader from a list of account balances and explanatory notes.
- Be able to understand and comment on the basic information conveyed by a profit and loss account.
- Combine skills gained as a result of studying Chapters 6 and 7 to draw up a set of financial statements comprising a profit and loss account and balance sheet.

Profit and loss

As noted in the previous chapter, an organisation run on commercial terms will attempt to make profits. In straightforward terms, it does this by selling goods and/or services at prices that will allow it to cover all the expenses of the business, with a surplus remaining.

- Revenue (also referred to as 'sales' or 'turnover') is the amount of goods and/or services sold, expressed in monetary terms.
- Expenses are the amounts incurred by the business in purchasing or manufacturing the goods sold, and other expenditure on items such as rent and telephone charges.
- Profit is the surplus remaining when revenue exceeds expenditure (a desirable state of affairs in a commercial organisation).
- Loss is the deficit that occurs when expenditure exceeds revenue (a state of affairs that cannot persist for a long period in a commercial organisation).

The profit and loss account summarises the revenue and expenses of an organisation over a period of time. It shows the performance of the business over the period. It gives the reader information showing how well or how badly the business is doing. Note that 'profit and loss account' is the description that is usually used in the UK; however, the term income statement is also used, especially internationally.

Categories of commercial activity

Commercial activities can be broadly classified into three types, as follows:

- trading
- manufacturing
- service.

Trading organisations operate as 'middlemen'. Typically, they buy in goods that have been manufactured by another individual or organisation and then sell them on at a higher price to someone else. Salma's kitchenware business, which we examined in the previous chapter, is a trading organisation. Her business has nothing to do with the manufacturing of kitchenware items; she buys in finished goods and aims to sell them at a profit.

Manufacturing organisations are often complex operations. They manufacture goods that are either sold directly to the public or to trading organisations which then sell them on. For example, a factory manufactures woollen coats which it sells to fashion shops. The factory business sells at prices that cover the various costs of manufacture plus a profit. The shop owners sell at a higher price than they are charged by the factory business, and so they, too, make a profit. By the time the customer in the shop buys the coat, at least two organisations have made a profit on the transaction.

Service organisations sell services rather than goods. For example, a solicitor is not concerned at all with the sale of goods. He or she makes a surplus out of the provision of professional services.

Some organisations have a mixture of activities. Take, for example, a commercial tennis club. It sells annual subscriptions to a range of services such as use of tennis courts and tennis coaching. It also sells a range of shoes and clothing that it buys in from all the well-known sports clothing manufacturers. The club, therefore, operates both trading and service activities.

Profit and loss account for a sole trader

Later, we will examine the financial statements of other types of business. For the moment, however, we will concentrate on drawing up a profit and loss account for a trading business.

The profit and loss account of a trading business splits into two parts: first, the profitability of the buying and selling processes are shown in the trading account, to arrive at a figure of gross profit, and then all the other expenses of the business are deducted to arrive at a net profit.

The basic layout of the profit and loss account is as follows:

	£
Sales	—
Less: cost of sales	(—)
Gross profit	—
Various expenses	(—)
Net profit	—

First, we will look at the calculation and presentation of the upper part of the profit and loss account to arrive at gross profit. This part of the financial statement is known as the trading account.

Example 7.1

Mary has a shop that sells cookers. For the sake of simplicity we will assume that she sells only one type of cooker at a price of £195 each. She buys all the cookers from one manufacturer at a cost of £135 each. Each cooker therefore produces a profit of £60 (£195 less £135). If Mary bought and sold only one cooker the basic trading account information would be as follows:

Mary: Trading account

	£
Sale of cooker	195
Less: cost of cooker	135
Profit	60

The standard terminology used in drawing up a trading account is to describe the deduction for the cost of the goods as cost of sales, and the profit shown in the trading account as **gross profit**. We can restate Mary's trading account using this standard terminology:

Mary: Trading account

	£
Sales	195
Less: Cost of sales	135
Gross profit	60

Naturally, if Mary is trying to make a profit out of her business she will hope and expect to sell more than one cooker. If she sells 100 cookers during the course of the month of May 20X2 her trading account will be as follows:

Mary: Trading account for the month ending 31 May 20X2

	£
Sales: 100 cookers @ £195	19 500
Less: cost of sales (100 cookers @ £135)	13 500
Gross profit	6 000

Note that this trading account statement has a proper heading showing Mary's name and the period covered by the statement. It is necessary to show this information so that the reader of the financial statement can be quite sure about the scope of the information covered. Note also the use of the terminology: sales, **cost of sales** and **gross profit**.

? Self-test question 7.1 (answer at the end of the book)

This question tests the understanding of the key elements of the trading account. Jules sells leather bags from his market stall. The bags are all to the same design but are produced in a range of different colours with slightly different fastenings. During the month of December 20X5 he sells 66 bags at £23 each. He has bought the bags for £14.50 each. Show Jules's trading account for the month.

Movements in stock

In most trading businesses a stock of goods has to be held at all times, so that goods can be displayed and so that there are enough items in stock to satisfy potential demand. For example, in the cooker business outlined above, Mary has found that she needs to have at least five cookers on display at any time in order to show minor differences in styling and colours to her potential customers. Also, she needs to have a further 20 cookers in stock to cope with potential demand. Stock is replaced when necessary in order to ensure that there are always at least 25 cookers on the premises. The factory from which she orders guarantees rapid delivery so Mary does not have to keep a large amount of stock on the premises.

Example 7.2

Let's explore this example further by looking at some transactions during the month of June 20X2. At 1 June Mary has 30 cookers in stock. During June she sells 76 cookers. She orders 35 cookers which are delivered on 10 June and a further 40, delivered on 24 June. How many cookers does Mary have in stock at 30 June? In order to answer this question we can construct a stock movement account:

	Units	£
Opening stock: 30 cookers @ £135	30	4 050
Add purchases: (35 + 40) 75 cookers @ £135	75	10 125
Less: items of stock sold: 76 cookers @ £135	(76)	(10 260)
Closing stock: 29 cookers @ £135	29	3 915

Note that items sold are expressed in terms of the price Mary pays, so that like is compared with like. This account would form part of Mary's business record-keeping but would not be shown as part of the financial statements.

We can use the information about stock movements to draw up a more informative trading account for Mary for the month of June 20X2.

Mary: Trading account for the month ending 30 June 20X2

	Units	£	£
Sales:			
76 cookers @ £195	76		14 820
Cost of sales:			
Opening stock: 30 cookers @ £135	30	4 050	
Add: purchases: 75 cookers @ £135	75	10 125	
	105	14 175	
Less closing stock: 29 cookers @ £135	(29)	(3 915)	
Cost of sales: 76 cookers @ £135	76		(10 260)
Gross profit for month			4 560

Because this is a simple example we can double check the gross profit. Mary has sold 76 cookers and we know that the gross profit on each is £60.

$$76 \times £60 = £4560$$

so the answer is correct.

Note that the column containing the cost of sales calculation has been pulled to the left-hand side: this is simply to make the trading account easier to read and understand.

? **Self-test question 7.2** (answer at the end of the book)

At 1 January 20X6 Jules has 36 handbags in stock. Usually, January is a poor month for sales. This January is no exception and he sells only 42 bags at £23 each. However, Jules decides to improve the display by buying in several of each of the full range of colours. He buys in total 68 bags in January, at a cost of £14.50 each.

Prepare a stock movement account for Jules, showing the number of units of stock and monetary amounts. Also, prepare a full trading account for the month of January, assuming that all handbags are sold for £23.

Calculating cost of sales

The example of Mary's cooker business has been kept deliberately straightforward in order to illustrate the calculation of cost of sales. However, most businesses, even small ones, would trade in more than one product. It would become very complicated to calculate precise numbers of units in the trading account. It is also unnecessary.

Most businesses have periodic stocktaking, usually to coincide with the date at which the accounts are drawn up. This allows them to keep track of stock, to identify those items that are not selling, to dispose of any damaged items found, and to generally make sure that there have not been any significant losses through poor accounting or theft. Stocktaking identifies the quantities of stock, which can then be valued by reference to how much it cost. Therefore, at the date of the profit and loss account and balance sheet, a valuation of stock is established. Purchases in the period are calculated from delivery records and from the invoices that suppliers send for payment.

Because the stock value at the beginning and the end of the accounting period are established, and because the total purchases are known, it is easy to calculate cost of sales as follows:

	£
Opening stock	—
+ Purchases	—
– Closing stock	(—)
Cost of sales	—

At this point it may be helpful to check this simplified layout against the trading account for Mary in Example 7.2 – note that it shows the same basic components. Now we will look at Mary's trading account for a one-year period.

Example 7.3

Mary's accounting year ends on 31 October. In respect of the year to 31 October 20X2 she will need information about:

Opening stock on 1 November 20X1
Closing stock on 31 October 20X2
Purchases for the whole year.

At 1 November 20X1 her opening stock value was £4725. At 31 October 20X2 her closing stock value was £6480. During the year she received total purchases of cookers of £153 900. She sold 986 cookers at the normal selling price of £195 and a further 141 at £175 in a special Christmas promotion. This is all the information that is needed to calculate Mary's gross profit for the year.

Mary: Trading account for the year ending 31 October 20X2

	£	£
Sales		
986 cookers @ £195	192 270	
141 cookers @ £175	24 675	
		216 945
Cost of sales		
Opening stock at 1 November 20X1	4 725	
Add: purchases during year	153 900	
	158 625	
Less: closing stock at 31 October 20X2	(6 480)	
		(152 145)
Gross profit for year		64 800

Calculating net profit

Earlier in this chapter we looked at the basic layout of a profit and loss account, which was as follows:

	£
Sales	—
Less: cost of sales	(—)
Gross profit	—
Various expenses	(—)
Net profit	—

The calculation of gross profit has now been covered comprehensively. Provided we know the expenses of the business we can deduct them from gross profit to arrive at the net profit for the period.

Typical business expenses

Expenses vary from one sort of business to another, in both type and importance. For example, one of the main expenses in a road haulier's business will be the costs of fuel and other costs associated with running a fleet of haulage vehicles. By contrast, fuel and motoring costs in a business like Mary's cooker business are likely to be minor.

Expenses could include the following:

- *Cost of premises*: rental, business rates, insurance, electricity, gas, water and repairs.
- *Selling costs and costs of distributing goods*: haulage costs, delivery services, costs of sales' staff salaries and commissions.
- *Administration costs*: telephone, stationery, administrative staff salaries, accountants' and legal fees, computer costs.
- *Finance costs*: bank charges and interest on loans.

In the next example we will continue to look at Mary's business.

Example 7.4

In the year to 31 October 20X2 Mary's business expenses are as follows:

- *Staffing costs*: Mary works in the shop by herself on quieter days, but she employs an assistant for three days per week, and on some extra days in the run-up to Christmas. She pays the assistant £28 per day and he is employed for a total of 165 days during the year to 31 October 20X2.
- *Premises costs*: Mary pays an annual rental for the shop of £17 500, including business rates, any major repair costs and service charges. In addition, in the year to 31 October 20X2 she pays general business insurance of £1350, electricity bills of £1207 and water rates of £795.
- *Administration*: Mary does all of the basic bookkeeping herself, and pays an accountant £585 to produce the final accounts and the tax computation for the Inland Revenue. She spends £103 on stationery, stamps and so on. Her phone bills for the year to 31 October 20X2 come to £312, and she spends £132 on other odds and ends (usually known as 'sundry' expenses) for use in the business. Her membership subscription to the trade association, the Cooker Association of Retailers and Manufacturers (CARM), costs £87 per year.
- *Finance costs*: bank charges total £85. Mary has not borrowed any money so there are no interest charges.

From this information it is possible to complete Mary's profit and loss account to arrive at her net profit for the year, as follows:

Mary: Profit and loss account for the year ending 31 October 20X2

	£	£
Sales (detailed calculation given earlier)		216 945
Less: cost of sales (detailed calculation given earlier)		(152 145)
Gross profit		64 800

	£	£
Expenses		
Staffing costs (165 days @ £28 per day)	4 620	
Rental of premises	17 500	
Business insurance	1 350	
Electricity	1 207	
Water rates	795	
Accountant's fees	585	
Stationery	103	
Telephone	312	
Sundry expenses	132	
CARM subscription	87	
Bank charges	85	
		(26 776)
Net profit for year		38 024

Note that the expenses are set off in a separate column towards the left hand side of the page; this is to make the statement easier to read.

Mary has made £38 024 out of her business in the year to 31 October 20X2. Out of this she will have to pay tax, but for the sake of simplicity we are going to ignore tax in most of the examples in this book. Ignoring tax, what happens to the £38 024? In the previous chapter we noted that the balance sheet of a sole trader includes a capital account. This account shows the total resources of the owner which are tied up in the business. It includes: capital introduced, plus profits retained in the business, minus drawings, minus any losses made by the business.

So, to answer the question, Mary's net profit of £38 024 goes into her capital account. It is up to her, the owner of the business, to decide how much, if anything, she will withdraw from the business. If it is her only source of income she will almost certainly have to take money out of the business to live on.

Towards the end of this chapter we will examine an example of how the profit and loss account and the balance sheet fit together.

What does the profit and loss account mean?

The profit and loss account and other financial statements are prepared for a purpose; that purpose is to communicate information to people who need to know about the business. So, what information does Mary's profit and loss account communicate? An obvious and important piece of information is that the business is profitable in the year to 31 October 20X2. If this is a typical year, it is possible to draw the general conclusion that the business is currently successful, and may continue to be successful into the future. This general conclusion could be taken a little further by examining gross profit and net profit.

Mary is interested in assessing whether the general trend in her business profitability is upwards or downwards. She supplies the key figures from the profit and loss account for the previous year's trading to 31 October 20X1: sales were £197 535, gross profit was £57 300, expenses totalled £24 904 and net profit was £32 396. This information can be summarised alongside the comparable figures for 20X2:

	20X2 £	20X1 £
Sales	216 945	197 535
Less: cost of sales	(152 145)	(140 235)
Gross profit	64 800	57 300
Various expenses	(26 776)	(24 904)
Net profit	38 024	32 396

Gross profit analysis

Gross profit is an important element in judging how well or badly a business has performed. However, one isolated figure has little significance on its own. We need to make comparisons between at least two figures.

Comparing two consecutive years

The increase in gross profit is £64 800 – £57 300 = £7500. This is sufficient information to be able to calculate the percentage increase in gross profit from 20X1 to 20X2, as follows:

20X1 gross profit   = £57 300
Increase in gross profit   = £7 500

$$\text{Percentage increase} = \frac{£7\,500}{57\,300} \times 100 = 13.1\% \text{ (to one decimal place)}$$

If we were further informed, for example, that the Cooker Association of Retailers and Manufacturers published figures to its members showing that there had been an increase in the gross profit on cooker sales across the UK of 10% between 20X1 and 20X2, we could see that Mary's business has done rather well, and certainly better than average. Mary could achieve this better than average performance by either increasing her sales prices by a rate that is slightly above average, or by negotiating lower prices than average with the supplier, or by a combination of the two factors. As a sole trader, she may well charge higher prices than a large retailer, but customers may be prepared to pay a little more for better advice and after-sales service.

Gross profit margin

'Gross profit margin' is a way of expressing, by means of a percentage, the relationship between gross profit and sales. It simply shows gross profit as a percentage of sales.

Two figures are needed to calculate a gross profit margin: sales and gross profit. Mary's trading account shows both, so we can apply the following formula:

$$\frac{\text{Gross profit}}{\text{Sales}} \times 100 = \text{Gross profit margin \%}$$

In Mary's case:

$$\frac{£64\,800}{216\,945} \times 100 = 29.9\% \text{ (to one decimal place)}$$

Does this tell us anything useful? Again, not unless we have more information to compare it with. Calculating the comparable ratio for 20X1 uses the gross profit and sales figures for 20X1:

$$\frac{\text{Gross profit}}{\text{Sales}} \times 100 = \text{Gross profit margin \%}$$

$$\frac{57\,300}{197\,535} \times 100 = 29.0\% \text{ (to one decimal place)}$$

To summarise, Mary's gross profit margin in 20X1 was 29.0% and in 20X2 was 29.9%. The gross profit margin in her business has improved. This means that the difference between the selling price and the cost of sales has increased. This may be as a result of selling prices increasing, cost prices reducing, or a combination of the two.

Net profit analysis

We can analyse net profit in the same way as gross profit.

Comparing two consecutive years

Net profit for the year is £38 024, and for 20X1 was £32 396. The fact that it has increased is good news for Mary, but we can extend the analysis further to look at the percentage increase in the same way as we did for gross profit: the increase is £38 024 – £32 396 = £5628.

$$\text{Percentage increase} = \frac{5\,628}{32\,396} \times 100 = 17.4\% \text{ (to one decimal place)}$$

The figures for gross profit increased by 13.1% but net profit has increased by an even greater percentage. Why? The answer lies somewhere in the figure for expenses. In 20X1 expenses totalled £24 904, increasing to £26 776 in 20X2, an increase of £1872.

$$\text{Percentage increase} = \frac{1\,872}{24\,904} \times 100 = 7.5\% \text{ (to one decimal place)}$$

We could extend the analysis further by looking at the percentage increases and decreases in the separate categories of expense. The basic analysis shows that, although expenses have increased, the level of increase is much lower than the level of increase in gross profit. As a result net profit shows a substantial increase.

Net profit margin

Net profit margin is a way of expressing, by means of a percentage, the relationship between net profit and sales. It shows net profit as a percentage of sales. In Mary's business the net profit margin for 20X2 is as follows:

$$\frac{38\,024}{216\,945} \times 100 = 17.5\% \text{ (to one decimal place)}$$

The net profit margin for the previous year, 20X1 is as follows:

$$\frac{32\,396}{197\,535} \times 100 = 16.4\% \text{ (to one decimal place)}$$

These calculations show that net profit margin has increased. The conclusion is that, on the basis of the analysis of gross profit and net profit, Mary's business performance seems to have improved substantially.

It is possible to take this type of analysis much further, given more information. In later chapters we will examine more closely the meaning of financial information. However, it is never too soon to start thinking about the information content of financial statements.

Profit and loss accounting in a service business

A service business does not trade in goods and therefore does not need to produce a trading account. In this section of the chapter we will look at the example of a business that supplies services only.

Example 7.5

Tony is a chartered surveyor who supplies property advice services to clients investing in commercial property. He also acts as a commercial property agent, handling the selling of office and retail buildings. He makes commission on any successful sales. He employs a full-time personal assistant and, in the year to 31 December 20X7 he has employed a student from the local college's estate management course on a day release basis. Other expenses incurred in his business include motor expenses for his large BMW (Tony clocks up around 50 000 miles each year in taking prospective clients to view industrial estates and business parks), entertaining, the cost of office premises, large phone bills for office phone and mobile, and sundries such as professional subscriptions and stationery.

Tony is a sole trader, trading as Aisgarth & Co. He provides the following list of income and expense items from which to draw up a profit and loss account for the year ending 31 December 20X7.

	£
Premises rental	12 570
Electricity bills	2 907
Personal assistant's salary	15 788
Income: commissions on commercial property sales	68 360
Motor expenses	15 370
Office and general insurance	1 003
Professional indemnity insurance (PII)*	1 880
Entertaining	9 351
Telephone charges	3 775
Income: fees for professional advice	23 333
Student's wages	1 200
Sundry office expenses	3 720

*Many qualified professionals, such as surveyors and accountants, are obliged under the regulations of their professional body, to take out special insurance against possible liabilities for professional negligence.

From this list of balances we can draw up Tony's profit and loss account for the year to 31 December 20X7 as follows:

Aisgarth & Co.: Profit and loss account for the year ending 31 December 20X7

	£	£
Fees for professional services	23 333	
Commissions	68 360	
		91 693
Expenses		
Premises rental	12 570	
Electricity	2 907	
Personal assistant's salary	15 788	
Student's wages	1 200	
Motor expenses	15 370	
Insurance	1 003	
PII	1 880	
Entertaining	9 351	
Telephone charges	3 775	
Sundry office expenses	3 720	
		67 564
Net profit for year		24 129

Note that sole traders can trade under a business name, like Tony's. It is quite common for professional businesses like accountants, solicitors and surveyors to trade as 'Something & Co.', even though there is only one sole trader involved.

We can work out a net profit margin figure for Tony's business

$$\frac{£24\ 129}{91\ 693} \times 100 = 26.3\%$$

However, in a business like this, the net profit margin may fluctuate quite significantly from one year to another. Expenses are likely to be similar from year to year, but income may vary. Commercial property transactions are usually large, and the commission on a single transaction may amount to many tens of thousands of pounds. However, Tony may have to do a lot of entertaining and travel (both of which, as shown in the profit and loss account, cost the business significant sums) in order to bring off just one deal. Without having other years' results for comparison it is not possible to say whether 20X7 was a good, bad or middling year for Tony.

Preparing the profit and loss account and balance sheet

In this section of the chapter we will prepare the two financial statements for one business in order to demonstrate how they fit together.

Example 7.6

Nellie sells boots from her market stall and also carries out a boot repair service. This activity has never made much of a profit, but some of Nellie's long-standing customers continue to expect the service. Nellie's year-end is 31 May, a time of year when boot sales are low, and when she has very little stock on hand. She counts and values her stock on 31 May 20X1 and arrives at a value of £2904.

You are employed in the office of Naylor & Co, Nellie's accountants. Your boss, Nasser, asks you to prepare her accounts for the year to 31 May 20X1. As well as the information about stock you are given the following list of items as at the year-end date.

	£
Stock at 1 June 20X0	2 672
Stall rental and service charge	3 844
Bank interest received	320
Sundry expenses	313
Saturday assistant's wages	1 200
Repairs income	1 801
Purchases	42 640
Creditors	2 497
Accountant's fees and other administration	862
Insurance	574
Cash at bank	3 422
Drawings	14 257
Repairs expenses	1 742
Motor expenses	1 252
Sales of boots	63 060
Capital at 1 June 20X0	6 060
Fixed assets – display stands	960

Nasser will be having a meeting with Nellie next week to talk about her business. She feels that she isn't doing as well as in previous years. Her gross profit for the year end 31 May 20X0 was £22 831 on sales of £67 760. In addition to preparing the accounts, Nasser would like you to calculate the actual and percentage changes in gross profit and sales between 20X0 and 20X1, and to compare the gross profit margins between the two years. He would also like you to make some preliminary comments on Nellie's business performance.

Step 1: Prepare the accounts

The first step is to prepare the profit and loss account and balance sheet for Nellie's business. The list that she has provided is a jumbled mixture of profit and loss account and balance sheet items, so a useful preliminary step is to identify a category for each item depending upon whether it goes in the trading account, the rest of the profit and loss account or the balance sheet. For balance sheet items the terminology used in Chapter 6 can be used:

fixed assets
current assets
current liabilities
long-term liabilities
capital

	£	Category
Stock at 1 June 20X0	2 672	Trading account
Stall rental and service charge	3 844	Profit and loss account
Bank interest received	320	Profit and loss account
Sundry expenses	313	Profit and loss account
Saturday assistant's wages	1 200	Profit and loss account
Repairs income	1 801	Profit and loss account
Purchases	42 640	Trading account
Creditors	2 497	Balance sheet: current liabilities
Accountant's fees and other administration	862	Profit and loss account
Insurance	574	Profit and loss account
Cash at bank	3 422	Balance sheet: current assets
Drawings	14 257	Balance sheet: capital
Repairs expenses	1 742	Profit and loss account
Motor expenses	1 252	Profit and loss account
Sales of boots	63 060	Profit and loss account
Capital at 1 June 20X0	6 060	Balance sheet: capital
Fixed assets – display stands	960	Balance sheet: fixed assets
Stock at 31 May 20X1	2 904	Trading account AND balance sheet: current assets

Note that closing stock always appears in both the trading account and the balance sheet as a current asset. Stock that remains unsold at the balance sheet date is deducted, as we have seen, in arriving at the cost of sales figure. However, it is also an asset of the business, because it can be sold to make money in the following accounting period.

Having categorised all the items the next stage is to pick out those that appear in the trading account, so as to be able to prepare the trading account. Then, immediately below it, the rest of the profit and loss account items are listed, ending with net profit. Remember that a heading with the name of the business (in this case Nellie simply uses her own name – which is common among sole traders) and a description of the financial statement are always required.

Nellie: Profit and loss account for the year ending 31 May 20X1

	£	£
Sales		63 060
Less: cost of sales		
Opening stock	2 672	
Add: purchases	42 640	
	45 312	
Less: closing stock	(2 904)	
		(42 408)
Gross profit		20 652

	£	£
Boot repairs: income	1 801	
Boot repairs: expenses	(1 742)	
		59
Other income – bank interest received		320
		21 031
Expenses		
Stall rental and service charge	3 844	
Motor expenses	1 252	
Saturday assistant's wages	1 200	
Insurance	574	
Accountant's fees and other administration	862	
Sundry expenses	313	
		(8 045)
Net profit		12 986

Once all of the balances have been put into the profit and loss account the remainder should all relate to the balance sheet, which can then be prepared.

Nellie: Balance sheet at 31 May 20X1

	£	£
Fixed assets		960
Current assets		
Stock	2 904	
Cash	3 422	
	6 326	
Current liabilities		
Creditors	(2 497)	
Net current assets (£6 326 – 2 497)		3 829
Net assets		4 789
Capital		
Opening capital balance 1 June 20X0	6 060	
Add: net profit for the year	12 986	
	19 046	
Less: drawings	(14 257)	
Closing capital balance 31 May 20X1		4 789

The capital account shows the resources committed to the business by its owner. The balance on the capital account increases or decreases in the following ways:

Capital introduced, plus Profits retained by the business, minus Drawings, minus any losses made by the business. Nellie's capital account, as shown in the balance sheet at 31 May 20X1, has been increased by the amount of net profit for the year (calculated in the profit and loss account) and has been decreased by the drawings she made from the business.

Step 2: Calculate the actual and percentage changes in gross profit and sales

Change in sales: sales have decreased from £67 760 to £63 060, a decrease of £4700. The percentage change is calculated as follows:

$$\frac{4700}{67\,760} \times 100 = 6.9\%$$

Change in gross profit: gross profit has decreased from £22 831 to £20 652, a decrease of £2179. The percentage change is calculated as follows:

$$\frac{2\,179}{22\,831} \times 100 = 9.5\%$$

Gross profit margins compared:

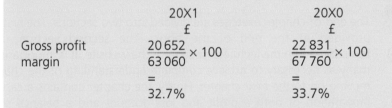

	20X1	20X0
	£	£
Gross profit margin	$\frac{20\,652}{63\,060} \times 100$	$\frac{22\,831}{67\,760} \times 100$
	=	=
	32.7%	33.7%

Step 3: Comment on Nellie's accounts

Sales and gross profits have both fallen between 20X0 and 20X1. The gross profit margin is poorer in 20X1 than in the previous year. We do not have net profit information available. Nellie may be able to pinpoint reasons for the decline in trade, and Nasser needs to make some suggestions as to how she might be able to increase sales in future. For example, a change of suppliers might improve gross profit margin.

Other observations: the boot repair service is making virtually nothing. Nellie's time could perhaps be better used elsewhere and she may like to consider finally ceasing to offer the service. Nellie's drawings are in excess of the net profit generated by the business. There may be specific reasons why this level of drawings has been made during this recent financial year, but Nellie really should be considering ways of reducing drawings if possible, at least until her trade has recovered its previous levels.

Chapter summary

This chapter has explored the basics of preparing a profit and loss account. Students should now understand the principal components of the profit and loss account, and should be ready to undertake the end-of-chapter exercises.

The chapter has covered not only preparation of the profit and loss account but also has started to consider the information content of the statement. Calculation of changes in certain items has been covered, as have calculations of gross and net profit margin. Students should be able to comment on the basic information conveyed in the profit and loss account.

Finally, the chapter drew upon knowledge and skills gained as a result of studying Chapter 6 to produce both a profit and loss account and a balance sheet from a set of given information.

The end-of-chapter exercises are divided into two sections. The first section has answers provided at the end of the book. The second section, in the white box, has answers on the lecturers' section of the website. It is important to work through as many as necessary to achieve complete understanding of the chapter content, before moving on to the next chapter. Finally, the chapter contains a case study that requires preparation of both a profit and loss account and a balance sheet for a business, together with some commentary about the significance of the figures. Answers to the case study requirements can be found on the students' section of the website.

Website summary

The book's website contains the following material in respect of Chapter 7:

Students' section

- Quiz containing ten multiple choice questions and answers
- Five longer questions with answers
- Answer to case study at end of this chapter.

Lecturers' section

- Answers to exercises 7.10–7.15
- Five longer questions with answers.

Exercises: answers at the end of the book

7.1   Jackie sells garden furniture in sets comprising a dining table and four chairs. She purchases each set for £75 from the manufacturer and retails a set for £132. At the beginning of June 20X1 Jackie has 30 sets in stock. At 30 June 20X1 the stock room contains 42 sets. She sells 35 sets during the month.

1.   How many sets of dining table and chairs has Jackie purchased during the month?

a) 107

b) 47

c) 23

d) 37

2.   What is Jackie's cost of sales figure for the month?

a) £4425

b) £4620

c) £2625

d) £1875.

3.   What is Jackie's gross profit for June?

a) £2745

b) £1425

c) £6783

d) £1995.

7.2   Jay's business is shoe retailing. He has bought in a special purchase of 1000 pairs of trainers for £8500. He sells 750 pairs quite quickly at a retail price of £15.50 per pair. Then, in order to clear the stock out of the shop, he reduces the selling price to £12.50 and clears a further 200 pairs. The remaining 50 pairs are put into a bargain bin at a price of £5 per pair and these sell during the shop's autumn sale. What is Jay's gross profit on this line of trainers? How much gross profit would he have made if he had been able to sell the whole consignment at £15.50 per pair?

7.3   During the year Jake sells 8000 units of stock at £42.50 each. The gross profit on each unit is £17.50. He purchased stock at a total cost of £197 300 and still had £17 400 in stock at the year-end. What was Jake's opening stock?

7.4   Jethro sells an extensive range of children's toys. He likes to be well informed at all times about the performance of his business. Part of the routine work of his administrative assistant is to draw up a monthly trading account so that Jethro can check on gross profit levels. Information about sales and purchases relating to a three-month period, October–December 20X2, is as follows:

	October £	November £	December £
Sales	39 370	48 998	56 306
Purchases	37 085	40 830	6 250

Stocks at the beginning of October are valued at £30 863. Stocks at the end of each of the three months are as follows: October £43 258; November 53 190; and December 23 980.

Draw up a trading account for Jethro's business for each of October, November and December 20X2.

7.5 Leon runs a retail grocery business dealing in luxury and delicatessen goods. In 20X6 sales are £295 993, with cost of sales at £242 085. The equivalent figures for 20X5 are sales of £287 300 and cost of sales of £235 920. Calculate:

1. Leon's gross profit margin in both years.

2. The increase in sales.

3. The percentage increase in sales.

4. The increase in gross profit.

5. The percentage increase in gross profit.

7.6 The summarised results of Louise's business for the three years to the end of 20X8 are as follows:

	20X8 £	20X7 £	20X6 £
Sales	291 318	282 400	269 340
Cost of sales	(213 916)	(206 420)	(196 071)
Gross profit	77 402	75 980	73 269
Expenses	(52 394)	(51 720)	(49 270)
Net profit	25 008	24 260	23 999

Calculate the gross and net profit margins for each year and comment briefly on the general trends in the business trading results.

7.7 Madigan & Co. is the trading name of Basil Madigan, a chartered accountant. He runs a small city centre office employing a part-qualified accountant as an assistant and a secretary, both on a full-time basis.

In the year to 31 March 20X5 fees from Madigan's clients total £95 311. The assistant's salary is £19 300 and the secretary is paid £11 150. Basil's one-room office is in a run-down office building at a comparatively low rental of £10 310, which includes energy costs and business rates. There is also an annual service charge (to cover repairs, caretaking and so on) which this year comes to £3790. Basil pays general insurance of £794, plus professional indemnity insurance (PII) of £1250. Subscriptions and professional registration charges are £952. Business travel expenses (mileage claims for use of own car by himself and his assistant) come to £1863. Entertainment is £342.

Telephone charges are £1103 for the year and other administration charges are £1575. Stationery is £761 and sundry expenses total £715. Basil has made donations to local charities out of the business account to the sum of £120.

Prepare the profit and loss account for Madigan & Co. for the year ending 31 March 20X5.

7.8   Norbert runs a small wholesaling business selling imported Italian coffee machines to retailers. His business is run from a small warehouse with an office at the side on an industrial estate on the edge of a large city. The industrial estate is largely deserted at night and the crime rate is high for theft and criminal damage. Norbert has recently joined a scheme run by the local authority on behalf of tenants of its industrial units; he makes an annual contribution to a fund, which pays for improved lighting and security patrols.

Norbert's accounting year-end is 31 March. He provides you with a list of figures relating to the most recent year which ended on 31 March 20X7. You are required to prepare a profit and loss account and balance sheet from the figures.

	£
Delivery van	5 020
Sales for the year	351 777
Staff costs: storeman's wages	12 090
Electricity	2 821
Cash at bank	3 444
Capital at 1 April 20X6	18 011
Administrative costs	3 810
Opening stock at 1 April 20X6	20 762
Fixed assets in warehouse and office	3 900
Drawings	25 219
Sundry expenses	1 406
Warehouse and office rental	10 509
Insurance	3 909
Debtors	36 623
Water rates	1 226
Security services charge	2 937
Purchases	255 255
Bank charges	398
Creditors	31 950
Delivery expenses	8 630
Part-time admin assistant's wages	3 779

Norbert has counted and valued the coffee machines on the premises at the 31 March 20X7. The total value is £22 446.

Prepare the profit and loss account and balance sheet for Norbert's business for the accounting year to 31 March 20X7.

7.9   Refer to the example of Mary's cooker business used earlier in the chapter. Briefly describe the principal group of users of financial information who are likely to have an interest in Mary's financial statements, and the reasons for their interest. (You may find it helpful to refer back to the list of user groups provided in Table 5.1 in Chapter 5.)

Exercises: answers available to lecturers

7.10 Jin-Ming's mail order business sells trampolines. The selling price is £400 for a standard size trampoline and £550 for a large one. The opening stock at 1 January 20X3 is 6 standard trampolines and 5 large. The cost of the trampolines to Jin-Ming is £260 (standard) and £330 (large). In the year to 31 December 20X3 Jin-Ming sells 30 standard and 17 large trampolines. He could have sold more of the large size but the manufacturer stopped making them part-way through the year. Jin-Ming's purchases for the year totalled £14 880 including the purchase of 12 large trampolines.

a) Draw up Jin-Ming's trading account for the year ending 31 December 20X3.

b) Calculate the gross profit on the sale of large and standard trampolines respectively.

7.11 Jodie is a wholesaler of electrical discount goods. She buys in end-of-line and seconds quality stock from manufacturers and sells it on to small electrical retailers. She has to take advantage immediately of any special offers that manufacturers make available; if she does not the manufacturers will sell to one of her competitors. Therefore, her stock levels can fluctuate substantially from one week to the next. The level of sales is not steady from month to month; it depends upon what is in stock and whether there is much demand for the items Jodie currently has in her warehouse. At the beginning of March Jodie's stock is valued at £93 882 and comprises principally kettles, toasters and dishwashers. An unexpected surge in demand by small retail wholesalers for these items results in a high level of sales in March of £89 907. By the end of March stock has dropped to £34 920. At the end of April, as the result of a special purchase of electric blankets it has gone up to £82 860 dropping back only slightly to £75 918 at the end of May. Jodie knows that she will find it difficult to dispose of most of this stock before the end of the summer. Sales for April are £31 241 and for May, £40 270. Purchases for each of the three months are: March £3074; April £65 747; and May £18 911.

a) Draw up trading accounts for each of the three months.

b) Discuss the business and financial problems Jodie would encounter in running this type of wholesaler operation.

7.12 Lulu's sales in 20X3 are £115 399. The following year, 20X4, sales increase by 4.3%. In 20X5 sales are 7.8% higher than they were in 20X3. Gross profit margin in each of the three years is:

20X3: 19.3%
20X4: 21.4%
20X5: 18.7%

Calculate cost of sales for each of the three years, 20X3, 20X4 and 20X5 (working to the nearest £).

7.13 In 20X8 Lola's net profit margin has fallen to 9.8% from 10.2% in the previous year. Her gross profit margin, on the other hand, has increased from 30.2% to 33.8%. Sales in 20X7 were £148 360 and in 20X8 were £153 062.

From this information prepare summary profit and loss account statements for 20X7 and 20X8 showing sales, cost of sales, gross profit, expenses and net profit. (Work to the nearest £.)

7.14 Mahbub runs a recruitment agency. The agency's income is earned in the form of commissions from clients who pay a percentage of the first year's salary of new employees recruited by the agency. In the year to 31 December 20X7 the total of commission income earned is £115 900. Mahbub is very pleased with this record level of commission; it is 25% higher than total commissions in the previous year.

Expenses, however, have also increased. Premises costs total £16 506, staff costs are £29 900 and administration costs are £15 981. In the year to 31 December 20X6 the equivalent expenses totals were: premises £13 370; staff costs £28 807; and administration costs £12 773.

From the information given above, prepare Mahbub's profit and loss account for both 20X7 and 20X6. Calculate the percentage increase or decrease in net profit.

7.15 Some elements included in the profit and loss account and balance sheets of trading businesses are not usually present in the accounts of service businesses. Identify and briefly describe the principal differences between the accounts of trading and service businesses.

!   CASE STUDY 7.1   Preparing and using accounts

Jimmy Bowden has run a bicycle shop for several years in rented shop premises. He sells new and reconditioned second-hand bikes and also runs a repair service, with the help of a part-time assistant. The business has been moderately profitable and has provided Jimmy with enough to live on. His wife, Sophie, works as a local government officer and between them they have been able to afford to take out a mortgage on a house and go on holiday at least once a year. Jimmy, however, is concerned that his business is in decline. Local parking restrictions near to his shop have increased and people are parking in a multi-storey at the other end of town. Before the restrictions were imposed they used to park in a large free car park in the next street to Jimmy's shop, and so a lot of people would pass his shop on the way into town. This no longer happens and Jimmy thinks

that general awareness of the existence of his business has declined. While he still gets a lot of trade from cycling enthusiasts, his sales of children's bicycles have declined and he didn't sell as many as expected just before Christmas. Jimmy suspects that a lot of this trade has been transferred to the bicycle and car maintenance retailing chain store in the town's main shopping centre.

Sales of more expensive bikes to cycling enthusiasts are the more profitable end of Jimmy's business. His stocks of this type of bike are at around the usual level at 28 February, which is Jimmy's year-end. However, the stock room is crammed full of the cheaper bikes reflecting the fact that Christmas sales were lower than expected.

It is now early March 20X5. Jimmy is anxious to get the annual accounts prepared so that he can assess the overall effects of the downturn in trade on his profitability. He is worried about both the immediate and the longer-term future of his business. The business bank account balance at 28 February 20X5 is quite a bit lower than it was at the previous year-end.

Jimmy provides the following list of figures for incorporation into the profit and loss account and balance sheet:

	£
Sales	143 520
Opening stock	9 274
Fixed assets	3 823
Opening capital balance 1 March 20X4	19 776
Cash in the bank account	1 685
Rental expense	16 500
Insurance	2 023
Electricity	2 056

	£
Trade creditors	8 229
Debtors	1 800
Drawings	23 153
Bank interest received	118
Purchases	103 221
Income from repairs services	4 389
Repairs service expenses – bicycle parts	1 317
Administration, finance and sundry expenses	2 278
Assistant's wages	8 902
Closing stock*	16 337

*Jimmy counted and valued the stock on 28 February.

He asks you, a local business adviser, to do two things:

1. Prepare a profit and loss account for the year ending 28 February 20X5 and a balance sheet at that date.

2. Prepare a brief report on the profitability of the business compared to the previous year with some recommendations as to possible courses of action in the future. To help with this he provides the following information about the year ending 28 February 20X4:

Bicycle sales for the year to 28 February 20X4	£164 728
Gross profit on bicycle sales	£49 418
Gross profit margin	30%
Profit on repairs service	£3 422
Total expenses	£27 263
Interest received	£260
Net profit	£25 837
Net profit margin	15.7%

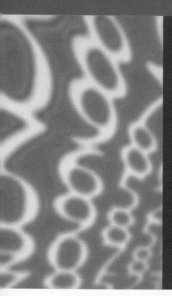

CHAPTER 8

Adjustments to the profit and loss account and balance sheet
Part 1

Aim of the chapter

To enable students to understand the use of various accounting adjustments and their effect on the profit and loss account and balance sheet.

Learning outcomes

After reading the chapter and completing the related exercises, students should:

- Understand the treatment in the profit and loss account of complexities such as discounts and returns of goods.
- Appreciate and be able to apply some of the important conventions in accounting for recognition of income and expenses.
- Understand the need for provisions against certain current assets, and be able to make appropriate adjustments to the profit and loss account and balance sheet.

The chapter is divided into the following principal sections:

- Consideration of some additional items that may be included in the profit and loss account – namely, returns of goods, discounts and delivery charges.

- An introduction to some of the main conventions in accounting, including the important principle of matching (accruals).
- Adjustments that may be required in respect of stock and debtors.

Some further complexities in preparing the profit and loss account

In this section we will extend the knowledge gained in the previous chapter to encompass three further items that may be included in the profit and loss account: returns; discounts; and delivery charges.

Returns

The majority of the examples in Chapter 7 involved the purchase and sale of items of stock, and in all cases it was assumed that the transactions were straightforward in that no items were ever returned. However, while transactions are often completed without error or dispute, this is not always the case. A retail customer, for example, may buy a pair of jeans but find, on examining the purchase at home, that the zip is broken. The jeans are taken back to the shop and either a replacement is provided or a refund paid. The same can happen, although usually on a larger scale, with the purchase and sale of items in business. The goods are not what was ordered, the quality level of the goods is insufficiently high, the quantity is wrong, or a combination of any and all of those factors. Where a return of purchased items is made there are implications for the profit and loss account of both the vendor and the purchaser.

Example 8.1	John runs a business selling artists' easels and other art equipment. Imran purchases 30 easels from him at a cost of £45 each: total = £1350. The transaction is added to John's sales, and added to Imran's purchases. Upon close examination of the easels Imran discovers that five are missing essential bolts and screws. He decides to return them to John. The effect of this return is that John's sales and Imran's purchases are reduced by the same amount: $5 \times £45 = £225$.

Where returns are a fairly frequent occurrence, as will be the case in many businesses, a total of items returned is built up during the year and will feature in the list of balances from which the profit and loss account is drawn up. Sales returns must be deducted from sales, and purchases returns must be deducted from purchases in drawing up the trading part of the profit and loss account. Rather than setting these figures off against each other, it is conventional to show the total for sales and then deduct the total for returns.

Discounts

Trade discounts

A trade discount is a special kind of discount given, for example, to long-standing customers, or to customers who purchase a very high volume of goods. This type of discount is normally given via reduced prices, thus resulting in a relatively lower cost of purchases for the recipient. Large businesses are often able by this means to buy goods at lower unit prices than small businesses, and so obtain a competitive advantage. If they pass on the discounts via lower prices to their customers then they may be able to gain market share at the expense of their smaller competitors.

Where discounts like this are given or received, there is no special adjustment to be made in the profit and loss account. The amounts invoiced already reflect the reduction. However, the issue of trade discounts may be relevant when analysing the meaning of profit and loss account statements, especially when comparing one business with another.

Financial discounts

Many businesses trade on credit – that is, they do not demand immediate payment but instead are prepared to wait for a period. The acceptable period varies from one business to another, and will depend upon the norms in that particular industry. A frequently encountered arrangement is to require payment within 30 days of invoice. For example, goods are dispatched to a customer on 15 May and an invoice is sent on 17 May; until the invoice is paid the amount is recorded as a debtor. The invoice specifies that payment should be made within 30 days; it is therefore expected that payment will be received by 16 June. Some customers will pay within the time allowed; others will take longer; and some may not pay at all (a problem we will examine in more detail later in this chapter).

Business people in most trades and professions have to accept the necessity for trading on credit. However, they will seek to minimise the length of time they have to wait for their money, and one way of actively encouraging early payment is to offer an incentive in the form of a discount. The cost of the discount has to be carefully balanced against the benefit of receiving the cash earlier than it would be received if there was no discount.

Example 8.2

Fernando runs a small business manufacturing and selling gloves. His customers are mainly retail businesses, many of which do not pay within his stipulated terms of credit, which are receipt of cash required within 30 days of invoice. In order to encourage earlier payment, Fernando decides to set up a discount incentive. Customers who pay within 30 days are entitled to reduce the invoice amount by 0.5%.

On 1 October he sends an invoice to one of his biggest customers for £3000 with a note about the discount. The value of the sale recorded in Fernando's accounting records on that day is £3000. Thirty days later, a cheque arrives for

£2985, i.e. £3000 less 0.5% of the invoice value. The discount is, therefore, £15. How should Fernando record it?

The discount is an expense of Fernando's business – a type of finance charge paid in order to get the money into his bank account sooner than he would have done otherwise. Therefore, it is included as an expense in his profit and loss account. Where a business receives financial discounts, they are included as part of its other income, below the trading account details.

Delivery charges

Some businesses incur the expense of distributing their goods to customers. Typical expenses would include road or rail haulage costs, handling costs and import duties. In some cases the selling business pays such costs and they appear in the expenses section of the profit and loss account. Where the purchasing business pays these costs, they are added to the cost of the purchases and appear in the trading account.

Example 8.3

Brooklyn imports Brazilian footballs in cartons of 100, each carton costing £52. In addition, he must pay import duty of £5 per carton. On 15 August he orders 16 cartons. How much is added in to his total of purchases for the year?

	£
Cost of 16 cartons @ £52 per carton	832
Import duty: 16 cartons @ £5 per carton	80
Total added to purchases for the year	912

So, in summary, accounting for delivery and similar charges varies depending upon whether the selling organisation or the purchasing organisation is paying the cost.

The following example incorporates several of the adjustments we have examined so far in this chapter.

Example 8.4

Bennie runs an art shop that sells all kinds of artists' materials, and also lines in greetings cards, books and office stationery. As well as over-the-counter sales for cash, he also supplies local art colleges and schools with art materials and equipment. This type of sale is made on credit. Bennie requires payment within 30 days, but finds that colleges and schools are slow to pay. During the year to 31 October 20X5 he introduces an early payment discount scheme: all credit customers paying within one month are entitled to deduct 1.25% of the invoice value. Some of the schools and colleges take advantage of the scheme and Bennie allows total discounts of £196 during the year. Other relevant points are:

▶

- Bennie himself receives discounts for early payment from some of his suppliers. The total for the year is £98.
- During the year he buys in some easels from John, but finds them to be faulty. Several sub-standard easels have to be returned to John; the cost of the easels is £853.
- One of the art colleges supplied by Bennie returns to him a large order of paint because it is infested with weevils. The value of the amount returned, at selling price, is £590.
- Generally, delivery charges are included in the price of the goods that Bennie buys. However, he imports a range of fragile pastel sticks from France. He pays a courier firm for special delivery of these items so that they will not be damaged in transit. The total for this type of delivery for 20X5 is £150.

The following is a list of all Bennie's sales and expenses items (including the items described above) for 20X5:

	£
Insurance	2 984
Discounts allowed to colleges and schools	196
Stock at 1 November 20X4	16 037
Subscription to Chamber of Commerce	100
Delivery van expenses	760
Shop rental	18 300
Sales	159 760
Sundry expenses	1 982
Purchases	94 736
Courier service – pastel imports	150
Returns of goods sold to college	590
Electricity and other premises costs	3 598
Assistant's wages	10 920
Discounts received for early payment	98
Returns of easels to John	853
Accountancy fees	570
Stock at 31 October 20X5	18 006

This example is more complicated than any encountered so far. The additional adjustments mean that more items are included in the trading account. As a first step, then, each of the items is classified as belonging either to the trading account or to the rest of the profit and loss account, as follows:

	£	Category
Insurance	2 984	Profit and loss account
Discounts allowed to colleges and schools	196	Profit and loss account
Stock at 1 November 20X4	16 037	Trading account
Subscription to Chamber of Commerce	100	Profit and loss account
Delivery van expenses	760	Profit and loss account

	£	Category
Shop rental	18 300	Profit and loss account
Sales	159 760	Trading account
Sundry expenses	1 982	Profit and loss account
Purchases	94 736	Trading account
Courier service – pastel imports	150	Trading account
Returns of goods sold to college	590	Trading account
Electricity and other premises costs	3 598	Profit and loss account
Assistant's wages	10 920	Profit and loss account
Discounts received for early payment	98	Profit and loss account
Returns of easels to John	853	Trading account
Accountancy fees	570	Profit and loss account
Stock at 31 October 20X5	18 006	Trading account

Several items in the above list are included in the trading account. If we separate them out, we can deal with them first:

	£	Category
Stock at 1 November 20X4	16 037	Trading account
Sales	159 760	Trading account
Purchases	94 736	Trading account
Courier service – pastel imports	150	Trading account
Returns of goods sold to college	590	Trading account
Returns of easels to John	853	Trading account
Stock at 31 October 20X5	18 006	Trading account

Of the above seven items, two relate to sales transactions: £159 760 of sales and £590 of sales returns. These will be presented as follows:

	£
Sales	159 760
Less: sales returns	(590)
	159 170

The remaining items relate to the cost of sales calculation. The basic calculation remains as:

$$\text{Opening stock} + \text{Purchases} - \text{Closing stock}$$

But the calculation of purchases has become a little more complicated

	£	£
Cost of sales:		
Opening stock		16 037
Add purchases:		
Purchases	94 736	
Add: courier charges	150	
Less: purchase returns	(853)	

	£	£
		94 033
		110 070
Less: closing stock		(18 006)
Cost of sales		92 064

Note that the detail of the purchases calculation has been pulled over to the left-hand side for greater clarity.

The remainder of the profit calculation follows the same approach as in the previous chapter, so should not be especially difficult. Once all the figures are put together Bennie's profit and loss account looks like this:

Bennie: Profit and loss account for the year ending 31 October 20X5

	£	£	£
Sales			159 760
Less: sales returns			(590)
			159 170
Cost of sales:			
Opening stock		16 037	
Add purchases:			
Purchases	94 736		
Add: courier charges	150		
Less: purchase returns	(853)		
		94 033	
		110 070	
Less: closing stock		(18 006)	
Cost of sales			(92 064)
Gross profit			67 106
Discounts received			98
			67 204
Expenses			
Shop rental		18 300	
Electricity and other premises costs		3 598	
Assistant's wages		10 920	
Insurance		2 984	
Discounts allowed		196	
Accountancy fees		570	
Delivery van expenses		760	
Sundry expenses		1 982	
Chamber of Commerce subscription		100	
			(39 410)
Net profit			27 794

Note the following:

1. Discounts received are a type of income. However, they are not included in the trading section of the profit and loss account, but are added on to gross

profit. This is because the level of discounts received has no bearing on the trading activities of the business; they are received as a result of good financial management.

2. Delivery van expenses are the expenses that Bennie has to pay for running a van to deliver goods to his customers. These costs are obviously not being passed on to customers and therefore have to be paid for out of the proceeds of Bennie's business.

3. Bennie's profit and loss statement looks quite complicated because it has three columns of figures. Figures are indented like this in order to make the statement easier for the reader to understand.

Accounting conventions

Recognition and realisation

Accounting conventions help to determine the amounts at which items should be stated in the financial statements, and, indeed, whether or not those amounts should be included at all.

This section considers the issue of recognition of income and expenses. Recognition occurs when items are brought into the accounting statements. In some cases the point at which items should be recognised is straightforward. A sale made for cash is recognised at the point where the exchange of goods for cash takes place. So, for example, in the case of Bennie's art shop all the sales he makes for cash up to closing time on 31 October 20X5 are included in the accounts for that year.

However, Bennie makes both cash sales and sales on credit. At what point should sales on credit be recognised in the accounts? The accounting convention on this point is that income should be recognised at the point at which the goods are supplied or services rendered. So, for example, goods that are delivered to the local art college on 31 October 20X5 with a sales value of £366 are included in Bennie's total sales for the year ending on that date. Goods delivered on the next day (1 November 20X5) will be included in total sales for the next accounting year (the year ending on 31 October 20X6).

It is important to appreciate that this convention (known in accounting terminology as the realisation convention) means that the total recorded for sales in an accounting period will not usually be the same as the cash received. The goods Bennie delivers to the art college on 31 October are included in sales at a value of £366. However, payment for these goods will not be received until after the year-end. Any amounts due at the year-end are debtors and will be included as assets in the business's balance sheet.

Similar considerations apply in respect of expenses. In Bennie's case all goods delivered up to the close of business on 31 October 20X5 are included in his total purchases for the year. Bennie has almost certainly not yet paid for all of the purchases. Any amounts still to be paid at the year-end are creditors and will be included as liabilities in the business's balance sheet. So, the total for purchases and expenses recorded in an accounting period will not be the same figure as cash spent.

In summary, accounting income is not the same as cash received, and accounting expenditure is not the same as cash paid.

Matching (accruals)

The matching, or accruals, convention is very important in the calculation of profit. The effects of transactions should be recognised in the accounting period in which they occur, which is not necessarily the period in which they are invoiced or paid. In the last chapter we established the basic foundation for calculating profit:

$$\text{Sales} - \text{Expenses} = \text{Profit}$$

In order to calculate profit with as much precision as possible, it is important to match sales and expenses. That means setting off against sales for an accounting period all the expenses that have contributed to making those sales. So, for example, in a business like Bennie's which pays rent, the matching convention requires that one year's rent is matched against one year's sales in working out the profit for that year. If only nine months rent is included the expenses figure will not be large enough and profit will be overstated. If 15 months rent is included the expenses figure will be too large and profit will be understated.

Expenses are recorded as they are paid or when bills are received. When drawing up the year-end accounts it is important to examine the detail of the amounts recorded for expenses to ensure that expenses and income are matched as closely as possible. Note that the matching convention is also referred to as the accruals convention. The importance of matching is illustrated in the following example.

Example 8.5

Gregory runs a small business supplying leather goods on credit to small shops and market stalls. The business is run from a warehouse on a trading estate. Gregory pays rental for the warehouse, and the usual type of expenses such as insurance and telephone.

Gregory's accounting year-end is 30 June. The annual warehouse rental is paid in quarterly instalments in advance. So, for example, Gregory pays rental on 29 September every year, which will cover October, November and December. Any increases in rental take effect from 1 January in the calendar year.

Gregory has the following rental arrangements with his landlord for 20X6 and 20X7: in 20X6 the total annual rental is £12 000, but in 20X7 there is a substantial increase to £14 400. What is the total of rental expense for Gregory's business in the year ending 30 June 20X7?

Following the matching convention in accounting, Gregory's sales for the year ending 30 June 20X7 must be matched with the expenses that have been incurred in order to achieve those sales. Between 1 July 20X6 and 31 December 20X6 (a period of six months) the cost of the warehouse rental was £12 000/2 = £6000. Between 1 January 20X7 and 30 June 20X7 (a period of 6 months) the cost of the warehouse rental was £14 400/2 = £7200. The total rental expense to be matched against Gregory's sales for the year is therefore £6000 + £7200 = £13 200.

The calculations may be easier to understand with the aid of a diagram (Figure 8.1).

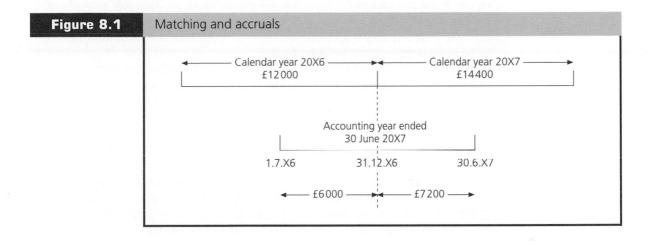

Figure 8.1   Matching and accruals

Comprehensive example – matching

In the next example we will look at the adjustments that may be required to the financial statements because of the timing of the recording of expenses. Parts 1 and 2 of the example examine the detail of the adjustments and then, in Part 3, we look at the effect on the accounts overall.

Example 8.6

Part 1

Graham has a consultancy business with a year-end of 31 December. He receives quarterly bills for telephone call charges. At the 31 December 20X6 year-end the total in his account books for his business telephone call charges is £6840. This is the total of three separate payments made during the year:

1. Payment on 13 April 20X6 of £2175 for the bill covering 1 January to 31 March.
2. Payment on 30 July 20X6 of £2444 for the bill covering 1 April to 30 June.
3. Payment on 18 October 20X6 of £2221 for the bill covering 1 July to 30 September.

By 31 December 20X6 Graham has received no bill for the last quarter of the year. This is not surprising as the bill will cover the period up to and including 31 December and so Graham would not expect to receive it until several days after the year-end. However, Graham must include the amount of the final quarter bill in his accounts to 31 December 20X6 so that the total charge for telephone expenses reflects all of the charges for calls made in the year. If he fails to include an appropriate amount, expenses will be understated and, consequently, profit will be overstated.

In drawing up the accounts, then, Graham must add the appropriate amount to telephone expenses. If he receives the bill before he completes the accounts he can make an exact adjustment. If not, he must make a reasonable estimate of the likely cost. Unless the final quarter is unusual in some way, Graham could estimate based upon the previous quarters' bills. An estimate of around £2200 to £2300 would probably be appropriate.

Suppose that Graham receives the bill in good time before the accounts are finished. The total amount of call charges is £2237 for the quarter. Graham adds this to the charges for the first three quarters: £6840 + £2237 = £9077 total telephone expense for the year.

There is another adjustment to be made as well, this time to the balance sheet. The three bills already paid have depleted the bank balance. The new bill will deplete the bank balance at some point in January or February 20X7, but at the date the accounts are drawn up (31 December) the payment transaction has not yet occurred. Graham, therefore, must show the telephone bill as a creditor at the year-end. This particular type of creditor is known in accounting terminology as an accrual, and it is included in the balance sheet under current liabilities.

Part 2

Telephone charges are billed after the calls have been made. The phone company extends credit to its customers, and other utilities companies commonly do the same (unless the customer is known to be very bad at paying up, in which case the companies will insist on payment in advance or via pay meters). Some types of expense, however, may be payable in advance, and matching problems may therefore occur.

Graham pays his business buildings and contents insurance on 1 July each year, in advance. The amount paid on 1 July 20X6 covers the whole year from 1 July 20X6 to 30 June 20X7. Only half of the amount paid, therefore, relates to the year to 31 December 20X6.

At 31 December the balance on Graham's insurance account is £3901, which includes the bill paid on 1 July 20X6 for £2644. Half of this (£1322) relates to the next following accounting year (20X7). This is known in accounting terminology as a **prepayment** – a type of current asset. It will be included in the balance sheet at 31 December 20X6 under current assets of the business.

The total expense for Graham's business insurance for the year comprises £1322 for the second half of the year, plus the amount relating to the first six months of the year:

	£
Insurance expense in Graham's records at 31 December	3 901
Less: amount relating to 20X7	1 322
Insurance expense for inclusion in the 20X6 accounts	2 579

Because we know that the insurance expense relating to the second six months of the year was £1322 we can work out (£2579−£1322) that the expense for the first six months of the year was £1257.

Part 3 – the full accounts

Next we will look at how the accrual and prepayment adjustments explained above fit into Graham's accounts for the whole year.

The following is Graham's list of balances at 31 December 20X6, before any adjustments for accrual and prepayment items. Each item is identified as to whether it belongs in the profit and loss account or balance sheet:

	£	
Consultancy income	103 907	Profit and loss account
Secretarial assistant's salary	18 742	Profit and loss account
Entertaining expenses	961	Profit and loss account
Fixed assets	3 336	Balance sheet
Cash at bank	12 906	Balance sheet
Travel expenses	1 888	Profit and loss account
Telephone	6 840	Profit and loss account
Interest received	360	Profit and loss account
Debtors	14 820	Balance sheet
Creditors	1 793	Balance sheet
Capital at 1 January 20X6	21 130	Balance sheet
Office premises – rent and other expenses	23 590	Profit and loss account
Sundry office expenses	2 553	Profit and loss account
Insurance	3 901	Profit and loss account
Accountant's fees	772	Profit and loss account
Drawings	36 881	Balance sheet

The adjustments for the accrual and the prepayment must be made before Graham's profit and loss and balance sheet are drawn up.

1. *Accruals adjustment*: £2237 is added to telephone expenses and an accrual for £2237 appears in the balance sheet, included under current liabilities.
2. *Prepayment adjustment*: £1322 is deducted from insurance expenses and a prepayment for £1322 appears in the balance sheet, included under current assets.

Using all of the above information, Graham's accounts can be drawn up:

Graham: Profit and loss account for the year ending 31 December 20X6

	£	£
Consultancy income		103 907
Interest received		360
		104 267
Expenses		
Office premises: rent and other expenses	23 590	
Secretarial assistant's salary	18 742	
Entertaining expenses	961	
Telephone (£6840 + £2237)	9 077	
Travel expenses	1 888	

Sundry office expenses	2 553	
Insurance (£3901−£1322)	2 579	
Accountant's fees	772	
		(60 162)
Profit for the year		44 105

Graham: Balance sheet at 31 December 20X6

	£	£
Fixed assets		3 336
Current assets		
Debtors	14 820	
Prepayment	1 322	
Cash at bank	12 906	
	29 048	
Current liabilities		
Creditors	1 793	
Accrual	2 237	
	4 030	
Net current assets (£29 048−£4 030)		25 018
Net assets		28 354
Capital		
Opening capital balance 1 January 20X6	21 130	
Add: net profit for the year	44 105	
	65 235	
Less: drawings	(36 881)	
Closing capital balance 31 December 20X6		28 354

The following should be noted:

1. After the adjustments are made the balance sheet still balances. The first adjustment, for the accrual, is an addition to expenses and a reduction in profits for the year. Consequently, the capital side of the balance sheet is reduced. However, there is a balancing reduction in net assets because we have included a creditor in the form of an accrual. The second adjustment, for the prepayment, is a deduction from expenses and an increase in profits for the year. Consequently, the capital side of the balance sheet is increased, but there is a balancing increase in net assets because we have included a current asset in the form of a prepayment.

2. Note the position of the new items. Prepayments are usually recorded immediately below debtors in the balance sheet list of current assets. Accruals are recorded immediately below creditors as part of current liabilities.

The accounting adjustments that arise because of the matching convention can be difficult to assimilate at first. However, there are several examples at the end of the chapter which will help to reinforce understanding.

Current asset adjustments

In this section of the chapter we will examine the range of adjustments that may have to be made, in certain circumstances, to stock and debtors.

Stock

The value of stock at the year-end is determined by the following calculation:

Number of items in stock × Value of individual items

The number of items is usually established by means of a stocktake carried out on the last day of the year. Value is generally, but not always, cost. As we saw, earlier in the chapter, it may be necessary to add in certain items (such as import duties, for example) to the cost of purchasing goods. Also, it can happen that stock loses some part of its value before it can be sold. This can happen because the stock is accidentally damaged or where, by its nature, it does not hold its value for long.

The fundamental rule to be applied to stock valuation is that stock is valued at the lower of cost and net realisable value. Net realisable value is the amount for which the stock could be sold, less any incidental expenses of sale. It is important to compare cost and net realisable value, to ensure that the balance sheet does not contain stock at over-valued amounts. The following example illustrates the point.

Example 8.7

Taruni runs a wholesale business dealing in novelty items and toys. Following a massive televised talent show a new band, Neolithic Hamster, has been formed. Its first two releases have done really well, and the band's promoters have rushed out a range of supporting merchandise – T shirts, cuddly hamster toys and so on. This type of merchandise presents a difficult problem for Taruni in judging just how much to keep in stock. While the band remains popular the merchandise will sell very well and there is likely to be a strong demand for it. However, the market for such items is fickle and unreliable because the public tends to grow tired of manufactured bands within a couple of years at most.

Neolithic Hamster, it emerges, has a shorter shelf life than average. After only six months, public interest dwindles to nothing. Taruni has miscalculated her purchasing and is now left with 3000 giant cuddly hamsters. They originally cost her £6.50 each from the manufacturer and she was able to sell them to shops for £9.50 each at the height of the interest in the band. In order to be able to value the hamsters still in stock at her year-end date (31 August) Taruni needs to know whether she will be able to sell them at a price above £6.50, the original cost to her. If so, she will value the stock at cost price – i.e. £6.50 × 3000 = £19 500.

Taruni makes enquiries. Unfortunately, hers is not the only business trying to unload hamsters in a hurry. The promoters misjudged the whole merchandising promotion and arranged for the production of far too many tie-in goods. Finally, in early September, Taruni finds a man who runs several street market stalls. He is prepared to take the hamsters off her hands for a price of £2 each, and he even offers to come and collect them in his van from her warehouse. In the circumstances Taruni feels she has little choice but to accept the offer. It is clear that Taruni will make a loss on the stock. At 31 August the stock items were no longer worth £6.50 each. She must value at the lower of cost or net realisable value – i.e. at the lower of £6.50 or £2.

Sales for the year are £265 331. Opening stock was £42 307, purchases amounted to £165 956 and closing stock, apart from the hamsters, was £19 952. As noted above, if the hamsters are valued at cost the total value is £19 500. If they are value at net realisable value, the total value is £2 × 3000 = £6000.

In the table below we will assess the effect on Taruni's gross profit of valuing the hamsters at cost and at net realisable value.

	Hamsters at cost £	Hamsters at net realisable value £
Sales	265 331	265 331
Cost of sales		
Opening stock	42 307	42 307
Add: purchases	165 956	165 956
Less: closing stock (19 952 + 19 500)	(39 452)	—
Less: closing stock (19 952 + 6 000)	—	(25 952)
	168 811	182 311
Gross profit	96 520	83 020
Gross profit margin	36.4%	31.3%

The difference between the two figures for gross profit is £13 500 – that is, the loss per item of £4.50 × 3000 units of stock. This has been a very costly error in purchasing.

Businesses involved in the sale of fashionable items always face the risk that their stock will go out of fashion before it can be sold. Purchasing in such businesses involves a high level of skill, judgement and experience. However, the risk is likely to be absorbed to some extent by charging high prices for the goods while the fashion still lasts.

Debtors

Earlier in this chapter the issue of income recognition was discussed. The realisation convention in accounting requires that income from a transaction is recognised at the point when the goods are dispatched or when services are rendered. In a commercial environment it is very often the case that there is a time lag between the supply of goods (or provision of services) and the receipt of payment.

Once goods have been dispatched a sales invoice follows. The risk for the business selling the goods, of course, is that the purchaser will subsequently fail to pay for the goods. Businesses can take certain precautions against this happening: for example, they can contract with credit agencies to obtain advice on whether or not to offer credit to prospective purchasers. Larger businesses employ their own credit control staff to investigate credit ratings and to chase up unpaid debts. Nevertheless, even in the best organised businesses unpaid invoices can become a problem.

Debtors in the balance sheet represent the total value of unpaid sales invoices. A business problem arises if some debtors will not, or cannot, pay their debts. There is also an accounting problem to be solved. In order to help ensure that the balance sheet provides information that is useful and reasonably accurate, debtors should be stated at their 'recoverable amount' – that is, the amount that can be expected to be paid within a reasonable time after the balance sheet date.

Accounting adjustments are made to cover, broadly, two eventualities:

1. *Bad debts*. These are debts that will almost certainly not be paid.
2. *Doubtful debts*. These are debts that may not be paid.

Example 8.8

Hilda runs a business that supplies water filter equipment. She allows customers 30 days credit. At her year-end, 31 May 20X9, the total of her debtors list is £38 384. She has problems with two of the debtor balances, as follows:

1. £1200 is owed by Jimbo Associates. Jimbo, head of the business, has disappeared to South America taking with him all the cash that was left in his business and leaving many angry creditors behind. It emerges that police in several countries wish to interview him. His creditors, who include Hilda, are unlikely ever to receive payment. From Hilda's point of view this is a bad debt.
2. Hilda sells goods at a total price of £3985 to a firm, Bernini & Co. on her normal terms of trade which are payment within 30 days of receipt of invoice. Three months pass and by her year end, 31 May, Hilda has still not been paid. For the last month she has rung Bernini & Co every week and every Monday Mr Bernini gives her his personal assurance that the cheque will be in the post by Friday. Hilda is beginning to have doubts about these assurances and intends to threaten Bernini with legal action if the debt is not settled.

There is a difference between the debts described above. In the first case Hilda will never receive the money. In the second case, there is a possibility that Mr Bernini will be sufficiently impressed by the threat of legal action to pay up without further fuss.

How should these debts be recorded in Hilda's accounts? In the first case, the debt has ceased to be an asset. It is a **bad debt** and it should be excluded from the total of debtors. In the second case, it is not clear whether or not the debt can be recovered. Hilda will treat this item as a **doubtful debt**. The appropriate accounting treatment is to make a **provision** against the doubtful debt. The provision is deducted from debtors in the year-end balance sheet. Debtors will be shown as follows at 31 May in Hilda's balance sheet:

▶

	£
Debtors (£38 384−£1200)	37 184
Less: provision	(3 985)
	33 199

The £1200 due from Jimbo is excluded altogether. The debt due from Bernini remains in the list because it might be recovered in due course, but is deducted from the total in the form of a provision.

The £1200 represents an actual loss of profit. The asset of debtors is reduced and so, consequently, is Hilda's profit. The £3985 is a potential loss of profit. It is recognised, for the time being, as a deduction from profit for the year ending 31 May 20X9.

Next, we will look at how these adjustments fit into Hilda's accounts for the whole year. She has the following list of balances at 31 May 20X9, before making any adjustments to the debtors. Each item is identified as belonging in the trading account, the rest of the profit and loss account or the balance sheet.

	£	Category
Stock at 1 June 20X8	34 401	Trading account
Sundry administration expenses	1 270	Profit and loss account
Cash at bank	1 700	Balance sheet
Drawings	38 380	Balance sheet
Premises costs	26 670	Profit and loss account
Marketing expenses	2 190	Profit and loss account
Travelling expenses	1 630	Profit and loss account
Purchases	281 830	Trading account
Debtors	38 384	Balance sheet
Fixed assets	18 361	Balance sheet
Staffing costs	21 010	Profit and loss account
Telephone	2 620	Profit and loss account
Creditors	34 600	Balance sheet
Capital at 1 June 20X8	49 855	Balance sheet
Sales	389 005	Trading account
Delivery van expenses	2 967	Profit and loss account
Insurance	2 047	Profit and loss account
Stock at 31 May 20X9	35 433	Trading account *and* balance sheet

From the balances and the information about bad and doubtful debts the following accounting statements can be drawn up for Hilda's business.

Hilda: Profit and loss account for the year ending 31 May 20X9

	£	£
Sales		389 005
Cost of sales		
Opening stock	34 401	
Add: purchases	281 830	
	316 231	

	£	£
Less: closing stock	(35 433)	
		(280 798)
Gross profit		108 207
Expenses		
Premises costs	26 670	
Staffing costs	21 010	
Marketing expenses	2 190	
Delivery van expenses	2 967	
Travelling expenses	1 630	
Telephone	2 620	
Insurance	2 047	
Sundry administration expenses	1 270	
Bad debts	1 200	
Provision for doubtful debts	3 985	
		(65 589)
Net profit		42 618

Hilda: Balance sheet at 31 May 20X9

	£	£	£
Fixed assets			18 361
Current assets			
Stock		35 433	
Debtors	37 184		
Less: provision	(3 985)	33 199	
Cash at bank		1 700	
		70 332	
Current liabilities			
Creditors		(34 600)	
Net current assets (£70 332−£34 600)			35 732
Net assets			54 093
Capital			
Opening capital balance 1 June 20X8		49 855	
Add: net profit for the year		42 618	
		92 473	
Less: drawings		(38 380)	
Closing capital balance 31 May 20X9			54 093

The following should be noted:

1. After the adjustments are made in respect of debtors, the balance sheet still balances. Assets are depleted by the amount of the adjustments, but so is

profit. The reduced profit decreases the capital side of the balance sheet by the same total amount.
2. The total for debtors includes the amount owed by Bernini & Co. The debtors total will continue to include this debt until either: (a) it is paid; (b) Hilda concludes that the debt has gone bad.

Let us look at the two possibilities in turn. If the debt is paid by Bernini & Co. the asset of debtor (£3985) will be replaced by the asset of cash. The provision for the doubtful debt would no longer be necessary and it would have to be removed from the accounts. This essentially involves reversing the original adjustment. The provision would cease to exist and profit would be increased by £3985 in the following period.

If Hilda concludes that the debt has gone bad, the provision will prove to have been necessary. The debt would be removed from the list of debtors and the provision would also be removed. We can see from the balance sheet above that the net effect of this adjustment on assets would be nil.

Specific and general provisions

The type of provision for doubtful debts made by Hilda in the case above is 'specific'. That means that the provision relates to a certain specific debt. Sometimes, however, businesses make 'general' provisions against doubtful debts.

Example 8.9

Walter sells goods on credit. Usually the invoices are for small amounts and at any time Walter has about 500 debtors who owe him money. He knows, on the basis of many years' experience, that a few of the debtors will not pay up, but it is not usually possible to identify them specifically. He has calculated that, on average, about 1.5% of the value of debtors will not be paid.

Walter's accountant recommends that at his year-end, 30 September 20X1, he should make a general provision for doubtful debts. The total of debtor balances at that date is £52 250. The general provision is calculated at 1.5% of £52 250, or £784 to the nearest £. Walter's accountant makes the adjustment. Profit for the year is reduced by £784, and debtors are shown in the year-end balance sheet as follows:

	£
Debtors	52 250
Less: provision	(784)
	51 466

At 30 September 20X2 Walter's debtors total is £59 942, and his accountant again advises him to make a general provision of 1.5%, which is £899 (to the nearest £). What accounting adjustment is necessary for this? Walter has £784 recorded as a provision in his accounts. The accounting adjustment to be made at 30 September 20X2 is £899−£784 = £115. Therefore, £115 is added to the

existing provision and is deducted from the profit for the year. Debtors are shown in the year-end balance sheet as follows:

	£
Debtors	59 942
Less: provision	(899)
	59 043

Chapter summary

This chapter has explained the accounting treatment of returns of goods, discounts received and allowed, and of delivery charges.

The concept of income and expense recognition was introduced. The realisation and matching conventions in accounting were dealt with in detail, using a comprehensive example to explain the necessary accounting adjustments.

Adjustments to the value of stock and debtors have been examined in depth. The distinction between the accounting treatment of bad debts and of doubtful debts has been explained, and finally, in the case study, the potential impact of bad debts upon a small business was considered.

A great deal of quite complex material has been covered in this chapter. Students should ensure that they complete as many of the end-of-chapter questions as necessary in order to be sure of completely understanding all the principles and practices described in the chapter.

The end-of-chapter exercises are divided into two sections. The first section has answers provided at the end of the book. The second section, in the white box, has answers on the lecturers' section of the website. Finally, the chapter contains a case study that requires the preparation of a full set of accounts (profit and loss account and balance sheet), and analysis of the problems facing a small business with a substantial bad debt.

Website summary

The book's website contains the following material in respect of Chapter 8:

Students' section

- Quiz containing ten multiple choice questions and answers
- Eight additional questions with answers
- Answers to case study at end of this chapter.

Lecturers' section

- Answers to exercises 8.11 to 8.18
- Six additional questions with answers.

Exercises: (with answers at the end of the book)

8.1 Oscar's trading company prepares accounts to 31 December. In the year to 31 December 20X1 the following trading transactions occur:

	£
Sales	72 411
Purchases	53 005
Sales returns	361
Purchases returns	1 860

Stock at 1 January 20X1 was £4182, and at 31 December 20X1 it was £5099. What is Oscar's gross profit for the year?

a)   21 822

b)   18 102

c)   18 824

d)   22 544.

8.2 Omar imports onyx picture frames from India. He prepares accounts to 30 April each year. In the year ending 30 April 20X7 he records the following totals for trading transactions:

	£
Sales	347 348
Purchases	240 153
Import duties	6 043
Sales returns	2 971
Purchases returns	1 800

Omar's opening stock at 1 May 20X6 was £43 730 and his closing stock at 30 April 20X7 was £41 180. What is Omar's gross profit for the year?

a)   97 431

b)   99 773

c)   109 517

d)   91 388.

8.3 Poppy imports and sells display fireworks. She supplies her customers on credit terms, requiring payment of invoices within 30 days. In order to encourage early payment she offers customers a discount of 0.5% of invoice value for receipt of payment within 30 days.

The following is a list of Poppy's account balances for all sales and expenses items at 28 February 20X2:

	£
Staffing costs	9 777
Opening stock at 1 March 20X1	7 140

Sales returns	3 997
Import duties	9 911
Rental	17 211
Discounts allowed	716
Telephone charges	1 227
Purchases	123 057
Insurance	8 204
Marketing	1 888
Administrative expenses	922
Electricity	1 604
Delivery van expenses	2 107
Sales	220 713
Stock at 28 February 20X2	7 393

Prepare Poppy's profit and loss account for the year ending 28 February 20X2.

8.4 Pookie's business involves telephone sales, so her business phone bills are high. Her accounting year ends on 31 August, and in the year to 31 August 20X8 she has received bills for phone charges as follows:

Date received	Date paid	Period covered	Amount (£)
9 October 20X7	15 October 20X7	1.7.X7–30.9.X7	9 760
5 January 20X8	15 January 20X8	1.10.X7–31.12.X7	12 666
6 April 20X8	14 April 20X8	1.1.X8–31.3.X8	8 444
8 July 20X8	12 July 20X8	1.4.X8–30.6.X8	9 530

Pookie estimates that her telephone charges for July and August will be two-twelfths of the total of the charges for the 12 months to 30.6.X8.

To the nearest £, what is the telephone expense for inclusion in Pookie's profit and loss account for the year ending 31 August 20X8?

a)   £40 400

b)   £40 626

c)   £47 133

d)   £33 667

8.5 Patience pays a subscription to a business trade association annually in advance. The subscription is due on 30 September each year, to cover one year running from 1 October. Patience's accounting year runs to 28 February. The subscriptions paid in September 20X6 and 20X7 are as follows: 20X6 = £644; 20X7 = £796.

What are the amounts included in prepayments for this expense at 28 February 20X7 and 20X8? (Work to the nearest £.)

a)   20X7 = £268; 20X8 = £332

b)   20X7 = £376; 20X8 = £464

c)   20X7 = £376; 20X8 = £332

d)   20X7 = £268; 20X8 = £464

8.6 Simon trades in soft furnishings from shop premises in the centre of a small town in northern England. He provides basic summaries of his transactions for his accountant, Bernie, who prepares his final accounts and tax computation. The business year-end is 31 July.

Simon's income and expense transaction totals for the year ended 31 July 20X4, before any necessary year-end adjustments, are as follows:

	£
Delivery expenses	2 490
Opening stock at 1.8.X3	38 888
Income from curtain-making service	6 519
Costs of curtain-making service	2 797
Shop rental	18 750
Business rates	3 510
Assistant's wages	22 379
Insurance	4 478
Electricity	2 064
Travelling expenses	603
Sales	317 342
Telephone	1 035
Purchases	230 133
Discounts received	377
Trade subscriptions	165
Charitable donations	500
Closing stock at 31.7.X4	39 501

Note the following additional information:

1. Of the £4478 included above for insurance, £501 relates to the period after 1 August 20X4.

2. Simon has two very trustworthy assistants working in the shop. As well as wages, he pays each of them an annual bonus of 0.5% of total sales (not including income from the curtain-making service). An accrual needs to be made for this item.

3. Electricity charges of £377 require accrual.

4. Bernie always makes an accrual for his own fees when drawing up Simon's accounts. He estimates that the fee required for the year ended 31 July 20X4 will be £800.

5. In conversation, Simon mentions that he has been having a lot of trouble with the occupants of the shop next door who regularly leave rubbish scattered on the forecourt that serves both shops. Simon has taken legal advice to see whether he can obtain a legal injunction, but he has not yet received a bill from the solicitor for work done. At Bernie's request Simon contacts the solicitor for an estimate of the fees at 31 July 20X4. The solicitor tells Simon that time charges for consultation and correspondence amount to about £350. Bernie and Simon agree that an accrual should be made for this amount.

Prepare a profit and loss account for Simon for the year ending 31 July 20X4 and calculate the totals for accruals and prepayments for inclusion in the balance sheet at that date.

8.7 Ted sells belts and accessories to fashion stores around the country, buying in most of his goods from China. Long experience in the business has developed his judgement in purchasing; he needs to be able to judge fashion trends at least six months in advance. Even Ted, however, makes mistakes.

In his accounting year to 31 December 20X5, Ted buys in a range of coordinating accessories in hot pink. By the middle of the year Ted realises that he has misjudged the market. This year's colours are sludgy browns and greens and there is no demand for pink. In total Ted's purchases for the year are £379 322. Of these, £21 900 related to the pink items and £17 750 of the stock remains unsold at the year-end. Ted's sales are £599 790 for the year. Total opening stock (which included no pink items, and which was valued at cost) was £49 071, and total closing stock is £62 222 including the unsold £17 750 of pink items. Ted has had an offer from a discounter of £6000 for all the pink items that remain in stock.

Draw up a trading account that values closing stock at the lower of cost or net realisable value. Calculate Ted's gross profit margin and compare it to the gross profit margin that would have been achieved if the whole of closing stock were valued at cost.

8.8 Ulrich prepares his accounts to 31 July each year. At 31 July 20X1 his debtors list totals £397 700. Included in the list is a debt of £17 000 owing by Gayle Associates. Gayle Associates has recently ceased to trade and Ulrich has been told by Gayle's administrator that there is little likelihood of him ever recovering the £17 000 owing to him.

There is a recession in the general economy and Ulrich is concerned that some of his other debtors could run into difficulties. He decides to make a general provision for doubtful debts of 1% of debtors whose balances have been outstanding for more than three months at 31 July 20X1 (excluding the £17 000 owed by Gayle). He has never previously made a provision against debtors.

An analysis of Ulrich's debtors at 31 July 20X1 shows the following:

	£
Outstanding for one month or less	169 930
Outstanding for between one month and three months	143 370
Outstanding for over three months	67 400
Gayle Associates	17 000
	397 700

How will debtors be presented in Ulrich's balance sheet at 31 July 20X1? What is the effect of bad and doubtful debts on Ulrich's profit for the year?

8.9 Ursula is a wholesaler trading in stationery supplies. She sells to offices and shops around the country and at any one time has up to 350 debtors due to pay her. She allows 30 days credit but finds that her bigger customers are quite likely to exceed this limit.

At 31 December 20X2 Ursula has the following balances in her accounts:

	£
Assistant's wages	10 008
Fixed assets	23 360
Opening stock at 1 January 20X2	31 090
Discounts allowed	1 046

Creditors	25 920
Discounts received	361
Electricity	4 850
Business and water rates	3 899
Warehouse rental	11 070
Telephone	2 663
Debtors	50 354
Opening capital at 1 January 20X2	70 219
Cash at bank	361
Insurance	3 414
Delivery costs	4 490
Drawings	33 988
Administration charges	3 242
Purchases	239 285
Sales	326 620
Closing stock at 31 December 20X2	30 048

Note the following additional information:

1.   Ursula has recently been informed that a debtor of hers, Wainwright, has left the country owing large amounts of money. Ursula is relieved that the outstanding debt is no more than £672 because, in the past, she has sold large quantities of stationery to Wainwright. Ursula is advised by her accountant that the debt should be treated as completely irrecoverable, and should be written off.

2.   At 31 December 20X2 there are accrued charges for electricity of £338.

3.   The accountant's fees in respect of the year are likely to be in the region of £700. This amount should be accrued.

4.   Two debtors are giving Ursula some cause for concern. Wilson has been owing £398 for almost six months. Wilson assures Ursula via frequent phone calls that the payment will be made when he gets back on his feet after a devastating fire at his offices. And £700 is owed for stationery supplies to a friend of Ursula who started a new business a few months ago. The friend assures Ursula that the bill will be paid, but Ursula knows from mutual friends that the new venture is not going well. Ursula decides to make a provision against both of these amounts.

5.   Of the insurance balance of £3414, £622 relates to the next accounting year and should be treated as a prepayment.

Prepare a profit and loss account for Ursula for the year ending 31 December 20X2, and a balance sheet at that date, incorporating all the adjustments noted.

8.10   Briefly explain the following accounting terms, providing an illustrative example in each case:

a)   Recognition

b)   Accruals

c)   Net realisable value

Exercises: (answers available to lecturers)

8.11 Olivia's trading company prepares accounts to 31 August each year. In the year ending 31 August 20X4, the following trading transactions occur:

	£
Sales	193 306
Purchases	144 315
Sales returns	1 836
Purchases returns	63

Opening stock at 1 September 20X3 was £16 399 and closing stock at 31 August 20X4 was £17 041. What is Olivia's gross profit for the year?

a)   47 797

b)   51 469

c)   47 860

d)   51 658.

8.12 Ophelia imports glass ornaments from Norway. She prepares accounts to 30 June each year. In the year ending 30 June 20X9 she records the following totals for trading transactions:

	£
Sales	83 722
Purchases	65 277
Special charges for safety packaging	604
Sales returns	426
Purchases returns	291

Opening stock at 1 July 20X8 was £5799. Closing stock at 30 June 20X9 was £5904. What is Ophelia's gross profit for the year?

a)   18 084

b)   18 437

c)   18 663

d)   17 811.

8.13 Paolo trades in promotional goods. His customers order items like mouse mats, biros, playing cards, golf balls and so on, printed with their own logo. Paolo keeps a stock of blank goods. When he receives an order from a customer he sends the plain items of stock to a local printer who adds the customer's logo and address details. The business is run from a shed in Paolo's back garden at home. The shed is supplied with electricity; the cost of the electricity is billed together with Paolo's domestic supply. He estimates that one-sixth of the bill is attributable to electricity used in the shed. His electricity bills for the year to 31 March 20X6 total £3072.

Apart from the electricity, Paolo's records show the following items of sales and expenses for the year:

	£
Discounts allowed to customers	88
Travelling expenses	3 914
Sales	118 242
Opening stock at 1 April 20X5	5 918
Cost of printing	17 291
Telephone	1 671
Mobile phone call charges	419
Purchases	43 947
Discounts received from suppliers	133
Accountancy and tax advice	800
Office sundry expenses	977
Marketing	2 663
Interest received	204
Purchases returns	1 774
Closing stock at 31 March 20X6	4 261

Prepare Paolo's profit and loss account for the year ending 31 March 20X6.

8.14 In 20X7 the gas bills for Peregrine's business are received and paid as follows:

Date received	Date paid	Period covered	Amount (£)
4 March 20X7	10 March 20X7	1.12.X6–28.2.X7	841
6 June 20X7	20 June 20X7	1.3.X7–31.5.X7	790
6 September 20X7	15 September 20X7	1.6.X7–31.8.X7	654
9 December 20X7	20 December 20X7	1.9.X7–30.11.X7	752

Peregrine prepares accounts to 31 December each year. He estimates that gas used in December 20X7 would be billed at about £300.

What figure for gas expense should be included in Peregrine's accounts to 31 December 20X7? (Work to the nearest £.)

a) £2 737

b) £3 037

c) £3 057

d) £2 457.

8.15 Paula's business expenses for 31 October 20X1 are summarised as follows:

	£
Insurance	7 280
Phone	2 017
Other expenses	36 470

Examination of the detailed transactions in the insurance account shows the following:

	£
Insurance charges for seven months to 31 May 20X1	2 660
Paid 3 June for one year from 1 June 20X1 to 31 May 20X2	4 620
	7 280

Examination of the detailed transactions in the phone account shows the following:

	£
Bill for period 1 November 20X0–31 January 20X1	690
Bill for period 1 February 20X1–30 April 20X1	627
Bill for period 1 May 20X1–31 July 20X1	700
	2 017

The bill for the three-month period to 31 October 20X1 was not received until after the year-end. The amount of the bill was £696.

What is the total amount of Paula's business expenses for inclusion in her profit and loss account for the year ending 31 October 20X1?

a) £45 767

b) £43 768

c) £43 072

d) £41 825.

8.16 Sylvester runs a consultancy business, employing two members of staff as consultants and a secretarial assistant. Because he has done an accountancy course, he is able to prepare his own accounting records and statements. He consults an accountant periodically for tax advice. Sylvester's accounting year-end date is 31 January.

In the year to 31 January 20X8 Sylvester has built up the following income and expenditure balances on his accounts:

	£
Staff consultants' salaries	47 090
Secretarial assistant's salary	14 441
Premises expenses – office rental	12 750
Premises expenses – other	4 419
Consultancy fees	239 000
Telephone – office	4 200
Mobile phone	2 419
Entertainment	3 007
Membership subscriptions	1 136
Administration costs	3 422
Sundry expenses	1 620
Electricity	5 187

Note the following additional information:

1. Sylvester pays the two assistant consultants a basic salary plus a bonus based upon performance. The bonus for each consultant for the year ended 31 January 20X8 will be the higher of 10% of total consultancy fees billed in the year and £24 500. The bonus element of salaries must be accrued for at the year-end.

2. £366 of the membership subscriptions relate to the period after 31 January 20X8.

3. Office telephone charges include bills for the 10 months to 30 November 20X7. Phone charges for the business vary very little from month to month and the charges for December and January should be in line with previous months.

4. Sylvester rings his accountant for an estimate of costs in relation to tax advice for the year. The accountant suggests that an accrual of £400 will probably be appropriate.

Prepare Sylvester's profit and loss account for the year ending 31 January 20X8.

8.17 Umberto makes a provision of 1.5% against his total debtors each year. In the year to 31 August 20X7 he has used up £650 of this provision because a debtor has gone out of business. Umberto's debtors at 31 August 20X6, before provision, were £366 000. At 31 August 20X7 debtors before provision are £390 000.

How are debtors presented in Umberto's balance sheets at 31 August 20X6 and 31 August 20X7? What is the effect of the provision for doubtful debts on Umberto's profit and loss account for the year ending 31 August 20X7?

8.18 Identify and explain the fundamental rule that is applied to the valuation of stock.

! CASE STUDY   A problem debtor

The case study brings together several of the adjustments examined in the chapter. Richard studied hotel management many years ago at college. After leaving, he spent two years as a sous-chef at a large hotel in London, but soon grew tired of the hectic pace of work. While on holiday in Italy he bought a very stylish pan from a range of well-designed kitchenware. On his return to the UK he decided he would like to buy another pan from the range, but was unable to find a stockist. He made enquiries and discovered that no one in the UK was currently importing the range. He persuaded his mother to lend him some cash and started a business importing kitchenware, initially only from Italy, but as the business developed, from other countries as well.

The business has been successful. Richard has always managed to make a profit, but he is not very careful with money. He spends a lot, and he has never quite been able to follow his original intention, which was to invest part of the profits in expanding the business. Still, he has always prided himself on being able to provide a high standard of living for his family. However, more recently Richard has fallen into difficulties. Four years ago his wife, Hermione, discovered that he was having an affair with an Italian sales rep. Horrified and upset, she refused to believe his assur-

ances that the affair was over and that it would never happen again. She turned him out of the house and demanded a divorce. Richard feels that he has done rather badly out of the divorce, under the terms of which Hermione kept the family home, and Richard has had to pay what he considers to be an unreasonably large sum of maintenance for the three children of the marriage. He now lives in a small rented flat.

A few months after the divorce Richard met up, by complete coincidence, with Charlie, a former friend from college, on a train journey to London. After college Charlie spent several years working as a chef in France and Switzerland, but had now returned to the UK to start a private restaurant school. He is delighted to find that Richard deals in high quality kitchen supplies, and promises that he will place all his contracts for equipment with Richard's business. Charlie and Richard discover that they are both keen Formula One enthusiasts and, after that chance meeting, they see each other regularly at races and social events. Because he knew Charlie at college and considers him to be a good friend, Richard is quite relaxed about supplying goods on credit. Charlie explains that he will be a bit short of money for the first few months in the new business, but he will pay Richard whatever he is able to spare: 'Once the business is on its feet, there'll be no problem at all . . .'.

Charlie's business starts up in July 20X3, and Richard supplies all the equipment for the demonstration kitchen in the school at a cost of £23 000. At first the business seems to be doing well, and Charlie is so confident about it that he starts up another, bigger, branch in another city only six months later, in December 20X3. Again, Richard supplies all the equipment, this time at a cost of £27 600, although this time he does say to Charlie that he would like to have some of the debt paid off soon. Charlie has not been able to pay him anything at all in the first few months of his business. As the months go by, Richard notices that he's not seeing Charlie around so much, and even starts to suspect that Charlie is avoiding him.

Richard, in the meantime, has his own money troubles. Hermione has pestered him for extra money to take herself and the children on an exotic cruise. Because Richard still feels guilty about the failure of the marriage he gives in and pays over £7500 out of his drawings from the business. Feeling depressed, Richard decided to cheer himself up by going on a skiing holiday in Colorado with his new girl-friend. Somehow, the drawings from the business seem to be much higher, and, for the first time ever, Richard needs a business overdraft. The bank manager is happy to oblige and, because interest rates are low, Richard is not really worried about it. He knows that his cash position will be back to normal as soon as Charlie pays him.

In late October 20X4 Richard is alarmed to find an article in the trade press about Charlie. Headlined 'Charmer Charlie in closure chaos', the article reports the sudden closure of the restaurant schools. Irate clients, all of whom had paid in advance for courses, have been trying to gain entry to the schools, the doors to which are permanently locked. Richard rings the journalist responsible for the article. Off the record, the journalist confirms that this latest enterprise is not the first business failure that Charlie has experienced. He is notorious in some circles for his ability to charm people into lending him money. Several years ago he started a restaurant business with money that he persuaded friends to contribute. The restaurant was not a success and Charlie went abroad still owing his ex-friends large sums of money. There is some speculation now that the Fraud Squad is interested in Charlie's activities.

Richard rings Charlie on his business telephone line, but the line does not appear to be working. There is no reply from Charlie's mobile phone. In desperation he rings a chef who has been working at one of the schools. The chef is extremely angry. He hasn't been paid for over a month and he has no idea of Charlie's present whereabouts.

Richard is not very good at keeping track of his financial affairs. A bookkeeper maintains the basic records of the business and, once a year, his accountant, Frank, prepares a profit and loss account and balance sheet at 31 December. At this point, in October 20X4, Richard really does not know how the business stands, but he is aware that he is close to the business overdraft limit of £24 000. For the first time in the history of the business his Italian supplier, Giovanni, has rung him asking politely when he is likely to be paid. Richard does not have an immediate answer to the question, but tells Giovanni that he will call him back in a couple of days.

Richard visits Frank with a list of balances prepared by the bookkeeper as at the end of September 20X4. Richard is, by now, extremely anxious and asks Frank to prepare financial statements as at the end of September as soon as possible, and to advise him on the impact there will be upon the business if the money owed by Charlie cannot be recovered. Richard is desperate to have Frank's opinion on whether or not the business can survive.

The list of balances is as follows:

	£
Interest paid and bank charges	1 560
Sales	250 836
Delivery expenses	2 612
Stock at 1 January 20X4	17 881
Creditors	51 760
Discounts allowed	870
Discounts received	183
Import duties related to purchases	1 536
Purchases	140 255
Premises rental and other charges	31 580
Overdraft	23 861
Debtors (including £50 600 owed by Charlie)	93 242
Staff wages	23 391
Administration charges	7 726
Capital at 1 January 20X4	64 084
Drawings	61 760
Fixed assets	8 311
Closing stock at 30 September 20X4	19 870

The bookkeeper sends a note with the balances to say that the telephone bill for the quarter to 30 September 20X4 still needs to be paid and is not included in the total for administration charges above. The bill is for £422. In addition, Frank thinks that it would be sensible to make an accounting adjustment for an accrual for his own fees. He has not sent a bill to Richard for a while and he estimates that about £1300 will be due for tax work already carried out and for the work of preparing these interim accounts. These two items (£422 + £1300) will create a total accrual to be included in balance sheet liabilities of £1722.

Requirements
a) Prepare a profit and loss account for Richard's business for the nine months ended 30 September 20X4, and a balance sheet at that date, without making any adjustment in respect of the amounts owed by Charlie.
b) Show the effect on the profit and loss account and balance sheet of treating the amounts owed by Charlie as a bad debt.
c) Discuss the prospects for the business as revealed by the accounts prepared in part b).
d) Suggest possible ways in which Richard could obtain further finance to support his business.

@ The answers and discussion relating to these requirements can be found on the student section of the book's website.

CHAPTER 9

Adjustments to the profit and loss account and balance sheet
Part 2

Aim of the chapter

To enable students to understand the use of adjustments for depreciation and amortisation and their effect on the profit and loss account and balance sheet of sole trader businesses.

Learning outcomes

After reading the chapter and completing the related exercises, students should:

- Understand the need for depreciation and amortisation in financial statements.
- Understand the distinction between tangible and intangible fixed assets.
- Be able to incorporate adjustments for depreciation and amortisation into a profit and loss account and balance sheet.

Depreciation and amortisation

In Chapter 8 we examined the matching (also known as accruals) convention in accounting. It is important to set off against sales for an accounting period all the expenses which have contributed to making those sales. We looked at examples of the adjustments for prepayments and accruals which are necessary to ensure that matching is done as precisely as possible. There is one further important category of adjustment that must be made under the matching (or accruals) convention: adjustment for the depreciation or amortisation of fixed assets.

Fixed assets are purchased for use in the business; they are used in the ordinary activities of the business to generate sales. For example, a business that delivers goods to its customers needs delivery vans. The vans are fixed assets in that they are used within the business over a long period of time. However, they do not last forever; eventually they will accumulate a high mileage and will become unreliable. It is likely that, before this point is reached, the business will dispose of them and buy new replacements.

The costs of running the fleet of delivery vehicles must be matched against the sales generated in an accounting period. Some of the costs are obvious: there is fuel, insurance, service and repair to consider. However, in order to fully meet the obligation to match costs against sales, it is conventional in accounting to include in costs an estimate of how much of the value of fixed assets has been used up in an accounting period. The next example illustrates how such an estimate would be arrived at in practice.

Example 9.1

Quickwash is a commercial laundry service used, principally, by hotels and restaurants. Dirty towels, sheets, tablecloths and so on, are collected in one of the Quickwash fleet of delivery vans, and are taken to the laundry on an industrial estate where they are washed, dried and pressed. The clean items are then delivered by van to the client, usually within 24 hours.

The delivery vans are essential to the running of the business. Experience has shown that even the high quality vans used by the business tend to start needing replacement parts after three or four years. The laundry business is highly competitive and Quickwash cannot afford to upset customers by being late with deliveries because a van has broken down. Therefore, Quickwash's management has a policy of replacing the vans every three years.

At the beginning of January 20X1 Quickwash buys a van at a cost of £20 000. Management's policy means that the van will be used for no more than three years. It will be sold second-hand and replaced in January 20X4. As explained in earlier chapters, the cost of the van will be included in the fixed assets section in the balance sheet. Initially, the amount included will be £20 000. However, by the end of the first year, some of that value has been used up in the course of Quickwash's business activities. Depreciation is a measure of the amount of value used up.

How do we calculate depreciation?

It is important to realise that depreciation is an estimate, not an exact figure. Quickwash's management knows the exact amount spent to acquire the van, and also knows that the van will be kept in the business for three years. However, they do not know exactly how much the van can be sold for at the end of the three-year period. Suppose that, based upon past experience, it is expected that the second-hand van can be sold for approximately £5000 at the end of the three-year period. What is the total value used up over three years?

	£
Cost of van	20 000
Expected proceeds from sale after three years	5 000
Value used up over three years	15 000

So £15 000 represents an estimate of the van's depreciation over a three-year period. This is a cost of running the business which, in order to comply with the matching convention, should be set off against the sales that are generated over that period.

How is depreciation spread over the three-year period?

A straightforward way of spreading depreciation is to split the total figure equally over the accounting periods that benefit from the use of the fixed asset. This approach would produce an annual figure for depreciation on this van of £5000. There are other ways of spreading the cost of depreciation, and later in the chapter we will examine one other popular method.

The equal split of depreciation over accounting periods is known as the straight-line method of depreciation. It is the most commonly used method in the UK.

? Self-test question 9.1 (answer at the end of the book)

This question tests understanding of the process involved in estimating depreciation.

Salvatore runs a small haulage business. The business owns two heavy goods vehicles, one driven by Salvatore himself and the other by his assistant, Ginette. Business is booming and Salvatore decides to buy a new HGV, and to employ another driver. On 1 January 20X4 he spends £65 000 on a new vehicle. He plans to use it for four years and then to sell it. He hopes to be able to sell it for approximately £25 000.

Estimate the annual depreciation charge for the new vehicle using the 'straight-line' method of depreciation.

Impact of depreciation on the accounts

In order to apply the matching convention, the annual charge for depreciation must be set off against sales in the accounting period. In the profit and loss account, therefore, depreciation is shown as an expense.

Depreciation, however, also has an impact upon the value of fixed assets shown in the balance sheet. Over time, the value of fixed assets is depleted as they are used up in the course of business. Depreciation is, therefore, deducted from the initial cost of the asset each year.

Example 9.2

Using the information in the Quickwash example above, we will look at the impact on the profit and loss account and balance sheet of the business in the three years of the life of the asset. Quickwash's accounting year ends on 31 December.

Year 1

The asset is acquired on 1 January 20X1 at a cost of £20 000 paid out of the business bank account. Quickwash reduces the current asset of cash at bank and fixed assets are increased by the same amount. (Remember the accounting equation that was explained in Chapter 6.)

At 31 December 20X1 the van has been in use for one year. In Example 9.1 we estimated an annual depreciation charge of £5000 per year. So, in Quickwash's profit and loss account for the year ended 31 December 20X1 an expense of £5000 will be included. The inclusion of this amount reduces profit by £5000.

In the balance sheet at 31 December 20X1 the van is recorded at its value after taking into account the depreciation charged:

	£
Van at cost	20 000
Less: depreciation	5 000
Net book value of van	15 000

Some points to note:

1. It is conventional to show the original cost value of fixed assets, less a deduction for depreciation.
2. Cost less depreciation is described as 'net book value'.
3. Quickwash owns several vans; the cost and depreciation of this particular van will be included in an overall total for vans.
4. The value of the van in the balance sheet has been reduced from £20 000 to £15 000. At 31 December 20X1 it might be possible to sell the van on the open market for more or less than £15 000. Net book value is not the same as market value.

Year 2

At 31 December 20X2 the van has been in use for two years. The profit and loss account should include the amount of depreciation for the year; this is the amount that has to be matched against sales. An expense of £5000 is therefore included in the total expenses, while profit, as in the previous year, is reduced by £5000.

In the balance sheet at 31 December 20X2 the net book value of the van has reduced, as more of its value is used up in the course of the business activities.

	£
Van at cost	20 000
Less: depreciation	10 000
Net book value of van	10 000

Note that after each year of use in the business the net book value of the asset diminishes.

Year 3

At 31 December 20X3 the van has been in use for three years. The profit and loss account should include the amount of depreciation for the year; this is the amount that has to be matched against sales. An expense of £5000 is therefore included in the total expenses, while profit, as in the previous year, is reduced by £5000.

In the balance sheet at 31 December 20X3 the net book value of the van has reduced, as more of its value is used up in the course of the business activities.

	£
Van at cost	20 000
Less: depreciation	15 000
Net book value of van	5 000

At this point in time the van is ready for disposal. It is shown in the balance sheet at a net book value of £5000, which is the value that Quickwash's management originally estimated it could be sold for after three years. It is unlikely that their estimate would turn out to be precisely correct; later in the chapter we will examine what happens when a fixed asset is sold for more or less than the original estimate.

Summary

For each year that the van is used in Quickwash's business a charge of £5000 is made to the profit and loss account. This charge reduces profit by £5000 and represents an estimate of the depletion in value of the van each year.

In the balance sheet at each year-end the following values are included:

	20X1	20X2	20X3
	£	£	£
Van at cost	20 000	20 000	20 000
Less: accumulated depreciation	5 000	10 000	15 000
Net book value	15 000	10 000	5 000

Note that the total for depreciation increases each year as the asset is used up. The net book value decreases by a corresponding amount.

Intangible assets and amortisation

At the beginning of the chapter the term 'amortisation' was introduced. Amortisation works in the same way as depreciation but is applied to intangible fixed assets, rather than tangible fixed assets.

So far, the examples in this book have mostly used tangible fixed assets. 'Tangible' means capable of being touched; it is a piece of accounting terminology used to refer to assets that have a physical presence, such as the vans in the Quickwash example earlier. 'Intangible' refers to assets that have a value to the business, but which do not exist physically. Examples of tangible fixed assets include land and buildings, plant and machinery, office equipment, vans, lorries and cars, and computer equipment. Examples of intangible fixed assets include brands, mineral extraction rights, patents and licences, lease premiums on property and newspaper titles.

The examples of tangible fixed assets probably need no further explanation. The intangible fixed assets are, perhaps, less familiar, and so brief explanations follow.

Brands

Brands can be immensely valuable to the business that owns them. Examples of world famous brands include Coca-Cola, Microsoft, Hoover and McDonald's. Brand names can be bought and sold; there are firms of specialist valuers who can assist in fixing an appropriate price. If a business buys a brand name it is buying an intangible asset that is likely to produce income for the business over a long period.

Mineral extraction rights

Where a piece of land contains valuable minerals, its owner may make profits by extracting the ores, processing and selling them. Alternatively, the owner may licence another firm or person to extract the ores over a period of time by granting a licence over the extraction rights. The purchaser of the licence is buying a fixed asset, although it is not tangible. The asset consists of the transfer of certain rights over a piece of land, not the land itself.

Patents and licences

The inventor of a useful and potentially money-making process may decide to set up a manufacturing business to exploit the value of the process (think, for example, of the Dyson bagless vacuum cleaner). The inventor lays claim to ownership of the knowledge by registering a patent which affirms his or her rights over the knowledge. Rather than setting up in manufacturing, however, he or she may grant the right to use the process to a manufacturer in exchange for cash. The manufacturer in this case is buying the rights of access to the inventor's knowledge; such rights are often known as patent rights.

Lease premiums on property

Lease premiums are another example of rights of access. Where a business buys, say, shop premises or a warehouse on a freehold basis, it acquires tangible assets.

However, it may instead choose to invest in a lease of the premises instead. The lease represents the right to occupy the premises. Often in such cases a large sum of money must be paid over at the start of the lease and then, subsequently, regular rental is paid in addition. The large initial sum constitutes an intangible asset; rights of occupation have been purchased.

Newspaper titles

Newspaper titles are similar to brands, and can be very valuable assets. Such titles are a type of intangible asset in that they are usually very well known, with loyal readerships and with a reputation for a particular type of journalism. It is possible to buy and sell titles (sometimes known as 'mastheads'); if such a title is bought it constitutes an intangible asset.

Accounting for amortisation

The accounting procedure adopted in accounting for amortisation is identical to the procedure for depreciation, which we examined earlier in the chapter. Note, however, that amortisation is almost invariably estimated using the straight-line method. The following example will illustrate how to account for amortisation.

Example 9.3

Bright & Shoesmith is a pharmaceutical manufacturing business. It is not involved itself in pharmaceutical research and development; instead it buys rights, in the form of licences to manufacture medicines, from the large pharmaceutical development firms. On 1 January 20X4 it concludes its negotiations with Exnox Worldwide to buy a licence to manufacture Nox, a sleeping pill. The contract for the licence stipulates that it lasts for a period of four years and that a manufacturing royalty of 25.6p per packet of 20 pills will be payable over the whole period of the contract. An up-front payment of £3 600 000 will be paid by Bright & Shoesmith for the licence.

In this case, Bright & Shoesmith is acquiring an intangible fixed asset in the form of a licence for the sum of £3 600 000. It is clearly laid down in the contract terms that the licence will last for exactly four years. After four years, the intangible asset will be completely used up and there will be no value left in it. Over that four-year period, Bright & Shoesmith will receive revenue from the sale of the sleeping pills and this is the period over which the cost of acquiring the licence must be matched (in accordance with the matching convention).

Applying the straight-line method, amortisation of the licence fee amounts to £900 000 for each of the four years (£3 600 000/4). In each of the four years amortisation of £900 000 will be charged as an expense in the profit and loss account of Bright & Shoesmith.

Bright & Shoesmith's year-end is 31 December. The intangible fixed asset will appear as follows in the end-December balance sheets of the business:

	20X4 £	20X5 £	20X6 £	20X7 £
Intangible fixed assets				
Licence at cost	3 600 000	3 600 000	3 600 000	3 600 000
Less: accumulated amortisation	(900 000)	(1 800 000)	(2 700 000)	(3 600 000)
Net book value	2 700 000	1 800 000	900 000	—

After four years the licence has no value remaining in the balance sheet. This is correct because, by that time, Bright & Shoesmith no longer has the right to manufacture the sleeping pills.

Note that part of the deal with Exnox is that a royalty must be paid on each packet of pills manufactured. This type of arrangement is quite commonly found in licence agreements. The royalty is part of the cost of manufacturing the pills, and it will be set off against revenue in arriving at a figure for profit. It has no bearing on accounting for the amortisation of the licence.

Another method of depreciation

We have examined the straight-line method of depreciation in detail in this chapter. Straight-line is the method of depreciation most often encountered in practice, and it is the method that is almost invariably adopted in accounting for amortisation. However, there are several other possible ways of estimating depreciation. The most common, apart from straight-line, is the reducing balance method. This method applies a given percentage to the net book value at each year-end to estimate the depreciation expense. This is illustrated in the following example.

Example 9.4

Boris runs a small manufacturing company that makes soft drinks and packages fruit juice for sale to supermarkets and other retailers. He runs a fleet of four delivery vehicles. At 1 April 20X1 he buys a new replacement vehicle at a cost of £15 000. Boris adopts the reducing balance method for depreciation on the vehicles, at a rate of 25% per annum. What is the depreciation expense for each of the three years to 31 March 20X2, 20X3 and 20X4, and what is the net book value to be included for this van at each year-end?

Year 1

The first year of ownership is the year to 31 March 20X2. The depreciation expense for the delivery vehicle is 25% of the original cost of the asset: 25% × £15 000 = £3750. This will be shown as part of the expense of depreciation in the profit and loss account.

In the balance sheet at 31 March 20X2 the vehicle will be included as follows:

	£
	£
Vehicle at cost	15 000
Less: depreciation	3 750
Net book value of vehicle	11 250

Year 2

For the second year of ownership the depreciation expense for the delivery vehicle is 25% of the net book value at the beginning of the accounting year: 25% × £11 250 = £2813 (to the nearest £). This will be shown as part of the expense of depreciation in the profit and loss account.

In the balance sheet at 31 March 20X3 the vehicle will be included as follows:

	£
Vehicle at cost	15 000
Less: depreciation (£3750 + £2813)	6 563
Net book value of vehicle	8 437

Year 3

For the third year of ownership the depreciation expense for the delivery vehicle is 25% of the net book value at the beginning of the accounting year: 25% × £8437 = £2109 (to the nearest £). This will be shown as part of the expense of depreciation in the profit and loss account.

In the balance sheet at 31 March 20X4 the vehicle will be included as follows:

	£
Vehicle at cost	15 000
Less: depreciation (£3750 + £2813 + £2109)	8 672
Net book value of vehicle	6 328

Summary

The depreciation charge to profit and loss for the vehicle is as follows for each of the three years:

20X2 = £3 750
20X3 = £2 813
20X4 = £2 109.

In the balance sheet at each year-end the following values are included:

	20X2	20X3	20X4
	£	£	£
Vehicle at cost	15 000	15 000	15 000
Less: accumulated depreciation	3 750	6 563	8 672
Net book value	11 250	8 437	6 328

The following points should be noted:

1. Each year the depreciation charge to profit and loss falls. This may reflect the pattern of usage of the fixed asset more accurately than the straight-line method, depending upon how the asset is used up. Cars and other vehicles frequently lose a substantial amount of value in the first year of ownership from new, so the reducing balance method may be more realistic for such assets.
2. It takes many years of depreciation before the asset value is reduced to nil.
3. As with the straight-line method of depreciation it is possible to build in to the calculation the expected proceeds of sale at the end of the planned period of ownership. This requires the use of a mathematical formula. In this book none of the exercises will require use of the formula to calculate an appropriate rate of depreciation: the rate will be given in all cases.
4. Businesses may select a combination of methods for depreciating different types of fixed asset. Having selected a method, or methods, to apply to different assets it would be expected that the business would use the methods consistently. This is so that realistic comparisons between different years' results are made possible.
5. The cost in the balance sheet of £15 000 does not change.

? Self-test question 9.2 (answer at the end of the book)

Silvio runs a mobile hairdressing business. His annual mileage is high and he expects to keep his car for no more than three years. On the advice of his accountant, Silvio applies the reducing balance method of depreciation to his car over the three years of ownership at a rate of 30% per annum. He buys a new car on 1 May 20X6, the first day of his accounting year, for £17 209. Calculate the depreciation on the car for Silvio's accounts for the three years ending 30 April 20X7, 20X8 and 20X9, and show how the car will appear in Silvio's business balance sheet on each of those dates. Calculate all figures to the nearest £.

Land and buildings

In almost all cases land is not subject to depreciation as it does not wear out. Only in exceptional cases is it necessary to charge depreciation on land. For example, land containing mineral deposits is likely to have an enhanced value. If the minerals are mined, the land will tend to lose value, and in this case it may be appropriate to reduce the value over time by charging depreciation.

Some buildings have a longer useful life than others, but all eventually wear out. Therefore, it is appropriate to charge depreciation, although it will usually be over a long period, such as 50, 75 or 100 years.

The role of judgement in estimating depreciation

In each of the examples used in the chapter up to this point we have referred to the need to 'estimate' depreciation. Depreciation is one of the many areas in accounting where precision is impossible. When an asset is purchased it is impossible to be precise about how long it will remain in use in the business. The longer the life of the asset the more imprecise the estimate will be. For example, a building estimated to last 75 years might last 102 years (or 78, or 93, etc.); in any case, the people who are making the estimates will probably not be around to answer for the quality of their judgement when the building eventually falls down.

Judgement is involved in estimating both the useful lifespan of the asset and any monetary value for which the asset could be eventually sold. As we have seen, depreciation has a direct impact on profitability. It is an aspect of accounting that is, consequently, subject to manipulation. A business that is going through hard times may wish to exaggerate the estimated useful lives of fixed assets so as to spread depreciation over a longer period (and thus minimise the impact on profits). It can be very difficult to challenge the judgements made by business managers in this respect.

Sale of a fixed asset

Upon sale, the fixed asset is exchanged for the asset of cash (or possibly a debtor if it is agreed that the cash does not have to be paid straight away). If the net book value of the asset is the same as the price agreed for the sale, then the exchange of one type of asset for another is straightforward. However, in most cases the net book value of the asset will be higher or lower than the cash price. In such cases, either a profit or a loss on sale will arise. Examples 9.5 and 9.6 illustrate the calculation of profits and losses on sale.

Example 9.5

Ibrahim runs a juice bar. His business is doing well and he has decided to buy a new improved juicing machine. He advertises the old machine in the paper for sale at £750. Takis, a restaurant owner, rings up and offers him £650 in cash for the old machine, an offer Ibrahim decides to accept. The net book value of the machine in the accounts is £475. What is Ibrahim's profit on sale, and how will the transaction be recorded in his accounts?

The profit on sale is the proceeds of £650 less the net book value of £475: i.e. a profit of £175. Tangible fixed assets are reduced by the net book value (£475) and cash at bank is increased by £650. The profit of £175 is shown in the profit and loss account, thus increasing Ibrahim's capital. In summary, in terms of the accounting equation, assets (overall) increase by £175, as does capital.

Note that the 'profit' is really just an adjustment reflecting the actual outcome of the judgements made about depreciation at the start of the useful life of the asset. 'Profit' in this context arises where the asset has been over-depreciated.

188 SECTION 2 FINANCIAL ACCOUNTING

Example 9.6

Adebola's delivery service is run using two delivery vans. Her business policy is to replace the vans every four years. One of the vans, which was bought four years ago at a cost of £12 750, is due for replacement. Adebola depreciates the vans using the reducing balance method at a rate of 25% per annum. She accepts an offer of £3650 for the van. What is Adebola's profit or loss on sale of the van?

First, we must calculate the net book value of the van after four years:

	£
Van at cost	12 750
Year 1 depreciation (25% × £12 750)	3 188
Net book value at end of year 1	9 562
Year 2 depreciation (25% × £9562)	2 391
Net book value at end of year 2	7 171
Year 3 depreciation (25% × £7171)	1 793
Net book value at end of year 3	5 378
Year 4 depreciation (25% × £5378)	1 345
Net book value at end of year 4	4 033

The proceeds of the sale of the van are less than the net book value after four years. Therefore, Adebola makes a loss on sale of £3650 − £4033 = £383. Tangible fixed assets are reduced by £4033 and the asset of cash is increased by the sale proceeds of £3650. The loss of £383 is included in Adebola's profit and loss account for the year, thus decreasing her capital. In terms of the accounting equation, then, assets decrease by a net amount of £383 and capital is reduced by the same amount.

Note that the 'loss' on sale of the asset is really the amount by which the asset has been under-depreciated.

? Self-test question 9.3 (answer at the end of the book)

Sergio sells one of the machines from his factory for £3010. The machine was bought new exactly five years ago for £15 000 and has been depreciated using the reducing balance method at a rate of 30% per annum. Calculate Sergio's profit or loss on sale of the machine.

Buying and selling assets during the year

In all the examples in the chapter up to this point it has been assumed that fixed assets are bought on the first day of the year and are held for an exact number of years. However, businesses may buy or sell assets at any time during the accounting period. Where this happens, a business must decide not only on the method of depreciation to be adopted but also on how the rate is to be applied in the year of acquisition or disposal of an asset.

Example 9.7

Angelina has a card shop that uses several display stands. She decides to replace all the stands at the same time as the shop frontage is refurbished as part of a new look for the shop. She spends £8780 on new stands on 1 May 20X3. Her accounting year-end is 31 December. The stands should last for five years before they require replacement and Angelina decides to apply the straight-line method of depreciation.

Her accountant advises her that she must decide on how she will apply the depreciation method in 20X3. She can either:

a) apply a policy of charging a whole year's depreciation in the first year of ownership, regardless of the actual date of acquisition of the assets; or
b) apply a policy of charging depreciation in respect of the number of months she has owned the assets.

What will be the difference in the depreciation charge under approaches a) and b)?

With a) – a full year's depreciation in the accounting year ending 31 December 20X3 – depreciation will be:

$$\frac{£8780}{5} = £1756$$

The balance sheet at 31 December would include the following:

	£
Display stands at cost	8 780
Less: depreciation	1 756
Net book value	7 024

Under approach b) depreciation would be charged for only eight months:

$$\frac{£8780}{5} \times \frac{8}{12} = £1171$$

The balance sheet at 31 December would include the following:

	£
Display stands at cost	8 780
Less: depreciation	1 171
Net book value	7 609

Usually, businesses will seek to be consistent in the approach they adopt. So, if Angelina decides to adopt approach a) she should continue to do so. Also, businesses will adopt consistent approaches upon both acquisition and disposal of assets. So, if a full year's depreciation is charged as an expense in the year of acquisition, regardless of the actual date acquired, it would be consistent to charge none in the year of disposal. In answering questions on depreciation it is important to take careful note of how they are worded in order to adopt the correct approach.

So far, we have examined depreciation and amortisation calculations, and their presentation, in isolation. Questions 9.11 and 9.20, and the case study at the end of the chapter provide examples where depreciation is integrated into the accounts as a whole.

Chapter summary

This chapter has examined the accounting adjustments for depreciation and amortisation of fixed assets. The distinction between tangible and intangible assets was introduced, together with more detailed explanations of several examples of intangible assets.

 The end-of-chapter exercises are divided into two sections. The first section has answers provided at the end of the book. The second section, in the white box, has answers on the lecturers' section of the website. Finally, the chapter contains an extensive case study that examines the integration of a set of depreciation and amortisation adjustments into a profit and loss account and balance sheet.

Website summary

The book's website contains the following material in respect of Chapter 9:

Students' section

- Quiz containing ten multiple choice questions and answers
- Five additional questions with answers
- Answer to case study at the end of this chapter.

Lecturers' section

- Answers to exercises 9.13–9.21
- Six additional questions with answers.

Case study

Once Chapters 6–9 inclusive have been studied thoroughly, students may like to get some extra practice by using an additional case study – 'The Hayseed Gallery' – available on the website.

Exercises: answers at the end of the book

9.1 Valerie runs a small delivery business. She has a van that she replaces every four years. On 1 January 20X3 she sells her old van for £2000 and buys a new one for £14 460. She expects to be able to sell it for approximately £4000 in four years time.

Assuming that Valerie adopts the straight-line method of depreciation in her accounts what is her depreciation charge for the accounting year ending 31 December 20X3?

a)   £2 115

b)   £3 615

c)   £4 615

d)   £2 615.

9.2 Victoria owns a gym. In her financial year to 31 August 20X2 she buys a new exercise bike for £450. The date of purchase was 1 March 20X2. Victoria aims to keep gym equipment for three years. After three years she finds that the equipment is usually well worn and worth very little. She advertises old equipment to her members, and would usually expect to receive about £30 for an old exercise bike.

Victoria charges depreciation in her accounts on the straight-line basis, with a pro-rated charge in the first and final years of ownership, depending on the dates of acquisition and disposal. What is the depreciation charge in respect of the new exercise bike in the year to 31 August 20X2?

a)   £70

b)   £140

c)   £75

d)   £150.

9.3 Vinny is expanding his electrical components business. During his accounting year ending 31 December 20X6 he buys new machinery as follows:

- On 1 April a machine costing £10 300. The estimated useful life is five years, after which point Vinny expects that it will have a nil value.
- On 1 October a machine costing £8580. The estimated useful life is four years, and Vinny expects the machine to fetch £2000 on the second-hand market when the time comes to dispose of it.

Vinny charges depreciation in the accounts on the basis of the number of months of ownership of the asset in an accounting year. Working to the nearest £, what is the total depreciation charge for the new machines in the year ending 31 December 20X6?

a)   £3 705

b)   £2 081

c)   £1 956

d)   £2 779.

9.4 Having qualified as a mining engineer Violet decides that she would like to go into the gold-mining business. She spends a considerable period of time looking for mining opportunities. Finally she finds a piece of land in Wales that was formerly exploited for gold-mining. The activity had been abandoned some years ago because the yield was insufficient. However, Violet is convinced that the mine can once more be made profitable with the help of modern equipment and technology. She enters negotiations with the owners of the land. They refuse to sell it, but agree to grant Violet the rights for a three-and-a-half year period from 1 January 20X3. In exchange Violet agrees to pay £273 000, plus a fixed fee per kilo of gold extracted.

How will the purchase of the mineral rights be reflected in Violet's accounts for the year to 31 December 20X3?

9.5 Vincenzo's balance sheet at 31 August 20X7 shows the following balances in respect of fixed assets:

	£
Buildings at cost	306 000
Less: accumulated depreciation	(18 360)
Net book value	287 640
Motor vehicles at cost	48 770
Less: accumulated depreciation	(16 470)
Net book value	32 300
Fixtures and fittings at cost	12 720
Less: accumulated depreciation	(6 360)
Net book value	6 360

In the year ending 31 August 20X8 no purchases or sales of fixed assets are made. Vincenzo depreciates fixed assets as follows:

- Buildings at 2% per annum on cost on the straight-line basis.
- Motor vehicles at 25% per annum on the reducing balance basis.
- Fixtures and fittings (which were all purchased at the same time) over ten years on the straight-line basis.

First, calculate the total charge to Vincenzo's profit and loss account in respect of depreciation for the year ending 31 August 20X8. Secondly, show how fixed assets will be presented in Vincenzo's balance sheet at 31 August 20X8.

9.6 Wilma runs a wedding car service. Business is expanding and she is planning to buy a new vehicle. The basic list price of a new car is £24 400, but Wilma must pay an additional £800 for it to be sprayed white. She purchases the car on 1 March in time for the main spring and summer wedding season. Her year-end is 28 February. Wilma depreciates cars on the reducing balance basis at 15% per annum.

What will be the depreciation charge for the first year of ownership of the new car?

a) £3 660

b) £3 780

c) £3 540

d) £4 460.

9.7 At 1 January 20X3 William has the following balances in his books related to the fixed asset of cars:

	£
Cars at cost	38 370
Less: accumulated depreciation	(15 540)
Net book value	22 830

He acquires a new car on the same date for £14 447. No other cars are bought, or sold, during the rest of the accounting period which ends on 31 December 20X3.

William depreciates cars on the reducing balance basis at 25% per year. What is the total charge for depreciation on cars, to the nearest £, to be included in William's profit and loss account for the year ending 31 December 20X3?

a) £13 204

b) £9 319

c) £5 707

d) £9 592.

9.8 Xenia no longer needs a second van in her business, and so she decides to sell it. The van originally cost £8300 and by Xenia's year-end of 31 March 20X4 depreciation had accumulated of £6330. She sells the van for £2380 on 1 April 20X4. What is the profit or loss on sale of the van?

9.9 Xanthe runs a florist's shop. Her assistant goes out every day in the van delivering flowers. The van accumulates high mileage quickly and Xanthe usually replaces it every three years. The van cost £10 100 on 1 June 20X1 and Xanthe has depreciated it on the reducing balance basis at 30% per year for three years. She sells it on 1 June 20X4 for £3000. What is the profit or loss on sale of the van?

9.10 Ying runs a wholesale business supplying art equipment to retailers. She uses two computers to keep stock and other records – one in the office and one in the warehouse. In her accounting year ending 31 December 20X3 she decides to buy a new networked computer system, with terminals in both the office and warehouse. She is able to sell both of the old computers, one for £250 and the other, which is in slightly better condition, for £300. Both computers were bought on 1 January 20X1 for a total price of £3672. They have been depreciated on the straight-line basis over four years, with the assumption that their value will be nil at the end of the four-year period. Ying disposes of them on 1 July 20X3.

Ying charges depreciation for each full month of ownership of fixed assets. What is her profit or loss on sale of the computers?

9.11 Zoë starts up an independent fast food outlet on 1 January 20X4, trading as Zoë's Snacks. Her accountant has advised her that she should depreciate her machinery and fixtures over a period of between four and seven years on a straight-line basis. Zoë, who is a keen amateur accountant, decides to prepare her profit and loss account and balance sheet on the basis of straight-line depreciation over a four-year period. However, she is also interested to see what difference it would make to her profits if she depreciated machinery over the maximum advisable period of seven years. Her books show the following list of balances (before any adjustment for depreciation) at 31 December 20X4:

	£
Sales	132 614
Staffing costs	15 030
Rental of premises	7 400
Purchases	83 430
Electricity	2 961
Phone	1 806
Insurance	1 437
Sundry expenses	981
Accountant's fees	600
Machinery and fixtures at cost	28 760
Stocks of food etc	1 209
Cash at bank	3 406
Creditors	1 650
Capital introduced by Zoë	20 000
Drawings	8 453

The following are required:

a) Draw up the profit and loss account and balance sheet for Zoë's Snacks at 31 December 20X4 making adjustments for depreciation of machinery and fixtures on the basis of the straight-line method of depreciation over four years, with an estimated residual value of nil.

b) Calculate the increase or decrease in net profit that would arise if Zoë depreciated the machinery and fixtures on the basis of the straight-line method of depreciation over seven years.

c) Calculate the net profit margin on the basis of i) depreciating the fixed assets over four years; and, ii) depreciating the fixed assets over seven years.

9.12 Describe the effect of a charge for depreciation upon the components of the accounting equation.

Exercises: answers available to lecturers

9.13 Victor adopts the straight-line method of depreciation in his accounts. He purchases a new machine on 1 June 20X4 for £13 750. He expects to keep the machine for approximately six years, at the end of which time it will have a scrap value of about £250. Victor prepares accounts to 31 December each year.
What is the first year's depreciation charge, assuming that Victor charges a full year's depreciation in the year of acquisition of fixed assets and none in the year of disposal?

a)   £1 125

b)   £2 250

c)   £2 292

d)   £2 333.

9.14 Virginia runs a business that supplies food for office parties and similar functions. Food is delivered to the client's premises in vans which have been specially adapted to take shallow trays of food and which contain brackets for microwave ovens. The basic cost of a new van is £9570. When a new van is purchased Virginia sends it away for modification, which costs a further £1830. On 15 August 20X5 two new vans return with the modifications complete and Virginia puts them straight into service. Virginia expects to keep the vans for a period of six years. They are subject to severe wear and tear during their useful lives and she does not expect to get more than scrap value for them after six years. Therefore, she assumes a residual value of nil.

Her accounting year-end is 31 December. She charges depreciation on a straight-line basis. In the year of acquisition and disposal of fixed assets she charges depreciation for every full month of ownership in the accounting year. What is the depreciation charge (to the nearest £) for the two new vans in the year ending 31 December 20X5?

a)   £1 267

b)   £1 063

c)   £1 329

d)   £1 583.

9.15 Valda runs a marketing agency. She prepares her own accounts and is currently working on the profit and loss and balance sheet at 31 December 20X7. She purchased the freehold of a small office building on 1 January 20X2 for £364 000. The land value included in the purchase price is estimated at £50 000. Valda depreciates the buildings element of the freehold over 100 years, the expected useful life of the building.

Apart from the building, Valda's business owns fixtures and fittings that were purchased several years ago for £16 777. The fixtures and fittings are now fully depreciated. Also, the business owns two cars used for staff visiting clients. One car was bought in the accounting year ending 31 December 20X5 for £15 300 and the other in 20X6 for £17 660. Valda depreciates the cars on a straight-line basis over their estimated useful lives of four years. Both cars have an estimated residual value of £5000.

a)   Calculate the total depreciation charge to Valda's profit and loss account in respect of depreciation for the year ending 31 December 20X7.

b)   Show how fixed assets will be presented in Valda's balance sheet at 31 December 20X7.

9.16 Wally's business owns several machines that he depreciates on the reducing balance basis at the rate of 10% per annum. His balance sheet at 31 March 20X8 shows the following balances in respect of machines:

	£
Fixed assets	
Tangible fixed assets	
Machines at cost	288 994
Less: accumulated depreciation	(107 773)
Net book value	181 221

On 17 October 20X8 he buys a new machine for £14 800. There were no other additions or disposals of machines in the year. Wally's policy is to charge a full year's depreciation in the year of purchase of a new fixed asset, and none in the year of disposal. What is the charge for depreciation on machines (to the nearest £) to be included in Wally's profit and loss account for the year ending 31 March 20X9?

a) £28 899

b) £18 122

c) £18 739

d) £19 602.

9.17 Wilbur's celebration cake business is flourishing. He plans to move to new premises and to employ more staff. He finds a unit on an industrial estate with a seven-year lease, for which he is required to pay a lease premium of £21 000. The premium is paid on the date Wilbur and his business move to the new premises, 1 May 20X1. He is able to take quite a lot of equipment with him to the new premises, but needs to buy more. During the accounting year ending 30 April 20X2 he spends £8560 on new equipment. The cost of the equipment he transferred over to the new premises was £18 388, and its net book value at 1 May 20X1 was £7380.

Wilbur depreciates equipment on the reducing balance basis at 15% per year, with a full year's charge to depreciation in the year of purchase. The lease premium will be amortised over seven years on a straight-line basis. Assuming Wilbur has no other fixed assets, what amounts will be charged for depreciation and amortisation, to the nearest £, in Wilbur's profit and loss account for the year ending 30 April 20X2?

a) amortisation £3000 depreciation £2391

b) amortisation £1470 depreciation £4042

c) amortisation £3000 depreciation £4042

d) amortisation £1470 depreciation £2391.

9.18 Xavier depreciates his machinery over ten years using the straight-line method. On 31 December 20X7 he sells a machine that he has owned for exactly seven years. Its original cost was £73 730. The sale proceeds are £30 000. What is the profit or loss on sale of the machinery?

9.19 Xan has a machine at net book value of £13 338 in his accounts. If he sells the machine for £15 000 he makes a profit on disposal of £1662. Using the accounting equation, what is the effect on his assets, liabilities and capital?

a) assets increase; capital decreases; liabilities no change

b) assets decrease; capital increases; liabilities increase

c) assets increase; capital increases; liabilities no change

d) assets decrease; capital no change; liabilities decrease.

9.20 For several years Zak has run a contract office cleaning business. He employs several part-time staff who work at night and weekends. Zak has always run the business from rented premises; he has a small office to deal with the paperwork and a storage area where cleaning equipment and machinery is kept. He also runs three vans which deliver staff and their equipment to offices around the city.

Zak has the opportunity to buy the freehold office premises he currently occupies for £51 370. He would be able to obtain a commercial mortgage for £40 000 at a rate of 8% per annum. He would like some advice on whether or not to take out the mortgage to buy the premises.

Zak has the following balances in his books at 31 March 20X3:

	£
Capital at 1 April 20X2	21 410
Bank overdraft (note: overdraft limit £20 000)	10 447
Cleaning equipment at cost	6 400
Accumulated depreciation on cleaning equipment at 1 April 20X2	1 920
Office fixtures and fittings at cost	1 700
Accumulated depreciation on office fixtures and fittings at 1 April 20X2	1 660
Vans at cost	22 419
Accumulated depreciation on vans at 1 April 20X2	14 490
Debtors	13 796
Drawings	32 479
Creditors	1 624
Sundry stocks of cleaning materials	1 408
Sales	107 614
Premises rental	7 462
Electricity and other premises costs	2 444
Sundry office expenses	799
Staff costs	63 491
Accountancy and tax advice	1 200
Cleaning materials	5 177
Interest paid	390

Zak has not made any accounting adjustments in respect of depreciation in the above list of figures. He charges depreciation as follows:

- Cleaning equipment: straight-line basis over ten years. None of the equipment is fully depreciated at 31 March 20X3.
- Office fixtures and fittings: straight-line basis over ten years.
- Vans: 25% on the reducing balance basis.

There were no additions or disposals of fixed assets during the year ending 31 March 20X3.

a) Prepare Zak's profit and loss account for the year ending 31 March 20X3 and a balance sheet at 31 March 20X3

b) Advise him on whether or not, in your opinion, he should take out the mortgage and buy the premises.

9.21 Explain the purpose of making adjustments for depreciation in the accounts of businesses, briefly describing the process involved in determining the appropriate amount of depreciation.

CASE STUDY 9.1   Depreciation accounting

The case study at the end of Chapter 6 examined a new business start-up. This case study examines Isobel Buchanan's business at the end of its first year in trading. It is not necessary to refer back to the details given in Chapter 6; the case study that follows can be worked through without reference to the earlier one.

Buchanan International Designs is still in business at the end of the first year of trading. Initially the business was set up with £10 000 in cash contributed as capital by Isobel Buchanan. In addition, she received a loan of £40 000 from her Uncle Andrew and his wife Hannah. The loan was made at a commercial interest rate of 6%, with the agreement that it would be repaid at £5000 per year over eight years commencing on the 1 March 20X4. Andrew and Hannah would be willing to make a further £40 000 available in the form of a loan on similar terms if Isobel requires it.

Carpets and rugs are purchased in four sizes. Each size has a different purchase and selling price. The table below summarises the purchases, sales and closing stock at the year-end date, 28 February 20X2, together with the purchase and sales prices, which have remained at the same level throughout the year.

	Purchase price £	Selling price £	Number sold	Number in stock 28.02.X2
Small rugs	100	150	281	42
Larger rugs	300	420	103	8
Small carpets	750	1 035	16	6
Larger carpets	1 000	1 380	7	3

Isobel's best lines are undoubtedly the rugs. Carpet sales have been very disappointing. Although the carpets are useful for display purposes she has had very few customers who are prepared to spend over £1000 to buy one. A local businessman bought one of the larger carpets for his boardroom, and since then Isobel has been able to sell a few carpets on credit to other businesses. Isobel thinks it may be possible to expand this side of the business, but she would need to spend time away from the shop and this would mean employing a salesperson for the shop.

Isobel is concerned that she is not making sufficient profit on the carpets. Sales have been at a steady rate throughout most of the year and there is no indication that sales volumes are likely to increase very much; she has tried advertising in various outlets but without much obvious success. Most of her customers have come into the shop either because they were just passing or because they have heard about it from friends or colleagues. Isobel has added ranges of small bookcases, vases and ornaments to the stock in an attempt to increase sales. Sales of such items amounted to £3992 and related cost of sales was £2379. At 28 February 20X2 goods of this type in stock totalled £5300.

When the business started up Isobel took out a lease on shop premises for four years, paying a lease premium of £10 000. Annual rental, which covers rates and services charges, is £14 000 payable quarterly in arrears at the end of March, June, September and December each year. At 28 February 20X2 she had, therefore, paid four instalments, a full year's rental.

Isobel discovered shortly after setting up the business that many customers expected a delivery service to be available. She looked at the possibility of using commercial couriers but found that their charges were very high and that she was unlikely to be able to pass them on to her customers. Therefore, she has bought a second-hand van for £6500. Other fixed assets are display racks purchased in March 20X1 at a cost of £4500 plus sundry items of shop fittings, including a cash till, at a total cost during the year of £1630.

Andrew, who is a chartered accountant, suggests to Isobel that she should adopt the straight-line method of depreciation, with a full year's depreciation to be charged in the year of purchase of the assets. He tells her that the lease premium should be amortised over four years on the straight-line basis. Isobel decides that the other fixed assets, the display racks and other shop fittings, will probably last about five years, so she decides to apply a depreciation rate of 20% to them. She does not expect these assets to have any remaining value at the end of five years. On Andrew's advice Isobel decides to depreciate the van using the reducing balance method at 25% per year.

Other items for inclusion in the accounts to 28 February 20X2 are as follows:

Interest received from the bank	651
Interest paid to Andrew and Hannah	2 400
Insurance paid	1 224
Electricity	1 681
Telephone charges	686
Staff (to cover Isobel's annual holiday)	300
Advertising	1 560
Motor expenses	551
Sundry expenses	3 446
Drawings	7 500
Cash at bank	13 323
Creditors for goods	6 327
Debtors	3 520

Of the insurance paid of £1224, £507 relates to the year commencing 1 March 20X2. At the year-end Isobel has received an electricity bill for £665 up to 28 February 20X2. This is not included in the total in the list above.

Requirements

a) Prepare a profit and loss account for Buchanan International Designs for the year ended 28 February 20X2 and a balance sheet at the same date.

b) Comment on the performance of the business in its first year, and assess the probability of it being successful in the future.

@ The answers and discussion relating to these requirements can be found on the student section of the book's website.

CHAPTER 10

Cash flow

Aim of the chapter

To understand the importance of cash in business, and to deepen understanding of the distinction between profit and cash.

Learning outcomes

After reading the chapter and completing the related exercises, students should:

- Understand the important role that cash plays in business.
- Understand the distinction between profit and cash.
- Be able to draw up a simple cash flow statement for a sole trader business.

The role of cash in business

Cash is the fundamental business resource. Without the availability of cash to pay creditors, to buy up new stock and invest in fixed assets, any business will, sooner or later, fail. Sources of cash include the following:

- Cash resources placed in the business by its owner.
- Cash borrowed from individuals, other businesses or lending institutions.
- Cash generated by the business itself.

All profitable businesses ultimately generate cash. However, a business can be profitable but, nevertheless, suffer potentially devastating shortages of cash. Later in this chapter we will examine how this apparently paradoxical position can arise.

In a well-managed business sufficient (but not too much) cash circulates as demonstrated in Figure 10.1. The upper part of the diagram shows the working capital cycle. Working capital comprises the rapidly changing items of stock, debtors, creditors and cash. There are, of course, other cash inflows and outflows in a business and these are shown in the lower part of the diagram.

It is important to keep working capital in a business tightly under control. What are the consequences if the components of working capital are mismanaged? In the next section of the chapter we will look at the problems that can arise when the individual components of working capital are not at optimal levels.

Figure 10.1	The movement of cash around the business

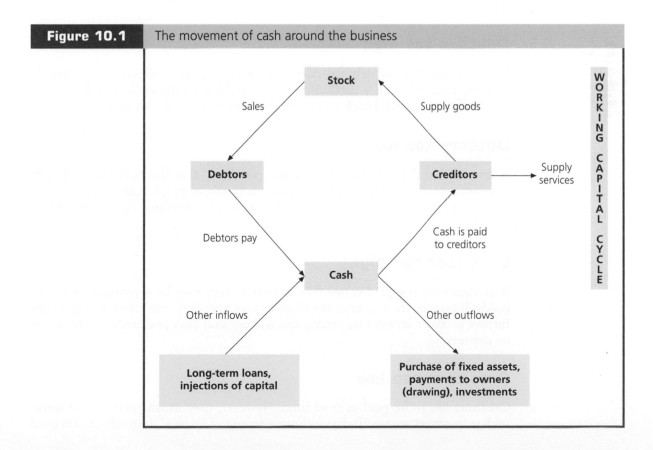

Mismanagement of working capital

In the following sub-sections we consider some of the consequences in cases where working capital is not managed properly.

Too much stock

A fairly common error in business is to tie up too much cash in the form of stock. This can lead to some of the following problems:

- If the stock comprises items that rapidly go out of fashion, the stock may lose most or all of its value before it can be sold.
- If the stock is perishable it may reach the end of its shelf life before it can be sold.
- It costs money to store stock safely. Additional costs may be incurred for no obvious benefit.
- If too much cash is tied up in stock it is not available for investment elsewhere in the business.

Too little stock

There may not be sufficient stock to fulfil orders; customers may therefore go elsewhere.

Debtors too high

Where a high level of debtors exists, the business is not collecting cash quickly enough. There may be a bottleneck in the working capital cycle which causes a shortage of cash, with knock-on effects on other parts of the business.

Debtors too low

A low level of debtors may indicate the possibility that the business is offering an insufficient level of credit to its customers. It may be possible to create a further inducement to buy goods from the business by extending the credit period available.

Creditors too high

If creditors are not paid reasonably promptly there may be a consequent loss of goodwill towards the business. In extreme cases, suppliers may refuse to supply any further goods or services on credit, and will demand cash payments in advance or on delivery.

Creditors too low

Creditors like to be paid in good time. However, they usually offer credit terms such as 'payment within 30 days following receipt of invoice'. It usually makes good business sense to pay towards the end of the time allowed and thus to take advantage of what is, effectively, a source of interest-free credit.

Cash too low

If the stock, debtor and creditor elements of working capital are mismanaged, the consequence may be that the cash level in the business is too low. It may become necessary to borrow cash, and borrowing, of course, costs money in the form of interest. Unauthorised overdrafts, in particular, can be very expensive, and good cash management involves anticipating any cash shortages and making appropriate arrangements in advance.

Cash too high

It may seem surprising that a business can suffer from the problem of too much cash, but it can happen. One of the reasons people go into business is to make profits in the form of a return on their investment. The return (or 'profit') made out of the initial investment in the business has to be greater than the return that can be made by leaving the money in a simple bank deposit account. Putting money into a bank account is easy, and requires virtually no effort on the part of the investor; by contrast, starting up a business requires a great deal of effort, and the investor expects a much greater reward.

If there is surplus cash in the business, what can be done with it? The simple, short-term answer is to place the money on deposit where it can earn interest. However, this is unlikely to represent a sufficient return, and the business owner will look for other opportunities for investment. Sometimes it makes sense to return the money in the form of a repayment of capital, so that the owner can invest in, for example, another business venture or a personal pension fund.

The distinction between profit and cash

In the long run, a profitable business will increase its supply of cash. However, and especially in the short term, profits are not the same as cash.

In Chapter 8 we looked at the concepts of recognition and realisation and concluded that accounting income is not the same as cash received, and accounting expenditure is not the same as cash paid. The matching (or accruals) concept requires that costs are matched against the income that they help to generate. In some cases this results in the recognition of income and costs that have not been received/paid in the form of cash. Annual charges for depreciation and amortisation, for example, are set against profits, but these charges do not involve any movement in cash.

Cash can be depleted or increased by transactions that do not affect the profit and loss account; for example, the purchase of fixed assets. When an item of machinery, for example, is purchased for use in the business, the asset of cash is replaced by a fixed asset. There is no immediate impact on profits, although they will be depleted over a period of time while the asset is depreciated. Table 10.1

looks at the implication for cash and profits of various transactions. Only in the case of the fourth transaction in the list – the sale for cash of £1600 – is the impact on cash and profit identical and simultaneous. All other cases result in a mismatch between cash and profit.

? Self-test question 10.1 (answer at the end of the book)

What is the effect on cash and on profit of the following business transactions?

1. Purchase of **raw materials** for cash of £1800.
2. Sale of old delivery van for £360.
3. Long-term loan from brother of £5000.
4. Payment of interest on bank overdraft of £150.
5. Amortisation charge of £8000 relating to patent rights.

Table 10.1

The impact of transactions on cash and profits

Transaction	Impact on cash	Impact on profits
Borrowing £10 000 at an annual interest rate of 10%. Loan to be repaid after five years.	Cash and long-term liabilities are both increased in the balance sheet by £10 000. After five years the loan will be repaid; cash and long-term liabilities will both be reduced by £10 000.	No immediate impact on profits. Each year for five years there will be an annual interest payment of £1000. This will decrease both cash and profit.
Purchasing a new car for £8000. The car is to be depreciated on the straight-line basis over four years, with the assumption of no residual value at the end of four years.	Cash is reduced and fixed assets are increased by £8000.	No immediate impact on profits. Each year for four years there will be a depreciation charge of £2000 (£8000/4), but this has no effect on cash.
Drawings of £3500.	Cash and capital are both reduced by £3500.	There is no impact on profit. Effectively, the owner is taking £3500 of his/her capital out of the business.

| Sale for cash of £1600. | Cash is increased immediately. | The sale is recognised immediately, and sales in the profit and loss account are increased by £1600. |
| Sale on credit for £1600. | Debtors are increased immediately. Provided that the debtor pays up, cash will be increased at some point in the near future. | The sale is recognised immediately, and sales in the profit and loss account are increased by £1600. |

Preparing a cash flow statement

So far in this section of the book we have examined the preparation of the profit and loss account and the balance sheet for sole trader businesses. It is also possible, and may very well be useful, to prepare a cash flow statement. This statement summarises the inflows and outflows of cash for an accounting period, usually of one year. Because, as we have seen, cash and profit are not the same, a cash flow statement can provide useful additional information that assists in understanding the performance and position of the business. Note that, except for some larger businesses (see Chapter 11 for more information), there is no absolute requirement to prepare a cash flow statement. However, it can provide some very useful information about a business that is not immediately obvious from a profit and loss account or balance sheet.

The procedures involved in preparing a cash flow statement will be illustrated first by reference to a new business start-up. Example 10.1 revisits the case of Isobel Buchanan, whose new business start-up was examined first in the case study in Chapter 6. Later, in the Chapter 9 case study, we examined the results of her first year in business. However, it is not necessary to revisit either of these chapters for information; the example sets out all the relevant details.

Example 10.1

Isobel's profit and loss account for her first year of trading, and her balance sheet at 28 February 20X2 are shown below. The expenses in the profit and loss account have been presented in a slightly different way in order to emphasise the totals for depreciation and amortisation, and for interest paid and received. Note that profit before interest is described as operating profit.

Buchanan International Designs: Profit and loss account for the year ending 28 February 20X2

	£	£
Sales		115 622
Cost of sales		(80 379)
Gross profit		35 243
Expenses		
Rental	14 000	
Insurance	717	
Electricity	2 346	
Telephone charges	686	
Staff	300	
Advertising	1 560	
Motor expenses	551	
Sundry expenses	3 446	
		(23 606)
Net profit before depreciation, amortisation and interest		11 637
Amortisation of lease	2 500	
Depreciation of display racks	900	
Depreciation of sundry fixtures and fittings	326	
Depreciation of van	1 625	
		(5 351)
Operating profit		6 286
Interest paid		(2 400)
Interest received		651
Net profit		4 537

Buchanan International Designs: Balance sheet at 28 February 20X2

	£	£
Fixed assets		
Intangible fixed assets		
Cost	10 000	
Less: accumulated amortisation	(2 500)	
		7 500
Tangible fixed assets		
Display racks at cost	4 500	
Less: accumulated depreciation	(900)	
		3 600
Sundry fixtures and fittings at cost	1 630	
Less: accumulated depreciation	(326)	
		1 304
Van at cost	6 500	
Less: accumulated depreciation	(1 625)	

	£	£
		4 875
		17 279
Current assets		
Stock	19 400	
Debtors and prepayments	3 520	
Prepayments	507	
Cash at bank	13 323	
	36 750	
Current liabilities		
Creditors	6 327	
Accruals	665	
	6 992	
Net current assets (£36 750 – £6992)		29 758
		47 037
Long-term liabilities		
Loan		(40 000)
		7 037
Capital		
Capital introduced		10 000
Add: profit for the year		4 537
Less: drawings		(7 500)
		7 037

Isobel started in business on 1 March 20X1 by putting cash into a new business bank account. The total cash deposited was £50 000, comprising a £40 000 loan from her uncle and aunt, and £10 000 of her own money. One year later we can see from her accounts that, although she has made a small profit of £4537, her bank balance has dwindled to £13 323, representing a drop of (£50 000 – £13 323) £36 677.

What has happened to the cash?

Isobel's balance sheet and profit and loss account convey a great deal of useful information, but are not obviously helpful in providing answers. A cash flow statement helps to answer the question by isolating the principal movements in cash.

Preparing a cash flow statement

Step 1

By convention, the first section in a cash flow statement examines profits adjusted for movements in working capital apart from cash (remember: working capital comprises items of stock, debtors, creditors and cash).

The starting point is operating profits. Isobel's operating profit (i.e. profit before interest) is £6286. This has been arrived at after deducting various items of depreciation and amortisation, which, as we saw earlier in this chapter, do not involve any movements in cash. Therefore, to get closer to a true cash figure, we add back those items that do not involve movements in cash:

	£
Operating profits	6 286
Add back: depreciation and amortisation	5 351
	11 637

Next, we adjust for investments in working capital in the form of stock, debtors and creditors:

- *Stock*. At the year-end of 28 February 20X2 Isobel has stock of £19 400. This will be converted into cash when sold, but that has not yet occurred. At 28 February 20X2 it represents a depletion of cash resources.
- *Debtors*. These are items that are waiting to be turned into cash; at the year-end £3520 of potential cash resource is locked up in debtors.
- *Prepayments*. These are amounts already paid for in cash, but for which services have not yet been received.
- *Creditors and accruals*. These are amounts yet to be paid by the business. Goods and services have already been received but have not yet been paid for. Cash balances will be lower once these amounts have been paid, but at the year-end point in time the cash to pay them has not yet left the business.

We add the following adjustments in respect of investments in working capital to the first section of the cash flow statement as follows:

	£	£
Operating profits		6 286
Add back: depreciation and amortisation		5 351
		11 637
Investment in working capital		
Stock	(19 400)	
Debtors	(3 520)	
Prepayments	(507)	
Creditors	6 327	
Accruals	665	
Net investment in working capital		(16 435)
Net cash outflow from operating activities		(4 798)

Step 2

The next step is to take into account all the other payments that have been made but which do not relate to changes in working capital:

1. *Interest received and paid*. Interest is separated out in a cash flow statement because it relates to financing, not operating activities. Interest received is £651 and interest paid is £2400.
2. *Capital expenditure*. In the first year in business, as is typically the case, Isobel has invested quite large sums in fixed assets. The total cash outflow relating to the investment of cash in fixed assets is:

	£
Intangible asset	10 000
Display racks	4 500

	£
Sundry fixtures and fittings	1 630
Van	6 500
Total	22 630

The cash outflow is shown separately in the cash flow statement.

3. *Other items.* Looking through the balance sheet at this point in the calculations we can see that most items have been taken into account in the cash flow statement. The only items remaining are the long-term loan (which involved a cash inflow of £40 000), Isobel's capital (a cash inflow of £10 000) and Isobel's drawings for the year (a cash outflow of £7500).

Step 3

We can now bring all the cash inflows and outflows together in a cash flow statement, as follows:

Buchanan International Designs: Cash flow statement for the year ending 28 February 20X2

	£	£
Operating profits		6 286
Add back: depreciation and amortisation		5 351
		11 637
Investment in working capital		
Stock	(19 400)	
Debtors	(3 520)	
Prepayments	(507)	
Creditors	6 327	
Accruals	665	
Net investment in working capital		(16 435)
Net cash outflow from operating activities		(4 798)
Interest		
Interest received (cash inflow)	651	
Interest paid (cash outflow)	(2 400)	
		(1 749)
Capital expenditure (cash outflow)		(22 630)
Proprietor's drawings (cash outflow)		(7 500)
Loan (cash inflow)		40 000
Capital introduced (cash inflow)		10 000
Net cash inflow		13 323
Cash balance at 28 February 20X2		13 323

Comments on cash flow statement

What additional information is provided by the cash flow statement? The aim of the cash flow statement is to provide explanations for the overall movement in cash in the accounting period. Neither the profit and loss account nor the balance sheet provide that information. In the cash flow statement presented above we isolate the major movements in cash. The outflow of cash into investments in various types of fixed asset is shown to have accounted for a substantial proportion of total spending. Also, we can see that operating activities and the movement of cash round the working capital cycle resulted in a net cash outflow. Both of these substantial outflows (i.e. on fixed assets and on investments in working capital) would be quite normal in the first year of a business.

The business does not have an immediate cash shortage, but it will need to generate cash (and profits) in the longer term in order to survive.

Direct and indirect approaches to cash flow

The example above shows the so-called 'indirect' approach to preparing cash flow statements. The first part of the statement prepared under the 'indirect' approach shows the cash flows derived from operating activities by taking profit and adjusting for non-cash items (in this case, depreciation and amortisation) and for investments in working capital.

There is an alternative: the so-called 'direct' method. This takes receipts from sales less payments for costs and expenses to arrive at a net cash flow from operating activities. This method is probably simpler to understand. However, in practice, businesses often use the 'indirect' method because the figures can be derived directly from the profit and loss account and balance sheet.

The 'direct' method explained

In the next example, we will present cash flow information for the first year of Isobel's business using the 'direct' method of preparing a cash flow statement.

Example 10.2

Isobel's total receipts of cash from sales in the year were £112 102.

Total payments for stock and the various categories of expenses (but excluding depreciation and amortisation, of course, because these do not involve any cash movement) were £116 900. The cash flow statement prepared under the 'direct' method is as follows:

Buchanan International Designs: Cash flow statement for the year ending 28 February 20X2

	£	£
Receipts from operating activities		112 102
Payments in respect of operating activities		(116 900)
Net cash outflow from operating activities		(4 798)

	£	£
Interest		
Interest received (cash inflow)	651	
Interest paid (cash outflow)	(2 400)	
		(1 749)
Capital expenditure (cash outflow)		(22 630)
Proprietor's drawings (cash outflow)		(7 500)
Loan (cash inflow)		40 000
Capital introduced (cash inflow)		10 000
Net cash inflow		13 323
Cash balance at 28 February 20X2		13 323

Note that it is only the upper part of the statement that changes. All the information relating to cash flows on capital expenditure and so on remain exactly the same.

Cash flow statements in an established business

Example 10.3 shows how a cash flow statement is prepared for an established business. In such cases, the information required is:

The opening balance sheet

The profit and loss account for the year

The closing balance sheet.

Example 10.3

Horst is in business as a sole trader, trading under the name of Box Distributors. His accountant has prepared a profit and loss account for the business for the year ending 31 December 20X5 and a balance sheet at that date. Horst approaches you in your capacity as a small business adviser to give him some advice on his cash flow. He shows you the financial statements and says:

'I can't quite understand what's happened here. My sales for 20X4 were £600 227 and they've increased this year to £636 636. The business is really doing quite well. I had to replace one of the delivery vehicles during the year, because it was unreliable, but I thought I'd been quite sensible about covering that spending. I got £5200 for it and extended the long-term bank loan by another £5000 which should have more or less covered the cost of the new van which was £10 660. I've made a big effort to control my own spending – I decided not to replace the BMW this year, and we went camping in France instead of going on that luxury cruise we'd planned. So, drawings are only slightly higher than they were in 20X4. Despite all this restraint the overdraft was almost £8000 at the year end. What's happened?'

Horst's profit and loss account for the year ending 31 December 20X5 and his balance sheets at 31 December 20X5 and 20X4 are shown below.

Box Distributors: profit and loss account for the year ending 31 December 20X5

	£
Sales	636 636
Less: cost of sales	(452 483)
Gross profit	184 153
Selling and distribution expenses (excluding depreciation)	(62 466)
Administration expenses (excluding depreciation)	(55 892)
Depreciation of delivery vehicles	(6 313)
Profit on sale of delivery vehicle	336
Depreciation of warehouse and machinery	(11 876)
Operating profit	47 942
Interest paid	(2 104)
Net profit	45 838

Box Distributors: balance sheets at 31 December 20X5 and 31 December 20X4

	20X5 £	20X5 £	20X4 £	20X4 £
Fixed assets				
Delivery vehicles at cost	35 897		33 650	
Less: accumulated depreciation	(16 960)		(14 196)	
		18 937		19 454
Warehouse and machinery at cost	118 760		118 760	
Less: accumulated depreciation	(71 256)		(59 830)	
		47 504		59 380
		66 441		78 834
Current assets				
Stock	52 687		45 611	
Debtors and prepayments	78 490		65 442	
Cash at bank	—		371	
	131 177		111 424	
Current liabilities				
Overdraft	7 996		—	
Creditors and accruals	39 943		42 417	
	47 939		42 417	
Net current assets		83 238		69 007
		149 679		147 841
Long-term liability – Loan		(15 000)		(10 000)
		134 679		137 841
Capital				
Capital brought forward		137 841		128 069
Profit for the year		45 838		58 222
Drawings		(49 000)		(48 450)
		134 679		137 841

A detailed analysis of the delivery vehicle accounts shows the following:

Cost	£
Delivery vehicles at 1 January 20X5	33 650
Disposal of vehicle	(8 413)
Addition of vehicle	10 660
Delivery vehicles at 31 December 20X5	35 897

Accumulated depreciation	
At 1 January 20X5	14 196
Accumulated depreciation on disposal	(3 549)
Depreciation charge for year (to profit and loss account)	6 313
At 31 December 20X5	16 960

A delivery vehicle was sold for £5200 during the year.

The first step is to prepare a cash flow statement. This is set out below, followed by detailed notes on its preparation.

Box Distributors: cash flow statement for the year ending

31 December 20X5

	£	£	Note
Operating profit		47 942	1
Add back: Depreciation of delivery vehicles	6 313		1
Profit on sale of delivery vehicle	(336)		1
Depreciation of warehouse and	11 876		1
machinery		17 853	1
		65 795	
Changes in working capital			
Stock (52 687 – 45 611) (cash outflow)	(7 076)		2
Debtors and prepayments (78 490 – 65 442) (cash outflow)	(13 048)		2
Creditors (39 943 – 42 417) (cash outflow)	(2 474)		2
Net change in working capital		(22 598)	
Net cash inflow from operating activities		43 197	
Interest paid		(2 104)	3
Capital expenditure (cash outflow)		(10 660)	4
Proceeds of sale of fixed asset (cash inflow)		5 200	4
Proprietor's drawings (cash outflow)		(49 000)	5
Increase in loan (cash inflow)		5 000	6
Net cash outflow		(8 367)	
Change in cash balance:			
Cash at 1 January 20X5		371	7
Overdraft at 31 December 20X5		(7 996)	7
Decrease in cash – net cash outflow (£371 + 7996)		(8 367)	7

Notes on preparation of the cash flow statement

1. The starting point, as in the case of Isobel's business, is operating profit. We must then add back all the items in the profit and loss account that do not involve cash movements: in the case of Box Distributors these are the depreciation charges for delivery vehicles and for the warehouse and machinery. We also make an adjustment for the profit made on the sale of the delivery vehicle (it may be helpful to refer back to the section in Chapter 9 on selling assets). Remember that a 'profit' or 'loss' on the sale of an asset represents either under- or over-depreciation; neither is a cash flow. However, cash is received in exchange for the asset and this will be reflected further down in the cash flow statement.

2. The changes in working capital must be calculated and recorded in this part of the statement. Comparing the working capital (i.e. current assets and current liabilities sections) in the two balance sheets we can see that:

   a) Stock has increased by £52 687 − £45 611 = £7076; there has been an additional investment in working capital in respect of this item.

   b) Debtors have increased by £78 490 − £65 442 = £13 048; this means that the business has more capital tied up in debtors at the end of the year than at the beginning, and there has been, effectively, a cash outflow in this respect.

   c) Creditors have decreased by £39 943 − £42 417 = £2474; this means that the business is obtaining less finance from its creditors than previously. This is equivalent to an outflow of cash.

3. The interest paid figure is taken from the business's profit and loss account.

4. The cash outflow on fixed assets is the figure for capital expenditure which is found in the detailed analysis of the delivery vehicles account. The inflow arising from the sale of the vehicle is shown in a note below that analysis.

5. Drawings are an outflow of cash from the business.

6. We can see by comparing the two balance sheets that the long-term liability has increased by £5000 to £15 000. This means that there has been an additional inflow of cash during the year.

7. The net inflow or outflow of cash that is calculated in the cash flow statement should equal the change in the balance of cash between the two year-ends. In the case of Box Distributors there has been a net outflow of cash of £8367. The final section of the cash flow statement 'proves' this figure by calculating the difference between cash at bank on 31 December 20X4 (a balance of £371) and the overdraft at 31 December 20X4 (a balance of £7996).

The second step in the exercise is to provide Horst with some advice about his cash flow. We will analyse the situation and then make some recommendations for reducing the business's overdraft.

Analysis

The overall net outflow of cash is over £8000. The principal cash inflows and outflows which have contributed to the increased overdraft are as follows:

A substantial investment in working capital of over £22 000. The total for debtors has increased by over £13 000, suggesting that the business has become significantly less successful at collecting money owed for credit sales. Stocks have also risen by a very significant amount.

The net cash inflow from operating activities is less than the total of drawings for the year. Drawings are therefore being removed from the accumulated capital of previous years.

Capital expenditure movements are not particularly significant in the year; the expenditure on the new vehicle is more or less covered by the proceeds of the sale of the old vehicle plus the increased borrowing from the bank.

The business is significantly less profitable in 20X5 than in the previous year. Net profit for 20X4 was £58 222 on sales of £600 227, a margin of 9.7%. The comparable margin for 20X5 is 7.2% (£45 838/636 636 × 100). This suggests the need for better control of costs.

Action to reduce the overdraft

In the next accounting period the principal action points to address include the following:

- Control costs to improve the net profit margin
- Reduce debtors by improving collection procedures
- If possible, reduce the amount of drawings from the business
- Reduce the amount of stock held so that less cash is tied up in this part of the working capital cycle.

The high profit/no cash paradox

In this chapter we have seen that profitability and availability of cash do not necessarily go hand in hand in the short term. The dislocation between profits and cash can create major short-term problems, even for very successful businesses.

Example 10.4

Adèle sells computer equipment, trading as Business Computer Specialist. She started in business six years ago and has done well, making a profit each year. However, about 18 months ago her business was the first in the UK to be granted the franchise to sell the XBS 0980, a specialist business computer system. She has become established as the principal supplier of the XBS 0980 and is likely to be supplied first with the XBS 0990 when it becomes available in the UK in the spring of 20X7.

Despite more than doubling her sales and nearly doubling net profits, Adèle's business is short of cash. During her accounting year to 31 December 20X6 she had to negotiate an overdraft of £20 000 with the bank, the first time since starting the business that she had done this. Later in the year, the overdraft facility was increased to £40 000 and Adèle is concerned that if things don't improve she will need to borrow more money. She has spent a total of £89 950 on new fixed assets during the year. Two new sales reps needed company cars, a lot of additional fixtures and fittings were required in the larger rented offices the business moved to, and the nearby warehouse, which is owned by the business, was extended to house all the additional stock.

The business profit and loss accounts for the years ending 31 December 20X5 and 20X6 are shown below, as are balance sheets at both dates.

Business Computer Specialist: Profit and loss accounts (summarised) for the years ending 31 December 20X5 and 31 December 20X6

	20X6 £	20X6 £	20X5 £	20X5 £
Sales		895 755		401 003
Less: cost of sales				
Opening stock	35 901		32 412	
Purchases	597 136		252 499	
	633 037		284 911	
	(78 700)		(35 901)	
Cost of sales		(554 337)		(249 010)
Gross profit		341 418		151 993
Expenses	204 016		82 278	
Depreciation	13 700		7 796	
		(217 716)		(90 074)
Operating profit		123 702		61 919
Interest received		—		988
Interest paid		(2 709)		—
Net profit		120 993		62 907
Gross profit margin		38.1%		37.9%
Net profit margin		13.5%		15.7%

Business Computer Specialist: Balance sheets at 31 December 20X6 and 20X5

	20X6 £	20X6 £	20X5 £	20X5 £
Fixed assets				
At cost	218 420		128 470	
Less: accumulated depreciation	(44 620)		(30 920)	
		173 800		97 550
Current assets				
Stock	78 700		35 901	
Debtors and prepayments	95 514		34 996	
Cash at bank	—		12 804	
	174 214		83 701	
Current liabilities				
Bank overdraft	33 679		—	
Creditors and accruals	65 490		24 399	
	99 169		24 399	

Net current assets	75 045	59 302
	248 845	156 852
Capital		
Capital brought forward	156 852	120 945
Profit for the year	120 993	62 907
Drawings	(29 000)	(27 000)
	248 845	156 852

From this information we can draw up a cash flow statement for the year ending 31 December 20X6. This will help us to analyse the problems that Adèle currently faces.

Business Computer Specialist: Cash flow statement for the year ending 31 December 20X6

	£	£
Operating profit		123 702
Add back: depreciation		13 700
		137 402
Changes in working capital		
Stock (£78 700 – £35 901) (cash outflow)	(42 799)	
Debtors and prepayments (£95 514 – £34 996) (cash outflow)	(60 518)	
Creditors (£65 490 – £24 399) (cash inflow)	41 091	
Net change in working capital		(62 226)
Net cash inflow from operating activities		75 176
Interest paid		(2 709)
Capital expenditure (cash outflow)*		(89 950)
Proprietor's drawings (cash outflow)		(29 000)
Net cash outflow		(46 483)
Change in cash balance		
Cash at 1 January 20X5		12 804
Overdraft at 31 December 20X5		(33 679)
Decrease in cash – net cash outflow (£12 804 + £33 679)		(46 483)

Capital expenditure: We are told in the introduction to the case study that Adèle has spent £89 950 on new fixed assets. It is also possible to work the figure out from the accounts, as follows:

	£
Fixed assets at net book value 31 December 20X5	97 550
Reduced by annual charge for depreciation in 20X6	(13 700)
	83 850
Fixed assets at net book value 31 December 20X6	173 800
Difference = purchases of fixed assets	89 950

The cash flow statement shows the principal causes of the decrease in cash/increase in overdraft. The business is expanding very fast, needing more fixed assets; nearly £90 000 has been spent in the year in acquiring new fixed assets. The next largest item has been the investment in working capital necessary to cope with the very rapid increase in sales. More sales means more stock on hand, and consequently, higher debtors and creditors. If the expansion continues at its present rate the business may need further overdraft facilities and possibly longer-term loans to fund the acquisition of more fixed assets.

It can be very difficult in practice to manage businesses that are expanding as fast as Business Computer Specialist. The problems such businesses encounter include:

■ Need to take on more staff very quickly. Poor quality personnel decisions may be made when management is under pressure to employ more people in a hurry.
■ Insufficient management time. Where small businesses grow very fast, the original proprietor is often swamped by the sheer weight and pace of decision making. Usually, in such circumstances, it is necessary to employ staff at managerial levels, but it can be difficult to get staff of the right calibre into positions quickly enough.
■ Loss of control over costs and stock. A consequence of rapid expansion is often that costs get out of hand, because the business does not have systems in place to control them properly. In the case of Adèle we can see that her net profit margin has, in fact, fallen between 20X5 and 20X6 although gross profit margin has remained more or less constant. This suggests possible difficulties in controlling costs.
■ Failure to control debtors. Debtors should convert into cash quite easily but some debtors need chasing to make them pay up. Where management time is short, amounts owed by debtors may be allowed to build up to unacceptable levels.
■ Chronic shortage of cash to fund additional working capital and new investment in fixed assets.

Business success brings its own problems. Where businesses expand very rapidly they can become victims of their own success, and may even fail. Growing businesses may need to have controls over expansion to ensure that it does not happen too quickly. In Adèle's case, she needs, as a matter of some urgency, to prepare forecasts for the coming year in order to see just how much of a problem shortage of cash is likely to be. It may be time for her to consider recruiting a qualified accountant to the management team. She probably also needs to consider employing other specialists in areas such as sales and personnel.

Chapter summary

This chapter introduced the role of cash in business by, firstly, examining the operation of the working capital cycle, and the problems that can occur when working capital is mismanaged. It emphasised the important distinction between cash and profits. Because of the operation of the matching (or accruals) principle, accounting income is not the same as cash received, and accounting expenditure is not the same as cash paid.

The chapter proceeded to examine the preparation of a third important accounting statement: the cash flow statement. The cash flow statement for the first year of trading in a new business was demonstrated, and then the Box Distributors example for the chapter examined the preparation of the cash flow statement in an established business.

The final example in the chapter highlighted the problems that can occur where a profitable and successful business expands very quickly. The cash flow statement for such a business provides answers to the very basic question: 'where has all the cash gone?'

Students often experience some difficulty in understanding the preparation and significance of cash flow statements. By carefully working through the examples in this chapter, and then applying their knowledge to the questions at the end of the chapter, students should find that they are equipped with all the necessary skills to understand the cash flow statement.

The end-of-chapter exercises are divided into two sections. The first section has answers provided at the end of the book.

 The second section, in the white box, has answers on the lecturers' section of the website. Finally, the chapter contains a case study that examines the preparation of a cash flow statement for an established business, and the provision of advice to its proprietor.

Website summary

The book's website contains the following material in respect of Chapter 10:

Students' section

- Quiz containing ten multiple choice questions and answers
- Four additional questions with answers
- Answer to case study at the end of this chapter.

Lecturers' section

- Answers to exercises 10.5–10.9
- Six additional questions with answers.

Exercises: answers at the end of the book

10.1 Fergus's business enters into the following transactions in the year to 31 December 20X2:

- Fergus introduces additional capital of £10 000 in cash.

- Purchase on credit of goods for resale for £8000.

- Payment received from debtor for £1800.

- Purchase of a new machine for use in the business. The machine costs £12 000 and will be depreciated over ten years on the straight-line basis, assuming no residual value, with a full year's depreciation in the year of acquisition.

- Sales returns of £1000 in exchange for a cash refund.

- Drawings of £1300.

For each transaction show the impact on cash, other assets and liabilities, and the impact on profits.

10.2 Gilbert's business sells a fixed asset for cash proceeds of £1300. The asset originally cost £20 700, and accumulated depreciation at the point of sale was £18 210. Three of the following six statements are correct:

1. Profits increase by £1190.

2. Profits decrease by £1190.

3. Cash increases by £1300.

4. Cash increases by £1190.

5. The net book value of fixed assets decreases by £2490.

6. The net book value of fixed assets decreases by £1300.

Which statements are correct?

a) 1, 3 and 6

b) 2, 3 and 5

c) 1, 4 and 5

d) 2, 4 and 6.

10.3 Gaston's business prepares accounts to 31 December each year. In the year ending 31 December 20X4 stock, debtors and creditors are shown in the balance sheet, with comparative figures at 31 December 20X3, as follows:

	20X4	20X3
	£	£
Stock	37 669	31 470
Debtors and prepayments	21 777	19 303
Creditors and accruals	18 250	16 264

Gaston's net profit for the year ending 31 December 20X4 is £36 790, after adding interest received of £763 and deducting total depreciation charges of £4585.

What is the net cash inflow from operating activities for inclusion in Gaston's cash flow statement for the year ending 31 December 20X4?

a) £47 299

b) £29 340

c) £33 925

d) £34 688.

10.4 Henrietta runs a business, trading as Spicer & Co. She prepares accounts to 31 March each year. By the year-end 31 March 20X4 the business has run into overdraft. Henrietta asks you to prepare a cash flow statement for the business for the year ending 31 March 20X4 and she provides you with the following information:

Spicer & Co: Profit and loss account (summarised) for the year ending

31 March 20X4

	£
Sales	598 731
Less: cost of sales	(430 131)
Gross profit	168 600
Expenses excluding depreciation	(79 633)
Depreciation	(12 471)
Operating profit	76 496
Interest paid	(230)
Net profit	76 266

Spicer & Co.: Balance sheets at 31 March 20X4 and 31 March 20X3

	20X4 £	20X4 £	20X3 £	20X3 £
Fixed assets				
At cost	175 630		128 547	
Less: accumulated depreciation	(67 248)		(54 777)	
		108 382		73 770
Current assets				
Stock	40 747		36 600	
Debtors and prepayments	50 661		48 730	
Cash at bank	—		7 423	
	91 408		92 753	
Current liabilities				
Bank overdraft	1 348		—	
Creditors and accruals	36 644		35 191	
	37 992		35 191	

	£	£	£	£
Net current assets		53 416		57 562
		161 798		131 332
Capital				
Capital brought forward		131 332		111 335
Profit for the year		76 266		61 297
Drawings		(45 800)		(41 300)
		161 798		131 332

Note: There were no disposals of fixed assets during the year.

You are required to prepare a cash flow statement for Spicer & Co. for the year ending 31 March 20X4.

Exercises: answers available to lecturers

10.5 Flynn's business enters into the following transactions in the year to 31 March 20X5:

- Purchase of stock for cash of £1300.

- Sale of a fixed asset with a written down value of £300. The sale proceeds are £900.

- Sale on credit for £3500.

- Payment made to creditor for electricity bill of £6350.

- Drawings of £800.

- Purchase of a motor vehicle for use in the business. The vehicle costs £10 000 and is to be depreciated, with a full year's depreciation in the year of acquisition, at 25% per annum.

For each transaction show the impact on cash, other assets and liabilities, and the impact on profits.

10.6 Describe the problems that can arise where a business ties up too much of its cash in stock.

10.7 Grant's business makes an operating profit of £16 632 in the year ending 30 April 20X1. One of the deductions in arriving at operating profit was depreciation of £6650.

At 30 April 20X1 the balance sheet showed stock of £26 750, debtors and prepayments of £12 704 and creditors of £11 667. On 30 April 20X0 the corresponding figures were: stock £27 997; debtors and prepayments £11 940; and creditors £9975.

What is the net cash inflow from operating activities to be included in Grant's cash flow statement for the year ending 30 April 20X1?

a) £21 107

b) £18 807

c) £22 073

d) £25 457.

10.8 Gunter's business sells an item of machinery for £2660 on 30 June 20X6. The balances at the beginning of the accounting year (1 January 20X6) for the asset were: cost = £17 700; accumulated depreciation = £15 930.

Gunter charges depreciation on this class of asset at the rate of 10% per annum on cost, with a month's depreciation charged for each full month of ownership in the year of disposal. He has assumed a nil residual value for this asset.

Two of the following eight statements are correct:

1. Profits decrease by £890.

2. Profits increase by £890.

3. Profits increase by £1775.

4. Profits decrease by £1775.

5. Cash increases by £2660.

6. Cash increases by £1775.

7. Cash decreases by £2660.

8. Cash decreases by £1775.

Which statements are correct?

a) 1 and 7

b) 4 and 6

c) 2 and 8

d) 3 and 5.

10.9 Hamid prepares his business financial statements to 31 May each year. Because he attended an accounting course at college he knows how to prepare profit and loss accounts and balance sheets. However, the course did not include the preparation of cash flow statements and Hamid asks you to prepare a cash flow statement for his business for the year ending 31 May 20X2. He supplies you with the following information:

Hamid: Profit and loss account (summarised) for the year ending

31 May 20X2

	£
Sales	437 500
Less: cost of sales	(298 423)

	£
Gross profit	139 077
Expenses excluding depreciation	(62 505)
Depreciation	(7 662)
Operating profit	68 910
Interest received	634
Interest paid	(506)
Net profit	69 038

Hamid: Balance sheets at 31 May 20X2 and 31 May 20X1

	20X2 £	20X2 £	20X1 £	20X1 £
Fixed assets				
At cost	82 610		38 750	
Less: accumulated depreciation	(21 462)		(13 800)	
		61 148		24 950
Current assets				
Stock	26 980		27 420	
Debtors and prepayments	44 349		42 760	
Cash at bank	5 354		6 642	
	76 683		76 822	
Current liabilities				
Loan	—		5 000	
Creditors and accruals	23 730		28 459	
	23 730		33 459	
Net current assets		52 953		43 363
		114 101		68 313
Capital				
Capital brought forward		68 313		33 766
Profit for the year		69 038		63 291
Drawings		(23 250)		(28 744)
		114 101		68 313

Note the following:

1. There were no disposals of fixed assets during the year.

2. Following your request Hamid supplies the following information relating to cash receipts and payments during the year: cash receipts = £435 911; cash payments = £365 217.

   You are required to prepare Hamid's cash flow statement for the year ending 31 May 20X2 using a) the indirect method; and b) the direct method.

! CASE STUDY 10.1   Advising using cash flow statements

Delroy Desmond has run a pizza restaurant for several years, trading as Dezzie's. He also provides a pizza delivery service to homes and a lunchtime delivery service to local offices, some of whom are supplied on credit terms. In the year ending 31 March 20X4 he has opened a new branch in another town, obtaining a mortgage loan to purchase freehold premises and to pay for some alterations to the premises. Delroy did not spend much on fixtures and fittings; he had some unused tables, crockery and so on in the store room of the existing premises and he transferred these over to the new branch.

Delroy is keen to expand the business further and would like to draw up a formal expansion programme. He has commissioned a market research survey of a representative sample of his customers from a firm of consultants. The survey report quotes some of the more negative reactions of the customers:

- 'Not enough staff on at weekends.'
- 'I had to wait almost two hours for my pizza delivery last week.'
- 'Great pizzas – shame the restaurant's so tatty.'
- 'You'd never think it was a brand new restaurant – it looks like it could do with a refit already.'
- 'That manager was so rude, I didn't go back for six months.'
- 'The delivery man said his bike had broken down; that's why the pizzas were stone cold when I got them.'

The consultant concludes that, although the standard of the product is high and there are many satisfied customers, there are quite a lot of staffing and premises-related problems. He recommends re-equipping the restaurants and replacing the existing managers with higher paid staff. Delroy accepts both the criticisms and the recommendations but realises that he probably does not have enough cash to address all the problems straight away. Delroy has asked his accountant to prepare a cash flow statement in addition to the usual accounting statements. Details of his profit and loss account for the year ending 31 March 20X4 and his balance sheets at 31 March 20X4 and 31 March 20X3 are supplied below.

The following is required: prepare the cash flow statement (using the indirect method) for Dezzie's for the year ending 31 March 20X4; and summarise for Delroy the key points that emerge from the cash flow statement, advising him, as far as possible from the information given, on the financial implications of following the consultant's advice.

Dezzie's: Profit and loss account for the year ending 31 March 20X4

	£	£
Sales		341 077
Less: cost of sales		
Opening stock	5 630	
Purchases	91 889	
	97 519	
	(6 186)	
Cost of sales		(91 333)
Gross profit		249 744
Expenses		
Restaurant heat and light	18 450	
Premises costs	18 295	
Salaries and wages	78 904	
Delivery expenses	6 411	
Telephone charges	6 349	
Advertising and marketing	6 904	
General administration expenses	5 966	
Consultants' fees	12 500	
Insurance	3 690	
Accounting and taxation advice	3 850	
Legal fees	1 000	
Sundry expenses	775	
Depreciation on buildings	2 000	
Depreciation on fixtures and fittings	1 829	
Depreciation on delivery vehicles	4 763	
Profit on disposal of delivery vehicle	(520)	
		(171 166)
Operating profit		78 578
Interest received	(280)	
Interest paid	4 617	
		(4 337)
Net profit		74 241

Dezzie's: Balance sheets at 31 March 20X4 and 20X3

	20X4 £	20X4 £	20X3 £	20X3 £
Fixed assets				
Land and buildings	147 900		44 900	
Less: accumulated depreciation	(11 140)		(9 140)	
		136 760		35 760
Fixtures and fittings	18 290		16 251	
Less: accumulated depreciation	(12 419)		(10 590)	
		5 871		5 661

	£	£	£	£
Delivery vehicles	21 603		12 920	
Less: accumulated depreciation	(8 313)		(8 450)	
		13 290		4 470
		155 921		45 891

Current assets

Stock	6 186		5 630	
Debtors and prepayments	5 914		7 419	
Cash at bank	3 240		15 160	
	15 340		28 209	

Current liabilities

Creditors and accruals	8 510		6 340	

Net current assets

		6 830		21 869
		162 751		67 760

Long-term liability

Mortgage loan		(73 750)		—
		89 001		67 760

Capital

Capital brought forward		67 760		50 816
Profit for the year		74 241		59 444
Drawings		(53 000)		(42 500)
		89 001		67 760

Notes on the balance sheet

Land and buildings

Movements in the year ending 31 March 20X4 on land and buildings at cost and on accumulated depreciation are as follows:

	£
Cost	
Land and buildings at cost 1 April 20X3	44 900
Additions at cost	103 000
Land and buildings at cost 31 March 20X4	147 900

	£
Depreciation	
Accumulated depreciation 1 April 20X3	9 140
Depreciation for the year	2 000
Accumulated depreciation 31 March 20X4	11 140

Net book value at 31 March 20X4 is £147 900 – £11 140 = £136 760.

Fixtures and fittings

Movements in the year ending 31 March 20X4 on fixtures and fittings at cost and on accumulated depreciation are as follows:

	£
Cost	
Fixtures and fittings at cost 1 April 20X3	16 251
Additions at cost	2 039
Fixtures and fittings at cost 31 March 20X4	18 290

	£
Depreciation	
Accumulated depreciation 1 April 20X3	10 590
Depreciation for the year	1 829
Accumulated depreciation 31 March 20X4	12 419

Net book value at 31 March 20X4 is £18 290 − £12 419 = £5 871.

Delivery vehicles

Movements in the year ending 31 March 20X4 on delivery vehicles at cost and on accumulated depreciation are as follows:

	£
Cost	
Delivery vehicles at cost 1 April 20X3	12 920
Disposal of vehicle*	(6 500)
Additions at cost	15 183
Delivery vehicles at cost 31 March 20X4	21 603

	£
Depreciation	
Accumulated depreciation 1 April 20X3	8 450
Disposal of vehicle*	(4 900)
Depreciation for the year	4 763
Accumulated depreciation 31 March 20X4	8 313

*The vehicle was sold for £2120. The net book value at the point of sale was £6500 − £4900 = £1600. Profit on sale was, therefore, £2120 − £1600 = £520. (Note that this is included in the profit and loss account for the year.)

Net book value at 31 March 20X4 is £21 603 − £8 313 = £13 290.

CHAPTER 11

Financial reporting by limited companies

Aim of the chapter

To understand the nature of company financial reporting, including an appreciation of the accounting regulatory framework applicable to companies.

Learning outcomes

After reading the chapter and completing the related exercises, students should:

- Understand in outline the regulations relating to accounting by companies.
- Understand the roles of directors in respect of company financial reports.
- Be able to draw up a set of financial statements for a simple limited company.
- Understand the need for additional financial and non-financial reporting by listed companies.

Introduction to accounting by limited companies

Some of the chapters in Section One of this book touched on various matters relating to limited companies. In Chapter 1 we considered the different forms of business organisation, including limited companies. In Chapter 4 we examined issues relating to financing of limited companies through the stock market, and Chapter 5 touched on the separation between the ownership and the management of capital that is characteristic of larger companies, and identified the principal users of the financial information produced by companies. Some of the information in these earlier chapters is reviewed in this chapter in order to provide a context for the examination of the regulation and practice relating to'company financial statements, which is the principal focus of the chapter.

In this chapter we will examine in more detail the nature of limited companies and their accounting.

The limited company

The limited company has been an important form of business organisation since the middle of the 19th century in the United Kingdom. The need for this type of organisation developed as industrial organisations became larger, and as greater amounts of capital were required to fund the expansion of, for example, the railway system. It is unlikely that one single individual would be wealthy enough to fund a major institution like a railway or a bank, and so a legal mechanism that allows for ownership to be shared is very useful in the development of advanced economies. Most capitalist countries have adopted ownership vehicles akin to the UK limited company, and in most of Europe this development took place during the 19th century.

A company is a convenient form of organisation in that:

- It allows for investments of differing amounts to be made by a potentially very large group of individuals or organisations.
- In the form in which it is most commonly found in the UK and elsewhere, it offers investors the protection of limited liability. This useful mechanism ensures that investors are liable for no more than their original investment.
- A company is regarded as a 'person' in law. It can sue or be sued, can hold bank accounts and other forms of assets, and it can be named as a contracting party in legal contracts. The individuals investing in it are protected by the so-called 'veil of incorporation'.
- The structure of the capital of a limited company in the form of shares lends itself to shared ownership by many parties, and, in some cases, access to markets in which share capital can be easily exchanged for cash.
- It can offer certain tax advantages over sole trader and partnership forms of organisation.

Limited liability

Limited liability confers a great advantage upon investors in shares of companies. By contrast, a sole trader or a partner in a partnership is exposed to unlimited liability, to the extent of his or her own personal assets, in respect of business dealings.

There is, potentially, a corresponding disadvantage for the creditors of limited liability companies. Creditors of business organisations always face the risk that they will not be paid; but if a limited company fails to pay, the creditors may have very little chance of successfully pursuing an action against the company. If it has no assets, the creditors will simply not be paid. Consider the following example.

Example 11.1

On 1 June 20X4 Elba Limited places an order with a supplier, Tommy, to supply stock on credit to a value of £3000. Tommy supplies the goods, but then Elba goes out of business on 10 August 20X4, without having paid Tommy any of the money owing to him. Elba Limited has the following balance sheet at 31 May 20X4:

	£	£
Fixed assets		8 000
Current assets		
Stock	1 250	
Debtors	1 000	
	2 250	
Current liabilities		
Creditors	2 550	
Overdraft	6 300	
	8 850	
Net current liabilities		(6 600)
Net assets		1 400
Share capital		100
Accumulated reserves		1 300
Capital and reserves		1 400

By 10 August 20X4 Elba's position has deteriorated. The balance sheet shows the following position:

	£	£
Fixed assets		8 000
Current assets		
Stock	5 250	
Debtors	1 600	
	6 850	
Current liabilities		
Creditors	8 940	
Overdraft	8 300	
	17 240	

	£	£
Net current liabilities		(10 390)
Net liabilities		(2 390)
Share capital		100
Accumulated losses		(2 490)
Capital and reserves		(2 390)

Elba's bank manager refuses to extend the overdraft any further and the company must cease to trade.

Where does Tommy stand as regards recovering the money due to him? In this case he may recover some of his money, but probably not all of it. In total, there are creditors of £17 240, of which Tommy's amount due is £3000. The balance sheet shows total assets of £14 850, a shortfall of £2390. However, the asset values may not be realistic estimates of the amounts that can be recovered by selling the assets.

Fixed assets, as we know, are presented in the balance sheet at cost less depreciation. The net book value may be higher than the amounts for which the assets can be sold. The debtors figure of £1600 may not be fully recoverable, and perhaps the stock could not be sold for the full amount stated in the balance sheet.

Suppose the assets of Elba could be liquidated as follows:

	£
Fixed assets in a forced sale	6 000
Debtors – amounts actually receivable	1 400
Stock in a forced sale	4 500
Total amount of cash that can be raised	11 900

Against total liabilities of £17 240 there is a shortfall of £5340, or just over 30%. The creditors cannot be repaid in full, and are likely to receive at most about 70% of the value of the sums due to them. In practice, this proportion will be reduced by accountants' fees for doing the work of winding up the company (yes: the accountants are paid before the other 'ordinary' creditors) and by any amounts due to the Customs and Excise and the Inland Revenue (who take precedence over other creditors). Note that the shareholders in Elba would lose the whole of their investment in share capital. However, the share capital amounts only to £100, and the loss is small compared to the loss that will be suffered by Tommy and other creditors.

Information needs

Information needs of company creditors

The situation outlined in Example 11.1 may seem very unfair to creditors. How could Tommy have avoided losing money? Well, if he had been aware of Elba's weak position he could have either refused to trade with the company, or he could have insisted on receiving the cash in advance. Either way, he would have been protected from loss.

It is partly to protect creditors like Tommy that regulation exists to ensure that companies are obliged to make certain financial details available to the public. If creditors are in possession of accounting information they are able to make better decisions. Even so, creditors like Tommy are rarely in possession of all the relevant facts. Companies are obliged to make information available within ten months of their year-end (seven months for some larger companies); by the time the information becomes available the company's position may have altered very significantly.

Information needs of company shareholders

Companies, especially larger companies, are sometimes owned and managed by different people. Where company directors and shareholders are two different groups of people (or two groups that overlap only partially), it is important that the directors are held to account for the way in which they have managed the shareholders' investments. (This accountability is known by the rather old-fashioned term stewardship.) Therefore, there are regulatory requirements to ensure that shareholders receive information in a standard form about the companies they have invested in. If the shareholders are unhappy about the way in which directors have managed the company, they can vote the directors out of office and replace them. Although there may be many shareholders, especially in very large companies, directors are voted out of office comparatively rarely.

Information needs of people other than shareholders and creditors

There are other groups of people who may be interested in the information made available by companies (see also Chapter 5). These include employees, customers, financial journalists, the government, academics and the general public.

In the next section of the chapter the nature of company regulation, especially in respect of accounting, is examined in outline.

Regulation of company accounting and other issues

There are few regulations governing accounting by sole traders. By contrast, accounting and financial reporting by companies is subject to comparatively heavy regulation. Some of the principal sources and features of company regulation will be explained in this section.

Companies Acts

Since the mid-19th century the conduct of companies has been subject to legal regulation in the form of Acts of parliament. Currently in the UK there are two Companies Acts in force: the Companies Acts 1985 and 1989. It is principally the earlier Act that concerns us.

The 1985 Companies Act contains many complex legal regulations relating to:

- formation of new companies and types of company
- company constitutional arrangements including the issue of shares
- role of directors
- the audit of companies
- publication and presentation of accounting information.

The 1985 Act introduced many aspects of European company law into UK legislation; in particular, standard formats for the presentation of company profit and loss accounts and balance sheets were introduced. These will be examined in more detail later in the chapter.

A major review of company law took place in the UK between 1999 and 2001. Company law as it stands has been criticised for retaining the same basic structure originally established in the Victorian era. It is argued that Victorian company law was appropriate for the 19th century but, as it now stands, it is an encumbrance to a modern economy. The proposals, many of which are radical, are currently under review and may well be considered by parliament in the near future. However, at the time of writing, company law in the UK retains many very traditional features. Some of the principal elements are discussed in the following sub-sections:

Company formation and types of company

Setting up a limited company is quite straightforward and is an inexpensive procedure (it can cost less than £100). It is usually handled by a professionally qualified accountant or solicitor, or by one of the specialist company formation firms. Certain forms have to be registered with Companies House, and there are provisions to ensure that a company is not registered with a name identical to that of an existing company.

There are two principal types of company under English law (note that English law applies to England and Wales, while arrangements in Scotland and Northern Ireland may differ):

1. *The private company*: this has a minimum of one shareholder, and one director. The word 'limited' is attached to the name of the company (in English or Welsh).

2. *The public limited company*: this must be described in its memorandum of association (see below) as a public company, its name must end in 'public limited company' or 'plc' (or the Welsh equivalents) and it must have a share capital of £50 000, at least 25% of which has been issued for cash.

Larger companies tend to be plcs. However, comparatively large businesses may be private companies. In order to be permitted to issue shares to the general public a company must be constituted as a plc. Only plcs may be listed on a stock exchange, but not all plcs are listed. (See Chapter 4 for further discussion of listing.)

Company constitutional arrangements including the issue of shares

There are formal arrangements in law for company meetings. An annual general meeting (AGM) must take place (although there are certain exemptions for very small companies), and shareholders must be permitted to vote democratically on resolutions at that meeting. The normal agenda for an AGM includes the following:

- acceptance of the directors' report and the financial statements
- authorisation for payment of dividend (and confirmation of dividends already paid)
- election of directors
- appointment of auditors
- any other business.

All companies are required to issue a memorandum of association and articles of association. The memorandum sets out the purposes for which the company is set up (usually framed in very broad terms) and the authorised share capital. The articles of association contain the company's internal constitution, including, for example, appropriate arrangements for appointment of directors, voting by shareholders, powers of directors and directors' expenses, pensions and remuneration.

Note that the authorised share capital is the quantity of shares that the company is authorised to issue. It does not have to issue all of the authorised capital, and, indeed, many companies do not. Therefore, issued share capital may be a lesser amount. The most common type of share capital is ordinary share capital. Each share carries the right to vote at the AGM and the right to receive a dividend (if any). Each ordinary share has a nominal value, which is commonly one of the following: 5p, 10p, 25p, 50p or £1.

Decisions on the amount of ordinary dividend to be paid are made by the company's directors. Ordinary dividends for an accounting year are often paid in two instalments: an interim dividend and a final dividend. At the year-end the final dividend may not have actually been paid out, and if so, it is included as a creditor in the balance sheet under current liabilities.

Some companies issue preference share capital. This differs substantially from ordinary share capital, in that preference shares carry a fixed rate of dividend (and are described as, for example, 8% preference shares), and have no vote at the AGM. Such shares are referred to as 'preference shares' because their dividends have to be paid out in preference to any dividend on the ordinary shares. Because there is a fixed rate of return on preference shares, they are really more akin to a long-term loan. Some preference shares are cumulative; that is, if the company does not pay the dividend on the shares, the obligation to pay is carried forward to the next following year.

Example 11.2

Pauletta Limited has an authorised share capital of £40 000, split into shares of 25 pence each. Half of the shares are issued. In the year ending 31 December 20X4 a dividend of 4p per share is declared.

Li Ming owns 5000 shares in Pauletta Limited:

a) What is the nominal value of the issued share capital of Pauletta Limited, and how many shares are in issue?
b) What is the total value of the dividend declared for the year ending 31 December 20X4?
c) What is the value of Li Ming's dividend for the year ending 31 December 20X4?

Answer

a) Pauletta Limited's authorised share capital, in terms of numbers of shares is £40 000 / 25p = 160 000. Half of those shares are in issue, i.e. 80 000. The nominal value of those shares is 80 000 × 25p = £20 000.
b) The dividend is 4p per share; total value is 4p × 80 000 = £3200.
c) Li Ming's dividend is 4p × 5000 (the number of shares held) = £200.

Example 11.3

Birch and Beech Limited has both ordinary shares and preference shares in issue, as follows:

- authorised and issued ordinary share capital: 30 000 £1 shares
- preference share capital: £50 000 7% preference shares.

The directors of the company declare an ordinary dividend of 5% of nominal share value in the year ending 31 December 20X1. The preference dividend is also paid.
 What is the total amount of dividend payable by Birch and Beech Limited for the year ending 31 December 20X1?

Answer

	£
Ordinary dividend: £30 000 × 5%	1 500
Preference dividend: £50 000 × 7%	3 500
Total	5 000

Role of directors

Company directors have important responsibilities under the law, and an appointment as a director is not to be taken lightly. Directors are required to act in good faith in the interests of the company (which may not be the same as the interests of shareholders). If a company loses money through the actions of directors, it may be able to reclaim the money from the directors even if they acted in what they thought were the best interests of the company.
 In respect of accounting and related requirements, directors must:

- Keep adequate accounting records.
- Prepare accounts each year, which must be filed within certain time limits with the Registrar of Companies. The accounts must include a directors' report.
- Ensure that the company does not trade while insolvent (note that the example of Elba Limited used earlier demonstrates an insolvent company balance sheet at 10 August 20X4).

The accounts of a company must present a 'true and fair view' (this is a legal term which has existed in company law for over half a century) of the performance and state of affairs of the company. Although the directors themselves do not all necessarily take part in the preparation of the accounts (the task is often delegated to a finance director or company accountant) they nevertheless take complete responsibility in law for the preparation and filing of accounts. Fines are quite frequently levied on directors by Companies House in respect of late filing of accounts. Late filing is a criminal offence and guilty directors may end up with a criminal record.

Allowing a company to trade while insolvent can have very serious consequences for individual directors. Directors may be ordered by the courts to make contributions out of their personal resources if they have allowed the company to continue trading in circumstances where there is no reasonable prospect of avoiding liquidation. If it is proven that directors have deliberately defrauded creditors a criminal offence is involved; they may be disqualified as a director, fined or even imprisoned.

Claiming ignorance is no defence. If people are appointed as directors they should fully understand their responsibilities and the possible adverse consequences of failing to meet those responsibilities. All members of the board of directors are equally responsible in law.

Publication and presentation of accounting information

As illustrated in Example 11.1, publication of financial information is of great importance to many interested parties. Companies are required to file their annual accounts at Companies House where they are available for inspection by any interested party. However, the meaning of 'annual accounts' varies depending upon the size of the company. Small and medium-sized companies are entitled to take advantage of exemptions that allow them to file a quite limited amount of information at Companies House. Small companies, for example, are not required to file a profit and loss account, and are entitled to restrict the amount of information they provide in the balance sheet and supporting notes. Medium-sized companies, while they are required to file a profit and loss account, are permitted to start the profit and loss statement with gross profit, so that they do not have to disclose turnover.

In order to qualify as small or medium-sized, companies must meet two out of three criteria relating to turnover, balance sheet size and number of employees. The current criteria are shown in Table 11.1 below.

Table 11.1	Criteria for small and medium-sized companies		
	Turnover	Balance sheet total	Number of employees
Small company	Not more than £5.6 million	Not more than £2.8 million	Not more than 50
Medium-sized company	Not more than £22.8 million	Not more than £11.4 million	Not more than 250

The turnover and balance sheet total limits are changed from time to time.

The main reason for allowing small and medium-sized companies to file a reduced amount of accounting information is to ensure that competitors do not have access to information that may harm the interests of the business. The reduction in filing requirements does not save these companies much, if anything, in costs because a full set of accounts has still to be prepared for the shareholders.

Later in the chapter presentation requirements for company financial statements are examined in more detail.

The audit of companies

Until a few years ago, all limited companies required a formal audit by a qualified chartered or certified accountant. The auditor examines the books and records of the business, and compares them to the final accounts. He or she issues an audit report addressed to the company shareholders, which states whether or not the accounts present a true and fair view.

Gradually, over the last few years, the requirement for company audit has been progressively restricted because it was felt to be a bureaucratic burden for companies. Where there are only one or two shareholders, who are probably the company directors, it seems a waste of resources to have a formal audit. Currently small companies (see the previous section of the chapter for the definition of a small company) are exempted from the audit requirement. Small companies can, of course, choose to have an audit if they wish. Sometimes it can be useful to do so: if a small company wishes to borrow a substantial sum of money from a bank it may assist the case if there is a set of audited accounts available to show the bank manager.

Accounting standards

The Companies Acts contain various requirements as to the preparation and presentation of accounting information by companies. However, these requirements are often quite general in nature, and a need has emerged over the last 50 years or so for more detailed guidance on how specific accounting issues should be dealt with in the accounts of companies and other business organisations. The accountancy professional bodies have been responsible for providing an additional layer of accounting regulation in the form of accounting standards.

Before 1990 accounting standards were issued in the United Kingdom by the Accounting Standards Committee (ASC), which comprised senior members of the accounting profession. The ASC issued Statements of Standard Accounting Practice (SSAPs), some of which are still current (such as SSAP 9 dealing with the subject of accounting for stock).

Since 1990, accounting standards in the UK have been issued by the Accounting Standards Board (ASB), a more broadly based organisation that represents a wider constituency of interest groups than the accountancy profession. To date, 20 Financial Reporting Standards (FRSs) have been issued by the ASB. Many of these are on very complex topics beyond the scope of this book, but, for example, FRS 15 deals with accounting for fixed assets, including regulations relating to depreciation.

International accounting standards

International accounting standards have been issued since the 1970s when the International Accounting Standards Committee (IASC) was established. In recent years international standards have become increasingly important as the volume of global trading has increased. Where, as is more and more frequently the case, companies and individuals are investing in companies based in other countries, it becomes important that financial statements should be comprehensible and comparable internationally. One means of achieving this goal is to have an internationally accepted approach to accounting so that people can invest across borders with some confidence in the financial information they are using as a basis for decision making. The international standard setting body has therefore gained in importance and stature in recent years. In 2001, the IASC was replaced by the International Accounting Standards Board (IASB) which is now responsible for setting international standards, known as International Financial Reporting Standards (IFRS).

How important are international standards? The European Union has now decided that all listed companies in its member states should prepare their financial statements to comply with international standards from 2005 onwards. This means that companies listed on the UK Stock Exchange will no longer adhere to UK standards after 1 January 2005. UK standards will continue to exist for the guidance of unlisted companies and other types of entity, but their importance will diminish. The Department of Trade and Industry in the UK has decided that unlisted companies will have the option of complying either with UK standards or with international standards. Therefore, over time, it can be expected that fewer and fewer businesses will comply with UK standards.

Outside Europe, too, international standards are gaining in importance. Australia and New Zealand will shortly be adopting them, and there is a project underway in collaboration with the US standard setter to bring USA and international accounting practice closer together.

It is beyond the scope of this book to examine international standards in any detail. However, it is worth noting that the layout of the principal accounting statements prepared under international standards differs from the layout generally used in the UK (and in this book). Some of the terminology differs too: for example, a profit and loss account is known internationally as an income statement, stock is known as inventory, and trade creditors are trade payables. Many companies already use international accounting standards: for example, in Germany, there has been an option for some years for listed companies to report under German, US or international accounting rules. An example of a business that prepares its financial statements in accordance with international standards is Volkswagen AG. Their financial statements are available on the company's website at **www.Volkswagen.de** (the website can be viewed in English).

Accounting for limited companies

The basics of accounting remain the same, regardless of the form of organisation. The accounting equation, for example, which was explained in Chapter 6, holds good whether the accounting is for a sole trader, a partnership or a limited company. However, accounting for limited companies involves the introduction of some additional complexities into the profit and loss account and balance sheet.

Components of a set of limited company accounts

Under the law, a set of accounts for a limited company comprises the following:

- a profit and loss account
- a balance sheet
- notes to the accounts
- directors' report
- auditors' report (where applicable).

In addition, FRS1 requires the inclusion of a cash flow statement for companies that do not qualify as 'small' under the Companies Act.

The contents of the profit and loss account and balance sheet are dealt with in detail elsewhere in this chapter and in Section Two of this book. Notes to the accounts can be highly complex in practice. They contain a great deal of supporting explanatory detail about the figures in the accounts, much of which is required by law or by various accounting standards. There are quite extensive requirements, for example, relating to the disclosure of directors' remuneration.

The directors' report is a quite formal document, which must contain explanation and comment on a range of items, including:

- description of the principal activities of the company
- review of the development of the business
- a note of political and charitable donations.

Presentation of accounting information

As noted earlier in the chapter, UK company law prescribes formats for the profit and loss account and balance sheet statements. There are two permissible balance sheet formats, and four profit and loss account formats. However, in the UK, almost all companies adopt the same formats and these are shown, in outline, below.

Balance sheet

Fixed assets
   Intangible assets
   Tangible assets
   Investments

Current assets
   Stocks
   Debtors (including prepayments)
   Investments
   Cash at bank and in hand

Creditors: Amounts falling due within one year
   Bank loans and overdrafts
   Trade creditors

Other creditors, including taxation and social security
Accruals

Net current assets

Total assets less current liabilities

Creditors: Amounts falling due after more than one year
Capital and reserves

Share capital
Reserves

Note that the descriptions shown in bold type must, by law, be used where there are items falling under those classifications.

Profit and loss account

Turnover
Cost of sales
Gross profit or loss
Selling and distribution costs
Administrative expenses
Other operating income
Operating profit
Income from investments
Interest receivable and similar income
Interest payable and similar charges
Profit or loss on ordinary activities before taxation
Tax on profit or loss on ordinary activities
Profit or loss on ordinary activities after taxation
Dividends
Retained profit or loss

The following points should be noted concerning the balance sheet and profit and loss account formats:

1. None of the lines in the profit and loss account are specified in the legislation, and so it is not a legal requirement to adopt precisely these descriptions. However, the descriptions shown above are very commonly used in UK company accounting, and will be seen in most large company accounts.

2. In all the questions dealt with in earlier chapters in the book we have ignored the effects of taxation. Companies are subject to corporation tax and some of the examples in this chapter will include limited references to tax but no knowledge of corporation tax (or indeed any other tax) is required. In most cases, corporation tax will be a deduction from profit in the profit and loss account, with a corresponding liability in the balance sheet (corporation tax is payable nine months after a company's year-end, so the liability for tax is a current liability).

3. The formats for profit and loss account and balance sheet set out above are not complete; the Companies Act format contains more complex descriptions, some of which are beyond the scope of this book. Examples included in this and other chapters on company accounts will not usually contain any more complex descriptions than those set out above.

Accounting for share capital

As shown in the balance sheet format above, share capital is accounted for on a separate line. The amount shown is the nominal value of the share capital in issue (*not* the authorised share capital).

Example 11.4

Xenophon Limited has authorised share capital comprising 23 000 50p shares. Of these, 8000 have been issued. What is the amount of share capital to be shown in the balance sheet?

The nominal value of the issued share capital of the company comprises 8000 shares of 50p each: total value for inclusion in the balance sheet = £4000.

? Self-test question 11.1 (answer at the end of the book)

Uppingham Telephones Limited has the following balances in its books at 31 March 20X2:

	£
Intangible fixed assets	35 866
Premises at net book value	65 700
Vehicles at net book value	44 430
Fixtures and fittings at net book value	17 260
Stock at 31 March 20X2	42 370
Debtors	82 026
Cash at bank and in hand	13 222
Trade creditors	39 210
Long-term loan	15 000
Share capital: 20 000 £1 shares issued	20 000
Reserves at 1 April 20X1	161 479
Sales	717 216
Cost of sales	509 582
Selling costs	63 477
Distribution costs	54 460
Administrative expenses	24 512

The chief accountant must allow for a corporation tax charge for the year of £19 500. Also, the finance director has told her that a dividend of 25p per share should be included in the accounts.

You are required to prepare the profit and loss account for the year ending 31 March 20X2 for Uppingham Telephones Limited, and a balance sheet at that date in a format that complies with Companies Act presentation requirements.

Accounting for listed companies: Additional requirements

Listed companies may have thousands of shareholders, employees and creditors, and may be of interest to a very large group of people. The nature of the information published by such companies is clearly of great public significance. Listed companies vary greatly in size – some are surprisingly small – but all are subject to additional accounting requirements.

Listing regulations for quoted companies

Companies are described as 'listed' if they are quoted on a recognised stock exchange. Obtaining a quotation for a company opens up potentially vast sources of capital available through investment in the company's shares. The London Stock Exchange is a highly significant exchange. As well as listing UK based companies (2300 of them at the end of February 2004), the London Stock Exchange has listings for many multinational companies (434 of them at the end of February 2004), such as Volkswagen, Volvo and Sara Lee.

In order to allow investors to trade in shares with a reasonable degree of security, stock exchanges tend to be highly regulated. The London Stock Exchange is no exception; for listed companies there are additional accounting and disclosure requirements beyond those that apply to companies in general. For example, listed companies in the UK are required to issue interim reports which follow six months after the principal annual accounts. A few companies are required to report quarterly (i.e. every three months). In the USA listed companies are required, as a matter of course, to produce quarterly reports. UK listed companies must also issue a preliminary announcement of annual results as soon as they have been approved by the board of directors.

Listed company regulation (the 'listing rules') are handled by the Financial Services Authority (FSA), which took over this responsibility comparatively recently in May 2000.

The annual report for a listed company

The annual report produced by a listed company is often a very long and complex document. It contains all the minimum annual accounting requirements under company law (the profit and loss account, the balance sheet and so on) but also a great deal of additional information. Some of the additional disclosures are voluntary and some are required by other regulations. The annual report is viewed by many listed companies as an important public relations vehicle, and a great deal of care is put into design and presentation. The report is often expensive to produce because of the high quality of paper, photography and graphics used.

Example: EMI Group

The annual reports of EMI Group plc are usually produced to a very high standard. The report for the accounting period to 31 March 2003 is no exception. The report is 92 pages long, broken down as follows:

	No. of pages
Report overview	1
New music formats and revenue streams	2
Financial summary	1
Chairman's statement	2
Operating reviews	12
Financial review by finance director	4
Social responsibility section	4
Information about the board of directors	3
Directors' report*	1
Corporate governance	3
Remuneration report	11
Auditor's report	1
Principal financial statements*	6
Notes to the financial statements*	26
Five year summary of results	1
Investor information	1
Index	1
Photographs (throughout the report)	12

*only these items are legal requirements

Many items in the report are provided on a voluntary basis – for example, the photographs and the social responsibility section (some companies provide much more than others on issues such as social and environmental responsibility). Other items are required because EMI Group plc is a listed company. There are extensive additional disclosures on corporate governance and directors' remuneration. The background to these disclosures is explained in the next sub-section.

It should be noted that the annual report of EMI Group contains financial statements relating to all the companies in the EMI Group. Where a company owns several others it is usually necessary in law to prepare consolidated financial statements, which bring together the results and the assets and liabilities of all companies under common control. Therefore, the profit and loss account in EMI's accounts is referred to as a 'consolidated profit and loss account'. The latest annual report of the EMI Group can be accessed at the group's website: **www.emigroup.com**.

Corporate governance requirements

Corporate governance is the system by which companies are directed and controlled. In the UK corporate governance of listed companies became the subject of much debate during the 1990s. The debate was provoked by several major company scandals that took place towards the end of the 1980s. Failures of governance were implicated in many of the scandals, and there was a general feeling that listed companies had to improve the way their boards were run.

Various reports and recommendations on corporate governance were issued (the *Cadbury Report* in 1992 the *Greenbury Report* in 1995 and the *Hampel Report* in 1998). Finally, in 1998 the London Stock Exchange published the final version of the various reports combined in *Principles of Good Governance and Code of Best Practice*, better known as the 'Combined Code'.

The detailed contents of the Combined Code are beyond the scope of this book, but broadly the Code addresses four areas:

- directors
- directors' remuneration
- relations with shareholders
- accountability and audit.

Each listed company is required to produce, as part of its annual report, statements on its corporate governance and on directors' remuneration.

Accounting for listed companies: Non-financial information

The annual reports of listed companies tend to be lengthy documents as we observed above in the example of the EMI 2003 annual report. A document of 100 pages or so is quite usual, especially in the case of the largest and most publicly prominent businesses. There has been a noticeable trend in recent years towards an increase in the volume of information produced in annual reports. This is the result of a combination of factors, including the following:

- More disclosures required as a result of developments in corporate governance
- Increases in voluntary disclosures especially in respect of social, environmental and sustainability issues
- The introduction of more complex accounting standards that require additional explanatory notes to the financial statements.

All of these factors contribute to the inclusion of much more information that is not expressed in terms of figures, i.e. non-financial information. There are both advantages and drawbacks to the inclusion of this type of information:

Advantages

- Non-financial information can often help the less financially oriented user of financial statements to understand the performance and position of the company.
- It is quite often illustrated with photographs and graphs that can help to enhance understanding.
- The presentation of non-financial information often appears much more attractive and user-friendly when compared to the financial statement section of the report; therefore it is more likely to be read.

Drawbacks

- The sheer volume of information included in an annual report may be off-putting to readers.
- Non-financial information may be produced principally for public relations purposes and it may, for example, report selectively about aspects of the company's performance.

- Information in the form of graphs that accompany non-financial reports may be biased (there is academic research in this area that shows that graphs can be used to give a misleading impression).

The Operating and Financial Review (OFR)

The OFR is a special type of largely non-financial disclosure intended to set out the directors' analysis of the business, so as to provide both a historical analysis of events and an analysis of prospects for the future. The UK Accounting Standards Board (ASB) issued a statement on the OFR in 1993: it is a voluntary, not a mandatory, form of disclosure, but many listed companies in the UK have chosen to adopt it. In the recent Company Law Review (referred to earlier in the chapter) it was proposed that all companies over a certain size should produce an OFR.

The most recent statement on OFR issued by the ASB (in January 2003) suggests that the following content may be appropriate:

- Description of the business as a context for the rest of the review
- Objectives of the business, and management's strategy for achieving the objectives
- Measures used by management to assess the extent to which the objectives are achieved
- Operating review of the business's performance in the period
- Returns to shareholders (such as dividends)
- Dynamics of the business
- Commentary on the strengths and resources available to the business
- Commentary by the directors on how they have sought to maintain business performance and to improve it in the future
- Financial review
- Discussion of the cash inflows and outflows for the period under review
- Discussion of liquidity.

The best way to become familiar with the contents of an OFR is to read some examples. Because the inclusion of an OFR is voluntary, it will not be found in the annual report of all listed companies, although many include certain aspects of the OFR under different headings. A starting point could be the annual report of BAA plc which does include an OFR. It can be accessed on BAA's website at **www.baa.co.uk**.

Accounting for listed companies: Corporate reporting on the internet

As soon as the World Wide Web became widely accessible in the mid-1990s, large corporations began using it to disseminate information. At first it was used principally by US companies, but they were rapidly followed by listed companies around the world. These days, in the UK, most (although not all) of the companies listed on the Stock Exchange have a website, and in many cases the website is used in part for publishing information relevant to investors.

Companies have to be careful about what they publish on their websites. They cannot be seen to be creating false market expectations by the publication of exaggerated or inaccurate information. In most cases, the accounting information that is published on corporate websites comprises html or pdf files containing exactly the same information as contained in the annual or half-yearly report. Increasingly, however, companies are exploiting the internet in more creative ways to reach their actual and potential investors. Some examples of the type of information found on the investor section of corporate websites include the following:

- Webcasts of annual general meetings and/or the analysts' meetings where directors present and discuss the financial results
- Corporate videos with information about business activities
- Stockbrokers' forecasts
- Press releases containing, for example, the preliminary announcement of the financial results and significant events such as takeovers and share issues
- E-mail links to corporate officers who can deal with queries about the business.

This type of information can be very useful. For example, listed companies generally hold annual meetings with the financial analysts who are interested in the activities of the company (and who often work on behalf of institutional shareholders). Until recently, these meetings have taken place behind closed doors. Webcasts of the meetings allow private investors and anyone else who is interested to see the directors fielding questions from analysts and discussing the financial performance and prospects of the business.

The availability of information on the internet is particularly useful for investors outside the country where the company is based. Previously, it was often difficult to obtain the financial statements of overseas businesses, but these days, it is usually a matter of simply downloading and printing out the annual report.

Further developments in technology will allow for greater flexibility in the usage of corporate information available from websites. XBRL (Extensible Business Reporting Language) is a development of XML (Extensible Markup Language) specifically, as the name implies, for business reporting purposes. It allows the preparers of reports to 'tag' certain items of information so that they can be readily transferred into the user's software applications. If data can be transferred in a standard format, it can then be subject to analysis, summary and comparison to suit the needs of the financial statement user.

Accessing corporate websites

It is usually easy to find specific corporate websites these days. Putting the company's name into any of the reliable search engines is likely to find the site quickly. The London Stock Exchange website (**www.londonstockexchange.com**) contains links to UK listed companies' websites. However, it is worth bearing in mind that not all listed companies have set up websites, and if it is proving difficult to find a website address for a particular company, it may be that no website exists. If in doubt, try ringing the company (the phone number of UK based listed companies is available free of charge through the Hemmington Scott company information service (**www.hemscott.com**).

Chapter summary

This chapter contains information about the nature of companies in the UK, shares, directors, financial statements and the general regulatory structures surrounding financial reporting by companies. There is a great deal of very detailed regulation pertaining to companies, and this chapter provides only an outline of it. Some of the website references listed below provide more information for those students who wish to obtain further details.

The need for publication of accounting information by companies was explained at the outset of the chapter as part of an introduction to limited liability companies. It was followed by an explanation of some of the key features of the legal requirements relating to companies, including the role of directors and the company audit. UK and international ccounting standards form part of the overall structure of regulation; they were mentioned briefly, but detailed consideration of their requirements is beyond the scope of this book.

Company law requirements for the presentation of financial information in the profit and loss account and balance sheet were outlined.

The final section of the chapter examined the additional regulation of accounting information required in the case of listed companies. Students should appreciate the reasons why the requirements relating to this class of company are so much more stringent than those that apply to smaller, less economically significant businesses. Finally, the chapter covered non-financial disclosure, and the reporting of corporate financial information via the internet.

It may take time to assimilate the information contained in the chapter. Students can increase their familiarity with company financial reporting by working through the exercises at the end of the chapter. However, reading the financial press will also help. Reading the *Financial Times* (FT) may present some challenges to understanding at first, but it will undoubtedly increase general business knowledge very quickly. A good way to start may be to read the FT once a week, or to start with the business pages of any of the broadsheet newspapers (e.g. *The Times*, *Independent* or *Guardian*).

Internet resources

The internet can be used to find out a great deal of information about UK companies and company law.

www.londonstockexchange.com – a very comprehensive site containing detailed information about share prices, stock exchange statistics and data relating to individual companies.

www.dti.gov.uk – this is the website of the Department of Trade and Industry. It contains detailed reports on the recent Company Law Review.

www.companieshouse.gov.uk – the website of Companies House. Some of the detailed information about individual companies is obtainable only upon payment of a fee, but there is some free information about companies. Also, the site contains a very good Frequently Asked Questions section and a lot of information about the law relating to companies.

www.hemscott.com – this is the website of the Hemmington Scott company information service. It is a very extensive resource that offers a large amount of free information about every UK listed company (but note that it does not include information about overseas companies listed on the London Stock Exchange).

www.xbrl.org – this is the website of the non-profit-making organisation that promotes the development and usage of XBRL.

The end-of-chapter exercises are divided into two sections. The first section has answers provided at the end of the book. The second section, in the white box, has answers on the lecturers' section of the website. Finally, the chapter contains a case study that examines the preparation of the key financial statements in the form required for compliance with company law.

Website summary

The book's website contains the following material in respect of Chapter 11:

Students' section

- Quiz containing ten multiple choice questions and answers
- Five additional questions with answers
- Answer to the case study at the end of this chapter.

Lecturers' section

- Answers to exercises 11.8–11.13
- Four additional questions with answers.

Exercises: answers at the end of the book

11.1 Two of the following four statements are correct:

1.   Directors must prepare the company's accounts themselves.

2.   Directors take complete responsibility for the preparation of accounts.

3.   Directors may be guilty of a criminal offence if the accounts do not present a true and fair view.

4.   Directors may be guilty of a criminal offence if it is proven that they have defrauded creditors.

The correct statements are:

a)   3 and 4

b)   2 and 4

c)   1 and 2

d)   1 and 3.

11.2 Bayliss Chandler Limited has an authorised share capital of £30 000, split into 50p shares. Two-thirds of the shares are issued. In the year ending 31 May 20X3 a dividend of 6p per share is declared. Ambrose owns 10% of the issued shares in Bayliss Chandler Limited. What is the value of Ambrose's dividend for the year ending 31 May 20X3?

a)   £180

b)   £120

c)   £240

d)   £360.

11.3 Peachey plc has an authorised and issued share capital of £60 000 denominated in 25p shares. On 13 May 20X6 Carina, a shareholder, sells half of her total share-holding of 8000 shares to her sister Cathy.

Peachey's accounting year-end is 31 December. In the year ending 31 December 20X6 the company declares dividends of 10% of nominal value. Half the dividend is paid on 31 March 20X6 and the remainder on 30 September 20X6.

What amount of dividend do Carina and Cathy receive in the year ending 31 December 20X6?

a)   Carina receives £600; Cathy receives £200

b)   Carina receives £400; Cathy receives £400

c)   Carina receives £100; Cathy receives £100

d)   Carina receives £150; Cathy receives £50.

11.4 Butterthwaite plc has issued share capital on 1 January 20X1, as follows:

▪ ordinary share capital: 68 000 £1 ordinary shares

▪ preference share capital: £20 000 6% cumulative preference shares.

On 31 January the company issued a further 12 000 £1 ordinary shares. The interim (paid 30 April 20X1) and final ordinary dividend amount to 5p per share in total. In 20X0 the company failed to pay its preference dividend, but in 20X1 finds that it can meet its obligations in full.

What is the total amount of dividend payable by Butterthwaite plc in respect of the year ending 31 December 20X1?

a)   £5800

b)   £5200

c)   £6400

d)   £4600.

11.5 The directors of Solar Bubble plc, a trading company, have asked the company's chief accountant to prepare a draft profit and loss account for the year ending 31 January 20X4 in time for them to discuss it at their board meeting on 15 February. The directors prefer to have the information presented in the same way as in the annual financial statements.

The chief accountant identifies the following relevant balances:

	£
Administrative expenses	73 959
Opening stock	51 240
Interest payable	1 977
Sales	975 420
Selling and distribution costs	80 714
Purchases	603 493
Closing stock	57 210

Note the following:

1.   £6000 has to be accrued in respect of sales commission for the year ending 31 January 20X4.

2.   The corporation tax charge for the year is estimated at £60 625.

3.   A preference dividend on the £10 000 8% preference shares must be accrued, and also the directors have proposed paying a final dividend of 5p per share on the 100 000 ordinary shares in issue. No other dividends have been paid in the year.

4.   Of the administrative expenses, £1270 relates to prepayment of insurance.

The chief accountant will be using the following format for the draft profit and loss account:

Turnover
Cost of sales
Gross profit or loss
Selling and distribution costs
Administrative expenses
Operating profit
Interest payable and similar charges
Profit or loss on ordinary activities before taxation
Tax on profit or loss on ordinary activities

Profit or loss on ordinary activities after taxation
Dividends
Retained profit or loss.

You are required to prepare the draft profit and loss account for Solar Bubble plc for the year ending 31 January 20X4.

11.6 Brighton Magnets Limited has the following balances in its books at 31 August 20X9:

	£
Closing stock	186 420
Delivery vans at net book value	120 000
Secretarial costs	51 498
Electricity (admin. office)	12 491
Trade creditors	219 411
Factory and plant at net book value	2 518 000
Reserves at 1 September 20X8	1 557 172
Share capital: £1 ordinary shares	800 000
Administration office: phone charges	6 964
Interest payable	1 207
Salespersons' salaries	64 299
Delivery van depreciation	12 000
Other selling and distribution costs	5 911
Office rental	42 704
Other administrative expenses	36 075
Sales	3 796 842
Interest receivable	644
Depreciation of office computer equipment	8 390
Salespersons' commission	12 270
Office manager's salary	21 704
Directors' remuneration	59 200
Delivery van expenses	24 470
Debtors	321 706
Office equipment at net book value	151 020
Cash at bank	18 290
Cost of sales	2 712 350
Other operating income	12 900

Adjustments are required as follows:

1. Corporation tax on the profits for the year is estimated at £216 470.

2. Dividends of 5p per share should be included in the accounts.

You are required to prepare a profit and loss account for Brighton Magnets Limited at 31 August 20X9 and a balance sheet at that date. Both financial statements are to be presented in an appropriate Companies Act format.

11.7 Two of the following statements are correct:

1. Listed companies are obliged to produce a social responsibility report as part of their annual report.

2. Consolidated financial statements bring together the results and assets and liabilities of all group companies.

3. Compliance with the requirements of the Combined Code is compulsory for listed companies.

4. Listed company regulation is handled by the London Stock Exchange.

The correct statements are:

a) 1 and 2

b) 2 and 3

c) 3 and 4

d) 1 and 4.

Exercises: answers available to lecturers

11.8 Three of the following six statements are correct:

1. The audit report of a company states that the accounts are correct.

2. A private limited company does not have to make any information available to the public.

3. A public limited company must have an authorised share capital of £50 000.

4. The minimum number of shareholders in a private limited company is two.

5. Each ordinary share carries the right to a vote at the annual general meeting of the company.

6. A company does not have to issue all of its authorised share capital.

The correct statements are:

a) 1, 3 and 5

b) 1, 2 and 4

c) 2, 4 and 6

d) 3, 5 and 6.

11.9 Western Gadgets Limited has an authorised share capital of £24 000 denominated in 25p shares; 20 000 shares are issued. In the year ending 30 April 20X6 an interim dividend of 2p per share and a final dividend of 2.5p per share were paid.

Joan owns shares in Western Gadgets Limited with a nominal value of £1500. What is the value of Joan's dividend for the year ending 30 April 20X6?

a)	£270

b)	£150

c)	£225

d)	£67.50

11.10	Parlabane Limited has an authorised share capital of 50 000 50p shares. Of these, 42 500 have been issued. In the year ending 31 December 20X4 a dividend of 2p per share is proposed, but it has not been paid by the year-end.
Jonah owns 13 000 shares in Parlabane Limited. What is the total dividend payable and how much is payable to Jonah personally?

a)	Total dividend payable £850; payable to Jonah £260.

b)	Total dividend payable £1000; payable to Jonah £260

c)	Total dividend payable £425; payable to Jonah £130

d)	Total dividend payable £500; payable to Jonah £130

11.11	Penge and Purley plc have in issue at 31 December 20X8:

- 138 000 ordinary shares of 50p each

- 40 000 8% preference shares of £1 each, issued on 1 July 20X8.

Derek owns 3250 ordinary shares in the company, and 1000 of the £1 preference shares. An interim dividend of 2.7p per ordinary share was declared and paid, and a final dividend of 3.7p per ordinary share was proposed. The preference dividend was also paid. What is Derek's total dividend from the company for the year ending 31 December 20X8?

a)	£184

b)	£288

c)	£144

d)	£248.

11.12	Downside Green Limited has the following balances relating to its position at 31 December 20X5:

	£
Overdraft	7 746
Share capital	100 000
Loan repayable 31 December 20X9	100 000
Debtors	916 278
Cash in hand	260
Intangible fixed assets at net book value	80 000
Trade creditors	868 462
Reserves	1 850 824
Tangible fixed assets at net book value	1 082 184
Stocks	841 740
Fixed asset investments	24 860
Other creditors (all current liabilities)	18 290

The directors wish to see how the balance sheet will be presented when it is sent to shareholders. Downside Green's financial controller intends to use the following balance sheet format:

Fixed Assets
Intangible assets
Tangible assets
Investments

Current assets
Stocks
Debtors
Cash at bank and in hand

Creditors: Amounts falling due within one year
Bank loans and overdrafts
Trade creditors
Other creditors

Net current assets

Total assets less current liabilities

Creditors: Amounts falling due after more than one year

Capital and reserves
Share capital
Reserves

You are required to prepare the balance sheet for Downside Green Limited for the year ending 31 December 20X5 in the format requested by the directors.

11.13 True or False?

a) Listed company regulation is handled by the Financial Services Authority

b) Listed companies are required by law to disclose information about their sustainability policies

c) The Combined Code on Corporate Governance addresses issues related to directors' remuneration

d) XBRL is the listed company regulator in the USA.

CASE STUDY 11.1   Figures in the boardroom

Joe Daley is the managing director of Daley Limited, which operates a small group of retail food stores in the West Midlands. Daley's was set up by Joe's father Edward and his uncle Eric several years ago; both have more or less retired from the business but each retain shareholdings of 15% and both remain directors of the company, although they rarely attend board meetings these days. Joe himself owns 34% of the shares. The remaining 36% not owned by Joe, his father or his uncle, are accounted for as follows:

Joe's sister Carol	10%
Carol's husband Nasser	7%
Eric's son Gervase	19%

Carol, Nasser and Gervase are all directors, although Carol rarely attends meetings as she is very busy with her own fashion design business, producing expensive designs in limited editions for the extremely rich. The normal business of Daley Limited is conducted by Joe, Nasser and Gervase; Joe takes overall control of the direction of the company, Nasser is principally responsible for purchasing and Gervase spends most of his time in day-to-day management of the retail outlets.

Generally, the directors work well together, although problems can arise when either Edward or Eric, or both, want to get involved in day-to-day business issues. The younger generation of directors feel that Edward and Eric have lost their grip on the business and don't understand current business issues. Edward and Eric, on the other hand, while they don't always agree with each other, are united in feeling that 'the youngsters' are too hasty in making important business decisions.

An important decision faces the board. Sales have remained strong but the profit margins of the business have dropped each year for the last five years. In the year ending 31 December 20X5 the operating profit margin (operating profit as a percentage of sales) had dropped to 21.3%. Joe has proposed that the retail units expand their range into clothing; this would entail transferring about one-third of the floor space in the stores from food to clothing. It would also mean borrowing money in order to lease additional storage facilities and to finance the investment in stock. He estimates that further borrowing of £200 000 will be required, which should be obtainable at 7% interest. He has sounded out the opinions of the other directors:

- *Carol*: 'Yes, great idea. I can use my contacts in the industry to get us some really good deals.'

- *Nasser*: 'Well, it's a risk, and I don't want to borrow money unless it's absolutely necessary, but Carol knows about the fashion business; it's not as though we don't have expertise on the board.'

- *Gervase*: 'I really don't think it can work for us. It's true that Carol knows about fashion, but she doesn't have experience of the type of clothing retailing we'd be doing. I'm very much opposed to going into an area where we have no experience. We could severely damage food sales if we get this wrong.'

- *Edward*: 'We should stick to what we know. Eric and I built this business up from scratch and this idea could ruin it. If you paid more attention to the core business instead of dreaming up daft ideas, we'd be able to keep the margins up.'
- *Eric*: 'You must be out of your mind . . .'

A board meeting is scheduled for Friday 16 January 20X6 to discuss the proposal. Each director has a single vote, and because there are six directors, there is always the possibility of deadlock. Where that happens, Joe, as managing director, can use a casting vote, but has never previously needed to do so; usually only he, Gervase and Nasser attend meetings and they tend to agree on most issues. It seems likely that all the directors will attend this meeting.

The company's year-end is 31 December, and draft figures are now available. Joe asks the company accountant, Estelle, to pull together some draft accounting data using the standard format for publication (so that the directors will be able to compare the figures easily to those of previous years).

The list of balances at the end of December 20X5 is as follows:

	£
Share capital: 150 000 £1 shares	150 000
Sales	2 793 800
Rental received from letting part of office building	29 350
Office building at net book value	423 751
Retail units at net book value	1 744 850
Vehicles, fixtures, etc. at net book value	404 470
Accumulated reserves at 1 January 20X5	1 788 208
Long-term loan	500 000
Creditors	106 309
Cash at bank	76 360
Opening stock at 1 January 20X5	263 404
Closing stock at 31 December 20X5	279 800
Directors' remuneration	69 550
Other administrative expenses	386 024
Selling and distribution costs	100 470
Purchases of goods	1 715 027
Interest payable	38 850
Dividends paid: interim	58 500
Debtors	86 411

Joe tells Estelle to include a final, proposed, dividend in the accounts of 50p per share. A provision for corporation tax payable is also required, and Estelle estimates this at £158 888.

The requirement is to prepare the draft financial statements, using the standard format for company profit and loss accounts and balance sheets, and to advise Joe on the key issues (both financial and non-financial) he needs to consider in preparation for Friday's board meeting, including an assessment of his position should he fail to convince a majority of directors to vote in favour of his proposal.

CHAPTER 12

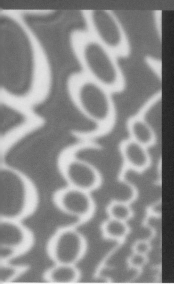

Understanding financial reports: Analysis of trends

Aim of the chapter

To develop a range of skills that assist in the understanding of financial reports for various types of business.

Learning outcomes

After reading the chapter and completing the related exercises, students should:

- Understand the potential usefulness of financial reports to various interest groups.
- Understand the principal features of the analysis of trends in financial statements.
- Be able to perform an analysis based on horizontal and/or vertical analysis of financial statements.
- Understand the problems that can arise in comparing businesses with each other.

Techniques of analysis will be developed further in Chapter 13.

Introduction

Probably the most important aim of this book is to help students appreciate that financial information actually means something. The formal figures that are set out in reports may not look very interesting in themselves, but the underlying reality that the numbers symbolise is almost always fascinating, especially for those involved.

The case studies used in earlier chapters have all attempted to illustrate the fact that accounting information is actually used by real people as a means of understanding what is going on in business. For example:

- Jimmy Bowden, in the case study for Chapter 7, needed accounting information to help him understand how much a downturn in trade had affected his business profitability.
- Richard, in the case study for Chapter 8, was anxious to find out whether or not his business could survive his disastrous decision to trade with a man who would not, in the end, pay him.
- Joe Daley, in the case study for Chapter 11, was preparing accounting information in advance of a board meeting that promised to be very difficult and contentious.

This chapter and Chapter 13 look much more closely at the analysis of financial information as a route to understanding. The two chapters cover a range of techniques and calculations. However, those students who are less than totally confident about their numeracy skills should not be put off; none of the techniques covered in the chapters involves anything more difficult than simple arithmetical skills of the type already utilised. The important skill, in fact, lies in the interpretation of the results; this is a skill best achieved through practice.

In this chapter we will first briefly examine the various groups of people who are interested in accounting information, the reasons for their interest, and the aspects that might be particularly useful to them. Then the chapter proceeds to examine simple analytical techniques that compare one figure or group of figures with another. (Note that this chapter of the book considers the analysis of the formal financial reports covered in Chapters 6–11 inclusive.

Usefulness of financial reports to various interest groups

Owners and investors

Previous chapters have included several examples of sole trader owners using periodic financial information to inform them about the progress of their business. However, it must be recognised that most unincorporated business owners will have available to them other, more comprehensive, sources of information about their business performance. For example, an annual financial statement does not provide any information about the state of the business's order book, but the current levels of demand for products and services would be regarded by business owners as an absolutely vital means of assessing business prospects. So, although it is not unrealistic to suggest that owners of businesses use annual financial reports as aids to understanding, it should be recognised that they have other, potentially more useful, sources of information available to them.

The situation is rather different, however, for investors in limited companies. Unless they are also directors, they do not have any privileges of access to information beyond their right to receive the annual report and accounts. An investor who buys 100 shares in Marks & Spencer plc, for example (or any other listed company), obtains some rights (the right to receive a part of any dividend declared and the right to vote at the annual general meeting). However, he or she does not have the right to wander in off the street to the company's head office demanding to see the monthly accounts.

Investors in companies who do not have access to information other than the annual report and accounts are likely to be interested in the answers to some or all of the following questions:

- How is my investment doing?
- Should I buy more shares/sell the shares I've already got/hold on to the investment I've already got?
- Is the dividend likely to increase?
- What are the chances of the company going out of business?

Potential investors in a business

People who are thinking of investing in a business will usually take steps to obtain the most recent financial reports. If the company is quoted, access to this type of information is usually very easy. Most quoted companies have websites, and many of them contain the most recent published financial reports for the company; they may also contain other useful pieces of information like the preliminary announcement of results and the six-monthly interim reports. Unquoted companies, as we saw in Chapter 11, are obliged to file accounting information with the Registrar of Companies, and it is possible to obtain copies of this information fairly quickly in exchange for a fee of a few pounds.

It may, however, be impossible to obtain any financial information about other forms of business because sole traders and partnerships are not obliged to make information public, although if a business is interested in attracting buyers there is an incentive to provide recent, reliable financial information to potential investors. But it should be recognised that financial information such as the profit and loss account and balance sheet is essentially backward looking; these statements report events that have already occurred, and these may not be a reliable guide to what is going to happen in the future.

Potential investors tend to be looking for answers to some or all of the following questions:

- What are the risks involved in this business? How likely would I be to lose money? Would my investment be safe?

- How much can I make from investing in this business? Will the return be better than I could make if I were to put the money into some other business, or leave it in the bank, or risk it on a bet on the horses/dogs/a card game?
- What are my chances of getting seriously rich?

Creditors

In Chapter 11 (Example 11.1) we looked at the case of Tommy, who supplied goods on credit to a limited company but was unable to obtain payment for them before the company became insolvent. Businesses and individuals who supply goods on credit to limited companies take the risk that they will not be paid. As noted in the discussion in Chapter 11, one of the ways of reducing the risk is to examine the financial reports of a company to assess its financial condition.

Suppliers of goods and services, like anyone else, are entitled to obtain the financial information that is filed at Companies House (although remember that this information is quite limited in the case of small companies). Alternatively, they may prefer to use the services of a credit agency, which, for a fee, supplies a detailed report on the creditworthiness of a named company. (See, for example, the range of services offered by Dun and Bradstreet: **www.dnb.com**.)

In the case of sole traders and partnerships, there is no publicly available source of financial information, and suppliers must base their decision on whether or not to offer credit on other factors: they may, for example, ask the trader or partnership to supply references from some reputable person like a bank manager.

If a bank or other financial institution lends to a business it becomes a creditor, possibly for the long term. In such cases, the bank is usually in a position to demand financial information, regardless of whether the business is a sole trader, partnership or company, and indeed, this may be part of the lending deal.

When undertaking an analysis of financial reports, creditors are interested in obtaining answers to the following questions:

- How likely is it that I will be paid?
- How likely is it that I will be paid on time?
- Will my interest (where applicable) be paid regularly?
- Is there a risk that this business will go bust before I get paid?

Financial statements, especially those produced by limited companies, tend to be principally oriented towards the information needs of investors and owners. However, other interested parties such as creditors will also find a great deal of information that is relevant to their needs.

Analytical techniques: Changes in figures

The most straightforward analytical technique can be one of the most effective: comparing two or more figures with each other to assess the differences between them.

| **Example 12.1** |

Ilse is a sole trader who runs a shop selling imported fabrics and furnishings. Her sales figures for the three years ending 31 March 20X4 are as follows:

	20X4	20X3	20X2
	£	£	£
Sales	217 300	209 220	204 240

It does not take a financial wizard to see that Ilse's sales have gone up between 20X2 and 20X4. Sometimes, this kind of straightforward pointing out of the obvious is all that's needed in financial analysis. However, the analysis could be refined, without much additional difficulty, by calculating the percentage increase year-on-year, as follows.

Between 20X2 and 20X3

Sales have risen by £209 220 − £204 240 = £4980, which can be calculated as a percentage of the 20X2 figure, as follows:

$$\frac{4\ 980}{204\ 240} \times 100 = 2.4\%$$

Between 20X3 and 20X4

Sales have risen by £217 300 − £209 220 = £8080, which can be calculated as a percentage of the 20X3 figure, as follows:

$$\frac{8\ 080}{209\ 220} \times 100 = 3.9\%$$

What does this mean?

By calculating the percentage increases we have added a little to our slender stock of knowledge about Ilse's sales. If we know, for example, from local Chamber of Commerce information, that traders in Ilse's part of town have experienced an average annual growth in sales of 8% between 20X2 and 20X4 it suggests that Ilse's business performance is in relative decline.

In order to increase the value of the information about Ilse's sales, we need some point of comparison. The point of comparison may come from outside the business (e.g. the information provided by the Chamber of Commerce) or from inside the business. For example, suppose Ilse tells you, as her new financial adviser, that she invested a lot of additional working capital in a new line of stock during 20X2 and 20X3, expecting to boost sales by 20% per annum, you might well conclude that her efforts to expand the business had been relatively unsuccessful. A great deal depends upon the context of the financial information.

Analytical techniques: Horizontal and trend analysis

Horizontal analysis is a fancy piece of terminology describing, essentially, the type of analysis we carried out above on Ilse's sales figures. Where there are at least two years' worth of information, it is possible to conduct some type of horizontal analysis. In some cases several years' worth of information is available, and it becomes possible to carry out a trend analysis. This type of analysis includes figures over several years and attempts to track longer-term business trends.

Moving rapidly up the size scale from Ilse's business we will now consider the publicly available information provided by the EMI Group plc. Listed companies commonly provide five-year summaries of information (sometimes the summaries even extend to a ten-year period). In the next example, we will examine some elements of the five-year record of information for EMI.

Example 12.2

The following table shows extracts from EMI Group plc's financial statements for the year ending 31 March 2003.

	2003 £m	2002 £m	2001 £m	2000 £m	1999 £m
Turnover	2175.4	2 445.8	2 672.7	2 386.5	2 373.5
Operating profit	254.0	190.9	332.5	290.6	269.7
Interest	77.3	83.2	103.6	73.7	72.0

This is just a small part of the information disclosed by EMI Group plc in its annual financial statements. What does it tell us?

Scanning the turnover line quickly, we can see that the business improved its sales each year to 2001 after which there has been a sharp decline. Operating profit fell back sharply in 2002, but has improved again in 2003. Interest charges peaked in 2001 but have fallen back in 2002 and 2003.

We can extend the horizontal analysis by calculating year-on-year percentage increases and decreases in the same way as for Ilse's business. The percentage changes can be neatly presented in a table like this one:

Annual percentage increases (decreases) in a selection of key figures:

EMI Group plc

	2003 %	2002 %	2001 %	2000 %
Turnover	(11.1)	(8.5)	12.0	0.5
Operating profit	33.0	(42.6)	14.4	7.7
Interest	(7.1)	(19.7)	40.6	2.4

The business appears to be experiencing some difficulties, although there has been a recovery in operating profit levels in 2003. The chairman's statement for 2003 sheds some more light on EMI's business performance. Although music publishing has managed to maintain turnover and profitability, there has been a significant fall in sales of recorded music. The chairman attributes the decline in sales to a combination of three factors: 'macro-economic effects in some regions, a growing impact of music piracy in all its forms and the disruptive impact of our restructuring activities, some of which took longer than originally planned'.

We can surmise from these comments, combined with the examination of a few key figures, that EMI Group plc is facing difficult trading conditions especially in its recorded music sector, but that it retains strengths in music publishing. If its restructuring activities are successful we could expect to see some further improvements in the 2004 results.

? Self-test question 12.1 (answer at the end of the book)

Jamal is a sole trader selling a range of pre-packaged foods. He has a small food processing factory and employs several staff. Three years ago in 20X4 he made the decision to employ a full-time sales manager. The manager, Jared, claimed at the interview that he would be able to achieve 15% sales increases each year.

Jared is asking for a substantial increase in his annual salary effective from the start of 20X8. He tells Jamal that he thinks he's worth it because of the contribution he's made to the business. The final accounts for the year ending 31 December 20X8 have just been finished in draft form by the accountant. Jamal is now reviewing his annual sales figures, which are available as far back as 20X0 when he started the business. The following table shows sales for each year:

Year	£
20X0	250 031
20X1	347 266
20X2	441 179
20X3	531 150
20X4	523 622
20X5	545 331
20X6	590 942
20X7	679 244
20X8	771 485

Examine the horizontal trends in Jamal's sales figures and, briefly, advise him on whether or not Jared's claim for an increased salary appears justified.

Some problems with horizontal analysis

There are two principal problems which are likely to arise in respect of horizontal analysis, relating to changes in the business and the effects of inflation.

Changes in the business

Very rapid changes can take place in business. These may mean that figures are not really comparable over a period of years. Also, new accounting rules and standards may make a difference to the presentation of figures. The figures of the EMI Group plc that we examined earlier have been adjusted for these effects so that a proper and meaningful comparison can be made. In the case of unlisted companies and smaller businesses, which do not usually include five years' worth of comparative figures in their financial statements, the analyst must be careful to make any necessary adjustments.

Failure to take the effects of inflation into account

Although it is possible to adjust accounting figures for the effects of inflation, this is not usually done in UK accounting. In recent years the general rate of inflation in the economy has not been high, and its effects are often regarded as negligible. However, this can be misleading, as the following example shows:

Example 12.3

A five-year analysis of the sales of Trevor Fine Art Productions Limited shows the following figures:

	20X8	20X7	20X6	20X5	20X4
	£	£	£	£	£
Sales	683 084	657 469	634 868	617 576	590 530
Percentage increase on previous year	3.9%	3.6%	2.8%	4.6%	—

Between 20X4 and 20X8 sales have increased in total by the following percentage:

$$\frac{£683\ 084 - 590\ 530}{590\ 530} \times 100 = 15.7\%$$

Looking at the individual years we can see that there has been an increase each year. So far, so good, but if we take inflation into account the picture changes somewhat. Suppose that in each year between 20X4 and 20X8 the average rate of inflation in the economy has been 3% per annum. We can see that in most years the sales increases were only slightly above inflation and the increase between 20X5 and 20X6 was actually a little below the rate of inflation. The sales increases are not as impressive as they first appear to be.

Analytical techniques: Vertical analysis and common size analysis

Vertical analysis is a simple analytical technique that can be useful and informative. It involves expressing each figure in the profit and loss account and balance sheet as a percentage of one key figure (sales in the profit and loss account and –

usually – net assets in the balance sheet). The next example explains the application of vertical analysis.

Example 12.4

Bore & Hole Limited makes mining equipment. The company profit and loss account and balance sheet for 20X6 are shown below, together with an extra column of percentage figures. In the profit and loss account all percentages are calculated by reference to the value of sales, and in the balance sheet by reference to the net assets total.

Bore & Hole Limited: Profit and loss account for the year ending 31 December 20X6

	£	%
Turnover	4 490 370	100.0
Cost of sales	(3 521 348)	(78.4)
Gross profit	969 022	21.6
Administrative expenses	(454 432)	(10.1)
Distribution and selling costs	(407 480)	(9.1)
Other operating income	16 210	0.4
Operating profit	123 320	2.8
Interest payable and similar charges	(33 900)	(0.8)
Profit on ordinary activities before taxation	89 420	2.0
Taxation	(26 461)	(0.6)
Profit on ordinary activities after taxation	62 959	1.4
Dividends	(40 000)	(0.9)
Retained profit for the year	22 959	0.5

Note that each item is calculated as a percentage of sales (to one decimal point): For example:

$$\frac{\text{Administrative expenses}}{\text{Sales}} \times 100 = \frac{454\ 432}{4\ 490\ 370} \times 100 = 10.1\%$$

Bore & Hole Limited: Balance sheet at 31 December 20X6

	£	£	%
Fixed assets		3 975 750	99.1
Current assets			
Stock	586 404		14.6
Debtors	430 580		10.7
Cash at bank	10 110		0.2
	1 027 094		25.5
Creditors: amounts falling due within one year	(599 212)		(14.9)

Net current assets	427 882	10.6
Total assets less current liabilities	4 403 632	109.7
Creditors: amounts falling due after more than one year	(390 000)	(9.7)
Capital and reserves	4 013 632	100.0
Share capital	800 000	19.9
Reserves	3 213 632	80.1
	4 013 632	100.0

What does the vertical analysis statement tell us? It is a single period statement only, so its information content is limited. The percentage column is helpful in that it tends to draw attention to the relative size of the figures. For example, we can see from the statement that operating profit as a percentage of sales is only 2.8%, and that retained profit is a mere 0.5% of sales. These percentages suggest that the business is not performing well.

Turning to the balance sheet we can see that it is dominated by fixed assets; this is a manufacturing business, and fixed assets could be expected to be high. Cash is negligible and the business has long-term borrowings of almost 10% of the net asset value.

Common size analysis extends vertical analysis across more than one accounting period. In the next example we will build on our knowledge of Bore & Hole Limited by examining the vertical analysis percentages in the company's profit and loss account over four years.

Example 12.5

The profit and loss account in Example 12.4 shows vertical analysis of all the items, based upon sales, for the year ended 31 December 20X6. Below, the comparative vertical analysis figures are repeated for the 20X6 profit and loss account, and are set alongside the comparative figures for the previous three years.

	20X6 %	20X5 %	20X4 %	20X3 %
Turnover	100.0	100.0	100.0	100.0
Cost of sales	(78.4)	(78.3)	(77.2)	(77.0)
Gross profit	21.6	21.7	22.8	23.0
Administrative expenses	(10.1)	(7.3)	(7.4)	(7.2)
Selling and distribution costs	(9.1)	(10.0)	(9.3)	(9.7)
Other operating income	0.4	0.4	—	—
Operating profit	2.8	4.8	6.1	6.1
Interest payable and similar charges	(0.8)	—	—	—
Profit on ordinary activities before taxation	2.0	4.8	6.1	6.1
Taxation	(0.6)	(1.4)	(1.8)	(1.8)

Profit on ordinary activities				
after taxation	1.4	3.4	4.3	4.3
Dividends	(0.9)	(2.0)	(2.0)	(2.0)
Retained profit for the year	0.5	1.4	2.3	2.3

This statement is expressed entirely in percentages; it gives no indication as to the value of each component. However, the statement does help understanding by presenting the trends in the figures quite clearly. For example:

■ *Gross profit* as a percentage of turnover has fallen in each of the four years. If this trend continues the business could ultimately fail.

■ *Administrative expenses* have remained at a fairly constant level compared to turnover for three out of the four years reviewed. Suddenly, however, in 20X6 the percentage leaps. There could be many explanations for this change; for example, perhaps there has been a change of management and the new management are not controlling costs very well. Or, there may have been a major new investment in fixed assets on which related depreciation charges are shown as part of administrative expenses.

■ *Interest payable* features for the first time in the 20X6 profit and loss account, suggesting that in previous years borrowings were either non-existent or negligible.

■ *Dividends* have remained at a constant percentage of turnover in three of the four years, but the proportion has fallen in 20X6. The shareholders may lose confidence in the company's management if this trend continues.

Overall, although we have relatively little information about the company (compared, for example, with what is available in a full set of financial statements) the common size profit and loss statement does allow the analyst to draw some tentative conclusions about the performance of the business over time.

Comparing businesses with each other

So far in this chapter we have analysed single businesses, generally by reference to the increases and decreases in elements of accounting information over time. However, interested parties will often need to make comparisons between businesses. They can do this by: (a) comparing the results and balance sheets of two or more businesses; (b) comparing the results and balance sheets of a business with industry averages.

Problems in comparison

The regulation surrounding accounting, especially accounting by limited companies, goes some way towards ensuring that financial statements are prepared to the same set of rules and in the same way. The Accounting Standards Board, for example, sets out four key characteristics that accounting information should have:

- relevance
- reliability
- comparability
- understandability.

Comparability is accorded a great deal of importance precisely in order to allow meaningful comparisons between accounting statements. However, despite the best intentions of the regulators, there are often problems in ensuring that a valid comparison can be made. Some of these are briefly described in the following sub-sections.

Differences in accounting policies

Accounting policies are the principles of accounting applied in preparing the financial statements. Despite a fairly extensive level of regulation, there are many areas in which a business can make legitimate choices about the amounts at which items are stated, and the way in which those items are presented. The following example will illustrate the point.

Example 12.6

Spanners Limited and Gasket Limited operate within the same business sector. A financial analyst is examining the results of the companies on behalf of a client. Extracts from their profit and loss accounts show the following information (together with vertical analysis percentages):

	Spanners Limited		Gasket Limited	
	£	%	£	%
Turnover	984 742	100.0	1 096 880	100.0
Cost of sales	673 938	68.4	756 993	69.0
Gross profit	310 804	31.6	339 887	31.0

The companies appear to be similar in size in that they generate similar levels of turnover, and the percentage of gross profit to sales is close. It seems a fair conclusion, on the face of it, that their performance is virtually identical. However, the analyst finds out that the companies' policies on inclusion of costs in cost of sales are not the same. Specifically, Spanners Limited includes depreciation of vehicles within cost of sales, whereas Gasket Limited includes the same type of cost within selling and distribution costs. Gasket's vehicle depreciation is £28 977 for the year under review.

In order to compare like with like the analyst must make an adjustment to Gasket's cost of sales:

Adjusted cost of sales = £28 977 + £756 993 = £785 970

Building this adjusted cost into the profit and loss analysis results in the following changes (vertical analysis percentages are recalculated for Gasket Limited):

▶

	Spanners Limited		Gasket Limited	
	£	%	£	%
Turnover	984 742	100.0	1 096 880	100.0
Cost of sales	673 938	68.4	785 970	71.7
Gross profit	310 804	31.6	310 910	28.3

The recalculation makes the comparison appear in a rather different light. Gasket's gross profit is 28.3% of sales, as compared to Spanners' at 31.6%.

Financial statement analysts have to be alert for this type of difference. As the example shows, application of different accounting policies can make a lot of difference. The example illustrates the point in relation to cost classification but there are many other potential areas of difference, including, for example, depreciation and amortisation methods.

Differences in business activities

No two businesses are entirely alike. Comparison of two apparently similar businesses can lead to incorrect conclusions if the differences between the two are not fully appreciated.

Example 12.7

A financial analyst is comparing the results of two companies for 20X7 and 20X6. Pool & Splash Limited and Dive & Float Limited are both involved in swimming pool installation and maintenance. The industry is prospering; a prolonged period of economic growth has led to many more people installing swimming pools in their own homes.

Sales figures for the two companies for 20X7 and 20X6 are as follows:

	Pool & Splash Limited		Dive & Float Limited	
	20X7	20X6	20X7	20X6
	£	£	£	£
Sales	1 662 997	1 357 549	1 842 791	1 543 360

The analyst calculates that the sales of Pool & Splash Limited have increased by 22.5%, whereas Dive & Float Limited's sales have increased by only 19.4%. On the face of it, Pool & Splash appears to have performed better in terms of sales growth. However, the picture changes when we are supplied with information about the breakdown of sales. Pool & Splash Limited's sales and maintenance contracts are in respect of domestic sales only. Dive & Float Limited, on the other hand, undertakes contract pool maintenance for local authorities. A breakdown of the sales figures shows the following:

	Pool & Splash Limited		Dive & Float Limited	
	20X7	20X6	20X7	20X6
	£	£	£	£
Sales – domestic	1 662 997	1 357 549	1 430 111	1 135 910
Maintenance contracts – local authorities	—	—	412 680	407 450
Total	1 662 997	1 357 549	1 842 791	1 543 360

From the more detailed figures the analyst can calculate a more meaningful comparison. Dive & Float's domestic sales have, in fact, increased by 25.9% as compared to Pool & Splash's increase of 22.5%.

Industry averages may be misleading

Comparison of a single company against a range of industry averages may be misleading.

Example 12.8

Wellington Burke Limited and Ashington Smith Limited are two companies operating in the same industry, but in different parts of England. According to a recent trade survey, the average increase in sales in the industry in the year ending 31 December 20X5 was 13.8%. The two companies show the following levels of sales growth over that period:

- Wellington Burke Limited = 14.2%
- Ashington Smith Limited = 11.6%.

It appears as though Wellington Burke Limited is the clear leader in terms of sales growth. However, the average increase in sales published in the trade survey masks wide regional variations.

- average growth in the north of England = 9.7%
- average growth in the south of England = 17.9%.

If we know that Wellington Burke's operates in the Home Counties, while Ashington Smith is based in Yorkshire, the comparison starts to look different. It appears that, in fact, Ashington Smith Limited may have outperformed other northern based firms in the industry, whereas, relatively speaking, Wellington Burke has underperformed in terms of sales growth.

Comparisons between businesses, then, must be approached with caution, because apparently obvious facts may be misleading.

? **Self-test question 12.2** (answer at the end of the book)

Barnes & Jack Limited and Carleen Baker Limited are competitors in the aquarium supply business. Both companies supply, install and maintain aquariums. Sales figures for the two companies for 20X6 and 20X5 are as follows:

	Barnes & Jack Limited		Carleen Baker Limited	
	20X6	20X5	20X6	20X5
	£	£	£	£
Sales	2 044 032	1 743 906	1 850 490	1 564 774

a) Which company has produced the more impressive growth in sales (calculate growth to one decimal place)?
b) Does the answer differ with the addition of the following information about sales?

Barnes & Jack Limited's sales are principally to the domestic and pet shop market. However, in addition, the company sells to zoos. Sales growth in the latter area has been slow in recent years due to cuts in public funding. Carleen Baker Limited would like to break into the zoo market, but currently supplies only the domestic and pet shop market.

Barnes & Jack's sales to zoos were £450 800 in 20X5, increasing to £488 307 in 20X6.

Chapter summary

In this chapter we first examined the usefulness of financial statements to certain interest groups: owners and investors, potential investors and creditors. The rest of the chapter was devoted to the study of a range of simple analysis techniques:

- *Horizontal analysis*: involving analysis of the financial statements of at least two consecutive accounting periods.
- *Trend analysis*: i.e. horizontal analysis taking place over several years.
- *Vertical analysis*: expressing figures in a financial statement as a percentage of one key figure (commonly sales in the profit and loss account and net assets in the balance sheet).
- *Common size analysis*: vertical analysis taking place over more than one accounting period.

We examined some of the problems of comparability that can arise when the analyst attempts to compare accounting information from two or more businesses:

- accounting policies may be different
- there may be differences between the activities of the businesses
- industry averages may be misleading.

 The end-of-chapter exercises are divided into two sections. The first section has answers provided at the end of the book. The second section, in the white box, has answers on the lecturers' section of the website. Finally the chapter contains a case study that involves analysing data from a very large UK business.

Website summary

The book's website contains the following material in respect of Chapter 12:

Students' section

- Quiz containing ten multiple choice questions and answers
- Four additional questions with answers
- Answer to the case study at the end of the chapter.

Lecturers' section

- Answers to exercises 12.7–12.10
- Four additional questions with answers.

Exercises: answers at the end of the book

12.1 Ronald's trading business operates from a shop in a large city centre. Extracts from Ronald's most recent profit and loss accounts for 20X4 and 20X3 show the following key figures:

	20X4	20X3
	£	£
Sales	110 450	95 544
Cost of sales	(72 058)	(62 075)
Gross profit	38 392	33 469

Ronald belongs to a trade association that has recently carried out a confidential survey of its members. The survey found that between 20X3 and 20X4 the average increases in sales and gross profitability of the membership were:

- increase in sales = 12.6%
- increase in gross profit = 15.2%.

Which of the following is correct? A horizontal analysis of Ronald's sales and gross profit figures shows:

a) Higher than average increase in sales, and lower than average increase in gross profit.

b) Lower than average increase in sales, and lower than average increase in gross profit.

c) Lower than average increase in sales, and higher than average increase in gross profit.

d) Higher than average increase in sales, and lower than average increase in gross profit.

12.2 Rory's profit and loss account statements show the following figures for the period 20X3 to 20X6 inclusive:

	20X6	20X5	20X4	20X3
	£	£	£	£
Sales	562 064	539 409	520 665	505 500
Cost of sales	(410 619)	(392 802)	(378 879)	(368 509)
Gross profit	151 445	146 607	141 786	136 991

Which of the following is correct? Analysed horizontally, these figures show:

a) A gradually increasing percentage of sales growth and a gradually increasing percentage of gross profit growth.

b) A gradually decreasing percentage of sales growth and a gradually increasing percentage of gross profit growth.

c) A gradually increasing percentage of sales growth and a gradually decreasing percentage of gross profit growth.

d) A gradually decreasing percentage of sales growth and a gradually decreasing percentage of gross profit growth.

12.3 Inge Larsen is the principal shareholder in Larsen Locations Limited. Her company provides services to businesses that are in the process of moving from one location to another. Inge and her staff plan the moves in detail, ensuring that all arrangements are made and that the move goes smoothly. Lately, the company has itself moved into larger premises and has taken on more staff.

Tom Wilton runs The Wilton Group plc, of which he is the major shareholder; the company's principal activity is similar to Larsen's. He is considering making an offer to Inge to buy the business from her, so that he can consolidate Wilton's position as market leader in the region. He does not want Inge Larsen to know anything about his possible interest in her company until he has completed some basic financial analysis.

Tom obtains Larsen's company accounts for the last three years from Companies House. Some of the extracted profit and loss account information is summarised in the following table:

	20X8 £	20X7 £	20X6 £	20X5 £
Sales of services	3 709 480	3 690 900	3 502 404	3 497 983
Administrative expenses	1 446 437	1 204 448	1 109 932	1 100 555
Operating profit	756 734	841 525	795 046	787 046

Over the period 20X5 to 20X8 The Wilton Group plc has experienced steady growth in sales, administrative expenses and operating profits of 2–3% per year.

You are required to analyse Larsen's sales, administrative expenses and operating profits horizontally, reporting briefly on how the trends in these items compare with those of The Wilton Group plc.

12.4 Chapter Protection Limited is a security firm. Its profit and loss account for the year ending 31 December 20X2 is as follows:

	£
Turnover	188 703
Cost of sales	(115 863)
Gross profit	72 840
Administrative expenses	(14 260)
Distribution and selling costs	(20 180)
Operating profit	38 400
Interest payable and similar charges	(1 200)
Profit on ordinary activities before taxation	37 200
Taxation	(7 450)
Profit on ordinary activities after taxation	29 750
Dividends	(10 000)
Retained profit for the year	19 750

You are required to prepare a vertical analysis statement of Chapter Protection's profit and loss account on the basis that the sales figure is 100%.

12.5 The following is a simplified extract from the balance sheet of Boots Group plc (the well known British high street chemist) at 31 March 2003 with comparative figures for 31 March 2002.

	2003 £m	2003 £m	2002 £m	2002 £m
Fixed assets		1 902.5		2 147.6
Current assets				
Stock	638.6		648.1	
Debtors	650.6		646.1	
Investments, deposits and cash	496.5		409.1	
	1 785.7		1 703.3	
Creditors: amounts falling due within one year	(1 112.7)		(1 174.7)	
Net current assets		673.0		528.6
Total assets less current liabilities		2 575.5		2 676.2
Creditors: amounts falling due after more than one year		(401.8)		(480.0)
Provisions for liabilities and charges*		(173.8)		(177.9)
Net assets		1 999.9		2 018.3
Share capital		203.5		223.2
Reserves and similar items		1 796.4		1 795.1
		1 999.9		2 018.3

*Provisions for liabilities and charges – we have not met this item previously. In this particular case the provisions relate to liabilities for future taxation and for costs that will be incurred in reorganising the group's activities.

The chief executive's review for the year refers to the recent sale of Halfords, and to the group's strategy to simplify its operations and to concentrate on its core activities. An extract from the chairman's statement emphasises the same theme: 'The past three years have seen Boots transforming itself. It is now a much simpler and more focused business, and we are continuing to increase the pace and improve the effectiveness of change.'

Required: prepare a common size statement showing the balance sheet items for 2003 and 2002 on the basis that net assets = 100.0%. Comment upon any significant changes which emerge from the analysis.

12.6 Causeway Ferguson plc is a trading company specialising in the supply of tea and coffee and related products. Jason has a small shareholding in the company that was left to him by a relative. He has never taken much interest in the company's activities but has noticed that the company pays a regular twice yearly dividend that never seems to vary much.

Jason has recently started reading the financial press on a regular basis and one day he finds a brief news item about tea and coffee suppliers. Causeway Ferguson is mentioned in passing: 'Causeway Ferguson, a fine old name in British tea supply, is quietly withering away. Its lacklustre management team has failed to tackle new competitors in the market – at this rate, it starts to look like a modest takeover target for one of the food industry big boys.'

Jason never throws anything away, and after a search, manages to dig out from a dusty pile of papers a set of unopened annual reports from Causeway Ferguson going back over four or five years. He gives the reports to his cousin, Jasper, who is a trainee accountant, and asks him to comment on the company's trading over the last few years.

Jasper extracts the following profit and loss account information from the annual reports:

	20X7	20X6	20X5	20X4	20X3
	£000	£000	£000	£000	£000
Turnover	13 204	13 561	13 602	12 430	12 003
Cost of sales	(8 012)	(8 217)	(8 213)	(7 401)	(7 085)
Gross profit	5 192	5 344	5 389	5 029	4 918
Administrative expenses	(2 184)	(2 101)	(2 097)	(2 010)	(1 975)
Selling and distribution costs	(2 086)	(2 001)	(1 977)	(1 972)	(1 951)
Operating profit	922	1 242	1 315	1 047	992
Taxation	(277)	(373)	(395)	(314)	(298)
Profit on ordinary activities after taxation	645	869	920	733	694
Dividends	(250)	(240)	(240)	(230)	(230)
Retained profit for the year	395	629	680	503	464

The requirement is to prepare a horizontal trend analysis statement and a common size statement and to comment on the key features that emerge from the analysis of these statements. Does the newspaper report appear credible in the light of the analysis?

Exercises: answers available to lecturers

12.7 Rasheda's sales for 20X2 were £206 400, and for 20X3 were £214 656. Her gross profit margins were 20X2 = 36.3% and 20X3 = 36.4%. Rasheda expects sales in 20X4 to increase by the same percentage as between 20X2 and 20X3. Gross profit margin should improve to 36.5%.

What is Rasheda's expected gross profit in 20X4 (to the nearest £)?

a) £78 349

b) £78 135

c)   £81 483

d)   £81 363

12.8 Reva has a jewellery business in a well-established shop. Her most recent profit and loss accounts show the following key figures:

	20X5	20X4
	£	£
Sales	696 400	585 702
Cost of sales	(416 447)	(352 007)
Gross profit	279 953	233 695

A recent survey by the Jewellers' Guild shows that average jewellery sales increased by 17.3% in 20X5 over the previous year. Also, it was found that the average gross profit margin in 20X5 among the survey respondents is 38.3%.

Which of the following is correct? An analysis of Reva's figures shows:

a)   A higher than average increase in sales, and a higher than average gross profit margin.

b)   A lower than average increase in sales, and a lower than average gross profit margin.

c)   A higher than average increase in sales, and a lower than average gross profit margin.

d)   A lower than average increase in sales, and a higher than average gross profit margin.

12.9 Isaac Prentiss Limited produces parts and components for ships' engines. The business requires a continuing investment in new machinery in order to keep production as efficient as possible. Isaac Prentiss is the founder and principal shareholder of the business, although he no longer takes an active part in management. Isaac is concerned because he feels that the business is borrowing too much.

   Burgess, the managing director, assures Isaac that sales and operating profits continue to improve and that the borrowing is necessary to fund the general expansion of the business, including the acquisition of new fixed assets. In order to reassure Isaac, Burgess prepares the following statement of key extracts from the financial statements for the last five years:

	20X8	20X7	20X6	20X5	20X4
	£000	£000	£000	£000	£000
Sales	1 635	1 421	1 254	1 181	1 133
Operating profit	303	254	223	203	199
Interest payable	(245)	(181)	(177)	(171)	(151)
Fixed assets	5 314	4 190	3 633	3 237	2 950
Borrowing	3 944	2 921	2 766	2 510	2 431

You are required to analyse the company's figures horizontally over the five-year period and write a brief report to Isaac on the results of the analysis. You should refer particularly to Isaac's concerns about the business borrowing.

12.10 Starkey Wilmott Limited has the following balance sheet at 31 March 20X3:

	£	£
Fixed assets		704 710
Current assets		
Stock	369 440	
Debtors	416 700	
Cash at bank	81 450	
	867 590	
Creditors: amounts falling due within one year	(390 900)	
Net current assets		476 690
Total assets less current liabilities		1 181 400
Creditors: amounts falling due more than one year		(200 000)
		981 400
Capital and reserves		
Share capital		50 000
Reserves		931 400
		981 400

You are required to prepare vertical analysis statements of Starkey Wilmott's balance sheet at 31 March 20X3 based upon (i) net assets = 100.0% and (ii) fixed assets = 100.0%.

CASE STUDY 12.1   Financial analysis: BAA plc

The case study for this chapter is relatively short; it is intended to demonstrate some aspects of the trend analysis of financial statements in the context of real company results.

This case study examines some information taken from the annual report of BAA plc for the year ending 31 March 2003. BAA plc owns and runs seven airports in the UK, and has stakes in several others around the world. The following table presents extracts in respect of the most recent five years from the ten-year financial summary provided in the 2003 annual report.

	2003	2002	2001	2000	1999
Passengers served (in millions)	127.7	121.9	124.7	117.8	112.5
	£m	£m	£m	£m	£m
Sales turnover	1 933	1 989	2 261	2 192	2 013
Profit on ordinary activities before taxation	524	505	547	494	507
Taxation	(162)	(151)	(155)	(115)	(115)
Profit before dividends	374	165	389	259	398
Fixed assets	7 994	7 122	6 883	6 467	6 457
Total assets less current liabilities	8 583	7 577	6 676	6 394	6 221
Creditors due after more than one year	(3 787)	(3 129)	(2 225)	(1 877)	(1 987)
Shareholders' funds [total net assets]	4 575	4 737	4 826	4 517	4 234

Tutorial notes:

1. Note the inclusion of non-financial information in the form of passenger statistics. Many companies include non-financial statistics to help to illustrate trends in their activities.

2. Not all of the lines from the profit and loss account and balance sheet are included in the summary information. Generally, companies include the key figures such as sales turnover and shareholders' funds.

Working to one decimal place for all percentages, the following are required:

1. Calculate and put into a table the percentage increases and decreases from year to year for each line of the figures presented above by BAA plc (i.e. conduct a horizontal trend analysis).

2. Calculate and put into a table common size statistics, as far as it is possible from the figures presented above. Exclude the passenger statistics. Base the profit and loss account common size percentages on sales, and the balance sheet common size percentages on shareholders' funds (net assets).

3. Comment on the fluctuations and trends revealed by the horizontal trends and common size statements.

CHAPTER 13

Understanding financial reports: Using accounting ratios

Aim of the chapter

To add to the range of skills developed in the previous chapter in order to understand financial reports for various types of business.

Learning outcomes

After reading the chapter and completing the related exercises, students should:

- Understand the usefulness of accounting ratios in financial analysis.
- Be able to calculate a range of accounting ratios.
- Be able to use their knowledge of accounting ratios to assist in the analysis of financial statements.

Financial ratio analysis techniques

The simple analysis techniques explained in the previous chapter can be of great assistance in understanding a business. Sometimes, however, it helps to build in some ratio analysis techniques.

There is nothing particularly remarkable about a ratio: it simply expresses the relationship between one quantity and another. Taking a very simple example: a basket of fruit contains eight apples and four oranges. The ratio of apples to oranges can be expressed in an arithmetical term as 8:4. It is common to reduce the smaller part of the ratio to one, so the ratio of apples to oranges is expressed as 2:1.

Not all of the techniques and calculations commonly included under the term 'financial ratio analysis' actually involve the calculation of a ratio of the 2:1 type calculated above. The same relationship could be expressed by a percentage (e.g. '33.3% of the fruit in this basket is oranges'). However, all of the techniques result in ways of expressing the relationships between two or more figures.

A typical set of financial statements contains many figures, and it is possible to calculate almost infinite permutations expressing their relative dimensions. Some, however, are very obviously of more use than others; it is important that the figures being compared do have some genuine relationship. In the rest of this chapter we will examine some of the more commonly considered relationships between items in the financial statements.

It can be helpful, when trying to understand accounting ratios to group the various categories of financial relationships together. We will examine ratios in five principal categories:

- *Performance ratios* – used to assess the relative success or failure of business performance.
- *Liquidity ratios* – used to assess the extent to which a business can comfortably cover its liabilities.
- *Efficiency ratios* – used to assess the extent to which asset and liability items are well utilised and well managed.
- *Investor ratios* – used to assess various items of particular interest to investors.
- *Lending ratios* – used to assess the relationship between financing via loan capital and financing via equity capital.

A word of caution about financial ratio analysis

Some of the ratio calculation techniques explained here may appear quite complicated, especially for students whose arithmetical skills are rusty. However, the purpose of their calculation, and the overriding purpose of this section of the book, is to assist in *understanding* financial information. Students often concentrate on trying to memorise the ratio formulae and either forget, or have never properly understood, what the relationship between the figures means. Therefore, in each example, we will search for the meaning in the expression of the relationship between figures.

Performance ratios

Students may be relieved to discover that they have already studied several aspects of the financial analysis of performance. Earlier chapters introduced the idea of a significant relationship between (a) sales and gross profit and (b) sales and net profit. In many examples and case studies used up to this point in the book, gross profit margins and/or net profit margins have been calculated, and students should by now be accustomed to the idea that these margin calculations can express financial relationships between sales and profits in ways that are actually quite helpful.

Return on capital employed

Return on capital employed (also known as ROCE) is widely used as a means of assessing the performance of a business. ROCE looks at the level of profits generated compared to the amount of capital invested in the business. Unfortunately, although the ratio is easy to calculate, it does present problems in that it can be difficult to decide what is included in 'return' and in 'capital employed'. An example should help to illustrate the issue.

Example 13.1

Bilton Burgess plc is a trading company occupying its own freehold premises. It has recently obtained a listing on a stock exchange. The company has the following summarised profit and loss account for the year ending 31 December 20X5 and balance sheet at that date:

Bilton Burgess plc: Profit and loss account for the year ending 31 December 20X5

	£000	£000
Sales		1 600
Cost of sales		
Opening stock	100	
Add: purchases	994	
	1 094	
Less: closing stock	(104)	
		(990)
Gross profit		610
Various expenses		(319)
Operating profit		291
Interest payable and similar charges		(80)
Profit on ordinary activities before taxation		211
Taxation		(64)
Profit on ordinary activities after taxation		147
Dividends		(40)
Retained profit for the year		107

▶

Bilton Burgess plc: Balance sheet at 31 December 20X5

	£000	£000
Fixed assets		1 813
Current assets		
Stock	104	
Debtors	170	
Cash	10	
	284	
Creditors: amounts due within one year	97	
		187
Net current assets		
Total assets less current liabilities		2 000
Creditors: amounts due after more than one year		(800)
		1 200
Capital and reserves		
Share capital: £1 ordinary shares		300
Reserves		900
		1 200

Return on capital employed measures the profit made by the business against the funds invested:

$$\frac{\text{Profit}}{\text{Investment}}$$

Which profit figure should be used? There are several to choose from:

- gross profit (£610 000)
- operating profit (£291 000)
- profit on ordinary activities before taxation (£211 000)
- profit on ordinary activities after taxation (£147 000)
- retained profit (£107 000).

And how much has been invested? Should we include total net assets/shareholders' funds (£1 200 000) or total assets less current liabilities (which is the same as the total of shareholders' funds and loan capital) at £2 000 000?

There are no definitive right answers; it depends upon which ratio is the most useful for the analysis. For example, if the analyst is looking at a set of accounts on behalf of a shareholder, he or she will be most interested in the return made by the shareholders' total investment. However, it is important to make sure that the 'return' matches the 'capital employed'. And what are 'shareholders' funds'? Shareholders' funds are the sum of the amount of the original investment in share capital, plus the total of whatever profits have been retained in the business. In this example, £300 000 of share capital plus £900 000 of retained profits.

In the case of Bilton Burgess plc pre-tax ROCE (return on shareholders' funds) equals:

$$\frac{\text{Profit before taxation and after interest}}{\text{Shareholders' funds}}$$

$$= \frac{211}{1\,200} \times 100 = 17.58\%$$

The correct figure to use here is £211 000 because it is what is left to the shareholders after interest has been deducted from profit.

Post-tax ROCE might also be helpful in the analysis. Post-tax ROCE equals: (return on shareholders' funds)

$$\frac{\text{Profit after taxation and after interest}}{\text{Shareholders' funds}}$$

$$= \frac{147}{1\,200} \times 100 = 12.25\%$$

Both pre-tax and post-tax ROCE could be useful to shareholders in order to compare the return on their investment in Bilton Burgess plc with other possible investments.

A third possibility is to look at the overall return against total investment in the business. Total investment in the case of Bilton Burgess plc is the total of shareholders' funds and long-term loan capital. The matching profit figure is the operating profit before any deduction for interest. ROCE (on total capital invested) equals:

$$\frac{\text{Profit before interest and tax}}{\text{Shareholders' funds and long-term capital}}$$

$$= \frac{291}{2\,000} \times 100 = 14.55\%$$

This is a very useful measure of business performance because it focuses purely on performance rather than bringing in considerations related to the method of financing the business operations.

ROCE may seem rather confusing. Try to focus upon the objective of the analysis and, above all, ensure that, where comparisons are being made, the ratio is calculated on a consistent basis. Students sometimes want to know which of the calculations explained above is 'right'. The answer is that the ROCE calculations are tools to be used for the purpose of analysis. The 'right' ROCE in any given situation depends upon the focus of the analysis. It is important from the outset to try to focus on the meaning of the figures and remember that accounting is an art rather than a science.

? **Self-test question 13.1** (answer at the end of the book)

The following figures are extracted from Augustus Algernon Limited's profit and loss account and balance sheet for 20X4:

	£
	£
Operating profit	186 000
Interest	(24 000)
Profit before taxation	162 000
Taxation	(48 000)
Profit after taxation	114 000

From the balance sheet:

	£
	£
Share capital	120 000
Reserves	1 000 000
Long-term loan	480 000

Calculate the following:

■ Pre-tax ROCE, where capital employed is shareholders' funds (i.e. share capital plus reserves).
■ Post-tax ROCE, where capital employed is shareholders' funds (i.e. share capital plus reserves).
■ ROCE on total capital invested, where total capital invested is shareholders' funds plus long-term loan.

Liquidity ratios

Liquidity ratios are used to assess the extent to which a business can comfortably cover its liabilities. The emphasis in this group of ratios is especially on current liabilities. Long-term liabilities, by definition, do not have to be settled in the immediate future. Current liabilities, on the other hand, have to be settled within, at most, one year of the balance sheet date, and usually much more quickly. If the business fails to settle its current liabilities it is in danger of failing altogether. Can the business meet its liabilities as they fall due? Two ratios are used to provide answers to this question: the current ratio and the quick ratio. We will use data from the Bilton Burgess plc accounts provided in Example 13.1 to illustrate the calculation of these important ratios.

Example 13.2

Current ratio

The current ratio assesses the relationship between current assets and current liabilities. If current liabilities had to be settled in full, would there be sufficient current assets to cover them? Bilton Burgess's current assets are £284 000 and its current liabilities are £97 000. The formula for the current ratio is:

$$\frac{\text{Current assets}}{\text{Current liabilities}}$$

$$= \frac{284\ 000}{97\ 000} = 2.93$$

It is customary to express this relationship in the form of a ratio – i.e. current assets: current liabilities – which in this case is 2.93:1. Current assets are 2.93 times as large, in total, as current liabilities. Another way of looking at this information is to say that, for every £1 of current liabilities that has to be met by the business there is £2.93 in current assets.

Does the current ratio for Bilton Burgess look reasonable? Well, the business does not appear to be in danger of going under because of inability to meet its current liabilities. If all the creditors were to arrive in a group on the company's doorstep demanding immediate payment, there is actually only £10 000 in the bank with which to pay them. However, this is an unlikely scenario. Given a month or so, many of the debtors will pay up in cash, and working capital will continue to cycle around the business as described in earlier chapters. It is reasonable to conclude that Bilton Burgess does not have any obvious liquidity problems.

Is there any 'gold standard' figure for the current ratio? Current ratios vary widely between industries, and there is no ideal figure (although some textbooks suggest that there is). It is best used as a point of comparison: for example, if we know that the current ratio for Bilton Burgess at 31 December 20X4 was 2.63, we can compare the two figures at consecutive year-ends and conclude that the current ratio has improved from 2.63 to 2.93.

Quick (acid test) ratio

The analysis of liquidity can be further refined by examining the quick ratio, which is also referred to as the acid test ratio. This works on the assumption that it takes longer to turn stock into cash, and so it leaves stock out of the analysis. The formula for the quick ratio is:

$$\frac{\text{Current assets} - \text{Stock}}{\text{Current liabilities}}$$

For Bilton Burgess plc:

$$= \frac{284 - 104}{97} = 1.86$$

Expressed in the form of a ratio this is 1.86:1. For every £1 of current liabilities there is £1.86 in cash or debtors available. If this ratio drops below 1:1 there may potentially be problems in meeting liabilities. However, it is difficult to generalise about this point. A business that generates cash quickly (like a food retailer, for example) can operate on a very low quick ratio. The quick ratio calculated for Bilton Burgess does not suggest that the company has any immediate problem in meeting its liabilities. As with the current ratio, the quick ratio is most informative when used in comparisons.

? Self-test question 13.2 (answer at the end of the book)

Arbus Nugent Limited has the following figures for current assets and current liabilities in its balance sheets at 31 December 20X8 and 31 December 20X7:

	20X8	20X7
Current assets		
Stock	34 300	31 600
Debtors	42 950	42 610
Cash	10 370	640
	87 620	74 850
Creditors: amounts due within one year		
Trade creditors	31 450	32 970

Calculate the current ratio and the quick ratio for Arbus Nugent for both years, working to one decimal place. Have the ratios improved or worsened?

Efficiency ratios

Efficiency ratios are used to assess the extent to which asset and liability items are well managed and well utilised. We will consider efficiency measurement related to four items: fixed assets, stock, debtors and creditors. The following example uses the Bilton Burgess plc data given in Example 13.1.

Example 13.3

Fixed asset turnover ratio

Fixed assets are employed in the business in order to generate sales and, ultimately, profits. It can be interesting and useful to gauge the success with which fixed assets are employed to produce turnover. The **fixed asset turnover ratio** examines the efficiency with which fixed assets have been utilised in the business. The formula is:

$$\frac{\text{Turnover (sales)}}{\text{Fixed assets}}$$

Applying the formula to the relevant figures for Bilton Burgess plc, fixed asset turnover equals:

$$\frac{\text{Sales}}{\text{Fixed assets}}$$

$$= \frac{1\,600}{1\,813} = 0.88$$

A helpful way of looking at this result is to think of it in terms of amount of sales generated per £ of investment in fixed assets. Each £ invested in fixed assets in Bilton Burgess plc produces, on average, sales of 88p.

Again, there is no 'gold standard' for this ratio. Businesses differ from each other in the extent to which they use fixed assets. Some businesses are largely people-based; because the value of people does not appear on business balance sheets, such businesses are likely to produce a high level of sales relative to very low investment in fixed assets. Bilton Burgess plc owns its own premises and therefore fixed assets are higher than in an equivalent business where the buildings are rented. When comparing the fixed asset turnover of two businesses, caution must be exercised to ensure that like is compared with like.

Stock turnover

Where stock is a significant factor in a business, its management is of prime importance. Holding too much stock costs money (because of storage costs, insurance, working capital tied up); holding insufficient stock may also lead to problems where there is a delay in supplying customer orders. The **stock turnover ratio** gauges the average length of time that an item of stock spends on the premises before it is sold. There are two related calculations:

$$\text{Stock turnover} = \frac{\text{Cost of sales}}{\text{Average stock}}$$

$$\text{Stock turnover in days} = \frac{\text{Average stock}}{\text{Cost of sales}} \times 365 \text{ days}$$

Extracting the relevant figures from Bilton Burgess's accounts, average stock is taken as the average of opening and closing stock:

$$\frac{\text{Opening stock} + \text{closing stock}}{2} = \frac{100 + 104}{2} = 102$$

The average could be more accurately calculated if more information were available; for instance, if monthly stock figures were available, a fairly accurate average stock figure for the year could be calculated by adding together the monthly figures and dividing by 12.

Bilton Burgess plc stock turnover ratio equals:

$$\frac{\text{Cost of sales}}{\text{Average stock}}$$

$$= \frac{990}{102} = 9.7 \text{ times}$$

This means that on average stock is replaced 9.7 times in a year. The additional calculation expresses the same information in a slightly different (possibly more helpful) way:

$$\text{Stock turnover in days} = \frac{\text{Average stock}}{\text{Cost of sales}} \times 365 \text{ days}$$

$$= \frac{102}{990} \times 365 \text{ days} = 37.6 \text{ days}$$

This means that, on average, an item of stock spends 37.6 days in Bilton Burgess's warehouse.

As with previous ratio calculation results, it is difficult to assess the significance of this figure without some point of comparison. If we know that in the previous year stock turnover in days was 32.7 days, we can conclude that the stock turnover ratio appears to have worsened. Also, much depends on the nature of the stock. If Bilton Burgess is in the fresh fruit supply business, 37.6 days would appear to be an excessive stock turnover; on the other hand, if it supplies electrical components, there is probably nothing out of the ordinary with a measure of 37.6 days.

Debtors turnover ratio

The debtors turnover ratio assesses the length of time that debtors take to pay. The calculation of this ratio is as follows:

$$\text{Debtors turnover ratio} = \frac{\text{Average debtors}}{\text{Credit sales}} \times 365 \text{ days}$$

In the case of Bilton Burgess plc we have no data available about the opening figure for debtors. In such cases we can use the closing figure, but it must be interpreted with some caution.

Extracting the relevant figures from the Bilton Burgess accounts, and assuming that all sales are made on credit (i.e. there are no sales made for cash):

$$\frac{\text{Debtors}}{\text{Credit sales}} \times 365 \text{ days}$$

$$= \frac{170}{1\,600} \times 365 \text{ days} = 38.8 \text{ days}$$

(Note that this is sometimes referred to as the debtors collection period.) This figure would be useful for making a comparison over time; if we had sufficient information we would be able to say whether or not this was an improvement over the previous year's figure.

The length of time debtors take to pay is related to the business's policy on offering credit. Let's suppose that Bilton Burgess's sales invoices state: 'Payment must be received within 30 days of despatch of goods'. The debtors turnover ratio tells us that, on average, customers exceed the credit terms by 8.8 days. It may be that, by improving its credit control procedures, Bilton Burgess would be able to reduce its debtors turnover figure.

Creditors turnover ratio

The **creditors turnover ratio** measures the length of time, on average, that a business takes to pay its creditors. Its calculation is very similar to that used for the debtors turnover ratio:

$$\text{Creditors turnover ratio} = \frac{\text{Average creditors}}{\text{Purchases}} \times 365 \text{ days}$$

In the case of Bilton Burgess plc we have no information available about the opening balance of creditors. In such cases it is usually acceptable to use closing creditors, but the results of the calculation need to be treated with caution.

Extracting the relevant figures from Bilton Burgess's accounts we can calculate the ratio as follows:

$$\frac{\text{Creditors}}{\text{Purchases}} \times 365 \text{ days}$$

$$= \frac{97}{994} \times 365 \text{ days} = 35.6 \text{ days}$$

Given that many businesses stipulate payment within 30 days, Bilton Burgess is probably not taking an unreasonably long time to pay its creditors.

Where the creditors turnover ratio is very high, or where it has risen significantly over the previous period(s), it may indicate possible liquidity problems. To some extent, it is good management practice to take advantage of this source of interest-free credit. However, it must be kept within reasonable limits. If a business takes an unreasonably long time to settle its creditors, there may be a consequent loss of goodwill and the business may find it difficult to obtain supplies on credit.

? Self-test question 13.3 (answer at the end of the book)

Armitage Horobin Limited is a trading company that makes all its sales on credit. Its profit and loss account and balance sheet for the accounting years 20X4 and 20X3 are as follows:

Armitage Horobin Limited: Profit and loss accounts for the years ending 31 March 20X4 and 20X3

	20X4 £000	20X4 £000	20X3 £000	20X3 £000
Sales		283.4		271.1

	20X4 £000	20X4 £000	20X3 £000	20X3 £000
Cost of sales				
Opening stock	23.7		21.2	
Add: purchases	184.8		177.5	
	208.5		198.7	
Less: closing stock	(25.9)		(23.7)	
		(182.6)		(175.0)
Gross profit		100.8		96.1
Various expenses		(75.9)		(73.0)
Operating profit		24.9		23.1
Taxation		(4.9)		(3.7)
Retained profit		20.0		19.4

Armitage Horobin Limited: Balance sheets at 31 March 20X4 and 20X3

	20X4 £000	20X4 £000	20X3 £000	20X3 £000
Fixed assets		289.2		275.3
Current assets				
Stock	25.9		23.7	
Debtors	33.0		28.2	
Prepayments	1.0		1.5	
Cash at bank	6.0		4.2	
	65.9		57.6	
Creditors: amounts falling due within one year				
Trade creditors	24.5		20.6	
Accruals	1.3		3.0	
	25.8		23.6	
Net current assets		40.1		34.0
Total assets less current liabilities		329.3		309.3
Capital and reserves				
Share capital		40.0		40.0
Reserves		289.3		269.3
		329.3		309.3

Calculate the following efficiency ratios:

- fixed asset turnover
- stock turnover
- debtors turnover
- creditors turnover.

In each case state whether the ratio shows an improvement or not.

Investor ratios

Investor ratios, as the name implies, are those ratios that are likely to be of particular interest to investors and potential investors. In Chapter 12 we identified some of the questions investors are likely to ask:

- How is my investment doing?
- Should I buy more shares/sell the shares I've already got/hold on to the investment I've already got?
- Is the dividend likely to increase?
- What are the chances of the company going out of business?

The group of accounting ratios classified in this section under the heading 'investor ratios' may help to suggest answers to some of these questions. Although the ratios covered in the section may be of particular interest to investors, they are likely also to provide information that is useful to other people who have some reason for wanting to know more about a business.

Note that several of the ratios that follow in this section can be calculated only for limited companies. They are not applicable to sole trader and partnership businesses.

As with the other main groups of ratios, we will use the information given for Bilton Burgess plc in Example 13.1 to illustrate calculations.

Example 13.4

Dividend per share

This ratio calculates the amount in pence of the dividend for each ordinary share:

$$\frac{\text{Dividend for the year}}{\text{Number of shares in issue}}$$

The relevant figures for Bilton Burgess are:

$$\frac{40}{300} = 13.3p \text{ per share}$$

Note that, in this case, the number of shares is the same as the value in the balance sheet, because the shares are of £1 each. Care must be taken where the shares are, for example, 50p shares. In this example, if the shares were of 50p nominal value there would be twice as many to take into the calculation.

Dividend cover

Dividend cover calculates the number of times the current dividend could be paid out of available profits.

$$\frac{\text{Profits after tax attributable to ordinary shareholders}}{\text{Dividend}}$$

For Bilton Burgess:

$$\frac{147}{40} = 3.67$$

What does this mean? Remember that the directors determine the level of dividend payout; usually they will seek to ensure that it is comfortably within available profits and that a good proportion of profits is retained in the business. The dividend cover calculated for Bilton Burgess tells us that the directors could pay the current level of dividend 3.67 times out of available profits.

As with all ratios the dividend cover ratio is of limited use on its own. However, it does suggest, in this case, that dividend cover is comfortable. If dividend cover equals one it means that all available profits for the year are being paid over to shareholders in the form of dividends. This would be a matter of concern for two reasons: (a) no profit is being retained in the business; and (b) it may not be possible to sustain this level of payout in future years.

Earnings per share

The dividend per share is the amount that is actually paid out per share to investors in the company. Earnings per share is the amount that is theoretically available per share. It is calculated as follows:

$$\frac{\text{Profits after tax attributable to ordinary shareholders}}{\text{Number of shares in issue}}$$

This gives earnings per share (often abbreviated to eps) in pence.

The relevant figures for Bilton Burgess are:

$$\frac{147}{300} = 49\text{p per share}$$

(Note that even where eps is greater than 99p the amount is always expressed in pence.) It is worth emphasising again that the eps of 49p per share does not end up in the pockets of the Bilton Burgess shareholders; it is a theoretical figure that expresses the amount of earnings available to shareholders. The amount that does end up in the pockets of the shareholders is (usually) a lesser amount: the dividend.

Price/earnings ratio

This is a very important stock market ratio. It expresses the relationship between earnings per share (which we have just looked at) and the price of the share. Because the calculation involves a share price, it can be performed only for companies listed on a stock exchange for which a share price is available. This ratio cannot, therefore, be calculated for most businesses, such as sole traders, partnerships and unlisted companies.

In order to calculate the ratio for Bilton Burgess plc (which, remember, is a listed company) we would need to obtain a current share price. Bilton Burgess plc is a fictional company; if it were a real UK listed company, a current share price could easily be obtained for it by looking in the companies listings in the *Financial Times* or by accessing the London Stock Exchange website.

Suppose that the current share price of Bilton Burgess plc is £6.40 per share. (Yes, these are £1 shares, but the value at which they are traded on the stock exchange depends upon the market's perception of the value and the prospects of the company.) The price/earnings (or P/E ratio, as it is often known) for Bilton Burgess is:

$$\frac{\text{Price per share}}{\text{Earnings per share}}$$

$$\frac{640p}{49p} = 13.1 \text{ (to one decimal place)}$$

So what does this mean? The P/E ratio for Bilton Burgess tells us that investors are currently prepared to pay 13.1 × the company's earnings for a single share. On its own, as with most ratios, it has little significance. However, it is very useful for making comparisons with other listed companies, and, especially, with companies in the same industry sector.

Suppose that Bilton Burgess's two main competitors are both listed companies, and that their P/E ratios are:

Abacus Casement plc = 18.4
Carew Grapeshot plc = 10.3

Investors are prepared to pay up to 18.4 × earnings for a share in Abacus Casement plc, which suggests that they regard the company more highly than Bilton Burgess. Carew Grapeshot plc, on the other hand, has a lower P/E than Bilton Burgess; investors are prepared to pay only 10.3 × earnings for a single share.

The P/E ratio is a measurement of the market's perception of a company's shares. A high P/E ratio suggests that the shares are regarded as highly desirable; this is often because they are perceived as relatively low risk. Low P/Es, on the other hand, suggest an unfashionable share that is downgraded by the market.

The following table shows a sample of real companies' P/E ratios in February 2005. All are 'household name' shares that appear under the 'general retailers' classification.

Examples of P/E ratios of companies listed on the London Stock Exchange

Company	P/E
Boots	15.6
Dixons	18.6

Company	P/E
Kingfisher	12.7
Marks & Spencer	19.2
Ted Baker	24.7
Woolworths	14.7

It should be noted that appearances can be deceptive. A sudden fluctuation in share price can result in a significant change to the P/E so that at any point in time, the P/E may not be representative.

Market capitalisation

Market capitalisation is not a ratio calculation, but it is a piece of information that is likely to be of interest to investors and potential investors in a listed company. Market capitalisation is the current share price multiplied by the number of shares in issue. It provides a guide as to the market's view of the current value of the company. For Bilton Burgess:

Price £6.40 × number of shares in issue 300 000 = £1 920 000

? Self-test question 13.4 (answer at the end of the book)

Armley Regina plc is a listed company with a current share price at 31 December 20X3 of £5.08 per share. The company has 1 000 000 50p shares in issue. Other relevant data for the company at 31 December 20X3 is as follows:

	£000
Profit after taxation (all attributable to ordinary shareholders)	680
Dividends	(220)
Retained profit for the year	460

Calculate the following:

- dividend per share
- dividend cover
- earnings per share
- price/earnings ratio
- market capitalisation.

Lending ratios

Gearing

A **gearing ratio** expresses the relationship between two different types of financing of a company: (a) financing through equity (i.e. ordinary) shares; and financing through long-term loans, i.e. debt.

Equity is contributed to a company by its ordinary shareholders who are able to vote in the annual general meeting, and who have a right to a share of any ordinary dividend that is declared by the company directors. Any undistributed profits are regarded as part of equity financing.

Debt is finance in the form of loans. Lenders are usually entitled to interest at a fixed rate on the loans, but, unlike shareholders, they do not have a vote and are not entitled to any share of the dividend.

Note that in Chapter 11 we briefly looked at another type of capital: preference share capital. This is share capital that confers the right to a fixed rate of dividend (for example, 10% preference share capital). Preference shareholders do not have any right to a share of the ordinary dividend; even if the company does really well, and distributes a lot of money to its ordinary shareholders, the preference shareholders still receive only the fixed percentage to which they are entitled. Preference share capital has characteristics more akin to debt, and so for the purposes of the gearing calculation, it is usually regarded as debt.

Gearing has great significance for shareholders and potential shareholders. However, it is a ratio of general importance that is likely to be significant for many interest groups.

There is more than one way of calculating gearing:

$$\frac{\text{Debt}}{\text{Equity}}$$

or

$$\frac{\text{Debt}}{\text{Debt} + \text{Equity}}$$

The really important point in adopting one or other of these methods is to be consistent.

The effect of interest in the profit and loss account is measured by our last ratio: interest cover.

Interest cover

Interest cover is a measurement of the number of times interest could be paid out of available profits. Students who have understood the idea of dividend cover will recognise that interest cover performs a similar function. It is calculated as follows:

$$\frac{\text{Profit before interest and taxation}}{\text{Interest}}$$

As for previous groups of ratios we will use the Example 13.1 data from Bilton Burgess to illustrate the calculations.

Example 13.5

Gearing

The relevant figures for debt and equity for Bilton Burgess are:

- Debt (assuming that amounts due after more than one year all relate to long-term debt) = £800 000.
- Equity (share capital + reserves) = £1 200 000.

Gearing for Bilton Burgess is calculated as follows. Either:

$$\frac{\text{Debt}}{\text{Equity}}$$

$$= \frac{800\ 000}{1\ 200\ 000} = 66.7\% \text{ (to one decimal place)}$$

or

$$\frac{\text{Debt}}{\text{Debt} + \text{Equity}}$$

$$= \frac{800\ 000}{800\ 000 + 1\ 200\ 000} = 40\%$$

Interest cover

The relevant figures for Bilton Burgess are:

$$\frac{291}{80} = 3.64 \text{ times}$$

The effects of gearing

Why are ordinary shareholders interested in gearing?

A high level of debt capital relative to equity capital (i.e. a high level of gearing) means that the company faces a relatively high interest charge. Interest must be paid out of the store of available profits. If the interest charge soaks up most of the available profit there will be very little left over for the ordinary shareholders. Therefore, an investment in a highly geared company is usually seen as relatively risky for equity shareholders. However, a great deal depends upon the level of profits generated.

The following example illustrates the potential impact of gearing.

Example 13.6

Two companies, Basket Rabbitts plc and Telford Barron plc, have very similar operations and are of very similar sizes. However, their financing varies: Basket Rabbitts is highly geared and Telford Barron is low geared. Their total capital is as follows:

High gearing		**Low gearing**	
Basket Rabbitts plc	£	*Telford Barron plc*	£
Long-term debt finance		Long-term debt finance	
10% interest	40 000	10% interest	5 000
Equity finance	30 000	Equity finance	65 000
	70 000		70 000

Let's look at the effects of the gearing at three different potential levels of profit before tax:

	£
High level	12 000
Medium level	8 000
Low level	4 000

In all cases we will assume a tax rate of 30%.

1. High level of profit

High gearing		**Low gearing**	
Basket Rabbitts plc	£	*Telford Barron plc*	£
Profit before interest and tax	12 000	Profit before interest and tax	12 000
Less: interest £40 000 × 10%	(4 000)	Less: interest: £5 000 × 10%	(500)
Profit before tax	8 000	Profit before tax	11 500
Tax: £8 000 × 30%	(2 400)	Tax: £11 500 × 30%	(3 450)
Profit after tax attributable		Profit after tax attributable	
to ordinary shareholders	5 600	to ordinary shareholders	8 050

Post-tax return on equity shareholders' funds:

$$\frac{5\ 600}{30\ 000} \times 100 = 18.7\%$$

Post-tax return on equity shareholders' funds

$$\frac{8\ 050}{65\ 000} \times 100 = 12.3\%$$

2. Medium level of profit

High gearing		**Low gearing**	
Basket Rabbitts plc	£	*Telford Barron plc*	£
Profit before interest and tax	8 000	Profit before interest and tax	8 000
Less: interest £40 000 × 10%	(4 000)	Less: interest: £5 000 × 10%	(500)
Profit before tax	4 000	Profit before tax	7 500
Tax: £4 000 × 30%	(1 200)	Tax: £7 500 × 30%	(2 250)
Profit after tax attributable		Profit after tax attributable	
to ordinary shareholders	2 800	to ordinary shareholders	5 250

Post-tax return on equity shareholders' funds:

$$\frac{2\ 800}{30\ 000} \times 100 = 9.3\%$$

Post-tax return on equity shareholders' funds:

$$\frac{5\ 250}{65\ 000} \times 100 = 8.1\%$$

▶

3. Low level of profit

High gearing		**Low gearing**	
Basket Rabbitts plc	£	*Telford Barron plc*	£
Profit before interest and tax	4 000	Profit before interest and tax	4 000
Less: interest £40 000 × 10%	(4 000)	Less: interest: £5 000 × 10%	(500)
Profit before tax	—	Profit before tax	3 500
Tax	—	Tax: £3 500 × 30%	(1 050)
Profit after tax attributable to ordinary shareholders	—	Profit after tax attributable to ordinary shareholders	2 450

Post-tax return on equity shareholders' funds:

Post-tax return on equity shareholders' funds:

$$0\% \qquad\qquad \frac{2\ 450}{65\ 000} \times 100 = 3.8\%$$

The example illustrates that returns to shareholders in a highly geared company are more volatile than returns to shareholders in a low geared company. Highly geared companies are, therefore, seen by ordinary shareholders as more risky.

Chapter summary

A great deal of useful material on financial ratio analysis has been covered in this chapter. The following ratios were examined within five major groups:

- **Performance ratios**
  - Gross profit margins
  - Net profit margins
  - Return on capital employed.

- **Liquidity ratios**
  - Current ratio
  - Quick (acid test) ratio.

- **Efficiency ratios**
  - Fixed asset turnover
  - Stock turnover
  - Debtor turnover
  - Creditor turnover.

- **Investor ratios**
  - Dividend per share
  - Dividend cover
  - Earnings per share
  - Price/earnings ratio
  - Market capitalisation.

- **Lending ratios**
  - Gearing ratio
  - Interest cover.

Remember that the purpose in analysing accounting information is to understand it better. Ratio calculations can be a useful means to an end, but the key objective is to understand the meaning of the financial statements.

 The end-of-chapter exercises are divided into two sections. The first section has answers provided at the end of the book. The second section, in the white box, has answers on the lecturers' section of the website. Finally the chapter contains a long case study that examines many aspects of the analysis of financial reports.

Exercises: answers at the end of the book

The following information is relevant to questions 13.1 to 13.3 inclusive. Extracts from Sigmund & Son Limited's financial statements for 20X4 show the following:

	£000
Gross profit	616.4
Various expenses	(313.6)
Operating profit	302.8
Interest payable	(35.0)
Profit on ordinary activities before taxation	267.8
Taxation	(80.0)
Profit on ordinary activities after taxation	187.8
Dividends	(100.0)
Retained profit	87.8
Share capital	500.0
Reserves	1 790.0
Long-term loan capital	350.0

13.1 Calculate the pre-tax return on shareholders' funds (to one decimal place). Is it:

a)   13.2%

b)   10.1%

c)   26.9%

d)   11.7%?

13.2 Calculate the post-tax return on shareholders' funds (to one decimal place). Is it:

a)   3.8%

b)   8.2%

c)   3.3%

d)   7.1%?

13.3 Calculate the return on total capital invested (to one decimal place). Is it:

a)   8.2%

b)   11.5%

c)   13.2%

d)   10.1%?

13.4 Shania would like to invest in a company that will give her a good rate of return on her investment. She has collected information on four companies. Extracts from their most recent financial statements are given below:

	Ambit Ltd	Bolsover Ltd	Carcan Ltd	Delphic Ltd
	£000	£000	£000	£000
Operating profit	983.6	647.8	726.8	1 061.4
Interest	(180.0)	(107.0)	(151.0)	(206.0)
Profit before taxation	803.6	540.8	575.8	855.4
Taxation	(240.0)	(160.0)	(170.0)	(250.0)
Profit after taxation	563.6	380.8	405.8	605.4
Share capital	80.0	95.0	86.0	60.0
Reserves	4 550.0	3 881.0	3 928.0	7 000.0
Long-term loans	2 400.0	1 250.0	1 820.0	2 500.0

Which company currently has the highest pre-tax return on shareholders' funds?

a) Ambit Limited

b) Bolsover Limited

c) Carcan Limited

d) Delphic Limited.

13.5 Trixie Stores Limited has the following working capital items in its balance sheet at 31 December 20X4:

	£
Stock	18 370
Debtors	24 100
Cash in hand	70
Trade creditors	15 450
Bank overdraft	6 400

The current ratio (working to two decimal places) for Trixie Stores Limited is:

a) 1.95:1

b) 1.11:1

c) 0.51:1

d) 0.9:1.

13.6 Trimester Tinker Limited has the following working capital items in its balance sheet at 31 December 20X1:

	£
Stock	108 770
Debtors	94 300
Cash in hand	1 600
Trade creditors	110 650

The company belongs to a trade association that has recently published industry averages for key financial ratios based upon a survey of its members. The industry averages for current and quick ratios applicable to the business of Trimester Tinker Limited are:

Current ratio = 1.62:1

Quick ratio = 0.93:1

Which of the following statements is correct?

a) Trimester Tinker Limited's current ratio is higher than the industry average and its quick ratio is also higher.

b) Trimester Tinker Limited's current ratio is higher than the industry average but its quick ratio is lower.

c) Trimester Tinker Limited's current ratio is lower than the industry average and its quick ratio is also lower.

d) Trimester Tinker Limited's current ratio is lower than the industry average but its quick ratio is higher.

13.7 Upwood Sickert Limited has total sales in the year to 31 May 20X6 of £686 430. Extracts from the company's balance sheet at that date show fixed assets as follows:

	Cost £	Depreciation £	Net book value £
Plant and machinery	200 000	30 000	170 000
Vehicles	106 640	46 655	59 985

Calculate the fixed asset turnover ratio for the year (to two decimal places). Is it:

a) 2.24

b) 0.34

c) 0.45

d) 2.98?

13.8 A sole trader's stock at 31 December 20X7 is £405 000. By 31 December 20X8 stock has increased in value by 10%. Cost of sales for the year ending 31 December 20X8 is £1 506 700.
What is the business's stock turnover in days?

13.9 A company has debtors in its year-end balance sheet of £218 603. Sales for the year were £1 703 698; 70% of these were sales on credit. Debtor turnover in days is:

a) 46.8 days

b) 32.7 days

c) 66.9 days

d) 18.3 days.

13.10 The managing director of Winger Whalley Limited has just received a report from one of the accounting assistants employed by the business. The report shows key ratios and supplies explanations for any significant fluctuations. The MD is concerned to find that the debtors turnover period has worsened significantly in the period from 20X2 to 20X3 (it was 36.4 days at the end of 20X2 and is 41.2 days at the end of 20X3). The accounting assistant has supplied the following reasons for the fluctuations:

1. The company's credit controller did a parachute jump for charity about three months ago. The parachute failed to open properly, and because of her injuries she was away from work in the last three months of 20X3. The temporary staff agency was unable to provide a suitable replacement for her, and during most of the three-month period her work was simply not done.

2. Sales have increased by 4% in the course of the year.

3. During 20X3 the board decided to introduce a system of early settlement discounts. Debtors paying within 30 days would receive a discount of 0.5% of the value of their invoices.

4. A new order of sales invoice stationery was received part way through the year. Usually the sales invoice stationery is printed with 'SETTLEMENT REQUIRED WITHIN 30 DAYS', but the printers had omitted this by mistake. The office general manager decided to use the stationery anyway. Two of these reasons could be valid explanations for the increase in the debtors turnover period. The valid explanations are:

   a) 1 and 2

   b) 3 and 4

   c) 1 and 4

   d) 2 and 3.

13.11 A business has creditors at its year-end of £206 460. Purchases for the year are £1 952 278, of which 90% were made on credit. What is the creditors turnover period?

   a) 42.9 days

   b) 38.6 days

   c) 34.7 days

   d) 11.7 days.

The following information about Waldo Wolff plc, a quoted company, is relevant to questions 13.12–13.15 inclusive. Extracts from Waldo Wolff's accounts for the year ending 31 December 20X4 include the following useful information:

	£000
Operating profit	1 836.4
Interest payable	(220.0)
Profit before taxation	1 616.4
Taxation	(485.0)
Profit after taxation	1 131.4
Dividends	(300.0)

	£000
Retained profit	831.4

The company has 6 000 000 shares in issue. The shares have a nominal value of 50p each. The market price at 31 December 20X4 of a share in the company is £3.11.

13.12 The dividend per share is:

a)   10p

b)   5p

c)   50p

d)   100p.

13.13 The dividend cover ratio is:

a)   3.77

b)   5.39

c)   2.77

d)   6.12.

13.14 Earnings per share (in pence) is:

a)   18.86p

b)   26.94p

c)   13.86p

d)   37.71p.

13.15 What is Waldo Wolff plc's market capitalisation at 31 December 20X4?

13.16 At 30 April 20X6 Wilson Streep plc has a market capitalisation of £6 303 000 with 3 300 000 ordinary 50p shares in issue. The profit attributable to ordinary shareholders in its profit and loss account for the year ending 30 April 20X6 is £750 090. What is the company's P/E ratio?

a)   16.1

b)   4.2

c)   8.4

d)   3.8.

13.17 Brazier Barkiss plc has the following capital structure at 30 April 20X6:

	£
Ordinary share capital (£1 shares)	1 000 000
Reserves	2 739 400
Long-term loans (10% interest rate)	2 000 000

Profit before interest and tax for the year ending 30 April 20X6 was £646 750 and interest payable was £200 000. Calculate the following ratios:

i) gearing (on the basis of debt/equity)

ii) interest cover.

13.18 The directors of the Cuttlefish Biscuit Corporation Limited have calculated a set of key accounting ratios for their biscuit manufacturing business. These are detailed in the following table, together with industry averages provided by the National Biscuit Manufacturers' Federation.

	Cuttlefish	Industry average
Gross profit margin	32.3%	31.6%
Operating profit margin	16.2%	17.1%
Debtors turnover (days)	36.0	38.4
Stock turnover (days)	48.7	47.4
Creditors (days)	31.4	39.6
Gearing (debt/equity)	18.7%	29.4%

Write a brief report to the directors of Cuttlefish comparing the ratios for their company with the industry averages. Identify any areas in which you think they could make improvements.

13.19 Cryer Roussillon Limited is a trading company. Shortly before the beginning of the 20X5 accounting year (which ends on 31 December) a new managing director was appointed. He made the strategic decision to alter the company's range of products. Previously, the company had concentrated on lower margin products within its industry, but the new MD decided to move into higher quality products which produce better margins. He has made several other changes to the company. He persuaded the board of directors that the company should invest in some badly needed new fixed assets, and the company took out a long-term loan to help finance the acquisitions. He has also obtained the agreement of the other directors (all of whom are shareholders) not to propose any dividend this year, so that profits can be retained in the company to help finance future growth. The summarised financial statements for 20X5 and 20X4 are as follows.

Cryer Roussillon Limited: Profit and loss accounts for the years ending

31 December 20X5 and 31 December 20X4

	20X5 £	20X4 £
Sales	206 470	210 619
Cost of sales	(121 198)	(141 789)
Gross profit	85 272	68 830
Various expenses	(41 459)	(47 610)
Operating profit	43 813	21 220
Interest	(3 000)	—

	20X5	20X4
	£	£
Profit before taxation	40 813	21 220
Taxation	(8 100)	(3 180)
Profit after taxation	32 713	18 040
Dividend	—	(13 000)
Retained profit	32 713	5 040

Cryer Roussillon: Balance sheets at 31 December 20X5 and 20X4

	20X5	20X5	20X4	20X4
	£	£	£	£
Fixed assets		129 490		68 750
Current assets				
Stock	14 278		14 550	
Debtors	20 693		29 420	
Cash at bank	10 792		640	
	45 763		44 610	
Creditors: amounts falling due within one year	15 470	30 293	16 290	28 320
Total assets less currents liabilities		159 783		97 070
Long-term loan		(30 000)		—
		129 783		97 070
Capital and reserves				
Share capital		20 000		20 000
Reserves		109 783		77 070
		129 783		97 070

The managing director has asked you, as the company's financial adviser, to write a confidential report to the board commenting upon items of significance in the accounts. He would like you to calculate any key ratios that you consider to be important, and to provide an assessment of how the company is doing.

Exercises: answers available to lecturers

The following information is relevant to questions 13.20 to 13.22 inclusive. Extracts from Sinclair Salter Limited's financial statements for 20X3 show the following:

	£000
Gross profit	896.4
Various expenses	(606.8)
Operating profit	289.6
Interest payable	(93.0)

	£000
Profit on ordinary activities before taxation	196.6
Taxation	(60.0)
Profit on ordinary activities after taxation	136.6
Dividends	(40.0)
Retained profit	96.6
Share capital	100.0
Reserves	1 170.0
Long-term loan capital	900.0

13.20 Calculate return on total capital invested (to one decimal place). Is it:

a)   15.5%

b)   13.3%

c)   9.1%

d)   22.8%?

13.21 Calculate pre-tax return on shareholders' funds (to one decimal place). Is it:

a)   15.5%

b)   10.8%

c)   9.1%

d)   22.8%?

13.22 Calculate post-tax return on shareholders' funds (to one decimal place). Is it?

a)   15.5%

b)   9.1%

c)   10.8%

d)   6.3%?

13.23 Shirley has been thinking for a while about investing some surplus cash in an unlisted company that organises lettings of holiday properties in France. The company is run by an old friend of hers who is looking for additional investors in order to fund a planned expansion of the business. Shirley has received financial statements for the business for 20X6 and 20X5. The profit and loss accounts and extracts from the balance sheets are as follows:

	20X6	20X5
	£000	£000
Sales revenue	976.9	899.6
Gross profit	377.6	360.9
Various expenses	(102.5)	(98.6)

	20X6	20X5
	£000	£000
Operating profit	275.1	262.3
Interest payable	(18.7)	(16.5)
Profit on ordinary activities before taxation	256.4	245.8
Taxation	(77.0)	(74.0)
Retained profit	179.4	171.8
Share capital	80.0	80.0
Reserves	1 465.0	1 285.6
Long-term loan capital	319.0	276.0

Calculate (to one decimal place) the following financial ratios for Shirley:

i)   gross profit margin

ii)   operating profit margin

iii)   return on shareholders' funds

iv)   return on total capital employed.

Comment on any apparent changes in business performance between 20X5 and 20X6.

13.24 Tadcaster Terrier Limited has the following working capital items in its balance sheet at 31 May 20X1:

	£
Stock	88 700
Creditors	90 450
Debtors	85 210
Bank overdraft	16 790

The current ratio (working to two decimal places) for Tadcaster Terrier Limited is:

a)   1.62:1

b)   0.62:1

c)   1.9:1

d)   0.79:1.

13.25 Turnbull Taffy Limited's figures to 31 March 20X4 show the following working capital items:

	£
Stock	67 400
Debtors	42 660
Cash at bank	6 050
Trade creditors	58 760

The company's finance director is preparing a projected balance sheet for 31 March 20X5 as part of a package of information to be presented to a bank from which the company hopes to obtain a long-term loan. The finance director estimates that there will be the following changes to working capital between 31 March 20X4 and 31 March 20X5:

Stock will decrease by 10%
Debtors will decrease by 15%
Cash at bank will increase by 50%
Trade creditors will decrease by 5%.

Calculate (to two decimal places):

i)   The current ratio and the quick ratio at 31 March 20X4.

ii) The expected current ratio and quick ratio at 31 March 20X5 based on the finance director's estimates.

13.26 Uriah Westwood plc is an advertising agency operating from rented offices in the West End of London. Ulverstone Thunderbird plc is a company engaged in heavy engineering. It owns all its own plant and equipment and a small factory site in the north of England. Both companies have recently reported sales in the region of £10 million. The fixed asset turnover ratio for one of the companies is 1.14 and for the other is 10.62.

From the brief descriptions given, which of the two companies is more likely to have the higher fixed asset turnover ratio?

13.27 The following are extracts from the profit and loss accounts of a sole trader business for the years ending 31 December 20X8 and 20X7:

	20X8	20X7
	£000	£000
Opening stock	1 605.3	1 396.4
Purchases	19 360.4	19 568.9
Closing stock	(1 565.7)	(1 605.3)
Cost of sales	19 400.0	19 360.0

Calculate the stock turnover in days for both years. Has it improved or worsened in 20X8?

13.28 Whybird, a sole trader, has been advised by his accountant to keep an eye on the number of days his debtors take to pay. The accountant has explained how to calculate the debtors turnover period but Whybird doesn't really understand. He asks you to do the calculation for him. Extracts from the last two years' accounts show the following figures:

	20X5	20X4
	£	£
Sales	180 630	178 440
Less: returns	(1 300)	(1 060)
	179 330	177 380

	20X5	20X4
	£	£
Debtors	20 982	21 117
Less: provision for doubtful debts	(306)	(297)
	20 676	20 820

Calculate the debtors turnover period for Whybird for both years to one decimal place. Has the debtors turnover period improved or worsened in 20X5?

13.29 Wiswell Limited is a trading company. Its year-end accounts for 20X4 and 20X3 include the following relevant details:

	20X4	20X4	20X3	20X3
	£	£	£	£
Sales		1 936 000		1 877 200
Cost of sales				
Opening stock	145 550		136 200	
Add: purchases	1 042 255		1 025 666	
	1 187 805		1 161 866	
Less: closing stock	(160 370)		(145 550)	
		(1 027 435)		(1 016 316)
Gross profit		908 565		860 884
Stocks		160 370		145 550
Debtors		226 485		209 063
Creditors		160 479		151 742

Calculate the following ratios for both 20X4 and 20X3:

i) stock turnover in days

ii) debtors turnover in days

iii) creditors turnover in days.

Comment briefly on the significance of the changes in the ratios.

The following information about Worsley Bacup plc, a quoted company, is relevant to questions 13.30–13.33 inclusive. Extracts from Worsley Bacup's accounts for the year ending 30 September 20X9 include the following useful information:

	£000
Operating profit	986.7
Interest payable	(106.0)
Profit before taxation	880.7
Taxation	(240.0)
Profit after taxation	640.7
Dividends	(250.8)
Retained profit	389.9

The company has 2 200 000 shares in issue. The shares have a nominal value of 25p each. The market price at 31 December 20X4 of a share in the company is £7.66.

13.30 The dividend per share is:

    a)   45.6p

    b)   11.4p

    c)   25.0p

    d)   29.1p.

13.31 The dividend cover ratio is:

    a)   3.51

    b)   1.55

    c)   3.93

    d)   2.55.

13.32 Earnings per share (in pence) is:

    a)   17.72p

    b)   29.12p

    c)   116.49p

    d)   70.89p.

13.33 What is Worsley Bacup plc's market capitalisation at 30 September 20X9?

13.34 Watkinson Chapel plc is a listed company with a market capitalisation of £3 430 000 at 31 August 20X7. It has in issue 1 000 000 £1 ordinary shares, and profits attributable to ordinary shareholders for the year ending 31 August 20X7 are £243 700. What is the company's P/E ratio?

    a)   21.4

    b)   4.1

    c)   3.4

    d)   14.1.

13.35 Better Belter Limited has the following capital structure at 31 October 20X7:

	£
Ordinary share capital (£1 shares)	80 000
Reserves	696 400
Long-term loans (8% interest rate)	300 000

Profit before interest and tax for the year ending 31 October 20X7 was £35 000, and interest payable was £24 000. Calculate the following ratios:

    i)   gearing (on the basis of debt/equity)

    ii)   interest cover.

CASE STUDY 13.1   Analysing financial statements

This is a long case study that brings together the analysis techniques covered in both Chapters 12 and 13. Students should work through it carefully to ensure that they understand all aspects of the calculations and discussions, before attempting the end of chapter questions.

Having qualified as a physiotherapist, Louise Donovan now has a job in the physiotherapy department of a large city hospital. She is very careful with money and has managed to pay off all her student loans, as well as saving almost £5000 towards a deposit to buy a house. Louise's boyfriend, Ben, is not so good with money. Ben is an insurance broker and he earns more than Louise, but she quite often has to help him out with cash towards the end of the month. Louise is in love with Ben and would like them to get married as soon as they've saved up enough to get the house.

A couple of months ago Louise's grandma died. No one had realised until she died and the will was read that the old lady had also been a very efficient saver. She leaves Louise, her favourite granddaughter, £30 000. Louise is delighted by this unexpected piece of good news; now she has enough money for a deposit and she can go ahead and arrange the mortgage as soon as she and Ben have found the house they want. Ben, however, has other ideas. In his opinion, Louise should invest the money and he thinks he's found her a really good investment opportunity. Ben isn't too worried about buying the house; he's not sure that he's ready to settle down yet, and, besides, the way Louise has been saving, they'll have enough in another couple of years in any case. He occasionally feels guilty that he hasn't contributed any savings himself, but part of his salary is in commission, and he's planning to work really hard this year to find new clients.

The investment opportunity Ben has identified for Louise is in Fitton Parker Limited. Two brothers, Sam and Henry Fitton, and their friend Barney Parker started up the company six or seven years ago; they are all directors and each has a shareholding of 15 000 £1 shares. The company imports a basic range of sports clothing and footwear. It adds value to the range by imprinting logos and brand names, which it uses under licence, then re-sells to large retailers. Ben met Barney Parker by chance in a bar a few months ago, and Barney explained to him that the business is looking for some additional investors. The business has continued to be successful but is always short of cash. An additional infusion of cash would allow for the overdraft to be paid off (although the loan of £57 000 from Sam and Henry's father would have to remain for the time being) and would provide some additional cash for investing in new ranges and more effective advertising. There are several good opportunities that would be open to the business if only it had access to more ready cash. Ben was really impressed by the way Barney talked about the business, and promised to look round his own range of contacts to see if he could identify anyone who might be interested in this promising business opportunity.

Ben contacts Barney in November 20X4 to tell him that Louise may be willing to invest in Fitton Parker. Barney says that they've had some preliminary discussions with several potential investors, but that so far nothing definite has been decided. He tells Ben that Fitton Parker would issue a further 10 000 £1 shares to Louise in exchange for £30 000 in cash. As a result of the deal Louise would own just over

▶

18% of the company (she would have 10 000 new shares and Barney, Sam and Henry would continue to own 15 000 each: Louise would therefore own 10 000 out of the total number of issued shares of 55 000). Barney, Sam and Henry do not want any new investors to take an active part in the business, but propose to pay a decent level of dividend once the business has really taken off.

When Ben explains the proposition to Louise she is unimpressed at first. However, after a while, he manages to sell her the idea of investing in shares rather than property. 'This is a great opportunity, Lou; you could end up owning 18% of a really major business; if the prospects are as good as Barney says, they might be floating on the stock market in five years time, and you could be a millionaire.'

Patrick Donovan, Louise's father, is a man of strong views. One of his strong views is that Ben is not nearly good enough for Louise: 'He's a parasite and a loser, and they'll get married over my dead body', as he tells a friend. When Patrick hears about the investment plan he is horrified, and tells Louise that 'it's just another one of Ben's stupid ideas' and that she might as well throw the money away. This has the effect of making Louise more determined to stand up for Ben, and she tells Patrick that she's made up her mind to go ahead. Patrick tells her that she must, at least, get hold of the business accounts for the last couple of years and have a financial adviser go through them. He tells her that, if she insists on investing in shares (and he doesn't advise it) she should at least invest in listed company shares, then she would be able to sell them at any time.

Ben explains to Barney that Louise's father is causing trouble but that he'll probably come round if he sees some figures. After a few weeks, Barney produces profit and loss accounts and balance sheets for Fitton Parker for the three years ending 31 March 20X3. He tells Ben that each year's accounts were audited and there were no problems. The figures provided by Barney are as follows:

Fitton Parker Limited: Profit and loss accounts for the years ending

31 March 20X3 20X2 and 20X1

	20X3 £	20X2 £	20X1 £
Sales	596 860	491 383	415 985
Cost of sales	(402 964)	(325 089)	(271 588)
Gross profit	193 896	166 294	144 397
Selling and distribution costs	(76 990)	(60 930)	(52 538)
Administrative expenses	(33 750)	(31 695)	(32 772)
Directors' remuneration	(60 000)	(60 000)	(60 000)
Operating profit/(loss)	23 156	13 669	(913)
Interest payable and similar charges	(5 133)	(4 027)	(3 275)
Profit/(loss) on ordinary activities before taxation	18 023	9 642	(4 188)
Taxation paid	(3 350)	(2 406)	—
Retained profit for the year	14 673	7 236	(4 188)

Fitton Parker Limited: Balance sheets at 31 March 20X3 20X2 and 20X1

	20X3 £	20X3 £	20X2 £	20X2 £	20X1 £	20X1 £
Fixed assets		86 790		83 250		94 484
Current assets						
Stock	55 450		44 791		36 425	
Debtors	70 315		56 233		44 190	
Cash	—		806		—	
	125 765		101 830		80 615	
Creditors: amounts due within one year						
Trade creditors	47 491		34 750		31 418	
Overdraft	10 696		10 635		11 222	
	58 187		45 385		42 640	
Net current assets		67 578		56 445		37 975
Total assets less current liabilities		154 368		139 695		132 459
Creditors: amounts due after more than one year						
Long-term loan		(57 000)		(57 000)		(57 000)
		97 368		82 695		75 459
Capital and reserves						
Share capital £1 shares*		45 000		45 000		45 000
Reserves						
Profit and loss account brought forward	37 695		30 459		34 647	
Profit/(loss) for the year	14 673		7 236		(4 188)	
Profit and loss account carried forward		52 368		37 695		30 459
		97 368		82 695		75 459

*Authorised share capital is 80 000 £1 shares. Issued share capital is £45 000 i.e. £15 000 of shares issued to each of the Fitton brothers and to Barney Parker.

As Louise's financial adviser, analyse the financial statements of Fitton Parker and provide her with some advice on a recommended course of action. Include any reservations you may have about the information.

The website contains two extra case studies which can be attempted after studying both Chapters 12 and 13. The case studies both relate to the financial analysis of real companies:

- Games Workshop Group plc

- Tesco and Sainsbury's

Answers to self-test questions and exercises

Answers to self-test questions

CHAPTER 6

6.1
- Bank overdraft = Liability.
- Computer and printer used to keep the administrative records of the business = Asset.
- Plates and cups in the stockroom = Asset.
- Cash float kept in the till – £100 in various notes and coins = Asset.
- Loan of £20 000 from George's brother = Liability.

6.2
1. The total of assets in Saqib's business is £30 000 (Fixed assets) + £5000 (Stock) + £4000 (Debtors) + £3000 (Cash held in business bank account) = £42 000.
2. There is only one category of liability in the business: trade creditors of £6000. Therefore total liabilities are £6000.
3. Saqib's capital is stated in the question as £36 000.
4. Applying the accounting equation to Saqib's business: Assets (£42 000) – Liabilities (£6 000) = Capital (£36 000).

6.3

Assets – Liabilities = Capital

Therefore, Amy's capital can be calculated as:

£58 000 – £30 000 = £28 000

7.1

Jules: Trading account for the month ending 31 December 20X5

	£
Sales: 66 bags @ £23	1 518
Cost of sales: 66 bags @ £14.50	957
Gross profit	561

Note: the heading specifying the name of the business and the period covered by the trading account is essential information and must not be omitted.

7.2

Jules: Stock movement account for January 20X6

	Units	£
Opening stock: 36 bags @ £14.50	36	522
Add purchases: 68 bags @ £14.50	68	986
Less: items of stock sold: 42 bags @ £14.50	(42)	(609)
Closing stock: 62 bags @ £14.50	62	899

Note that this account is part of Jules's business records. It is not shown in his financial statements.

Jules: Trading account for the month to 31 January 20X6

	Units	£	£
Sales			
42 bags @ £23	42		966
Cost of sales			
Opening stock: 36 bags @ £14.50	36	522	
Add: purchases: 68 bags @ £14.50	68	986	
	104	1 508	
Less: closing stock: 62 bags @ £14.50	(62)	(899)	
Cost of sales: 42 bags @ £14.50	42		(609)
Gross profit for month*			357

*Check: each bag sold gives a gross profit of £23 – £14.50 = £8.50. If Jules sells 42 bags he expects to make a profit of 42 × £8.50 = £357.

CHAPTER 9

9.1

	£
Cost of Salvatore's new vehicle	65 000
Estimated sales proceeds after four years of use	(25 000)
Estimated total depreciation over four years	40 000

Spread evenly over four years, this produces a straight-line annual depreciation charge of £10 000.

9.2 **Year ending 30 April 20X7**: car depreciation expense in the profit and loss account will be £17 209 × 30% = £5 163. As regards the balance sheet:

	£
Car at cost	17 209
Less: depreciation	(5 163)
Net book value of vehicle	12 046

Year ending 30 April 20X8: car depreciation expense in the profit and loss account will be £12 046 × 30% = £3 614. As regards the balance sheet:

	£
Car at cost	17 209
Less: depreciation (5163 + 3614)	(8 777)
Net book value of vehicle	8 432

Year ending 30 April 20X9: car depreciation expense in the profit and loss account will be £8432 × 30% = £2530. As regards the balance sheet:

	£
Car at cost	17 209
Less: depreciation (5163 + 3614 + 2530)	(11 307)
Net book value of vehicle	5 902

9.3 To calculate Sergio's profit or loss on sale of the machine, first the net book value after five years' depreciation must be calculated:

	£
Machine at cost	15 000
Year 1 depreciation (30% × £15 000)	4 500
Net book value at end of year 1	10 500
Year 2 depreciation (30% × £10 500)	3 150
Net book value at end of year 2	7 350
Year 3 depreciation (30% × £7350)	2 205
Net book value at end of year 3	5 145
Year 4 depreciation (30% × £5145)	1 544
Net book value at end of year 4	3 601
Year 5 depreciation (30% × £3601)	1 080
Net book value at end of year 5	2 521

Sale proceeds are greater than net book value and so a profit on sale has been made of £489 (£3010 – £2521 = £489).

CHAPTER 10

10.1

Transaction	Effect on cash	Effect on profit
Purchase of raw materials for cash of £1800.	Cash is immediately reduced by £1800.	No immediate effect on profit. Raw materials go into stock, and at some point will enter the production process. After conversion to finished goods a sale of those goods will probably take place at which point the value of the raw materials is set off against sales in the form of cost of sales.
Sale of old delivery van for £360.	Cash is immediately increased by £360.	A profit or loss on sale (see Chapter 9) will be calculated by setting off the proceeds of sale (£360) against the written down value of the asset. The effect on profit would be £360 only if the written down value of the asset was nil.
Long-term loan from brother of £5000.	Cash and long-term liabilities are both immediately increased by £5000.	The loan itself has no effect on profit. Any interest paid on the loan will reduce profits.
Payment of interest on bank overdraft of £150.	Cash is reduced by £150 (or, more likely, the overdraft is increased by £150).	The interest paid reduces profits.

| Amortisation charge of £8000 relating to patent rights. | No effect on cash. | Profits are reduced by £8000. |

11.1 Workings for this question comprise the following:

1. *Selling and distribution costs*

	£
Selling costs	63 477
Distribution costs	54 460
	117 937

2. *Proposed dividend*. There are 20 000 shares in issue. A 25p dividend for each share gives a total of £5000 to be paid. Note that this will be included in current liabilities on the balance sheet.

3. *Tangible fixed assets*

	£
Premises at net book value	65 700
Vehicles at net book value	44 430
Fixtures and fittings at net book value	17 260
	127 390

4. *Other creditors*

	£
Creditor for corporation tax	19 500
Creditor for dividend	5 000
	24 500

5. *Reserves*

	£
At 1 April 20X1	161 479
Profit for the year	40 685
	202 164

Uppingham Telephones Limited: Draft profit and loss account for the year ending 31 March 20X2

	£
Turnover	717 216
Cost of sales	(509 582)
Gross profit	207 634
Selling and distribution costs (working 1)	(117 937)
Administrative expenses	(24 512)
Profit on ordinary activities before taxation	65 185
Taxation	(19 500)
Profit on ordinary activities after taxation	45 685
Dividends:	
Proposed (working 2)	(5 000)
Profit for the financial year	40 685

Uppingham Telephones Limited: Draft balance sheet at 31 March 20X2

	£	£
Fixed assets		
Intangible assets	35 866	
Tangible assets (working 3)	127 390	
		163 256
Current assets		
Stock	42 370	
Debtors	82 026	
Cash at bank	13 222	
	137 618	
Creditors: amounts falling due within one year		
Trade creditors	39 210	
Other creditors (working 4)	24 500	
	63 710	
Net current assets		73 908
Total assets less current liabilities		237 164
Creditors: amounts falling due after more than one year		(15 000)
		222 164
Capital and reserves		
Share capital		20 000
Reserves (working 5)		202 164
		222 164

CHAPTER 12 12.1

Horizontal trend analysis: Jamal's sales 20X0–20X8

Year	£	Percentage increase (decrease) on previous year
20X0	250 031	—
20X1	347 266	38.9
20X2	441 179	27.0
20X3	531 150	20.4
20X4	523 622	(1.4)
20X5	545 331	4.1
20X6	590 942	8.4
20X7	679 244	14.9
20X8	771 485	13.6

Since the business started sales have increased each year, apart from 20X4 when there was a small drop. Jared claimed at interview that he would be able to increase sales by 15% each year, but it is only in 20X7 and 20X8 that the increase has approached 15%. The early years of the business were characterised by very rapid sales growth, but this had clearly stopped by the time Jared was appointed. It is possible that Jared has made a major contribution to the improvements in sales, but the figures alone do not prove this conclusively.

Jamal's decision on Jared's salary increase will depend on the answers to some of the following questions:

■ To what extent has Jared been responsible for the recent improvements in sales trends?

- Are there other market factors at work (for example, has demand in the market for pre-packaged foods strengthened)?
- Has Jamal set performance targets for Jared, and have these been met?

12.2 *a) Sales increase*
The increase in the sales figures for the companies are:

Barnes & Jack Limited $= \dfrac{(2\ 044\ 032 - 1\ 743\ 906)}{1\ 743\ 906} \times 100 = 17.2\%$

Carleen Baker Limited $= \dfrac{(1\ 850\ 490 - 1\ 564\ 774)}{1\ 564\ 774} \times 100 = 18.3\%$

Carleen Baker's sales growth is slightly higher.

b) Extra information
The additional information allows for a more detailed breakdown of Barnes & Jack Limited's sales, as follows:

	Barnes & Jack Limited		
	20X6	20X5	Change
	£	£	%
Domestic and shop market	1 555 725	1 293 106	20.3
Zoos	488 307	450 800	8.3
	2 044 032	1 743 906	17.2

From this analysis, it appears that Barnes & Jack Limited have done slightly better in terms of sales growth than Carleen Baker Limited in the areas of their business that are directly comparable.

CHAPTER 13

13.1 Augustus Algernon Limited's pre-tax ROCE (return on shareholders' funds) equals:

$$\frac{\text{Profit before taxation and after interest}}{\text{Shareholders' funds}}$$

$$= \frac{162}{120 + 1\ 000} \times 100 = 14.46\%$$

Post-tax ROCE (return on shareholders' funds) equals:

$$\frac{\text{Profit after taxation and after interest}}{\text{Shareholders' funds}}$$

$$= \frac{114}{120 + 1\ 000} \times 100 = 10.18\%$$

ROCE (on total capital invested) equals:

$$\frac{\text{Profit before interest and tax}}{\text{Shareholders' funds and long-term capital}}$$

$$= \frac{186}{120 + 1\,000 + 480} \times 100 = 11.63\%$$

13.2

$$\text{Current ratio} = \frac{\text{Current assets}}{\text{Current liabilities}}$$

$$\text{Quick ratio} = \frac{\text{Current assets} - \text{Stock}}{\text{Current liabilities}}$$

For Arbus Nugent Limited for 20X8 and 20X7:

	20X8	20X7
Current ratio	$\dfrac{87\,620}{31\,450} : 1 = 2.8{:}1$	$\dfrac{74\,850}{32\,970} : 1 = 2.3{:}1$
Quick ratio	$\dfrac{87\,620 - 34\,300}{31\,450} : 1 = 1.7{:}1$	$\dfrac{74\,850 - 31\,600}{32\,970} : 1 = 1.3{:}1$

Both the current ratio and the quick ratio have improved.

13.3

Ratio	20X4	20X3
Fixed asset turnover	$\dfrac{\text{Sales}}{\text{Fixed assets}}$ $\dfrac{283.4}{289.2} = 0.98$	$\dfrac{271.1}{275.3} = 0.98$
Stock turnover	a) *Stock turnover:* $\dfrac{\text{Cost of sales}}{\text{Average stock}}$ Average stock $= \dfrac{23.7 + 25.9}{2} = 24.8$	Average stock $= \dfrac{21.2 + 23.7}{2} = 22.5$

Ratio	20X4	20X3
	$$\frac{\text{Cost of sales}}{\text{Average stock}}$$ $$\frac{182.6}{24.8} = 7.36$$ *b) Stock turnover in days =* $$\frac{\text{Average stock}}{\text{Cost of sales}} \times 365$$ $$\frac{24.8}{182.6} \times 365 = 49.6 \text{ days}$$	$$\frac{175.0}{22.5} = 7.77$$ $$\frac{22.5}{175.0} \times 365 = 46.9 \text{ days}$$
Debtors turnover	$$\frac{\text{Debtors}}{\text{Sales on credit}} \times 365$$ $$\frac{33.0}{283.4} \times 365 = 42.5 \text{ days}$$	$$\frac{28.2}{271.1} \times 365 = 38.0 \text{ days}$$
Creditors turnover	$$\frac{\text{Creditors}}{\text{Purchases}} \times 365$$ $$\frac{24.5}{184.4} \times 365 = 48.4 \text{ days}$$	$$\frac{20.6}{177.5} \times 365 = 42.4 \text{ days}$$

- Fixed assets turnover has hardly changed.

- Stock turnover has worsened in that stock is now held on the premises for an average of 49.6 days compared with 46.9 days in the previous year.

- Debtors turnover has worsened in that it is now taking debtors, on average, 42.5 days to pay, compared with 38 days in the previous year.

- Creditors turnover has improved, in that Armitage Horobin is taking advantage of the interest-free credit offered by creditors to a greater extent than in the previous year. However, 48.4 days may be regarded as too long a period to wait, on average, for payment, and there may be a loss of goodwill on the part of creditors towards the company.

Tutorial note: average stock has been used in the calculations because there was sufficient data available. In the case of debtors and creditors there was insufficient data, and so closing debtors and creditors have been used in the calculations. Although, ideally, averages should be used in the calculations, it is often not possible to obtain them.

13.4

$$\text{Dividend per share} = \frac{220\ 000}{1\ 000\ 000} = 22\text{p per share}$$

$$\text{Dividend cover} = \frac{680\ 000}{220\ 000} = 3.09\text{ times}$$

$$\text{Earnings per share (eps)} = \frac{680\ 000}{1\ 000\ 000} = 68\text{p per share}$$

$$\text{Price/earnings (P/E) ratio} = \frac{508\text{p}}{68\text{p}} = 7.5$$

$$\text{Market capitalisation} = £5.08 \times 1\ 000\ 000 \text{ shares} = £5\ 080\ 000$$

Answers to exercises

CHAPTER 1

1.1 The only correct statement is c): the sole trader is entirely responsible for the management of the business.

1.2 The only correct statement is d): partners are personally liable for the debts of the business.

1.3 The only correct statement is a): a limited company is a separate person in law.

1.4 Out of those listed the most appropriate form of finance for purchasing a new office building is a ten-year mortgage loan. The correct answer, therefore, is a).

1.5 Out of those listed, the most appropriate form of finance for the new office photocopier is a lease. The correct answer, therefore, is c).

1.6 *Advice to Arnold Tapwood:* It is not difficult to set up in partnership. By contrast with the establishment of a limited company, there is no requirement to submit information to the authorities. However, the partners would be well advised to consider drawing up a partnership agreement, for which they would require legal advice. Although the provisions of the Partnership Act 1890 apply where there is no partnership agreement, in most circumstances it is preferable to have a formal agreement. This would cover areas such as profit-sharing and arrangements in the event of a dispute between the partners.

1.7 Geoffrey will probably find it difficult to finance this business start-up because of its risky nature. He appears to be quite sure that lots of people will want to pay a subscription to his website, but he appears to have nothing but optimism to support this view. It is highly unlikely that a bank would be at all interested in making a loan in the circumstances.

Geoffrey has no existing resources to draw upon and his family have refused to put money into the business. It is remotely possible that grant finance might be available from a specialist organisation, and Geoffrey should explore this avenue. A further possibility is to join forces in partnership with another dangerous sports enthusiast who does have some resources to draw upon.

This appears to be a business proposition that will be very difficult to finance. If Geoffrey cannot find a business partner who is prepared to put some money into the venture, he may have to shelve the idea for the time being. If he gets a job, pays off his debts and saves some cash he might be able to finance the start-up himself at some point in the future.

CHAPTER 2   **2.1**   Erika: The main points for the business plan, and the related questions, are as follows:

Description of the service to be offered

Is the service highly specialised, or is it a more general design service? For example, the design services offered may be principally focused on, say, company identity and logo designs, or alternatively upon graphic input into advertising material. Or, Erika may be planning to cover a broad range of services, depending upon her talents and interests.

Market for the service

- Who will be the principal customers for the services offered?

- Has Erika investigated the market by carrying out any market research?

- Who are the principal competitors? Are they well established?

- How difficult will it be to break into the market for design services?

Profile of Erika

This will include training and education, relevant experience, age, an analysis of personal strengths and weaknesses, and a current portfolio of her best work.

- Does Erika have the appropriate profile of experience for the work she is planning to do?

- Is her portfolio up to date and does it contain examples of the type of work she will be undertaking to provide as a self-employed designer?

Initial investment required

This will be a particularly important section if Erika is planning to borrow money. Has she prepared a plan of her expenditure and income in the first year to 18 months following her business start-up? Relevant expenditure will probably include the following:

- office rental and business rates

- utilities bills (water, electricity, phone)

- advertising and marketing

- office equipment and computer

- insurance.

Also, how will Erika support herself in the early months of her new business? In this type of business, Erika will need to find the work, do it, submit it and then invoice the client. Under normal commercial arrangements payment will follow about a month later. So, there is a time lag of up to several months between initially being commissioned for the work and finally receiving payment. In the meantime, Erika needs to live off something, and this element must be built into her initial plans.

Detailed financial projections

If Erika is looking for business start-up finance she will need to prepare detailed financial projections in the form of a budget, showing the projected profit and loss and cash flow in the business. Once the business starts she will need to keep business accounting records and submit tax returns. She may need to register for VAT.

- Does Erika have financial management or accountancy skills?

- Will she need an accountant to provide accountancy and tax advice?

Other issues

Will any other professional services be required in the first year or so of the business? For example, Erika may need legal advice in negotiating a lease on her office. Is Erika planning to employ any staff?

2.2 There are several risks attached to Ben's business start up plan:

Risk of not obtaining work

Although Ben has a good contact list, they have all been made through Amis & Lovett, his employers. Much will depend on whether or not any of Amis & Lovett's existing clients will give their work to Ben's agency. If their relationship with Amis & Lovett is good, and they are satisfied with the work, they may be quite happy to stay with the larger agency. However, if they want to stay with Ben, they may be prepared to move their work to his new agency. Ben is taking a big risk.

Risk of running out of money

Even if the work does follow Ben, the nature of the type of service he offers means that he will not start receiving payment for his work for quite some time. He has £45 000 which sounds like a lot, but this may not keep him going for very long. If he has not already done so, he needs to make a realistic plan so that he can budget for the first year or so of his new business.

Risk of employing people

Ben is taking a risk by employing people straight away. He may not have enough work to justify employing anybody in the early months of the business. His employees will expect to be paid at the end of month, whether or not Ben has much work. He would probably be well advised to get the work first, and then employ staff.

CHAPTER 3

3.1 *Nancy*: As regards costs, because there is sufficient space for another person to work on the premises, there will be no significant additional premises costs involved. There will be a small additional cost in consumables such as hair products and electricity, but the main cost will be in paying the salary of the new stylist, plus any additional administrative costs. Nancy already employs one person, so presumably she or her accountant already operates a payroll system that makes sure that the employee and the Inland Revenue are paid the correct amount.

There are two main risks:

1. That there will not be sufficient extra business to keep the new stylist busy. Employing another person does not make financial sense unless the new employee can generate enough additional business to cover the costs of employing him or her;

2. That the new stylist will prove to be unsatisfactory in some way. Perhaps there will be personality clashes with Nancy or with the customers, or perhaps he or she will not produce work of sufficient competence. An employee who turns up late, or not at all, or who is unpleasant to clients will create problems.

As regards benefits, if the appointment of a new stylist turns out well, there could be two main benefits for Nancy and her business:

1. Additional profits could be generated that would increase Nancy's wealth. She could either draw down more money from the business or could invest the profits in further expansion, perhaps by moving to larger premises and employing more staff.

2. The range of services offered could be expanded and improved.

3.2 Oleander Enterprises Limited

Buying into another business

Buying into another company may be advantageous because Libby and Lisa will be buying up an established business with employees who have knowledge of holiday operations in Turkey. They will not need to start from scratch in finding out about a new country. However, Oxus Orlando is, essentially, a service business which is very dependent upon the quality of its employees. Loretta, the main director, plans to retire, so her expertise will be lost. If the key employees also choose to leave, there may not be much value left in the company, and Libby and Lisa may find out that they have paid too much for the investment.

Information needed

Libby and Lisa need to know:

■ The price of the investment in Oxus Orlando, which Loretta wishes to sell. (Note that Libby and Lisa would almost certainly need to have the investment independently valued.)

■ What they would get in exchange for the investment (for example, does the business own its own premises?).

■ How profitable Oxus Orlando is (they will be able to ascertain this information from the business's annual accounts).

■ Details about the employees of the business. How much are they paid, how long have they been in their current jobs and how likely is it that they will stay if the company changes ownership?

CHAPTER 4   **4.1**   Ashton Longton plc: The company has 8 000 000 shares in issue, each valued at £3.85. Market capitalisation is 8 000 000 × £3.85 = £30 800 000.

4.2 The Alternative Investment Market is a market for companies that do not currently wish to proceed to full listing. The correct answer, therefore, is a).

4.3 The rights issue gives the holder of 50 000 shares the right to buy 50 000/5 shares = 10 000 shares. Each new share costs £5.42, so the total amount payable to take up the rights is: 10 000 × £5.42 = £54 200. The correct answer, therefore, is c). (Note that if the issued share capital is £3 000 000 denominated in 50p shares, the total number of shares in issue is 6 000 000. The shareholder in this question holds 50 000 shares of 50p each.)

4.4 Brighton Bestwines plc: Potential drawbacks of quotation on the Alternative Investment Market include:

1. Additional regulation applies to quoted companies; for example, they have to produce additional published financial reports. The additional compliance costs often involve employing more staff to deal with the extra requirements.

2. Although the company could raise the capital it needs, there will be legal and other professional fees involved. These are likely to be around 10% of the amount raised. This means that, for every share sold at the target price of £2.50, approximately 25p will be spent on fees. The percentage could be even higher.

3. Many directors are uncomfortable with the additional attention paid to quoted companies by the media. They may have to start meeting journalists, and there may be additional costs involved if professional public relations advice is required. (Tutorial note: AIM quoted companies are generally subject to rather less attention than companies with a full listing, but financial journalists will obviously take some interest when things go wrong.)

4. The company's share price may fluctuate for reasons that are difficult to explain (because they are related to general market sentiment, or the unpopularity of the industry sector to which the company belongs, for example).

5. There is a potential drawback in allowing other parties to buy shares in that the company may lay itself open to takeover bids. However, in this case the shares issued for sale will amount to only one-third of the total share capital, so the company will be safe from takeover unless and until it issues more shares for sale.

CHAPTER 5

5.1 The only correct statement is d): a sole trader must submit a tax return annually.

5.2 The only correct statement is b): a limited company must send annual accounts to all of its shareholders.

5.3 Podgorny & Weaver Limited

List of amounts owed by retail businesses
The directors would be able to see if any of the retailers owed very large amounts. If, in addition, the list contained details of the length of time the amounts had

been outstanding, the directors would also be able to see if the amounts owing were significantly overdue for payment.

Summary of the value of goods held in stock

It is important for a fashion goods business not to carry excessive stocks of goods that may be about to go out of fashion. The business will lose money if the stock cannot be sold. The directors need this statement to assess the risk of having excess stocks.

Summary of the value of orders received in the last month

The directors need to assess whether the orders received meet their expectations. If the value of orders received is less than expected, the directors need to take action to address the problem.

Profit and loss account for the last month

The directors will be able to assess the performance of the business compared to their expectations, and perhaps, compared to the same month in the previous financial year.

5.4 Burnip Chemicals plc: the activist group would probably be looking for the following types of information:

- Details about the amounts of emissions.

- Details of the sums the company has paid in fines.

- Details of plans for improvements to the factory that will minimise the emission of toxic waste.

A company's financial statements contain principally information about the financial performance and condition of the business. Details about the amounts of emissions during the year are not financial items, and it is quite possible that the company would make no reference to the matter.

The amount of fines paid might be evident from the financial statements. However, the expenses listed in the profit and loss account are summarised information (it would not be feasible to list each individual payment), and the amount paid in fines might well not be evident. Details of planned improvements, similarly, may not be evident from the financial statements. Although annual financial statements can be of interest to activist groups, they do not necessarily provide a full picture. (Tutorial note: some companies voluntarily publish information about their environmental policies and performance in addition to their financial statements, but they are not obliged by law to do this.)

CHAPTER 6   **6.1**
- Cash kept in a tin in the factory office = Asset.

- Oven = Asset.

- Bank loan, repayable over five years = Liability.

- Plastic packaging for biscuits = Asset.

- Flour and sugar = Asset.

- Amounts payable to supplier of dried fruit = Liability.

6.2
- Value added tax (VAT) payable to Customs and Excise = Current liability.
- Office computer = Fixed asset.
- Amount due from Lomax plc for consultancy work carried out by Amir = Current asset.
- Bank overdraft* = Current liability.
- Bank loan to be repaid in three years' time = Long-term liability.
- Amount payable to stationery supplier = Current liability

*Tutorial note: some businesses have an almost permanent bank overdraft, which they effectively use as long-term finance. However, a bank overdraft is technically 'repayable on demand', meaning that the bank is entitled to demand repayment at any time. Because of this, bank overdrafts are always classified as current liabilities in the business balance sheet.

6.3 The accounting equation is:

$$\text{Assets} - \text{Liabilities} = \text{Capital}$$

Applying the equation to the information given in the question:

	£
Assets	83 000
Less Liabilities	(36 500)
= Capital	46 500

Brian's capital is £46 500

6.4 In this case we turn the accounting equation around to find liabilities:

$$\text{Assets} - \text{Capital} = \text{Liabilities}$$

	£
Assets	188 365
Less Capital	(43 650)
= Liabilities	144 715

The liabilities in Basil's business total £144 715.

6.5 In this question assets are split into fixed and current assets. However, the basic principle remains the same: Total assets minus Total liabilities = Capital.

	£
Fixed assets	12 000
Plus Current assets	8 500
= Assets	20 500
Less Liabilities	(17 300)
= Capital	3 200

Brenda's capital is £3200.

6.6   In this question four pieces of information are given. However, the basic accounting equation still holds good.

Total assets = £27 000 (Fixed assets) + £16 000 (Current assets) = £43 000

Total liabilities = £12 000 (Current liabilities) + £10 000
(Long-term liabilities) = £22 000.

Brigitte's capital in the business is Assets – Liabilities, i.e. £43 000 – £22 000 = £21 000.

6.7   Bryony's capital is £34 340 (i.e. answer d). This is calculated as:

Total assets = £35 840 (Fixed assets) + £16 500 (Current assets) = £52 340

Total liabilities = £12 000 (Current liabilities) + £6 000
(Long-term liabilities) = £18 000

Bryony's capital in the business is Assets – Liabilities, i.e. £52 340 – £18 000 = £34 340.

6.8   Reminder: the accounting equation =

Assets – Liabilities = Capital

or

Assets – Capital = Liabilities

- Assets = £39 497 (Fixed assets) + £26 004 (Current assets) = £65 501
- Capital = £33 058
- Total liabilities therefore = £65 501 – £33 058 = £32 443.

Total Liabilities = Current liabilities + Long-term liabilities

Therefore:

£32 443 = £16 777 + Long-term liabilities

Long-term liabilities therefore = £15 666.

6.9   The missing figure for Long-term liabilities is £9 276 (i.e. answer b). This is calculated as:

- Total assets = £36 609 (Fixed assets) + £38 444 (Current assets) = £75 053
- Capital = £39 477

Therefore:

Total Liabilities = £35 576 (£75 053 − £39 477)

Current liabilities are £26 300, therefore Long-term liabilities = £9 276 (£35 576 − £26 300).

6.10 a) Total assets = £18 337 (Fixed assets) + £12 018 (Stock) + £365 (Debtors) + £63 (Cash) = £30 783.

b) Total current assets = £12 018 (Stock) + £365 (Debtors) + £63 (Cash) = £12 446.

c) Total liabilities = £3 686 (Bank overdraft) + £2 999 (Creditors) = £6 685

d) Callum's capital can be found by using the accounting equation: £30 783 (Total assets) − £6 685 (Total liabilities) = £24 098.

6.11

Ciera's business: Balance sheet at 31 December

	£	£
Fixed assets		
Premises		39 000
Current assets		
Stock	18 600	
Debtors	6 500	
Bank	13 000	
	38 100	
Current liabilities		
Creditors	(23 700)	
Due to Inland Revenue	(3 800)	
	(27 500)	
Net current assets (£38 100 − £27 500)		10 600
		49 600
Long-term liabilities		(20 000)
Net assets		29 600
Capital		29 600

6.12 In transaction (1), Dan is using up £1500 of the amount in the business bank account, but at the same time is increasing fixed assets.

Increase fixed assets by £1500
Decrease bank account by £1500.

In transaction (2), Dan is using up £3000 of the amount in the business bank account, but at the same time is decreasing creditors.

Decrease creditors by £3000
Decrease bank account by £3000.

Dan's business: Balance sheet at 3 May

	£	£
Fixed assets (30 000 + 1 500)		31 500
Current assets		
Stock	15 000	
Debtors	5 000	
Bank account (18 000 – 1 500 – 3 000)	13 500	
	33 500	
Current liabilities		
Creditors (16 000 – 3 000)	(13 000)	
Net current assets (£33 500 – £13 000)		20 500
Net assets		52 000
Capital		52 000

Note that the capital in the business has not changed at all between 1 and 3 May

6.13   **Ernest's business: Balance sheet at 31 December**

	£	£
Fixed assets		
Gallery premises		68 000
Office equipment		2 260
		70 260
Current assets		
Bank	18 600	
	18 600	
Current liabilities		
Creditors: Payable to artists	16 560	
Creditors: Payable to printers	1 600	
	18 160	
Net current assets (£18 600 – £18 160)		440
Net assets		70 700
Capital		70 700

Once Ernest has paid the artists and the printers (and, presumably, he will have to in the very near future) he will be left with only £440 in the bank. This will not leave him with enough money to pay the costs, which are estimated at £4000, of the exhibition in January. He may be able to obtain the goods and services needed to put on the exhibition on credit (that is, he will not pay for them straight away), but he would be taking the risk that the exhibition is a failure. If it produces no money, or less than the £4000 or so needed to cover essential costs, then Ernest will be in a very difficult position.

He may be able to borrow some money to put the business on a better footing. The only substantial asset the business owns is the art gallery premises. It may be possible to secure a mortgage loan on the property so as to obtain some much-needed cash.

CHAPTER 7 **7.1.** 1. Jackie has purchased 47 sets during June – i.e. answer b). Explanation:

	No. of sets
Opening stock	30
Add: purchases (missing figure)	X
Less: closing stock	(42)
= Sets sold in June	35

The missing figure is 47.

2. Jackie's cost of sales is £2625 – i.e. answer c). Explanation:

	No. of sets	£
Cost of sales:		
Opening stock at 1 June 20X1	30	2 250
Add: purchases during month	47	3 525
	77	5 775
Less: closing stock at 30 June 20X1	(42)	(3 150)
	35	2 625

An even easier calculation is to take the number of sets sold (35) and multiply by the cost price (£75). This gives an answer of £2625.

3. Jackie's gross profit for the month of June is £1995 – i.e. answer d). Explanation:

	£
Sales (£132 × 35 sets)	4 620
Less: cost of sales (see answer 7.1.2)	2 625
Gross profit	1 995

Another way of calculating this is to work out the gross profit on one set (£132 – £75 = £57) and multiply it by the number of sets sold (£57 × 35 = £1995)

7.2 The sales revenue raised through selling the special purchase trainers is as follows:

	£
750 pairs @ £15.50 per pair	11 625
200 pairs @ £12.50 per pair	2 500
50 pairs @ £5 per pair	250
Total sales revenue	14 375

The cost of sales was the purchase price of £8500. There is no opening or closing stock. Gross profit is therefore: £14 375 – £8500 = £5875.

If Jay had managed to sell 1000 pairs at £15.50 the sales revenue would have been £15 500. Gross profit would therefore have been £15 500 less the cost of sales figure of £8500 = £7000.

7.3 We can construct Jake's trading account and use it to find the value of the missing figure of opening stock.

First we put in the total value for sales, and for gross profit. The difference between these two is cost of sales, i.e. £340 000 – £140 000 = £200 000. Then we can work in reverse order through the cost of sales calculation. Because closing stock is £17 400 the total value of opening stock + purchases must be £217 400 (i.e. we deduct closing stock of £17 400 to get cost of sales of £200 000). If the total value of opening stock plus purchases is £217 400 and we know that purchases for the year equal £197 300, then opening stock is the difference between these two figures:

£217 400 – £197 300 = £20 100

The missing figure (X) is £20 100.

Jake: Trading account for the year

	£	£
Sales: 8000 units @ £42.50		340 000
Cost of sales		
Opening stock (missing figure)	X	
Add: purchases	197 300	
	217 400	
Less: closing stock	(17 400)	
		(200 000)
Gross profit: 8000 units @ £17.50		140 000

7.4 Jethro: Trading accounts for October, November and December 20X2

	October £	November £	December £
Sales	39 370	48 998	56 306
Cost of sales			
Opening stock	30 863	43 258	53 190
Add: purchases	37 085	40 830	6 250
Less: closing stock	(43 258)	(53 190)	(23 980)
	24 690	30 898	35 460
Gross profit	14 680	18 100	20 846

7.5 Leon's trading results are as follows for the two years under review:

	20X6 £	20X5 £
Sales	295 993	287 300
Cost of sales	(242 085)	(235 920)
Gross profit	53 908	51 380

1. Gross profit margin in 20X6 =

$$\frac{53\ 908}{295\ 993} \times 100 = 18.2\%$$

Gross profit margin in 20X5 =

$$\frac{51\ 380}{287\ 300} \times 100 = 17.9\%$$

2. The amount of the increase in sales is £295 993 – £287 300 = £8 693

3. The percentage increase in sales is:

$$\frac{8\ 693}{287\ 300} \times 100 = 3\%$$

4. The amount of the increase in gross profit is £53 908 – £51 380 = £2 528

5. The percentage increase in gross profit is:

$$\frac{2\ 528}{51\ 380} \times 100 = 4.9\%$$

7.6 The table shows the gross and net profit margins for Louise's business for three years:

	20X8 £	20X7 £	20X6 £
Gross profit margin	$\frac{77\ 402}{291\ 318} \times 100$ $= 26.6\%$	$\frac{75\ 980}{282\ 400} \times 100$ $= 26.9\%$	$\frac{73\ 269}{269\ 340} \times 100$ $= 27.2\%$
Net profit margin	$\frac{25\ 008}{291\ 318} \times 100$ $= 8.6\%$	$\frac{24\ 260}{282\ 400} \times 100$ $= 8.6\%$	$\frac{23\ 999}{269\ 340} \times 100$ $= 8.9\%$

Louise's sales have increased in each of the three years, as have gross profit and net profit. However, the gross and net profit margins have fallen. Gross profit margin has declined from 27.2% in 20X6 to 26.6% in 20X8. Net profit margin is stable in the latest two years, but has declined from 8.9% in 20X6.

7.7 Madigan & Co: Profit and loss account for the year ending 31 March 20X5

	£	£
Fees from clients		95 311
Expenses		
Salaries: assistant	19 300	
secretary	11 150	

Office rental	10 310
Office service charge	3 790
Insurance	794
PII	1 250
Subscriptions etc.	952
Business travel	1 863
Entertainment	342
Telephone	1 103
Other administration expenses	1 575
Stationery	761
Sundry expenses	715
Charitable donations	120
	54 025
Net profit	**41 286**

7.8 First, categorise the accounting items for Norbert's business:

	£	Category
Delivery van	5 020	Balance sheet: fixed assets
Sales for the year	351 777	Trading account
Staff costs: storeman's wages	12 090	Profit and loss account
Electricity	2 821	Profit and loss account
Cash at bank	3 444	Balance sheet: current assets
Capital at 1 April 20X6	18 011	Balance sheet: capital
Administrative costs	3 810	Profit and loss account
Opening stock at 1 April 20X6	20 762	Trading account
Fixed assets in warehouse and office	3 900	Balance sheet: fixed assets
Drawings	25 219	Balance sheet: capital
Sundry expenses	1 406	Profit and loss account
Warehouse and office rental	10 509	Profit and loss account
Insurance	3 909	Profit and loss account
Debtors	36 623	Balance sheet: current assets
Water rates	1 226	Profit and loss account
Security services charge	2 937	Profit and loss account
Purchases	255 255	Trading account
Bank charges	398	Profit and loss account
Creditors	31 950	Balance sheet: current liabilities
Delivery expenses	8 630	Profit and loss account
Part-time admin assistant's wages	3 779	Profit and loss account
Closing stock	22 446	Trading account *and* balance sheet: current assets

Norbert: Profit and loss account for the year ending 31 March 20X7

	£	£
Sales		351 777
Less: cost of sales		
Opening stock	20 762	

	£	£
Add: purchases	255 255	
	276 017	
Less: closing stock	(22 446)	
		(253 571)
Gross profit		98 206

Expenses

Staff costs: storeman's wages	12 090
Warehouse and office rental	10 509
Insurance	3 909
Electricity	2 821
Water rates	1 226
Security services	2 937
Delivery expenses	8 630
Administrative costs	3 810
Part-time admin assistant's wages	3 779
Sundry expenses	1 406
Bank charges	398

		(51 515)
Net profit		46 691

Norbert: Balance sheet at 31 March 20X7

	£	£
Fixed assets		
Delivery van	5 020	
Fixed assets – warehouse and office	3 900	
		8 920
Current assets		
Stock	22 446	
Debtors	36 623	
Cash	3 444	
	62 513	
Current liabilities		
Creditors	(31 950)	
Net current assets (£62 513 – £31 950)		30 563
Net assets		39 483
Capital		
Opening capital balance 1 April 20X6	18 011	
Add: net profit for the year	46 691	
	64 702	
Less: drawings	(25 219)	
Closing capital balance 31 March 20X7		39 483

7.9 There will be relatively few users of Mary's accounting information. She herself, as the proprietor of the business, is likely to be the principal user. However, if she needs to borrow money at some point in the future, potential lenders are likely to be interested in seeing her financial statements in order to assess the ability of the business to make repayments of loans and to meet regular interest payments.

Tax collecting agencies such as the Inland Revenue will be interested in Mary's accounts as a basis for assessing the amount of income tax due on her profits. The only other group of users likely to have an interest in Mary's accounts is the supplier group. If other businesses supply goods to Mary on credit they are likely to be interested in the likelihood of being paid promptly.

CHAPTER 8

8.1

Oscar: Extract from profit and loss account for year ending 31 December 20X1

	£	£	£
Sales			72 411
Less: returns			(361)
Cost of sales			72 050
Opening stock		4 182	
Add: purchases	53 005		
Less: returns	(1 860)		
		51 145	
		55 327	
Less: closing stock		(5 099)	
			(50 228)
Gross profit			21 822

Therefore the correct answer is a).

8.2

Omar: Extract from profit and loss account for year ending 30 April 20X7

	£	£	£
Sales			347 348
Less: returns			(2 971)
Cost of sales			344 377
Opening stock		43 730	
Add: purchases	240 153		
Add: import duties	6 043		
Less: returns	(1 800)		
		244 396	
		288 126	
Less: closing stock		(41 180)	
			(246 946)
Gross profit			97 431

Therefore, the correct answer is a).

8.3   Poppy: Profit and loss account for the year ending 28 February 20X2

	£	£	£
Sales			220 713
Less: returns			(3 997)
			216 716
Cost of sales			
Opening stock		7 140	
Add: purchases	123 057		
Add: import duty	9 911		
		132 968	
		140 108	
Less: closing stock		(7 393)	
			132 715
Gross profit			84 001
Expenses			
Rental		17 211	
Staffing costs		9 777	
Insurance		8 204	
Delivery van expenses		2 107	
Discounts allowed		716	
Telephone charges		1 227	
Electricity		1 604	
Marketing		1 888	
Administrative expenses		922	
			43 656
Net profit			40 345

8.4   Telephone expense for inclusion in Pookie's accounts to 31 August 20X8:

	£
1/3 × £9 760 relating to September 20X7	3 253
October–December 20X7	12 666
January–March 20X8	8 444
April–June 20X8	9 530
July and August 20X8: (9 760 + 12 666 + 8 444 + 9 530)×2/12	6 733
	40 626

Therefore, b) is the correct answer.

8.5   The prepayment at 28 February 20X7 is 7/12 × 644 = £376. The prepayment at 28 February 20X8 is 7/12×796 = £464

Therefore b) is the correct answer.

8.6   Simon: Profit and loss account for the year ending 31 July 20X4

	£	£	£
Sales			317 342
Cost of sales			
Opening stock		38 888	
Purchases		230 133	
		269 021	
Less: closing stock		(39 501)	
			229 520
Gross profit			87 822
Discounts received			377
Income from curtain making service		6 519	
Costs of curtain making service		(2 797)	
			3 722
			91 921
Expenses			
Shop rental		18 750	
Assistants' wages	22 379		
Add: accrued commission	3 173		
		25 552	
Business rates		3 510	
Insurance	4 478		
Less: prepaid	(501)		
		3 977	
Electricity	2 064		
Add: accrual	377		
		2 441	
Telephone		1 035	
Travelling expenses		603	
Delivery expenses		2 490	
Trade subscriptions		165	
Charitable donations		500	
Accountant's fees		800	
Legal fees		350	
			(60 173)
Net profit			31 748

Total accruals:

	£
Assistants' commission	3 173
Electricity	377
Accountant's fees	800
Legal fees	350
	4 700
Prepayment: insurance	501

8.7   Ted: Extract from profit and loss account for the year ending

31 December 20X5

	Closing stock at cost	Closing stock at cost/net realisable value
	£	£
Sales	599 790	599 790
Cost of sales		
Opening stock	49 071	49 071
Add: purchases	379 322	379 322
Less: closing stock	(62 222)	—
Less: closing stock*	—	(50 472)
	366 171	377 921
Gross profit	233 619	221 869
Gross profit margin	38.9%	37.0%
*Closing stock at cost	62 222	
Less: pink items at cost	(17 750)	
Add: pink items at net realisable value	6 000	
Closing stock adjusted to net realisable value for pink items	50 472	

8.8 Ulrich will require a general provision of 1% of debtors outstanding for over three months: 1% × £67 400 = £674.

The debt due from Gayle will be treated as irrecoverable and will no longer appear in debtors. Debtors will be stated at £397 700 − 717 000 = 380 700. Extract from Ulrich's balance sheet at 31 July 20X1:

	£
Debtors	380 700
Less: provision	(674)
	380 026

Ulrich's profit for the year is reduced by (a) the amount of the bad debt = £17 000; and (b) the provision made for the first time this year = £674. In total, Ulrich's profit is reduced by £17 674.

8.9   Ursula: Profit and loss account for the year ending 31 December 20X2

	£	£	£
Sales			326 620
Cost of sales			
Opening stock		31 090	
Add: purchases		239 285	
		270 375	

	£	£	£
Less: closing stock		(30 048)	
			(240 327)
Gross profit			86 293
Discounts received			361
			86 654
Expenses			
Warehouse rental		11 070	
Business and water rates		3 899	
Electricity	4 850		
Add: accrual	338		
		5 188	
Insurance	3 414		
Less: prepayment	(622)		
		2 792	
Assistant's wages		10 008	
Telephone		2 663	
Delivery costs		4 490	
Administration charges		3 242	
Bad debt written off		672	
Provision for doubtful debts		1 098	
Accountant's fee accrual		700	
Discounts allowed		1 046	
			(46 868)
Net profit			39 786

Ursula: Balance sheet at 31 December 20X2

	£	£	£
Fixed assets			23 360
Current assets			
Stock		30 048	
Debtors*	49 682		
Less: provision	(1 098)		
		48 584	
Prepayment		622	
Cash at bank		361	
		79 615	
Current liabilities			
Creditors		25 920	
Accruals		1 038	
		26 958	
Net current assets (79 615 – 26 958)			52 657
Net assets			76 017

Capital

Opening capital balance 1 January 20X2	70 219
Add: net profit for the year	39 786
	110 005
Less: drawings	(33 988)

Closing capital balance 31 December 20X2   76 017

*The bad debt of £672 disappears completely from the records. Debtors in the accounts list were £50 354 but are reduced for presentation in the balance sheet to £49 682 (i.e. £50 354 – £672).

8.10 a) Recognition occurs when items are brought into the accounting statements. For example, when a business proprietor concludes that he is unlikely ever to recover the amount of a debt owing by a customer, a bad debt expense will be recognised in the profit and loss account.

b) The accruals convention in accounting requires that the effects of transactions should be recognised in the accounting period in which they occur. This may not necessarily be the accounting period in which the transactions are invoiced or paid. For example, where a business receives a shipment of goods on the final day of its accounting year, the increase in stock should be recognised within that accounting year. This is despite the fact that an invoice will not be received for the stock until after the year end.

c) Net realisable value refers to the amount for which an asset can be sold, net of any incidental expenses of sale. For example, an item of stock may be able to be sold for a gross sum of £13 000. However, shipping and insurance costs of £500 would have to be borne by the seller if the stock were sold. The net realisable value is therefore £12 500.

CHAPTER 9   **9.1**

	£
Cost of the new van	14 460
Less: expected sale proceeds in four years time	(4 000)
Depreciable amount	10 460

Spread evenly over four years this gives an annual depreciation charge of £10 460/4 = £2 615. The correct answer, therefore, is d).

9.2

	£
Cost of new exercise bike	450
Less: expected sale proceeds in three years time	(30)
Depreciable amount	420

Spread evenly over three years this gives an annual depreciation charge of £420/3 = £140. However, Victoria charges depreciation only for the period of ownership, which, in the year ending 31 August 20X2, is six months. The depreciation charge for the bike for this year is therefore £140/2 = £70. The correct answer, therefore, is a).

9.3 *Depreciation on machine one*:

$$\frac{£10\ 300}{5} = £2\ 060$$

This is a full year's depreciation, but Vinny would calculate depreciation only for the part of the year he had owned the asset. Therefore the charge for the year ending 31 December 20X6 would be:

$$£2\ 060 \times \frac{9}{12} = £1\ 545$$

Depreciation on machine two:

	£
Cost of new machine	8 580
Less: expected sale proceeds in four years time	(2 000)
Depreciable amount	6 580

Spread evenly over four years, this gives an annual charge of £6580/4 = £1645. However, the charge for the year ending 31 December 20X6 would be for the three months of ownership only:

$$£1\ 645 \times \frac{3}{12} = £411 \text{ (to the nearest £)}$$

The total depreciation charge for these two assets is £1545 + £411 = £1956. The correct answer, therefore, is c).

9.4 Violet has purchased an intangible asset in the form of mineral extraction rights. She has a licence to extract gold (if she can find it) from the land for three-and-a-half years only. At the end of that period she has no further rights over the land unless she renegotiates them. The initial payment of £273 000 will be spread over the three-and-a-half year period of ownership of the rights. As noted in the chapter, amortisation is almost invariably calculated on the straight-line basis.

In the first year of ownership Violet will charge amortisation in her profit and loss account of:

$$\frac{£273\ 000}{3.5 \text{ years}} = £78\ 000$$

The balance sheet will show the following in respect of mineral rights:

	£
Fixed assets	
Intangible fixed assets	
Mineral rights at cost	273 000
Less: accumulated amortisation	(78 000)
Net book value	195 000

9.5 The total charge for depreciation for the year ending 31 August 20X8 is as follows

	£
Buildings: £306 000 × 2%	6 120
Motor vehicles: £32 300 × 25%	8 075
Fixtures and fittings: £12 720 × 10%	1 272
	15 467

The presentation of fixed assets in Vincenzo's balance sheet at 31 August 20X8 is as follows:

	£	£
Fixed assets		
Buildings at cost	306 000	
Less: accumulated depreciation (18 360 + 6 120)	(24 480)	
		281 520
Motor vehicles at cost	48 770	
Less: accumulated depreciation (16 470 + 8 075)	(24 545)	
		24 225
Fixtures and fittings at cost	12 720	
Less: accumulated depreciation (6 360 + 1 272)	(7 632)	
		5 088
Total		310 833

9.6

	£
Basic cost of new wedding car	24 400
Additional cost of white spray	800
Total cost	25 200

The first year's depreciation on the reducing balance basis is £25 200 × 15% = £3 780. The correct answer, therefore, is b).

9.7

	£	£
Net book value of cars at 1 January 20X3	22 830	
Depreciation for the year: £22 830 × 25%		5 707
New car added on 1 January 20X3	14 447	
Depreciation for the year £14 447 × 25%		3 612
Total depreciation for the year		9 319

Another, quicker, way of doing the calculation:

	£
Net book value of cars at 1 January 20X3	22 830
Add: new car purchased on 1 January 20X3	14 447
Total depreciable value at 31 December 20X3	37 277

Depreciation: £37 277 × 25% = £9319. The correct answer, therefore, is b).

Tutorial note: in William's balance sheet the presentation will be as follows:

	£
Fixed assets	
Tangible fixed assets	
Cars at cost (£38 370 + £14 447)	52 817
Less: accumulated depreciation (£15 540 + £9319)	(24 859)
Net book value	27 958

9.8

	£
Sale proceeds	2 380
The net book value of the van is £8300 − £6330 =	1 970
Profit on sale	410

Tutorial note: this is a profit on sale because Xenia receives more for the van than the value (net book value) at which it is recorded in her accounts.

9.9 First, we need to work out the net book value of the van at 1 June 20X4.

	£
Cost on 1 June 20X1	10 100
Year 1 depreciation: £10 100 × 30%	(3 030)
Net book value at 1 June 20X2	7 070
Year 2 depreciation: £7070 × 30%	(2 121)
Net book value at 1 June 20X3	4 949
Year 3 depreciation: £4949 × 30%	(1 485)
Net book value at 1 June 20X4	3 464

Comparing the net book value with the sale proceeds of £3000 results in a loss on disposal of £464.

9.10 By the time she disposes of them, Ying has owned the computers for exactly two years and six months (1 January 20X1 to 1 July 20X3). The annual charge for depreciation is: £3672/4 = £918. Two-and-a-half years of charges = 2.5 × £918 = £2295.

The net book value of the computers at the date of disposal is:

	£
Cost	3 672
Less: accumulated depreciation	(2 295)
Net book value	1 377
Sale proceeds	550
Less: net book value	(1 377)
Loss on sale	827

In effect, Ying has underestimated the depreciation appropriate to these assets. Their value has dropped more quickly than she initially supposed.

9.11 a) *Working for depreciation*
Machinery at cost = £28 760. Straight-line depreciation over four years = £28 760/4= £7 190.

Zoë's Snacks: Profit and loss account for the year ending 31 December 20X4

	£	£
Sales		132 614
Less: cost of sales		
Opening stock	—	
Purchases	83 430	
Less: closing stock	(1 209)	
		(82 221)
Gross profit		50 393
Expenses		
Staffing	15 030	
Premises rental	7 400	
Electricity	2 961	
Phone	1 806	
Insurance	1 437	
Sundry expenses	981	
Accountant's fees	600	
Depreciation (see working above)	7 190	
		(37 405)
Net profit		12 988

Zoë's Snacks: Balance sheet at 31 December 20X4

	£	£
Fixed assets		
Machinery and fixtures at cost	28 760	
Less: accumulated depreciation	(7 190)	
		21 570
Current assets		
Stock	1 209	
Cash at bank	3 406	
	4 615	
Current liabilities		
Creditors	(1 650)	
Net current assets		2 965
		24 535
Capital		
Capital introduced		20 000
Add: profit for the year		12 988
Less: drawings		(8 453)
		24 535

b) Depreciation over seven years

If Zoë used a period of seven years over which to depreciate the machinery and fixtures, the depreciation charge would be:

$$\text{Cost } \frac{£28\,760}{7 \text{ years}} = £4\,109 \text{ (to nearest £)}$$

Effect on profit:

	£
Net profit as stated in the profit and loss account above:	12 988
Add back: depreciation over four years	7 190
Net profit before depreciation	20 178
Less: depreciation over seven years	(4 109)
Net profit adjusted for change in depreciation	16 069

Net profit is £12 988 if machinery and fixtures are depreciated over four years.

If the depreciation period is increased to seven years, net profit increases to £16 069 (an increase of nearly 24%).

c) Net profit margin

Net profit percentage is net profit as a percentage of sales. Net profit percentage with depreciation over four years:

$$\frac{£12\,988}{132\,614} \times 100 = 9.8\%$$

Net profit percentage with depreciation over seven years:

$$\frac{£16\,069}{132\,614} \times 100 = 12.1\%$$

Note that a change in the method of depreciation can make a large difference to net profit and to the net profit percentage.

9.12 The accounting equation is as follows:

$$\text{ASSETS} - \text{LIABILITIES} = \text{CAPITAL}$$

Depreciation does not affect liabilities, but it does affect both assets and capital. Depreciation is a way of matching the using up of an asset over its useful life with the sales generated by the asset. The net book value of the asset gradually reduces as the asset is used up. Each year the reduction in asset value is the same as the amount that is set against the business's sales. Both profit and assets are therefore reduced by the same figure. A reduction in profit results in a reduction in capital.

10.1 The following table details the impact of transactions on Fergus's business:

Transaction	Impact on cash, etc.	Impact on profits
Introduction of additional capital of £10 000 in cash.	Cash and capital are both increased by £10 000.	No impact on profits.
Purchase on credit of goods for resale for £8000.	Stock and creditors are both increased by £8000. There is no immediate impact on cash, but there will be an outflow of cash when the goods are paid for.	No immediate impact on profits. When the goods are sold, they will form part of cost of sales.
Payment received from debtor for £1800.	The asset of debtors is reduced by £1800 and there is a corresponding increase (inflow of cash) in cash of £1800.	No impact on profits. The sale to which the debtor relates would already have been recorded.
Purchase of a new machine for use in the business.	There is an outflow of cash of £12 000 and fixed assets are increased by £12 000.	No immediate impact on profits, but there will be an additional depreciation charge for the year of £1200 (i.e. £12 000 over ten years).
Sales returns of £1000 in exchange for a cash refund.	There is an outflow of cash of £1000.	Sales returns are increased by £1000. Sales returns are deducted from sales in the profit and loss account, and thus, reduce profit.
Drawings of £1300.	Cash and capital are both reduced by £1300.	There is no impact on profit. Effectively, Fergus is taking £1300 of his own capital out of the business.

10.2

	£
Fixed asset at cost	20 700
Less: accumulated depreciation	(18 210)
Net book value	2 490

The asset is sold for £1300; that is less than it is recorded at in the accounts. A loss is thus incurred on sale of £2490 − £1300 = £1190.

Profits are reduced by £1190 (statement no. 2), cash is increased by £1300 (statement no. 3) and fixed assets are reduced by £2490 (statement no. 5). The correct answer, therefore, is b).

10.3 The net cash inflow from operating activities in Gaston's business for the year ending 30 April 20X1 is calculated as follows:

	£	£
Operating profit (£36 790 – £763)		36 027
Add back: depreciation		4 585
		40 612
Changes in working capital		
Stock – increase (£37 669 – £31 470) (cash outflow)	(6 199)	
Debtors – increase (£21 777 – £19 303) (cash outflow)	(2 474)	
Creditors – increase (£18 250 – £16 264) (cash inflow)	1 986	
Net change in working capital		(6 687)
Net cash inflow from operating activities		33 925

The correct answer, therefore, is c).

10.4   Spicer & Co.: Cash flow statement for the year ending 31 March 20X4

	£	£
Operating profit		76 496
Add back: depreciation		12 471
		88 967
Changes in working capital		
Stock (£40 747 – £36 600) (cash outflow)	(4 147)	
Debtors and prepayments (£50 661 – £48 730) (cash outflow)	(1 931)	
Creditors (£36 644 – £35 191) (cash inflow)	1 453	
Net change in working capital		(4 625)
Net cash inflow from operating activities		84 342
Interest paid		(230)
Capital expenditure (cash outflow) (£175 630 – £128 547)		(47 083)
Proprietor's drawings (cash outflow)		(45 800)
Net cash outflow		(8 771)
Change in cash balance		
Cash at 1 April 20X3		7 423
Overdraft at 31 March 20X4		(1 348)
Decrease in cash – net cash outflow (£7423 + £1348)		(8 771)

CHAPTER 11

11.1 It is true that directors take complete responsibility for the preparation of accounts, but they do not have to actually prepare the accounts themselves. They may delegate the preparation to others, but the directors take ultimate responsibility for ensuring that the accounts present a true and fair view, and that they are filed on time. It is not a criminal offence to produce accounts that fail to present a true and fair view. However, directors can be subject to criminal sanctions for failing to prepare and file accounts, and they may be guilty of a criminal offence if it can be proven that they have deliberately defrauded creditors. Statements 2 and 4 are, therefore, correct, so the answer is b).

11.2 Bayliss Chandler Limited has 60 000 authorised shares (£30 000 / 50p) – two-thirds of these are in issue, i.e. 40 000 shares. Ambrose owns 10% of the issued capital, i.e. 4000 shares. He is entitled to a dividend of 6p per share: 4000 × 6p = £240. The correct answer, therefore, is c).

11.3 A holding of 8000 shares in Peachey plc is equivalent to a nominal value of 8000 × 25p = £2000. The total dividend payable for the year is 10% of nominal value, therefore the holder of 8000 shares will receive 10% × £2000 = £200, half on 31 March 20X6 and half on 30 September 20X6.

At 31 March 20X6 Carina owns all 8000 shares and will receive £100 in dividend. At 30 September 20X6 Carina owns 4000 of the shares and her sister Cathy owns 4000. Therefore, they share the dividend, receiving £50 each. In total for the year, Carina receives £150 in dividend and Cathy receives £50. The correct answer, therefore, is d).

11.4 Butterthwaite plc

	£
80 000 ordinary shares × 5p per share =	4 000
Preference dividend for 20X1: £20 000 × 6%	1 200
Arrears of preference dividend for 20X0	1 200
Total	6 400

The correct answer, therefore, is c).

11.5 Workings comprise the following:

1. *Cost of sales*

	£
Opening stock	51 240
Add: purchases	603 493
	654 733
Less: closing stock	(57 210)
Cost of sales	597 523

2. *Selling and distribution costs*

	£
As stated in the list of balances	80 714
Add: accrued commission	6 000
	86 714

3. *Administrative expenses*

	£
As stated in the list of balances	73 959
Less: prepaid insurance	(1 270)
	72 689

Solar Bubble plc: Draft profit and loss account for the year ending
31 January 20X4

	£
Turnover	975 420
Cost of sales (working 1)	(597 523)
Gross profit	377 897
Selling and distribution costs (working 2)	(86 714)
Administrative expenses (working 3)	(72 689)
Operating profit	218 494
Interest payable and similar charges	(1 977)
Profit on ordinary activities before taxation	216 517
Taxation	(60 625)
Profit on ordinary activities after taxation	155 892
Dividends:	
Preference £10 000 × 8%	(800)
Ordinary 100 000 × 5p	(5 000)
Retained profit	150 092

11.6 Workings comprise the following:

1. *Administrative expenses*

	£
Secretarial costs	51 498
Electricity (admin. office)	12 491
Office rental	42 704
Administration office: phone charges	6 964
Depreciation of office computer equipment	8 390
Office manager's salary	21 704
Directors' remuneration	59 200
Other administrative expenses	36 075
	239 026

2. *Selling and distribution costs*

	£
Salespersons' salaries	64 299
Delivery van depreciation	12 000
Other selling and distribution costs	5 911
Salespersons' commission	12 270
Delivery van expenses	24 470
	118 950

   Note: it is often a matter of judgement as to how expenses are allocated between selling and distribution cost and administrative expenses.

3. *Dividends payable*

   800 000 £1 ordinary shares at 5p per share = £40 000

4. *Tangible assets*

	£
Factory and plant at net book value	2 518 000
Delivery vans at net book value	120 000
Office equipment at net book value	151 020
	2 789 020

5. *Other creditors*

	£
Taxation	216 470
Dividend	40 000
	256 470

6. *Reserves*

	£
Reserves at 1 September 20X8	1 557 172
Profit for the year	482 383
	2 039 555

Brighton Magnets Limited: Profit and loss account for the year ending

31 August 20X9

	£
Turnover	3 796 842
Cost of sales	(2 712 350)
Gross profit	1 084 492
Selling and distribution costs (working 2)	(118 950)
Administrative expenses (working 1)	(239 026)
Other operating income	12 900
Operating profit	739 416
Interest receivable and similar income	644
Interest payable and similar charges	(1 207)
Profit on ordinary activities before taxation	738 853
Taxation	(216 470)
Profit on ordinary activities after taxation	522 383
Dividends:	
Proposed (working 3)	(40 000)
Profit for the financial year	482 383

Brighton Magnets Limited: Balance sheet at 31 August 20X9

	£	£
Fixed assets		
Tangible assets (working 4)		2 789 020
Current assets		
Stock	186 420	
Debtors	321 706	
Cash at bank	18 290	
	526 416	

Creditors: Amounts falling due within one year

Trade creditors	219 411
Other creditors (working 5)	256 470
	475 811

Net current assets	50 535
Total assets less current liabilities	2 839 555

Capital and reserves

Share capital	800 000
Reserves (working 6)	2 039 555
	2 839 555

11.7 ■ Statement 1 is false: listed companies are not obliged to produce a social responsibility report as part of their annual report.

■ Statement 2 is true: consolidated financial statements do bring together the results and the assets and liabilities of all group companies.

■ Statement 3 is true: compliance with the Combined Code is compulsory for all listed companies.

■ Statement 4 is false: listed company regulation is handled by the Financial Services Authority (although until recently it was handled by the London Stock Exchange).

Statements 2 and 3 are correct, therefore the correct answer is b).

CHAPTER 12

12.1 Ronald's percentage increase in sales is:

$$\frac{110\ 450 - 95\ 544}{95\ 544} \times 100 = 15.6\%$$

His increase in sales is, therefore, higher than average. Ronald's percentage increase in gross profit is:

$$\frac{38\ 392 - 33\ 469}{33\ 469} \times 100 = 14.7\%$$

His increase in gross profit is, therefore, lower than average. The correct answer, therefore, is a).

12.2 Horizontal analysis of Rory's profit and loss account data shows the following percentage changes (percentage increases over previous year)

	20X6	20X5	20X4
	%	%	%
Sales	4.2	3.6	3.0
Gross profit	3.3	3.4	3.5

The sales growth percentage is gradually increasing, while the gross profit growth percentage is gradually decreasing. The correct answer, therefore, is c).

12.3   Horizontal analysis of selected items from Larsen Locations Limited's
profit and loss account 20X5 to 20X8

	20X8 %	20X7 %	20X6 %
Sales of services	0.5	5.4	0.1
Administrative expenses	20.1	8.5	0.9
Operating profit	(10.1)	5.8	1.0

Larsen Locations has experienced more volatile change in sales, administrative expenses and operating profit than The Wilton Group plc. Sales in 20X7 increased by a greater amount than Wilton's sales, but there was a negligible rate of sales growth in 20X6 and 20X8. However, the most obvious difference is in the greatly increased level of administrative expenses in Larsen Locations 20X8 accounts. Presumably this increase arises because of the move to larger premises and taking on more staff. The increase in costs in 20X8 does not appear, as yet, to have produced a similar level of increase in sales. The higher costs appear to have resulted in a lower level of operating profit – a 10.1% decrease in 20X8 compared to the previous year.

12.4   Vertical analysis: Chapter Protection Limited's profit and loss account
for the year ending 31 December 20X2

	£	%
Turnover	188 703	100.0
Cost of sales	(115 863)	(61.4)
Gross profit	72 840	38.6
Administrative expenses	(14 260)	(7.6)
Distribution and selling costs	(20 180)	(10.7)
Operating profit	38 400	20.3
Interest payable and similar charges	(1 200)	(0.6)
Profit on ordinary activities before taxation	37 200	19.7
Taxation	(7 450)	(3.9)
Profit on ordinary activities after taxation	29 750	15.8
Dividends	(10 000)	(5.3)
Retained profit for the year	19 750	10.5

12.5   Boots Group plc: common size balance sheet statements
at 31 March 2003 and 31 March 2002

	2003 £m	2003 £m	2003 Common size %	2002 £m	2002 £m	2002 Common size %
Fixed assets		1 902.5	95.1		2 147.6	106.4
Current assets						
Stock	638.6		31.9	648.1		32.1

Debtors	650.6	32.5	646.1	32.0
Investments, deposits and cash	496.5	24.8	409.1	20.3
	1 785.7	89.2	1 703.3	84.4
Creditors: amounts falling due within one year	(1 112.7)	(55.6)	(1 174.7)	(58.2)
Net current assets	673.0	33.6	528.6	26.2
Total assets less current liabilities	2 575.5	128.7	2 676.2	132.6
Creditors: amounts falling due after more than one year	(401.8)	(20.0)	(480.0)	(23.8)
Provisions for liabilities and charges	(173.8)	(8.7)	(177.9)	(8.8)
Net assets	1 999.9	100.0	2 018.3	100.0
Capital and reserves				
Share capital	203.5	10.2	223.2	11.1
Reserves and similar items	1 796.4	89.8	1 795.1	88.9
	1 999.9	100.0	2 018.3	100.0

Commentary

All categories of asset and liability have decreased in the year, with the exception of investments and cash which now represents 24.8% of net assets compared to 20.3% in 2002. The group's decision to concentrate on its core activities appears to have resulted in a slight downsizing of operations. The balance sheet, therefore, is consistent with the information provided by the chief executive and chairman.

The most noticeable features of the common size statement are the scaling down of fixed assets as a proportion of total assets, and the fact that liabilities (both current and longer-term) represent a lesser proportion of the total assets figure.

12.6   Causeway Ferguson plc: Horizontal trend analysis (% changes over previous year), of profit and loss statements 20X3–20X7

	20X7 %	20X6 %	20X5 %	20X4 %
Turnover	(2.6)	(0.3)	9.4	3.6
Cost of sales	(2.5)	—	11.0	4.5
Gross profit	(2.8)	(0.8)	7.2	2.3
Administrative expenses	4.0	0.2	4.3	1.8
Selling and distribution costs	4.2	1.2	0.3	1.1
Operating profit	(25.8)	(5.6)	25.6	5.5
Taxation	(25.7)	(5.6)	25.8	5.4
Profit on ordinary activities after taxation	(25.8)	(5.5)	25.5	5.6
Dividends	4.2	—	4.3	—
Retained profit for the year	(37.2)	(7.5)	35.2	8.4

Causeway Ferguson plc: Common size analysis of profit and loss statements, 20X3–20X7

	20X7 %	20X6 %	20X5 %	20X4 %	20X3 %
Turnover	100.0	100.0	100.0	100.0	100.0
Cost of sales	(60.7)	(60.6)	(60.4)	(59.5)	(59.0)
Gross profit	39.3	39.4	39.6	40.5	41.0
Administrative expenses	(16.5)	(15.5)	(15.4)	(16.2)	(16.4)
Selling and distribution costs	(15.8)	(14.7)	(14.5)	(15.9)	(16.3)
Operating profit	7.0	9.2	9.7	8.4	8.3
Taxation	(2.1)	(2.8)	(2.9)	(2.5)	(2.5)
Profit on ordinary activities after taxation	4.9	6.4	6.8	5.9	5.8
Dividends	(1.9)	(1.8)	(1.8)	(1.9)	(1.9)
Retained profit for the year	3.0	4.6	5.0	4.0	3.9

Commentary

The following key features emerge from the horizontal and the common size analysis:

1. In each of the five years from 20X3 to 20X7 there has been a fall in the gross profit percentage. The falls from year to year are not dramatic but decline gradually.

2. There was some growth in sales until 20X6. The last two years show decreases. The decline in sales together with the steady decline in gross profit margin suggest that the company has some problems to address.

3. Administrative expenses and selling and distribution costs have increased each year. Usually the increases are small, but they represent significant amounts over a five-year period. In 20X7 both categories of cost increased by over 4%, and contribute significantly to the overall substantial drop in operating profit for the year.

4. Dividends have increased twice over the five-year period but the increases have been small. A steady or gradually increasing dividend tends to reassure shareholders.

5. While it might be premature to announce the 'withering away' of the company, some aspects of its performance would cause concern to a shareholder. The fact that there are new competitors in the market would explain the declining sales performance of the last two years. The gradual decline in gross margin, however, goes right back to the beginning of the five-year period and could not be solely attributable to competitive effects if the competitors have emerged only recently.

CHAPTER 13

13.1 Pre-tax return on shareholders' funds:

$$\frac{\text{Profit after interest and before taxation}}{\text{Shareholders' funds}}$$

$$= \frac{267.8}{2\,290} = 11.7\%$$

The correct answer, therefore, is d).

13.2 Post-tax return on shareholders' funds:

$$\frac{\text{Profit after interest and taxation}}{\text{Shareholders' funds}}$$

$$= \frac{189.8}{2\,290} = 8.2\%$$

The correct answer, therefore, is b).

13.3 Return on total capital invested:

$$\frac{\text{Profit before interest and taxation}}{\text{Shareholders' funds} + \text{Long-term borrowing}}$$

$$= \frac{302.8}{2\,290 + 350} = 11.5\%$$

The correct answer, therefore, is b).

13.4 The pre-tax return on shareholders' funds is calculated as:

$$\frac{\text{Profit before taxation and after interest}}{\text{Shareholders' funds}}$$

For each company:

Ambit Limited	Bolsover Limited	Carcan Limited	Delphic Limited
$\dfrac{803.6}{80.0 + 4550.0}$ $\times 100 = 17.4\%$	$\dfrac{540.8}{95.0 + 3881.0}$ $\times 100 = 13.6\%$	$\dfrac{575.8}{86.0 + 3928.0}$ $\times 100 = 14.3\%$	$\dfrac{855.4}{60.0 + 7000.0}$ $\times 100 = 12.1\%$

The company with the highest return is Ambit Limited, and so the correct answer is a).

13.5 Trixie Stores Limited:

Total current assets = 18 370 + 24 100 + 70 = £42 540

Total current liabilities = 15 450 + 6 400 = £21 850.

The current ratio equals:

$$\frac{\text{Current assets}}{\text{Current liabilities}} = \frac{42\ 540}{21\ 850} = 1.95:1$$

The correct answer, therefore, is a).

13.6 Trimester Tinker Limited:

Current assets = 108 770 + 94 300 + 1 600 = £204 670

'Quick' assets = 94 300 + 1 600 = £95 900

Current liabilities = £110 650.

$$\text{Current ratio} = \frac{204\ 670}{110\ 650} = 1.85:1$$

$$\text{Quick ratio} = \frac{95\ 900}{110\ 650} = 0.87:1$$

Trimester Tinker's current ratio of 1.85:1 is higher than the industry average of 1.62:1, while its quick ratio of 0.87:1 is lower than the industry average of 0.93:1. The correct answer, therefore, is b).

13.7 Upwood Sickert Limited's fixed asset turnover is calculated as follows:

$$\frac{\text{Sales turnover}}{\text{Fixed assets}}$$

The correct figure to take for fixed assets is net book value, i.e. £170 000 + £59 985 = £229 985.

$$\frac{686\ 430}{229\ 985} = 2.98$$

The correct answer, therefore, is d).

13.8 Key data for the sole trader is:

Opening stock = £405 000

Closing stock = £405 000 + 10% = £445 500.

Average stock for the year equals:

$$\frac{405\ 000 + 445\ 500}{2} = £425\ 250$$

Stock turnover in days equals:

$$\frac{425\ 250}{1\ 506\ 700} \times 365 \text{ days} = 103.0 \text{ days}$$

13.9 Only credit sales are taken into account when calculating the debtors turnover ratio. Credit sales for the year equal:

$$£1\ 703\ 698 \times 70\% = £1\ 192\ 589$$

Debtors turnover ratio:

$$\frac{218\ 603}{1\ 703\ 698} \times 365 \text{ days} = 46.8 \text{ days}$$

The correct answer, therefore, is a).

13.10 Winger Whalley Limited:

1. The absence of the credit controller on sick leave is likely to result in a slowing up of debtor payments. Many debtors will pay on time as a matter of routine, but some always need chasing. Unless a credit controller is chasing this latter group for payment they will delay or defer settling their debts. This is a valid reason.

2. An increase of 4% in sales is not likely to make any difference to the collection of debts. A very large increase might put pressure on administrative systems, but 4% is not likely to matter.

3. Early settlement discounts should have the opposite effect: debtors should pay up more quickly in order to take advantage of the settlement discount.

4. It is important to state the company's terms on the invoice stationery. If this is not done, new and occasional customers will simply not know the terms of trade, and may be inclined to take longer to pay. Other debtors may use the absence of stated terms as an excuse to take longer to pay.

Reasons 1 and 4 could be valid explanations. The correct answer, therefore, is c).

13.11 The calculation of the creditors turnover period ratio should include only purchases made on credit. Purchases made on credit equals:

$$90\% \times £1\ 952\ 278 = £1\ 757\ 050$$

Creditors turnover in days:

$$\frac{206\ 460}{1\ 757\ 050} \times 365 \text{ days} = 42.9 \text{ days}$$

The correct answer, therefore, is a).

13.12 Waldo Wolff's dividend per share:

$$\frac{\text{Dividend}}{\text{Number of shares in issue}}$$

$$\frac{300\ 000}{6\ 000\ 000} = 5\text{p per share}$$

The correct answer, therefore, is b).

13.13 Wablo Wolff's dividend cover ratio:

$$\frac{\text{Earnings after tax attributable to ordinary shareholders}}{\text{Dividend}}$$

$$\frac{1\ 131\ 400}{300\ 000} = 3.77$$

The correct answer, therefore, is a).

13.14 Waldo Wolff's earnings per share:

$$\frac{\text{Earnings after tax attributable to ordinary shareholders}}{\text{Number of shares in issue}}$$

$$\frac{1\ 131\ 400}{6\ 000\ 000} = 18.86\text{p per share}$$

The correct answer, therefore, is a).

13.15 Waldo Wolff's market capitalisation is the share price times the number of shares in issue:

$$£3.11 \times 6\ 000\ 000 = £18\ 660\ 000$$

13.16 Wilson Streep plc. First, calculate earnings per share:

$$\frac{\text{Earnings attributable to ordinary shareholders}}{\text{Number of shares in issue}}$$

$$= \frac{750\ 090}{3\ 300\ 000} = 22.73\text{p}$$

P/E ratio = price divided by earnings per share:

$$\text{Price per share} = \frac{\text{Market capitalisation}}{\text{Number of shares}}$$

$$= \frac{6\ 303\ 000}{3\ 300\ 000} = £1.91$$

$$\frac{\text{Price}}{\text{Earnings per share}}$$

$$= \frac{191\text{p}}{22.73\text{p}} = 8.4$$

The correct answer, therefore, is c).

13.17 Brazier Barkiss Limited

i) Gearing ratio

$$\frac{\text{Debt}}{\text{Equity}}$$

$$= \frac{2\ 000\ 000}{3\ 739\ 400} = 53.4\%$$

ii) Interest cover

$$\frac{\text{Profit before interest and tax}}{\text{Interest}}$$

$$= \frac{646\ 750}{200\ 000} = 3.23 \text{ times.}$$

13.18 Report to the directors of The Cuttlefish Biscuit Corporation Limited
Gross profit margin for Cuttlefish is better than the industry average, but net profit margin is worse. This suggests that the business is incurring higher costs on average, such as administration, selling and marketing costs, than its competitors. There may be good reasons in the short term why this should be so, but if business costs continue at a relatively high level the directors may wish to consider a range of possible cost reductions. In the meantime, it would be helpful to examine costs in detail to identify areas where savings are possible.

The debtors turnover ratio shows that Cuttlefish collects its debts more quickly than average in the industry. Given that most businesses will automatically take 30 days credit, 36 days is very good. There may be room for some improvement, however, and the directors may wish to consider, for example, introducing discounts for early settlement if they have not already done so.

Stock turnover is slightly worse than the industry average. It may be advisable to look more closely at the level of stocks held in the business and look for ways of managing stock more efficiently.

On average the industry takes a lot longer to pay creditors than Cuttlefish: 31.4 days would usually be considered a low turnover ratio where the industry trading terms are settlement within 30 days. The directors might consider extending this period by a few days; it would release some cash into the operating cycle, and could probably be done without endangering relationships with suppliers.

Cuttlefish's gearing ratio is low, compared to the industry. No particular action is recommended on this point, but if directors are looking for long-term finance for business expansion they should bear in mind that the business is not currently regarded as highly geared. Further long-term loans, within reasonable limits, would therefore be an option for consideration.

Generally, Cuttlefish appears to be doing well compared to industry averages.

13.19 Confidential report to the board of Cryer Roussillon Limited

Executive summary

The implementation of the range of new strategies has been very successful. The company is now more profitable than it was a year ago, and its balance sheet is healthy. The company should now concentrate on consolidating its position and should seek to expand sales volume.

The appendix to this report sets out a set of relevant ratio calculations.

Detailed report

The company's sales have dropped by almost 2% since last year. However, gross profit has improved by almost 24%, and the gross profit margin is now 41.3% compared to only 32.7% in 20X4. The company's strategy of pursuing higher margin sales appears to have paid off. It should now concentrate on increasing sales volume in those higher margin products. Operating expenses appear to be well under control; some effective cost-cutting appears to have taken place in 20X5.

The company has made a major investment in fixed assets: net book value has increased by 88% in the year. It is possible that the benefits to be obtained from these assets have not fed through into sales volumes and profits yet. The fixed asset efficiency ratio is notably poorer in 20X5 but could be expected to improve in 20X6 as the assets are utilised throughout the whole year.

Liquidity is not a problem. Liquidity ratios in both 20X4 and 20X5 are good, and the amount of cash at bank has increased very substantially. The directors' decision not to propose a dividend has helped, and means that spare cash is now available for extra investment.

Stock turnover has worsened to 43 days (from 37.5 in 20X4). The company must ensure that it is not over-stocking, and controls over stock levels perhaps need further attention. Debtors, on the other hand, appear to be better controlled in 20X5: debtor turnover has reduced, and appears to be at a quite satisfactory level.

The company has taken on long-term debt resulting in a relatively modest level of gearing. The level of gearing does not appear to be a cause for any concern at the moment.

Appendix

	20X5	20X4
Performance		
Gross profit margin	$\frac{85\ 272}{206\ 470} \times 100 = 41.3\%$	$\frac{68\ 830}{210\ 619} \times 100 = 32.7\%$
Operating profit margin	$\frac{43\ 813}{206\ 470} \times 100 = 21.2\%$	$\frac{21\ 220}{210\ 619} \times 100 = 10.1\%$
Return on shareholders' funds	$\frac{40\ 813}{129\ 783} \times 100 = 31.4\%$	$\frac{21\ 220}{97\ 070} \times 100 = 21.8\%$
Liquidity		
Current ratio	$\frac{45\ 763}{15\ 470} = 2.96$	$\frac{44\ 610}{16\ 290} = 2.74$
Quick ratio	$\frac{20\ 693 + 10\ 792}{15\ 470} = 2.04$	$\frac{29\ 420 + 640}{16\ 290} = 1.85$
Efficiency		
Fixed assets turnover	$\frac{206\ 470}{129\ 490} = 1.59$	$\frac{210\ 619}{68\ 750} = 3.06$
Stock turnover (days)	$\frac{14\ 278}{121\ 198} \times 365 = 43.0$	$\frac{14\ 550}{141\ 789} \times 365 = 37.5$
Debtors turnover (days)	$\frac{20\ 693}{206\ 470} \times 365 = 36.6$	$\frac{29\ 420}{210\ 619} \times 365 = 50.1$
Gearing		
Debt/equity	$\frac{30\ 000}{129\ 783} = 23.1\%$	Nil

Accounting policies Those principles of accounting that are selected by the managers of a business to be applied in the preparation of the financial statements.

Accounting standards Regulations containing detailed guidance and rules on the preparation of financial accounts. In the UK accounting standards are issued in the form of Financial Reporting Standards (FRSs) by the Accounting Standards Board (ASB).

Accruals An important accounting convention that involves the matching of sales and expenses, so that all of the expenses incurred in making a sale are deducted from it. Also referred to as matching.

Acid test ratio The ratio of current assets, excluding stock, to current liabilities (also known as the 'quick' ratio).

Amortisation A measurement of the amount of fixed asset value that has been used up during the accounting period (the term usually relates to intangible fixed assets).

Articles of association A document, required by company law, which sets out the constitution of the company.

Assets Resources controlled by a business that it will use in order to generate a profit in the future.

Audit An independent examination by a properly qualified professional auditor of the records and financial statements of a business. (Note that in the context of this book the entity is a business enterprise, but audit of charities, local government and central government, for example, also takes place.)

Audit report The report by an independent auditor on the financial statements of a business.

Authorised share capital The number of shares that a company is authorised to issue (this is not necessarily the same number that has actually been issued).

Bad debt An amount owed to a business that cannot be recovered.

Balance sheet A statement of the resources owned and controlled by a business at a single point in time. Most businesses prepare balance sheets at least annually.

Budget A statement, prepared in advance, usually for a specific period (e.g. for one year), of a business's planned activities and financial outcomes.

Business entity concept The business is regarded as separate from its owner(s).

Business plan A detailed document produced to support an application for business finance.

Capital Amounts invested by the owners of the business to which they subsequently have a claim.

Capital introduced The resources in the form of money and other goods put into a business by its owner(s) when it starts up.

Cash flow The movement of cash in and out of a business.

Cash flow statement A statement prepared periodically that summarises the cash flows in and out of a business.

Chairman's statement A written statement by a company chairman that accompanies the annual financial statements of all companies in the UK listed on the London Stock Exchange.

Charge A legal arrangement for security for a loan. A lender puts in place a charge over specified property of the borrower. If the borrower fails to repay the loan, the proceeds of sale of the property are used to reimburse the lender.

Common size analysis The application of vertical analysis across comparable figures for more than one accounting period.

Consolidated financial statements The financial statements for a group of companies, which combine together the profit and loss accounts and balance sheets of all the companies in the group.

Cost of sales The cost of buying in or manufacturing the goods that have been sold in an accounting period.

Creditors Amounts owed by a business to other people or organisations.

Creditors turnover ratio Assesses the length of time, on average, that a business takes to pay its creditors.

Current assets Assets held in the business for a short period of time only (examples include stock, debtors and cash).

Current liabilities Amounts that will have to be paid by the business in the near future.

Current ratio The ratio of current assets to current liabilities.

Debentures Company bonds that entitle their holder to eventual repayment of the value of the stock plus a regular annual rate of interest (debentures are sometimes referred to as 'loan stock').

Debt Finance in the form of loans.

Debtors Amounts owed to a business by other people or organisations.

Debtors turnover ratio Assesses the length of time, on average, that debtors take to pay.

Depreciation A measurement of the amount of fixed asset value that has been used up during the accounting period (the term usually relates to tangible fixed assets).

Directors The senior managers of a limited company. Directors have special responsibilities in law.

Dividend A payment periodically made by a limited company to its shareholders.

Dividend cover A ratio that calculates the number of times the current dividend could be paid out of available profits for the period.

Doubtful debt An amount owed to a business in respect of which recovery is doubtful.

Drawings The taking of cash (or other resources) out of an unincorporated business by its owner(s).

Equity The ordinary shareholders' interest in a company, comprising their original contribution in share capital plus any profits retained in the business.

Equity shares The share capital in a company that entitles its owner(s) to a share of the business's profits (in the form of dividend) and to voting rights.

Expenses The amounts incurred by the business in purchasing or manufacturing goods sold, and other expenditure on items like rent and telephone charges.

Factoring An arrangement to obtain cash from a factoring company in exchange for debtors of the business.

Financial accountants Specialists in the provision of financial information oriented towards interested parties external to the business.

Financial accounting The processes and practices involved in providing interested parties external to the business with the financial information that they need.

Financial reporting Reporting financial information to interested parties external to the business.

Fixed assets Assets that remain in the possession of the business over a long period of time, almost always in excess of one year.

Fixed asset turnover ratio Expresses the efficiency with which fixed assets have been used in a business to generate turnover.

Gearing The relationship between equity capital and loan capital in a company.

Gearing ratio The relationship between equity capital and loan capital expressed as a ratio.

Goodwill The intangible factors that add value to a business, such as brand names and customer loyalty.

Gross profit The amount of profit after deducting cost of sales from total sales.

Horizontal analysis Analysis of comparable accounting figures over a period of time.

Hostile bid A takeover bid which is not welcomed by the target company.

Income statement Profit and loss account (income statement is more widely used outside the UK).

Incorporation The process of setting up a limited company.

Intangible fixed assets Fixed assets that do not have a physical presence.

Interest cover A measurement of the number of times interest could be paid out of available profits.

Interim financial statements Financial accounts issued half-yearly (or in rare cases in the UK, quarterly) by companies listed on the London Stock Exchange.

International financing reporting standards (IFRS) Accounting standards issued by the International Accounting Standards Board (IASB).

Inventory Items bought by a business to sell on to somebody else, or to process or transform in some way to make saleable goods (more usually known as 'stock' in the UK).

Issued share capital The number of shares actually issued by a company (it can issue a quantity of shares less than or equal to the amount of authorised share capital).

Lease premium A substantial sum payable at the start (inception) of a lease.

Leasing A financing arrangement for obtaining the use of business assets without having to purchase them.

Lessee A person or business that obtains the use of an asset under a leasing arrangement.

Lessor A person or (usually) business that makes assets available to businesses under leasing arrangements.

Liabilities Amounts that the business is obliged to pay to other people or organisations.

Limited company A legal arrangement for regulating the ownership of business.

Limited liability The liability of the shareholders of a limited company is limited to the amount of their original investment.

Loan stock Company bonds that entitle their holder to eventual repayment of the value of the stock plus a regular annual rate of interest (loan stock is sometimes referred to as 'debentures').

Loss The deficit that occurs when expenditure exceeds revenue.

Management accountants Specialists in the provision of financial information for use within the business.

Management accounting Accounting carried out within a business for its own internal uses, to assist management in controlling the business and in making business decisions.

Market capitalisation The total value obtained by multiplying the number of shares a listed company has in issue by the market value of one share.

Market value [of a share] The price at which the share can be traded on the stock market.

Matching An important accounting convention that involves the matching of sales and expenses, so that all of the expenses incurred in making a sale are deducted from it. Also referred to as accruals.

Memorandum of association A document, required by company law, which sets out the purposes for which the company is established, and its authorised share capital.

Mortgage A loan secured on real estate.

Net profit The amount of profit after deducting both cost of sales and other expenses from total sales.

Nominal value The basic denomination of a share – for example, 50p or 25p.

Offer for sale A general invitation to both the public and financial institutions to buy shares in a company.

Ordinary share capital The shares in a company that confer the right to vote in company general meetings, and to receive a share of any dividend paid out by the company.

Partnership A business that is run by two or more people with a view to making a profit.

Placing Offering a limited group of prospective buyers the opportunity to buy new shares in a company.

Profit The surplus that remains after deducting business costs from business income.

Profit and loss account A statement prepared by businesses of all sizes, at least annually, which shows the total business revenue less expenses. The net total is the profit or loss of the business.

Prospectus A document produced in accordance with (in the UK) Financial Services Authority regulation. It is prepared by a company which offers its shares for sale to the general public, and contains a large amount of information about the history and prospects of the company.

Provision (in respect of a doubtful debt) An amount recognised in the profit and loss of a business as a deduction from profit. It is included where the recovery of one or more debts is doubtful. It may be specific to a particular debt, or may be general, based upon an estimate of the proportion of debts that are doubtful.

Quick ratio The ratio of current assets, excluding stock, to current liabilities (also known as the 'acid test' ratio).

Raw materials Materials that are bought in by a business and then put through a manufacturing process.

Realisation Converted or capable of being converted into cash.

Recognition The inclusion of items of, for example, income and expense in the financial statements. Recognition is an important accounting convention.

Reducing balance method [of depreciation] A method of estimating depreciation which results in a higher charge in the earlier years of an asset's useful life, with the charge progressively reducing towards the end of the asset's useful life.

Registered auditors Professionally qualified auditors who are authorised to conduct the audits of businesses and other organisations.

Retained profits The amount of profit left in a business (i.e. profit not distributed to the owners of the business).

Revenue The amount of goods and/or services sold in an accounting period by a business, expressed in terms of monetary amounts.

Rights issue An offer of shares made to existing shareholders in a company, in proportion to the number of shares already held (e.g. a one for seven rights issue involves offering one new share for every seven already held).

Security An arrangement between a lender and a borrower where specified items of property can be used to meet the loan if the borrower defaults (i.e. does not repay the loan).

Shareholders The investors in a limited company; each investor owns a share or shares in the company.

Sole trader A person who operates a business himself or herself, keeping any profits that are made.

Stewardship Taking responsibility for the management of resources on behalf of somebody else. (The principal example in this book is that of company directors managing a company on behalf of its shareholders.)

Stock Items bought by a business to sell on to somebody else, or to process or transform in some way to make saleable goods.

Stock turnover ratio Measures the length of time, on average, that an item of stock remains in the business before being sold.

Straight-line method [of depreciation] The method that charges depreciation evenly over all accounting periods that benefit from the use of a fixed asset.

Takeover bid A move to take over a majority of shares in a target company so as to gain control of it.

Tangible fixed assets Fixed assets that have a physical presence (unlike intangible fixed assets).

Trade creditors Amounts owing to people or organisations that have provided goods or services on credit.

Trading account The upper part of the profit and loss account where gross profit is calculated.

Trend analysis The analysis of comparable accounting figures over a period of time sufficient to establish reliable tendencies and trends.

Vertical analysis An accounting analytical technique that involves expressing all of the figures in an accounting statement as proportions of a key figure (for example, sales).

Working capital The elements of financing required for investment in items that move rapidly in and out of the business, for example, stock.

Working capital cycle The movement of the elements of working capital (debtors, creditors, stock and cash) around the business.

Index